Mordecai

THE MAN AND HIS MESSAGE

*The Story of
Mordecai Wyatt Johnson*

Mordecai Wyatt Johnson

Mordecai

THE MAN AND HIS MESSAGE

*The Story of
Mordecai Wyatt Johnson*

BY
❦ Richard I. McKinney

*To Dr. Orland Taylor
With best wishes,
Richard I. McKinney*

HOWARD UNIVERSITY PRESS
Washington, DC
1997

Howard University Press, Washington, DC 20017

No part of this book may be reproduced or utilized in any form or by any means, electronic or mechanical, including photocopying and recording, or by any information storage and retrieval system, without permission in writing from the publisher. Inquires should be addressed to Howard University Press, 1240 Randolph Street, N.E., Washington, DC 20017.

Manufactured in the United States of America.

This book is printed on acid-free paper.

10 9 8 7 6 5 4 3 2 1

Library of Congress Cataloging-in-Publication Data

McKinney, Richard I. (Richard Ishmael), 1906–
    Mordecai, the man and his message: The story of Mordecai Wyatt
Johnson / by Richard I. McKinney.
    p.   cm.
    Includes bibliographical references and index.
    ISBN 0-88258-197-X (cloth). — ISBN 0-88258-193-7 (pbk.)
    1. Johnson, Mordecai W. (Mordecai Wyatt), 1890-1976   2. Howard
University—Presidents—Biography.   I. Johnson, Mordecai W.
(Mordecai Wyatt), 1890–1976. II. Title.
LC2851.H817M35 1997
378.1'11—dc21
[B]
                                         96–47507
                                         CIP

Cover photograph courtesy of Moorland-Springarn Research Center, Howard University Archives, Howard University.

For George K. and Phyllis Zanaida

Keepers of the Dream

Contents

8
The Incisive Orator

9
Another Beginning

Bibliographical Notes

Bibliography

Notes

Photo Section

Appendixes

Index

Preface

*T*his is the story of Mordecai Wyatt Johnson, a very unusual man for his time. Although a nationally recognized platform speaker and a university president for more than three decades, he was a sometimes controversial figure. He made enemies—some bitter; he made friends—mostly loyal. With a powerful mind and a compelling platform presence, he was one of the most effective orators America has produced. Sometimes he appeared to be "called" to change America and to make a difference in the world.

This volume began as a project to gather materials for a short biographical sketch to introduce an edited volume of some of his sermons and addresses. As the work progressed, however, it became desirable to tell the story of his life in greater detail and to present some of his addresses and sermons in appendixes. Because of the impact he made during his long career, his story should be told to a wider public.

Those who knew Mordecai Wyatt Johnson referred to him as "Dr. Johnson" when they were in his presence. In speaking among themselves, however, they called him "Mordecai." I first met him during my student days at Morehouse College, to which he came annually as a speaker. Through the years, I came to know him personally.

I am indebted to many people who assisted me in the preparation of this study. Ms. Esme E. Bhan, Research Associate; Ms. Joellen El Bashir, Curator of Manuscripts; and Dr. Clifford L. Muse Jr., University Archivist of the Moorland-Springarn Research Center at Howard University, graciously provided a considerable amount of materials pertaining to

Dr. Johnson. Mr. Andy Simons, Reference Archivist of the Amistad Research Center at Tulane University, was most helpful in providing access to the file of the "Julius Rosenwald Papers, Re: Mordecai W. Johnson," from which most of the primary data in chapters 5 and 6 of this volume were derived. Mrs. Elaine Williams, Archivist of the Robert Woodruff Library of Atlanta University, extended courtesies during my research there. Dr. Norman J. Kansfield, Librarian, and Ms. Bonnie L. VanDelinder, Assistant Librarian for Public Service of the Ambrose Swasey Library at the Colgate-Rochester-Bexley Hall-Crozer-St. Bernard's School of Divinity, were generous in supplying important data, including a photocopy of Dr. Johnson's thesis for the Bachelor of Divinity degree. Ms. Deborah A. Terry, Assistant to the Registrar of Morehouse College, cordially provided photocopies of relevant pages of the catalogs of Dr. Johnson's years there.

The extended interviews with William H. Johnson, the son of Mordecai and Mrs. Johnson, and Dr. John Q. Taylor King, Dr. Johnson's stepson, were indispensable for information and insights into Mordecai's life. I am especially grateful to them.

In Paris, Tennessee, Mr. George E. Bass Jr. and Mr. Thomas McWherter were excellent guides during my visit there. In addition, Mrs. Robert H. Woodson, widow of Mordecai's boyhood friend; the Reverend V. Joseph Gardner Jr. of the Mt. Zion Baptist Church; and Bill Williams, editor and publisher of the local *Paris Post-Intelligencer*, were generous with their time and knowledge.

I am indebted to Ms. E. McKinney Johnson of Laney College and to Dr. Martina J. Bryant of Duke University for reading portions of the manuscript and making very helpful suggestions. Two former professors at Howard University gave invaluable recommendations: Dr. Herman Branson read a portion of the manuscript and Dr. Martha Putney read the original version of the entire manuscript. Their wise observations have been of immeasurable worth to this study. Of course, I take full responsibility for whatever limitations may be found here.

For their professional competence and painstaking work in the final editing phase of this project, I am deeply indebted to the late Ms. Eleanor Johnson and to Ms. Barbara Hart of Publications Professionals, LLC.

For permission to quote from copyrighted material, I thank the following: the Kennekat Press, publisher of E. R. Embree's *Thirteen Against the Odds*; the Judson Press, publisher of E. A. Jones's *A Candle in the Dark, A History of Morehouse College*; the University of Pennsylvania Press, publisher of Genna Rae McNeil's *Groundwork: Charles Hamilton Houston and the*

Struggle for Civil Rights; A. Leon Higginbotham, author of "An Open Letter to Clarence Thomas," *University of Pennsylvania Law Review* 140, no. 3 (January 1992); The *Afro-American* newspapers; the Robert W. Woodruff Library of Atlanta University Center, repository of the John and Eugenia Hope Papers; the Amistad Research Center at Tulane University; and the Moorland-Springarn Research Center at Howard University.

This book is basically a portrait of Mordecai Wyatt Johnson. The author intended to prepare a definitive biography based not just on the sources already mentioned, but primarily on the extensive files Dr. Johnson accumulated during his thirty-four years as president of Howard University. Unfortunately, those materials have not yet been made available to scholars. Certainly at some future time when access to them is permitted, a more complete account of Mordecai and his many associations with individuals, organized bodies, and the federal government, as well as his interactions with the Howard faculty and staff, can be written.

I could not have completed this book without the expert secretarial support of Mrs. Joyce A. Brown. Finally, I pay tribute to my wife, Lena Martin McKinney, whose encouragement and patience during this enterprise have sustained me.

R. I. M.

Baltimore, August 1997

1

The Early Years

$\mathcal{T}$he setting was London, England, 1959. He was an imposing figure, with a resonant voice that occasionally reverberated in the large hall where he was speaking. He had the bearing and authoritative manner of a diplomat; he was in fact a man with a mission. He was one of five speakers before the plenary session of the First Atlantic Congress sponsored by the North American Treaty Organization.

From a lifetime of personal encounters, he knew that his light skin color often belied the condition of his birth. He wanted his audience to know at the outset who and what he was. Identifying himself with the subjects of his message, he began by saying he was a member of the underclass, the son of ex-slaves. This revelation heightened the interest and expectations of his international audience. He pleaded with the European powers to understand the urgent need to take action to eliminate the evils of colonialism, especially against the encroachments of the Soviet bloc.

This charismatic orator was Mordecai Wyatt Johnson, electrifying an audience of diplomatic leaders and leaving an unforgettable impression. The *London Times* reported that he had "exploded" into the relaxed atmosphere of the group. *Le Monde* of Paris said that he "made himself the ardent and moving defender of the underdeveloped peoples, particularly those in Africa." The *New York Post* remarked that "many were moved . . . some with annoyance, but at the end the applause lasted for five minutes."[1] He had come a long way from his roots. Much had happened in his life since it had begun sixty-nine years earlier in a romantically named small town in the southern United States.

The name Paris, Tennessee, conjures up images of historical personalities, dramatic events, and exotic entertainment that characterize the "City of Light" in France for which it was named. Located in western Tennessee, Paris is the seat of Henry County, named for Patrick Henry, the great Revolutionary patriot and former governor of Virginia. The commissioners established it as the county seat on September 23, 1823. According to legend, each of the five commissioners appointed to select the county seat put a name in a hat, with the understanding that the town would be called the name drawn first. The name "Paris" won out, and that settled the matter. Henry County was "One of the most thriving and populated in west Tennessee, attracting a high grade of settlers."[2] Farming and mill work were the principal occupations. Today, on entering the small town one sees a large billboard sign reading, "Welcome to Paris, Home of the World's Biggest Fish Fry."

The town boasts of another distinction. Some years ago it sponsored a holiday honoring four educators who were born or grew up there. One honoree that day was Mordecai Wyatt Johnson, whom some of his admirers characterized as "One of the World's Greatest Educators." Not all of those who knew him shared this sentiment. In fact, some people hated him with a passion.

Mordecai's story begins with the last decade of nineteenth-century America. Reconstruction had ended. Only twenty-five years had elapsed since Confederate General Robert E. Lee surrendered to General Ulysses Grant under an apple tree in Appomattox, Virginia, thus effectively bringing an end to slavery in America. In Paris, Tennessee, as elsewhere in the South, many knew first hand and full well the contrast between freedom and bondage. For most of the 4.5 million former slaves, the opportunities for earning even a modest living consisted primarily of work as common laborers or domestic servants. Because of the establishment of schools by missionaries from the North, some African Americans had completed enough formal training to qualify as teachers at the elementary, secondary, and college levels. For most of the former slaves, however, the living was not easy.

The nation was still rebuilding after the ravages of the Civil War. The Deep South had begun enacting Jim Crow laws. President Benjamin Harrison was charting a new course for the nation. The United States had more than 63 million people, whose average annual income was $437. It was a time when Americans took the idea of progress for granted. An Atchison, Topeka, and Santa Fe train set a speed record of 78.1 miles per hour. Electric lights were installed in the White House, and some dedicated people organized the Women's Christian Temperance Union to fight the evils of drink.

By 1890 African Americans across the country had been gradually improving their condition. This was in large measure because of the establishment of churches and the work of missionaries. These missionaries from the North came to provide education for the freedmen, whom the law had forbidden to be taught to read and write.

After the Civil War ended, the freedmen lost little time in forming churches of their own, the only institutions they could claim exclusively for themselves. (Before emancipation, it had been illegal for slaves to hold formal religious services unless some trusted white overseer was present to monitor their activities. Religion had been the source of their strength for survival during the travails of slavery.) After gaining freedom, their first objective was to establish churches. These became not only places of worship, but also centers where they could learn to read. The churches also served as bases for the organization of small businesses, for the development of leadership, and for a liberating social life. The pastor was the leading figure in the black community and often served as a bridge between his people and the white majority.

Each of the well-established denominations responded to the need to provide education for the ex-slaves. Typical of the religious organizations active in this effort were the American Baptist Home Mission Society and the Woman's American Baptist Home Mission Society, which established or aided twenty-seven educational institutions before 1901.[3] This represented at least one school for the freedmen in each of the former slave states. The American Missionary Association was also active in this field. Under its auspices Fisk University was established in 1866 and soon developed a viable four-year college program. Among its 1888 graduates was W. E. B. Du Bois, who for decades was the foremost African-American intellectual.

Of the 102 historically black institutions of higher learning now surviving, 62 were established before 1890—46 by religious groups and 16 by the states. The establishment of thirty-five of these schools during the first ten years following the end of the Civil War shows the sense of pressing need to educate the freedmen.[4] In addition to the schools now surviving, other organizations established schools during that period, but many of these failed because of inadequate funding or were taken over by political entities. The schools established in the South with the help of missionaries from the North became the matrix for training teachers and preachers. Most of the founders of these institutions named them "college" or "university," although their major focus was on early and secondary education. They played a vital role in preparing a generation of leaders and raised the aspirations of hundreds of young African Americans. These schools also provided the tools by which the dispossessed could raise their quality of life.

The number of African Americans who entered the field of politics declined considerably during the early days of Reconstruction. Not long after the war many African Americans had been elected to political office. Some had gained seats in state legislatures; others had won seats in the U.S. Congress. However, by 1890 opposition groups curtailed whatever political power African Americans had achieved. The move toward keeping them in an inferior status was growing apace. Racism was rampant, expressed in gross intimidation (exacerbated by the violence of the Ku Klux Klan) and the disenfranchisement of blacks.

Most African Americans were limited to work requiring few skills, and whatever business opportunities existed for them were minor and targeted to a circumscribed clientele. The need was pressing for training in small business operations and for managing whatever funds could be earned.

Into this world on a Sunday night, January 12, 1890, Wyatt and Carolyn Johnson welcomed their first, and only, child together. They could hardly have imagined that he was destined to become a major, and sometimes controversial, educational and religious leader in America.

Wyatt J. Johnson had been born on a slave plantation in middle Tennessee sometime between 1822 and 1838. Prior to 1861 he was married to Nellie Biass. They had three children: Jonas W., Dora, and Sallie. Nellie died on July 21, 1885. In 1900 Jonas died, and thirteen years later Dora passed away. Three years after Nellie's death, Wyatt married Carolyn Freeman,[5] an attractive young woman thirty years his junior. She was quite light in color while Wyatt was dark.

Before his emancipation, Wyatt Johnson had several slave masters over a period of thirty to forty years, depending on the exact year of his birth. During the Civil War he served in the Confederate Army with his master and incurred injuries that troubled him for the rest of his life. Mordecai describes his father as standing five feet, six inches tall and as being erect in his bearing and strong in the shoulders and the arms. Wyatt had a booming voice that could be heard "as far as the eye could see." With his strong muscles he was able to lift heavy timbers and steel. Mordecai never saw him take medicine of any kind. He lived well-ordered life, rising at four A.M. to spend two hours doing chores before going into the upper room to pray. He was never late getting to his job. He was a stern disciplinarian, using corporal punishment when the severity of his son's infractions merited it. Mordecai said that it took him forty years to understand his father and what the man meant to him.

During his years as a slave, Wyatt knew what it meant to see families torn apart by slave trading; he witnessed and experienced many ignominies heaped on those who were considered mere chattel to be bought, bred, and sold like any commodity. He deeply resented these indignities, which he was powerless to rectify. All he could do to preserve the sense of his own manhood and worth was steel himself to bear the injustices with stoic strength.

Wyatt Johnson's abiding religious faith was introduced to him as he was growing up. He heard "exhorters" preach about the love and, particularly, the justice of God. He heard the sorrowful songs, the spirituals, and about some time when all God's children would eventually find peace and happiness. He may have imagined that some day he himself would stand before listeners and proclaim the good news of the Gospel.

Whenever the opportunity to get help arose, Wyatt would try to decipher a printed page, and eventually he learned to read. The Bible was one of his basic textbooks. A grown man when emancipation finally came with its freedom to learn without fear, Wyatt took advantage of every opportunity to improve his mind.

After emancipation, Wyatt Johnson moved from middle Tennessee to an area near Memphis. Later he settled in Henry County and made his living as an independent farmer, with his own tools and livestock. His ability to read broadened his employment opportunities. He gave up farming and worked for several mills, mainly Porter's, Dobbin's, and Parker's mills. His last employment was at the Paris Lumber Company, where he remained for twenty years. This thriving lumber company bought large quantities of rough lumber, cured it in the sun, and shaped it into barrel heads, staves, doors, window frames, and other items for frame-building construction. Wyatt Johnson and a white man named McAdoo were the leaders of the lumberyard crew. The two-man team was skilled in the intricacies of precision lumber processing. Wyatt's dependability and character won him the respect of his employers and co-workers. His friendship with his employer's family continued until his death.

Wyatt formally became a Christian before the Civil War. After the war he felt a call to the ministry and was ordained. He founded and built the Cedar Grove Baptist Church in Cottage Grove, Tennessee. In time he became pastor of the Mt. Zion Baptist Church in Paris. He was also the founder of the Obion River Baptist Association.

The Mt. Zion Church had its beginnings in 1866. Organized under the leadership of the Reverend Sanford Griffin, who had achieved the status of "exhorter" during his slave days, Mt. Zion continued to grow in membership. The tenures of its pastors were relatively short; the church also went through three name changes. The congregation had first adopted the name "Palmers Chapel." Later, after moving to a new location, the members changed the name to "Saint Elmore." Because he had been diligently preparing himself through the years, Wyatt Johnson became the sixth pastor of this congregation. Under his leadership, the church moved again, to its present location at 304 Rison Street, and was yet again renamed as "Mt. Zion." The new structure was far more substantial than those preceding it.[6] Wyatt Johnson used his house as security for the materials needed in this enterprise.

Meanwhile Wyatt was active in the Masonic Lodge. For a while he served as Worshipful Master of the local organization.

Carolyn Freeman Johnson is remembered as having possessed intelligence, patience, and love for her family. She enjoyed planting and maintaining beautiful flower beds around the home. She had learned to read the Bible and other literature and to develop an appreciation for music, but the limitations of her schooling prevented her from securing work other than that of a domestic servant for the well-to-do families in town.

The home in which Wyatt and Carolyn Johnson lived was a four-room frame structure with a basement. It was modest but comfortable. The Louisville and Nashville Railway line was close by, and they could often see men on handcars pumping their way to work at some not-too-distant site. The railroads, freight yards, and mills provided the main employment opportunities for the men in the community.

Mordecai had his father's first name, Wyatt, but for a very significant reason his parents chose "Mordecai" for his middle name. The biblical Mordecai was the wise and dedicated Jew, the cousin and adoptive father of Esther. The story is told in the book that bears her name in the Hebrew Bible.

The narrative describes how the biblical Mordecai, a leader of the colony of Jews living in Susa, the capital city of the Persian Empire, demonstrated a profound concern for the welfare of his people. When, by chicanery, all the Jews in the empire were marked for slaughter because of hatred for them and their minority status, Mordecai urged Esther, queen to King Xerxes, to use her influence to have the edict countermanded. He urged Esther to take the risk involved in saving her people by asking her the question: "Who knows whether you have not come to the kingdom for such a time as this?" In acceding to Mordecai's entreaty, Esther approached the king uninvited and decided, "If I perish, I perish!" In the end, through her careful planning and maneuvers, the Jewish people were saved and good triumphed over evil. As Esther became the heroine, Mordecai became the hero of this minority, the Jews. The biblical narrative closes with these words: "Mordecai was great among the Jews and popular with the multitude of the brethren, for he sought the welfare of his people and spoke peace to all his people." It is an inspiring tale, and Carolyn loved to read the story of "Moni-cai" to her young son. As Mordecai recalls:

> She said it came to her from a voice in the western part of the house, and that I heard it, and, child that I was, I moved definitely upon her breast and looked as if I was trying to rise. From that day until her death she never allowed me to forget this revelation. She suspected that it had to do with the Lord's preparation of my life for an unusual service to my own people. It was a long time—about ten years—when I was reading the Bible which my father kept on the center table in the upper room of the house into which he went every morning to pray. I then came upon the story of Esther and Mordecai, and for the first time I was not only deeply impressed but I was instructed as to the direction of my life which the revelation indicated I would take.[7]

Doubtless the story of the biblical Mordecai's dedication and concerns for a persecuted minority, as well as his mother's account of her revelation about this ancient hero, became an unconscious and sometimes a very conscious factor in Mordecai's own sense of mission. In his quest for a viable education, and in the acceptance or rejection of job opportunities, the thought of his having a special mission to carry out could have been the controlling element in his decisions. He liked the name "Mordecai," and in time he reversed the order of his given names.

Mordecai's mother read other biblical stories to her son—stories of courage and heroism, of strong characters overcoming great odds, of David conquering Goliath, of Daniel in the lion's den, of the three Hebrew children in the fiery furnace, and of the exploits of the great Hebrew prophets.

While Carolyn Johnson was gentle and caring in her attitude toward her son, Wyatt Johnson was a demanding taskmaster. A man of the old school, he believed that rigorous discipline was important in rearing children. He set chores for the child to do, and in the event of any shortcoming in Mordecai's performance, corporal punishment followed. Mordecai recalled that, unlike his mother, his father never formally engaged in the effort to educate him and that his father's "greatest ability was generally applied from the rear." This treatment hampered a close relationship between father and son. Not until Mordecai was in college was he comfortable having a one-on-one conversation with his father.

Meanwhile, as the child Mordecai developed, his imagination grew increasingly fertile. He reveled in the wonders of nature around him. He marveled at the flowers that blossomed as winter's cold subsided and at the songbirds—harbingers of spring—that heralded the renewed greening of the earth. Certainly he had the opportunity to watch men at work, those operating the fascinating machinery in the mill and others wheeling loads of cement for construction, and he observed with interest the rhythmic movements of carpenters hammering nails. He was transfixed by the hooting of the owl that occasionally came to roost in the nearby cedar trees at night, and he savored the taste of mulberries before the trees decayed and had to be cut down.

Mordecai also saw the domestics in the late afternoon, trudging home from the big houses, often carrying a pan of leftover food from their mistresses' kitchens to feed their families. Sometimes these pans were the primary source of food for all their relatives.

For a short time Mordecai's father gave him the opportunity to work at the lumber mill, moving small pieces of lumber from one pile to another. However, Wyatt summarily dismissed his prankish son when he learned that Mordecai was secretly putting small pieces of wood under the wheels of the conveyance for moving heavy stacks of lumber, making it difficult for the conveyance to be moved.

Every afternoon after school young Mordecai and Robert H. Woodson, his best friend (they were born three months apart), spent time together. They established a bond of camaraderie that was to continue until their deaths many decades later (and in the same year).[8]

The fathers of these two boys were also close friends. Robert's father, whose name was General Pillow Woodson, had donated his labor to the construction of the new church of his friend Wyatt Johnson. The builders made each stone in this structure by hand. The project represented a major achievement, of which the African-American community was rightfully proud. G. P. Woodson in time heeded the call to preach. In later years he, too, became pastor of the Mt. Zion Baptist Church, and served there for thirty-one years.[9]

Wyatt and Carolyn Johnson were well aware of their son's potential and his inquiring mind. Carolyn saw to it that Mordecai's schooling began early. Two dedicated teachers gave him a good start on his educational odyssey. The first was Miss Nora Porter, a young woman who took the boy on horseback to her private country school. There she taught him to read and write. She gave him an excellent foundation and instilled in him a strong interest in learning all he could. Soon Miss Porter was employed in the little public school for blacks in Paris, and Mordecai went along with her.[10] This school, a frame building consisting of three rooms and a hall, was located on an elevation called "Methodist Hill." To reach it, one had to walk through a sandy bottom for a quarter of a mile, then cross a stream on a plank at the lowest point. Instruction was limited to the elementary grades.

Mordecai had a very retentive, almost photographic, memory. Miss Porter, along with his mother, would select significant literary passages for him to memorize and recite without notes. He became the outstanding pupil in this regard. Miss Porter and the second of his effective early teachers, Benjamin F. Sampson, taught him how to speak looking directly at the audience, correcting a fault that characterized his early efforts.

Benjamin Sampson made a lasting impression on the young Mordecai. He was a man of unusual drive and talents who had moved to Paris after he was forced out of Memphis because of his aggressive stand on racial issues. Sampson, who told Mordecai that he had attended Oberlin College, rigorously drilled and motivated his pupils not only in the fundamentals of mathematics, but also, and especially, in public speaking and debating. According to Mordecai, Sampson gave these instructions among others:

> When you speak, pick out one boy in the room and deliver your speech to him. If he is moved, the whole crowd will be moved; if he laughs at your jokes, everybody will be laughing. If he gets bored or looks as if he didn't believe you, stretch out your hand, shake your fist at him, walk over and tower over him, do anything to hold him and make him believe you.[11]

Sampson taught his charges all the basic rules of debating, including anticipating the opponents' arguments and being prepared to respond to them effectively. This training at the elementary school level served Mordecai well during the remainder of his formal schooling and throughout his career.

Mordecai recalls that his history teachers in public school were not effective and that his best history teacher was a classmate who was a grown man named Caldwell, a rural teacher going to school to get more formal training. Sometimes he would meet Caldwell waiting for him on the way to school. The man would challenge Mordecai on some factual point. He carried a small book of facts with him to verify or give Mordecai the answers. These experiences whetted Mordecai's appetite for learning history, and he persuaded his mother to buy him a large book of facts, such as *The Book of Knowledge*. He began to compile his own book of facts. Mordecai maintained that Caldwell was "one of the best and most provocative teachers" he ever had.[12]

On completing the elementary grades at the school on Methodist Hill, Mordecai's next step was high school. His parents never considered that their son's formal education would be limited to the elementary grades, the highest level available to blacks in Paris. Consequently, they had to look elsewhere for a place where he could further his education.

One prominent school then was the Roger Williams University in Nashville, Tennessee, run under the auspices of the American Baptist Home Mission Society. As mentioned earlier, the society was active in establishing schools for the freedmen in the southern states. In 1867 the Reverend Daniel William Phillips, a Welshman who later settled in New England, had established the Nashville Normal and Theological Institute. In 1883 the American Baptist Home Mission Society assumed responsibility for the institution and obtained a charter for it under the laws of the state of Tennessee. It was renamed the Roger Williams University after the founder of the Baptist movement in America. The school became a thriving institution and attracted a sizable student body and some outstanding teachers. It also gained a reputation for producing some successful graduates: teachers, preachers, and other leaders. Among the teachers at Roger Williams early in the 1890s were John Hope, a Phi Beta Kappa graduate of Brown University, and Samuel H. Archer Sr., an alumnus of Colgate University. Both men later served as president of Morehouse College in Atlanta, Georgia, and were to exert a great influence on Mordecai.

In 1903 Wyatt and Carolyn Johnson sent Mordecai, then thirteen years of age, to Roger Williams University to begin his high school work. A teacher there, a relative of the Reverend G. P. Woodson, by then the pastor of the Mt. Zion Baptist Church, had heard that Mordecai was good at delivering speeches. She had written a speech for him to deliver at the Obion River Baptist Association and was so impressed by his delivery that she encouraged his mother to send him to Roger Williams. She emphasized that because he was a minister's son, his expenses would be only $9 a month. This included room, board, tuition, and laundry, and required one hour of work a day. This schooling was to be Mordecai's first experience of social equality between blacks and whites. G. P. Woodson also sent his son, Robert, to Roger Williams. However, he remained only one year.

Mordecai's first daily assignment was to sweep a long hall that the supervisor covered with sawdust to make sure that Mordecai swept every inch of the floor. He then got a job in the school printing shop and learned to set type, format pages, and operate the printing press. His skill served him well in his later educational endeavors.

At Roger Williams, Archer made a profound and lasting impression on Mordecai because of the clear and inspiring manner in which he taught mathematics. But, more important, Archer emphasized fairness, good sportsmanship, and integrity not only in athletics but also in the classroom. Mordecai developed a very close relationship with Archer that lasted through the years.

Tragedy struck the school, however. During Mordecai's third year (1904–1905) there, fire destroyed its buildings. The institution could not resume operations until two and a half years later.

During one or two summers young Mordecai worked as a clerk in a local grocery store. Among other things he learned how to cut precise weights of bacon from uncut slabs. He was especially excited when large numbers of people would come into town on Saturdays. He said of this experience:

> On Saturdays, when great crowds of people came to the county seat to the court house and on other business, it was my job to go out on one of the leading corners and cook and sell hamburgers. I had a great time doing this—meeting and serving all kinds of people, white and colored from all over Henry County. If I must say so, I could cook a mean hamburger.[13]

Mordecai lived the life of the average energetic boy. In his later years, writing about his medical history in connection with renewing his automobile driver's license, he described his boyhood years as follows:

> During my boyhood and adolescence I lived a vigorous life— fishing, hunting, horseback riding, swimming, engaging in playfully sustained fisticuffs, playing baseball, tin can hockey, football, basketball, and tennis. I have had many blows all over my body and on the head. I have had sprained ankles and a broken left forearm. I have had measles, mumps, attacks of malaria, [and] an attack of influenza (during World War I). I must also have had rheumatic fever in my boyhood, for I discovered by electrocardiograph about thirty years ago, a serious scar on the heart valve carried over from those earlier years.[14]

Apparently no childhood illness or activity affected him in his later years. He also maintained an interest in sports throughout his educational career.

With the burning of the buildings at Roger Williams University, Carolyn had to decide where to send her son to continue his education. Fortunately that decision was not difficult. In 1888 black Baptists in western Tennessee persuaded Peter Howe of Winona, Illinois, to contribute money to establish a school in Memphis to enable their people to prepare themselves in "academic, religious, and industrial training."[15]

Memphis, located on the banks of the Mississippi River about 121 miles southwest of Paris, had a sizable number of African Americans, many cherishing high hopes for themselves and their children. It was one of the largest cities in the South and flourished on an economy bolstered by heavy river commerce that included barges ferrying huge loads of cotton and other goods in both directions. At age sixteen, Mordecai was excited to be in this bustling city.

Although its corporate name was the Memphis Baptist Bible and Normal Institute, Mordecai's new school was called Howe Institute, in recognition of Peter Howe, its benefactor. (Unfortunately, for some reason Howe and his wife were slain in their home before the first building was completed.) This school developed a good reputation for its sound educational program. In time it boasted 500 students. The teachers taught with a sense of mission. Instruction included more than textbook training; emphasis also was placed on manners and decorum. The school was a good place for Mordecai to continue his educational odyssey.

Nevertheless, Mordecai spent only one semester at Howe Institute, where he learned, "in a ragged manner," to do the work at the level of third-year high school. He was not satisfied academically and wanted to change schools. Unfortunately, Roger Williams had not reopened since its disastrous fire.

Wyatt and Carolyn wanted their son's education to be continued in a Baptist-affiliated institution that offered high school and college work. The Atlanta Baptist College was the closest in this category. Therefore, Mordecai did not seriously consider African-American schools in Tennessee. Fisk University in Nashville was affiliated with the Congregational Church, Lane College in Jackson was associated with the Methodist Church, Knoxville College with the Presbyterians, and Le Moyne, also in Memphis, with the Congregationalists. Except for Fisk, the other schools were still fledgling institutions. At the same time, the Atlanta Baptist College had rapidly acquired a reputation as a school for men. The Johnsons decided that this was the school Mordecai should attend. Also, they were aware that their friend, the Reverend General Pillow Woodson [no known relation to the Woodsons in Memphis,

Tennessee] had sent his son Robert, Mordecai's best friend, to Atlanta Baptist College, where he was enrolled in the English Preparatory Course designed for students planning to enter high school. Robert had expressed great enthusiasm for the school. Moreover, Mordecai learned that his beloved professor at Roger Williams University, Samuel H. Archer, had gone to Atlanta Baptist College. All these factors were sufficient to convince the Johnsons that Atlanta Baptist College was the place for Mordecai.

That September, Mordecai and Robert Woodson boarded the train together in shared excitement over going to Atlanta. Bob was returning as a first-year student, while Mordecai was planning to enter as a high school senior, a decision that would be changed later.

Atlanta would be the largest city that Mordecai had ever seen. Even then, it was rapidly gaining a reputation as the "Gate City of the South." The city was strategically located on principal rail lines and highway routes and was steeped in southern history. General William Tecumseh Sherman had passed that way on his devastating march to Savannah, but the city had recovered rapidly. By 1894 ambitious plans were under way for sponsoring the largest exposition ever staged in the South. Atlanta staged this historically significant event the following year. The city was bustling with activity; the huge exposition had brought notoriety and visitors from all over the South. Business boomed.

During the exposition, Booker T. Washington, principal of Tuskegee Institute, made the famous speech that diffused the fear in the minds of many Southerners that African Americans would seek "social equality." In that speech, Washington said, "In all things that are purely social, we can be as separate as the fingers; yet as one as the hand in all things essential to mutual progress." That assertion was manifested a year later in the *Plessy* v. *Ferguson* decision of the Supreme Court, holding that in public transportation African Americans could be separated while the accommodations were "separate but equal."

Besides Atlanta Baptist College, other African-American institutions in Atlanta included Atlanta University, founded in 1865 by the Congregationalists; Clark University, founded in 1869 under the auspices of the Methodist Episcopal Church; and Morris Brown College, established in 1881 by the African Methodist Episcopal (AME) Church. The city was also the site of Spelman Seminary, now Spelman College, founded in 1881. Named for Laura Spelman, the mother of John D. Rockefeller Sr., the school was devoted exclusively to the education of young women. This school was of special significance to the men of Atlanta Baptist College, and, in more than one sense, was a sister institution. It, too, was under the auspices of the American Baptist Home Mission Society, and the two institutions were closely situated.

Although Mordecai had done third-year high school work at Roger Williams and at Howe Institute, the experience and results were unsatisfactory. So, in consultation with his advisor, he entered the third-year academy class at the college, a decision that he concluded was providential. The move to Atlanta Baptist College enabled him to have significant contact with Professor Benjamin Brawley, a renowned scholar in English. Brawley's instruction had a "creative effect" on Mordecai's use of the English language and on his speaking. That first year in Atlanta was pivotal. He realized that this was where he needed and wanted to be, and he looked forward to five more years there en route to obtaining his college degree.

At the close of that school year Mordecai returned to Memphis to find work for the summer. There he became manager of the Iroquois Cafe, owned by two young men whose primary interest in other projects kept them from operating it.

In Memphis, Mordecai joined the "Primrose Club," an organization of about forty young people whose families cherished high ideals and achievement for their children. The club sponsored many activities designed to be educational and to provide for a wholesome social life for its members. It sponsored musical programs and meetings where members discussed timely subjects and issues.

Memphis was also where the adolescent Mordecai first experienced profound love for a member of the opposite sex. During his early adolescence in Paris, Tennessee, however, he had not been immune to the attractions of pretty girls. In one memoir he tells of his admiration for the Bobo girls there ("two of the most beautiful feminine creatures in the world") and of Gladys Langford, a "very pretty" girl of his own age, whom he called his sweetheart while in elementary school. He tells of how he hoped his walk to school would coincide with hers so he could carry her books. Also, he recounts how, following Sunday School, he and his friends would rush over to Quinn Chapel AME Church hoping to see the beautiful girls before *their* Sunday School adjourned. Such experiences to him were "adventurous and thrilling to the nth degree."[16] They were exciting, but not profound.

Mordecai's experience that summer was of a different nature altogether. The home in which he had a room was directly across the street from that of a prominent family that included a daughter of striking beauty. From time to time her mother would send her over with a piece of cake for Mordecai's proprietress. (The mother may have sent the cake over to Mordecai; his notes are not clear on this point.) The daughter's name was Alice Clinton Woodson.[17] The friends of this young lady called her "Sweet Alice," which described her personality.

Alice's father, Benjamin F. Woodson, born in Ohio in 1844, was a graduate of Wilberforce University. He was of the family of Woodsons of whom Thomas Woodson was the first born. The Woodsons were said to be direct descendants of Thomas Jefferson through a liaison with his slave, Sally Hemmings.[18] She is believed by some to have been Thomas Jefferson's consort following the death of his wife when he was only thirty-nine years old. Although Jefferson survived his wife by forty-four years, he never re-married. Members of the Woodson family were instrumental in the founding of Wilberforce in 1856.

Benjamin Woodson had a successful practice in Memphis as an attorney and a contractor. Alice's mother, Alice Allen Woodson, was a native of Memphis and a member of the first class to enter Fisk University when it opened in 1866. Part of her maternal family descended from a long line of free blacks who had migrated from New Bern, North Carolina, to Ohio, and who had cherished their status of freedmen for almost two centuries.

Alice Woodson was also a member of the Primrose Club. She and Mordecai found many opportunities to know and appreciate each other in their school activities and as they helped to plan and to participate in the programs of the club. Evidently they spent much time together. In later years Mordecai described this relationship as follows:

> I came to know this girl. She was only 14 and I was 17. She became a beautiful friend and we had a very strong mutual affection for each other. I knew her only for one summer but the memory of that very natural, sweet, clean fellowship held my affection over a period of nearly sixty years when we separated by going to different schools far away from each other.[19]

Obviously that summer was an unforgettable one for Mordecai. He returned to Atlanta Baptist College to complete his high school work and begin his post-secondary studies. He was one academic year ahead of Alice. It was still too early in his life for a profound sense of a personal mission in the distant future. His focus was on the exciting present. In parting, he and Alice pledged loyalty to each other and vowed to keep in touch by mail. Each would be a constant inspiration to the other throughout the remainder of their student days.

2

Formative Years in Atlanta

*M*ordecai returned to his fourth-year class at the academy of Atlanta Baptist College with a renewed spirit and a determination to make his second year there better than the first. His summer in Memphis had been eventful. He had greatly enjoyed the company of old and new friends. He was able to save some money from his job at the cafe, thus easing his parents' financial obligations to the college. His job in the printing office on the campus would provide additional freedom from financial worry.

The college was on the verge of some significant developments. After a productive tenure as president of Atlanta Baptist College, Dr. George Sale had resigned. (Most of the institutions for African Americans established by northern missionaries still had white presidents.) The time was ripe for the first African-American educator to head the school. That year, the trustees appointed John Hope as acting president. He was a young, imaginative, and well-trained Phi Beta Kappa graduate of Brown University, where he had majored in the classics. Hope had taught at Roger Williams University in Nashville from 1894 to 1898 before transferring to Atlanta Baptist College.

A native of Augusta, Georgia, Hope was the son of James Hope, a successful Scotch businessman and an intelligent young woman possessing some African-American blood. They were devoted to one another, but Georgia laws prohibited them from marrying. Nevertheless, they established a happy home where they reared their three children.[1] John Hope was blue-eyed and blond, with no distinguishing Negroid features. He could have easily been assimilated into the white world, as were some of his relatives. Just before his graduation from Brown University, a faculty committee urged him to take a job in Providence on the staff of the *Providence Journal,* a position that could have separated him from the African-American community. Nevertheless he resolutely maintained a commitment to retain his identity and devote his talents to the service of African Americans.[2]

As acting president, Hope had the full cooperation of students, faculty, and members of the Atlanta community. Because this appointment represented an unusual achievement for an African American, and because the title "acting" suggested a trial period that might, or might not, lead to a regular appointment, the students, as reported by Mordecai, met and resolved that their deportment and overall performance would be of such a nature that it would not reflect negatively on his leadership.

Apparently Mordecai found keeping this resolution difficult. His imagination and adolescent energy sometimes found expression in impish ways and a mischievous disposition. The institution had a policy of placing younger students with older ones. His roommate then was William J. Harvey Jr., a college senior, who after graduation became an outstanding religious and educational leader. According to Harvey, Mordecai for a time was one of the most prankish boys on campus. On certain nights, said Harvey, Mordecai would secretly bring to his room some old Civil War cannonballs from a pile on the campus. After all the dormitory residents had retired, Mordecai would roll the balls down the stairs, causing quite a clamor. He then would rumple his hair, rub his eyes, hustle into bed, and pretend that he had been sleeping all the while when the dormitory monitor made the rounds looking for the culprit.[3]

The reasons for Mordecai's pranks can only be speculated on. Perhaps they were merely the boyish pranks of a fourteen-year-old or rebellion against certain rules with which he disagreed, or maybe he felt a sense of frustration on being separated from "Sweet Alice" back in Memphis. Nevertheless, the school had applied all appropriate sanctions against him without results. Acting President Hope wrote to his father about his behavior.

In a letter postmarked Paris, Tennessee, January 22, 1907, the Reverend Wyatt Johnson responded to President Hope's letter as follows:

> Prof. John Hope, Dear Brother. I received your letter yesterday relative to my boy. I wrote him a letter tonight which I think will have effect upon him. I am truly glad that you bear with him a little. I hope that you will have no further trouble with him along

these lines. If after he fails to obey all your rules let me know. I will have him to come home. He must by all means obey and I give him to understand that. I am your brother in Christ, W. J. Johnson.[4]

Thereafter, Mordecai modified his behavior and became an outstanding student in the academy.

During his first two years at Atlanta Baptist College, Mordecai registered and signed his name as Wyatt Mordecai Johnson. He later reversed the order of his given names and became known as Mordecai Wyatt Johnson.[5] No record exists as to the reason for that change. It may have indicated a desire for self-determination or his preference for the name "Mordecai." Then again, it may have been symbolic of an emotional distance from his father.

Atlanta Baptist College boasted of having inspiring teachers pledged to the task of making real men out of the youths who came under their tutelage. Certainly John Hope, Benjamin G. Brawley, and Samuel H. Archer Sr. were in this group. Archer's influence on Mordecai continued from their association at Roger Williams University. Archer was a master teacher and a rigorous disciplinarian, but he was always fair and considerate. Mordecai's appreciation of him may have been due in part to some consideration that Archer gave him during his mischievous days. Many years later, upon Archer's death in 1941, Mordecai's telegram of condolence to the family described Archer in part:

> He was a man who possessed a living and vigorous moral integrity of the most inspiring kind. For this I owe him the most precious debt which a man can owe to another. I shall be grateful to him as long as I live. I have named one of my sons after him and I shall continue to teach my students to know and revere him as I do.[6]

At the conclusion of his senior year at the academy of Atlanta Baptist College, Mordecai received a scholarship for attaining the highest academic average in the class. Clearly he had immersed himself in the academic life of the college and had refrained from his earlier infractions against school rules. In addition, Mordecai won three of the five other prizes and awards open to all the students in the academy: the prizes for excellence in debate, in English composition, and in Scripture reading.[7] As a result, when he entered his freshman college year in the fall of 1907, he had established his reputation as a highly competent student.

Besides Archer, among the other teachers who greatly influenced Mordecai were Benjamin G. Brawley in English, Matthew W. Bullock in geology and the social sciences, John Hope in philosophy, and Charles H. Wardlaw in geology. Each of these men played a role in guiding Mordecai's intellectual journey. From them he gained insights, inspiration, and solid academic grounding for the kind of leadership he was to exert as an adult.

While maintaining high academic standing in all of his courses, Mordecai participated in most of the co-curricular activities offered by the school. He was a varsity debater; co-editor of the student newspaper, the *Athenaeum* (produced in cooperation with Spelman students); and member of the glee club, where he sang in the bass section. He also was a star quarterback on the football team. In one game against Atlanta University, he made four touchdowns in a game ending with a score of 44 to 0.[8] Mordecai and his close friend, John W. Davis, who also played football, were members of the first varsity basketball team at Morehouse in 1910. Davis was Mordecai's classmate and close friend throughout most of their years at Atlanta Baptist College—a friendship that lasted all their lives. A native of Milledgeville, Georgia, Davis had attended Americus Institute in Georgia and was an excellent and hardworking student. He enjoyed the full confidence of the faculty and held some important campus jobs.

Along with programs for academic and athletic development, the institution fostered serious, required activities in which Mordecai had the opportunity to expand his religious perspectives. For example, the catalog of 1908–1909 states that "besides the daily morning and evening devotions, religious exercises are held as follows: Sunday, 1:30 P.M., Y.M.C.A.; 7:00 P.M., Preaching Service; Thursday, 6:45 P.M., Prayer Meeting."

Nevertheless, these religious exercises were not sufficient to discourage Mordecai from violating college rules again. When he was in his junior year, despite all of his academic, athletic, and other achievements up to that time, Mordecai committed a serious infraction against the strict college regulations. For many years card playing was prohibited in most, if not all, of the colleges founded by the northern missionaries. This offense was considered so serious that institutions suspended students who violated the rule. When a college official caught Mordecai playing cards in his room, he was suspended from the institution. The idea of suspending one of its most promising students was not a pleasant decision for the college. Nevertheless, in spite of Mordecai's excellent scholastic and overall reputation, the officials followed the rule. They did give some thought to the effect this would have on his parents, especially his mother, whose life revolved around her brilliant son. Accordingly, instead of sending him back home to Paris, Tennessee, the college allowed Mordecai to spend his suspension period with a relative in Chicago. During that time John Davis forwarded to Chicago all the letters

Mordecai's parents sent to him in Atlanta. Correspondingly, Mordecai wrote responses to these letters and sent them to Davis to be postmarked from Atlanta. His parents never had to deal with the heartache of their son's being suspended from college.[9]

When his suspension ended, Mordecai returned to the college, where the officials allowed him to remain on condition that he share a room with Davis. Because Davis had shown such trustworthiness and sense of responsibility, the faculty charged him with keeping Mordecai in line for the rest of his stay at the college. In later years, Mordecai said that he would have lost respect for the college if the officials had not suspended him for his infraction.

Mordecai caught up with his classwork and graduated with high honors in May 1911. Besides John W. Davis, others in Mordecai's class receiving the Bachelor of Arts degree included Philip M. Davis, who became principal of the Slater School in Birmingham, Alabama; Samuel A. Owens, who was appointed president of Florida Memorial College in Live Oak and who later helped found a college that bore his name in Memphis, Tennessee; and King D. Reddick, who was a Sunday School field worker in Alabama. At that commencement two other close friends of Mordecai were graduated from Morehouse Academy: J. B. Adams, who eventually became the pastor of the large Concord Baptist Church in Brooklyn, New York; and Mordecai's boyhood friend, Robert Woodson of Paris, Tennessee. Woodson, after completing his freshman college year in May 1912, enrolled in an embalming school in Cincinnati, Ohio. A year later, he established a successful undertaking business in his hometown.

During his six years at Atlanta Baptist College, Mordecai had excelled so as a scholar and leader that upon his graduation President Hope immediately hired him as an English instructor. For a while, he substituted for the great English teacher and dean, Benjamin Brawley, who went on leave during the 1911–1912 academic year. Later he taught economics, a discipline that remained an interest throughout his career. One of his responsibilities was to coach the debating team, a prestigious co-curricula activity in which he delighted. Ever since his introduction to public speaking and debating in elementary school, debating had been one of his favorite activities. For many years the institution was part of a five-member college debating consortium that included Fisk University and Talladega College. Under Mordecai's tutelage his teams won honors in intercollegiate competition.

Mordecai's undergraduate roommate, Davis, was also hired as an instructor at Morehouse upon graduation. Davis was to remain at Morehouse for five years, the last three as registrar.

In their second year of teaching at the college, Mordecai and Davis assisted the football coach, Samuel H. Archer. Frank Forbes writes that the 1912 team "not only won championship honors, but amassed a total of 205 points compared with a total of only nine for the five opponents—which establishes this team, up through this writing [1966] as the greatest offensive-defensive machine to ever represent Morehouse in football."[10]

Throughout his college career, Mordecai and Alice Woodson kept in close touch with each other. Through regular correspondence, he kept her informed of his various activities as student and teacher. He told her of the events on the campus and of his part in them. She wrote to him about her intramural activities and her delight to learn of his teaching position. The letters were regular and cherished by both Mordecai and Alice. Their correspondence served to sustain their relationship and their affection for one another.

After finishing high school in Memphis, Alice had enrolled at Howard University in Washington, D.C. She lived with her aunt and uncle, Dr. and Mrs. Jesse E. Moorland. Dr. Moorland, a trustee of Howard University, was active in the Young Men's Christian Association (YMCA) at the national level. After her freshman year, Alice transferred to Fisk University as a home economics major. Her mother had attended Fisk and was a member of the first class that entered the day it opened in 1866. Alice enjoyed Fisk, but she always looked forward to the day when she and Mordecai could be together again. Occasionally he managed to make brief visits to Nashville during her years there. They discussed getting married when she graduated in 1912, the year he completed his first stint as a college teacher.

Their relationship had progressed to the point where definite plans for their future were in order. Mordecai was prepared. Since his faculty appointment at Morehouse, he had been saving for the future. During his first year of teaching, he had scrupulously managed his finances. With the term behind him and the assurance of a permanent position, he was confident of his financial stability. His idea of having a special mission in life had not yet developed.

The letters he and Alice exchanged were full of hope and expectation. They had agreed that he would arrive in Nashville just prior to her graduation to make a formal proposal for marriage and so that they could discuss their prospects for the future. It was, therefore, with great pride and expectation that Mordecai prepared for his trip to Nashville to see the beautiful young lady who had inspired him since his adolescent days. They had agreed to announce their engagement after that visit.

Mordecai's trip to Nashville in May 1912 to propose marriage to Alice was destined to be memorable for both of them. One can imagine his impatience on the train and during the ride from the train station to the Fisk campus. Alice's letters had assured him that she was awaiting his arrival with similar expectation. And, to be sure, she was in her room waiting eagerly. With great anticipation, he climbed the steps of Jubilee Hall, the girls' dormitory, approached the matron's desk, and asked to see Miss Alice Woodson. For some strange reason—perhaps because she did not want young women at Fisk to be courted by anyone outside of Nashville—the matron told Mordecai that Miss Woodson was "out with her Meharry boy friend."[11]

Mordecai's shock at this announcement was profound, in view of his and Alice's past relationship and the plans for this visit. Despite all the professions of love through the years, all the wonderful but much too brief visits, and particularly the expectations for this special trip to Nashville, could she really be so callous and unfaithful? Perhaps. It was common knowledge that the men at the nearby Meharry Medical College generally dated Fisk women. Perhaps this was the ultimate proof. Besides, Mordecai had no reason to suspect the matron of lying.

Mordecai was profoundly hurt. He had never experienced rejection. Certainly he had all the credentials any aspiring bride could wish for. He was an outstanding scholar and athlete, a college graduate, and a college teacher with a promising future, and he had an acceptable physical appearance. He waited around a while in disbelief. But with the anguish of one who has been painfully betrayed by a very special friend, he decided to leave and return to Atlanta. Before departing, he left a message with the matron to give Alice: "Tell her I was here."

For her part, Alice, after getting dressed for what was to be one of the most important moments of her life, waited in her room for a long time after Mordecai was due to arrive. She came down from her room and asked the matron whether anyone had come looking for her. The deceptive matron, disregarding Mordecai's request to give Alice his message, said, "No, no one has come to see you tonight." Alice, too, was incredulous. Could it be that "Monty" [this and "Monnie" were his two nicknames] was unfeeling and unfaithful, that he had never been honest and sincere in his pledges of undying love? Had he changed his mind? She persuaded herself to believe that he must have been held up for some reason or that the train was late. She waited a while, but her beloved Monty did not show up. Thinking she had been jilted, she was both furious and heartbroken. She ran back to her room, sobbing.

As the Louisville and Nashville train rumbled back to Atlanta, Mordecai's mood was profoundly different from the anticipation he felt earlier. Instead of happy reflections on seeing Alice again and making plans for their marriage, his thoughts had to be of love betrayed, of how to assuage his anguish, and of how he now must reorganize his plans for the future. From that day forward Alice, no longer "Sweet Alice," must be simply a part of his past. The future would always be open to new possibilities.

After returning to Atlanta, Mordecai decided to write Alice to express his disappointment with her. With bitter eloquence he poured out his anger at her duplicity.

Alice's reply was not long coming. She asked Mordecai why he was continuing to try to deceive her. She stated that she had never left the dormitory the night he was supposed to be there and that the matron could attest to the fact. Certainly if he had really been there, the matron would have let her know. Not showing up was bad enough; pretending that he had come was even worse.

In such bitter exchanges, neither could be convinced of the other's sincerity. The avenues of communication between the two remained closed indefinitely.

3

Graduate School and Marriage

*M*ordecai Wyatt Johnson's apparent rejection by Alice Woodson could have resulted in a period of depression or the loss of a sense of personal worth. Whatever the psychological consequences, the experience seemed to stimulate his pursuit of learning. After settling his affairs, he set out for Chicago, where he stayed with relatives and took some courses at the University of Chicago. Doubtless, the start of a new educational odyssey refocused his mind and his energies. The change was good for him.

Johnson's first year of teaching led him to appreciate even more the importance of a thorough grounding in one's discipline. Chicago significantly challenged him intellectually. He welcomed the opportunity and buried himself in his studies.

The University of Chicago, formed in 1890 by the oil magnate, John D. Rockefeller Sr., was from the beginning a highly prestigious center of learning. Except for the well-established Ivy League schools of the East, it was the premier institution of the time. Students seeking unquestioned academic credentials were certain to obtain them upon satisfactory completion of their studies there. The university required even honors graduates from small and little-known colleges to take certain courses to meet the university's standards for an undergraduate degree.

At Chicago, Johnson spent time with outstanding scholars. Although he had earned a bachelor's degree from Atlanta Baptist College, another bachelor's degree from the University of Chicago would further validate his undergraduate credentials and enhance his career aspirations. Also, by broadening his intellectual horizons and immersing himself in his studies, he could be distracted from the disappointment resulting from his experience in Nashville some weeks earlier. An added incentive for studying at the University of Chicago was that his college roommate, John W. Davis, would also be enrolled there.

Johnson deliberately took courses that challenged his thinking. When he told some friends that he was going to the University of Chicago, they strongly urged him against it, on the grounds that the university was "a hotbed of atheism and communism." When they realized that he was determined to go, his friends urged him to avoid taking two courses: first, "that thing called evolution; it will ruin your religion" and second, "socialism . . . you will just be ruined in every way." Johnson duly ignored that advice. As he relates,

> When the dean of the graduate school said to me, "Johnson, you can take three courses. What are they?" I said, "Dean Small, I do not know what the third course is. I have not made up my mind yet, but the course in evolution and the course in socialism—I want them right away."
>
> So I took those two courses, and I will never forget as long as I live the profound creative contribution that those two courses gave to me. I did not become an indoctrinated member of the Socialist Party. I was not converted to the materialistic theory of history. I did not lose my belief in God, because in the light of evolution I saw that the universe was a magnificent thing that has taken hundreds of millions of years to grow. It enlarged my conception of God. After that I could not put Him in my vest pocket.[1]

At the end of the summer term, Johnson returned to Atlanta and busied himself preparing for the coming school year. Atlanta Baptist College was developing rapidly. In the fall of 1913 the trustees had the institution's charter altered. They changed the school's name to Morehouse College in honor of Henry Lyman Morehouse, the dedicated secretary of the American Baptist Home Mission Society under whose auspices the college operated. Everyone applauded the change. In commemoration, Johnson wrote the words of the first Morehouse song, set to the tune of an old English melody.[2] Many generations of Morehouse men have sung these words lustily:

Morehouse College, Morehouse College,
Morehouse College, bless her name.
Whether in defeat or victory,
We're loyal just the same.
And we'll cheer for Morehouse College
And for her we'll fight for fame.
And we'll sing her praises
Loud in every land,
Morehouse College, bless her name.

For a long time this song was the only musical tribute to the college until the creation of the much-loved "Morehouse Hymn," composed by J. O. B. Moseley of the class of 1929. In gatherings of the general alumni association, graduates often sing the older Morehouse song following the hymn.

Meanwhile, Johnson began to think about a social life, but not one that would involve the kind of commitment that characterized his earlier affair of the heart. Like other men of Atlanta Baptist College, he had responded to the charms of the young women at nearby Spelman Seminary. Now, however, he could entertain all notions of social relations with an open mind. During this his second year of teaching at the newly designated Morehouse, Johnson was struck by the beauty and other personal attributes of a young Spelman student enrolled in his history class. She was Anna Ethelyn Gardner, a native of Augusta, Georgia.

Anna Ethelyn (as an adult she used her middle name more often than the first) was one of two daughters of Robert and Elizabeth Gardner, a prominent family in the city. Robert Gardner was an industrious artisan, a brick mason who provided a comfortable living for his family. Elizabeth was a homemaker, noted for how well she cared her children. She also was a striking beauty, even in her final years.[3] Because they lived on Phillips Street, directly across from the Lucy Laney Normal and Industrial Institute, the Gardners were constantly reminded of the importance of education.

The African-American community in Augusta had a distinctive educational tradition. As many as six African-American men reared there became college presidents. Among these were John Hope of Morehouse College and Nathan W. Collier of Florida Memorial College.[4] Among other prominent African Americans whose roots were in Augusta were Channing H. Tobias of the National Council of the YMCA and Walter White, executive secretary of the National Association for the Advancement of Colored People (NAACP).

This determination to get an education was even more remarkable because the city of Augusta provided no four-year public high school for its black citizens until as late as 1943. Parents wanting full secondary education in Augusta for their children had to send them to one of the three private institutions that were available to African Americans. These were Paine College, supported by the Methodist Church; the Walker Baptist High School; or the Lucy Laney Normal and Industrial Institute, originally known as Haines Institute. Yet, however inspiring the history and success of these privately supported institutions were, many parents were unable to afford the tuition. The Gardners saw to it that their daughters received good academic preparation. Both Anna Ethelyn and her sister Mary attended Lucy Laney Normal and Industrial Institute. The Gardners lived next door to the school's founder, Miss Lucy Laney. She was a constant source of inspiration to the young women.

Miss Laney was a remarkable educator. She was the seventh child in a family of ten children. Her father was a Presbyterian minister born into slavery, but he purchased his freedom by using his skills as a carpenter. Even in her early years Miss Laney showed unusual intellectual abilities and promise. She was chosen to be a member of the first class at Atlanta University and graduated in 1873.[5] After establishing the school, she guided it through difficult times and became a role model for young and old alike. In an address during one of his visits to Augusta, Johnson called Miss Laney "Mother of the children of the people." These words are inscribed on her tombstone located on the grounds of the school.

The Gardner family attended the Union Baptist Church on Green Street, a congregation that included the more sophisticated and well-to-do among the African Americans in the community.[6] John Hope, his mother, his siblings, and some other relatives all belonged to this church. The ministers constantly encouraged the congregation's young people to seek an education. One of the ministers, the Reverend John Dart, impressed by Hope's intellectual promise, challenged him to go north to continue his education. Dart also helped to raise funds enabling Hope to make the trip. Hope enrolled in Worcester (Massachusetts) Academy, and secured a job in that area to help meet his expenses. On graduating from Haines Institute, Mary Gardner (Anna Ethelyn's sister) went to Paine College and majored in music. Anna Ethelyn went to Talladega College in Alabama to pursue a degree. After two semesters there she transferred to Spelman Seminary (now College) in Atlanta.[7] In his memoirs, Johnson recalls that it was probably at Talladega where he first met Anna Ethelyn, perhaps when he took the debating team there.[8]

Two years younger than Johnson, Anna Ethelyn Gardner had all the qualities of refinement that he admired. She was reserved, thoughtful, and unassuming, and her conversation was never trivial. The mutual attraction grew slowly but steadily, although Anna Ethelyn was careful not to appear aggressive in the relationship. After all, Johnson was the teacher and she was the student. At that time the rules at Spelman governing male-female relationships were scrupulously strict, especially regarding a romantic relationship between a teacher and student. Not until Anna Ethelyn graduated in 1914, with an A.B. degree, could the couple engage in a normal courtship.

Meanwhile, Johnson had begun to think seriously about his life work. He had considered a career in the ministry ever since his boyhood. The idea took hold when he listened intently to his father's powerful preaching and the Bible stories his mother read to him. By now, in his second year of teaching, he was twenty-three years old. The definitive decision regarding the course of his life came dramatically and unexpectedly. In the fall of 1912, his beloved mother, Carolyn, whose love and care had meant so much to him through the years, died. Now he had to come to terms with what, after all, his life should be about. Also, at that time he finally was able to speak comfortably man-to-man with his father. Before returning to Atlanta from the funeral, Johnson spent several nights seated in a cozy chair that his mother had given him. He wrestled with the crucial question of what direction his life should take. He described it to Mary White Ovington as follows:

> Always, I started with my death. Before, I had looked forward, now I looked back. If I were lying dead, as I had seen my mother lie, what in life would be worthwhile? What, of the many things that I had done, would justify my existence? What would have meaning?
>
> One night, as I rocked in my familiar seat, I had a vision. I was lying on my deathbed in a rough cabin, quite alone. The place was very still. Then, silently, the door opened and people came in, poorly dressed, plain people, who moved in line past my bed. And as they passed, each had something to say in affection and gratitude. I had helped one who was in trouble. I had comforted another. I had given wise counsel to a third. I saw the line distinctly, coming in and passing out, while I lay there, dying, on the coarse bed.
>
> [As] I went to sleep that night, I knew that I had found the meaning of life. It was service to the poor and afflicted.[9]

Through this moving spiritual awakening, Johnson recognized and affirmed the course his life would take. It doubtless reminded him of his mother's vision of the Old Testament Mordecai and the implication that he had a destiny to fulfill. He decided to return to Chicago in the summer of 1913 to complete work for his second bachelor's degree. He took courses in English (Daily and Fortnightly Themes), English Literature for Teachers, and Elementary French. He received the bachelor's degree in September of that year.

Johnson's next step was to go to a theological seminary to earn his academic credentials for the ministry. The nation's oldest and foremost Baptist-related theological school then was the Newton Theological Institution in Newton Centre, Massachusetts. Because his academic standards had always been high, it was natural that Johnson would want to attend that institution.

Founded in 1825, Newton boasted a strong faculty and curriculum. Its graduates were among the leading clergymen in the country. Between 1900 and 1926, however, the school followed a policy of denying admission to African-American students. The officials did not wish to discourage prospective white students from the South who might resent studying on an equal basis with blacks.[10] Thus, because of his racial heritage, Johnson was denied admission to his first choice for a theological school. This racial discrimination, especially by a supposedly *Christian* theological school, dramatized for him the need for what he was later to refer to as a "moral and spiritual engineer." Such a person would be in the vanguard denouncing this type of wrong and constantly calling attention to the social tenets of the Gospel.

Johnson was only one of several promising African-American young men who, because of their race, were denied admission to Newton Theological Institution during those years. Among these was Benjamin Elijah Mays, a Phi Beta Kappa graduate of Bates College. According to Mays,

> When the Newton "scout" came to Bates recruiting in the spring of 1920, he made it quite plain that Newton was not interested in Negro students, and advised me to go to Virginia Union University where I had spent my freshman college year. . . . So the famous Newton Theological Seminary was . . . prejudiced.[11]

After being discouraged officially from applying to Newton, Mays enrolled at the University of Chicago where he earned M.A. and Ph.D. degrees. Later he distinguished himself as a YMCA executive, dean of the School of Religion at Howard University, president of Morehouse College, and president of the Atlanta Board of Education.

The Newton Theological Institution also denied admission to Howard Thurman, an honor graduate of Morehouse College. Thurman writes,

> From high school days, I heard about Newton Theological Seminary. . . . The school carried an attractive advertisement in the *Watchman Examiner*, a Baptist journal that I had seen in our little academy library in Jacksonville. I wrote a letter to Newton Seminary inquiring about admission. In reply, I received a very cordial letter from the president expressing his regret that the school did not admit Negroes, and referring me to Virginia Union, a Baptist missionary college in Richmond, Virginia. The letter wished me well. It assured me that at Virginia Union I would be able to secure the kind of training I would need to provide *religious leadership for my people.*[12] [emphasis added]

Thurman matriculated at and graduated with high honors from the Rochester Theological Seminary and became one of the most distinguished spiritual leaders in America. In its April 6, 1953, issue, *Life Magazine* selected him as one of the "Great Preachers" of this century. Not until 1925, under a new and enlightened administration, did Newton change its racial admission policy.[13]

Throughout his life Johnson had to deal with the issue of race. He was ever mindful of the injustice of slavery, endured by his own father while a young man before the end of the Civil War. He was keenly aware of the discrimination that still hindered the advancement of black people. He was committed to pursuing a mission. That mission was to make a difference in society in whatever ways were open to him: as a pastor, on the public platform, or as an educator. He would fight against discrimination based on race, especially the institutional racism he encountered from his first choice of a theological seminary.

When the doors of Newton Theological Institution were closed to him, Johnson, at age twenty-three, applied to and was admitted to Rochester Theological Seminary, Rochester, New York, in September 1913. One of his Atlanta Baptist College schoolmates, Charles D. Hubert, had graduated from Rochester in 1912, and Johnson felt comfortable applying there. He had no certainty, however, of being admitted, because Rochester, as did certain other northern institutions, had a quota system for African Americans. In this instance, only two African Americans were admitted at a time.

Rochester had a rich tradition. In 1849 an organization of the Baptist clergy of the state of New York, sensing the need for providing sound professional theological training for young men headed for the ministry, formed the New York Baptist Union for Ministerial Education. In May of the following year this group was incorporated as a Board of Trustees for the founding of the Rochester Theological Seminary, which opened for instruction in November 1850.[14] Soon this institution established a reputation as an outstanding center for theological education. Some nationally known scholars were on the faculty. The curriculum was relevant for the times, and its graduates showed solid preparation wherever they served.

At Rochester, Johnson was influenced by some great teachers, notably Walter Rauschenbusch. It was this prophetic scholar who popularized the idea of the "social gospel." Born in 1861, he was a native of New York State. He received his early education in Germany, but returned to this country to complete his college and theological training at the University of Rochester and the Rochester Theological Seminary. He served on the faculty of the seminary from 1897 to 1918, during which time he exercised a powerful influence on theological thought in America. As no other American theologian had before him, Rauschenbusch interpreted the teaching of Jesus in terms of its demands for social reform. The ills of a rapidly expanding industrial society in this country were growing acute. Some industries were grossly exploiting their workers, as evidenced by factory "sweat shops," and workers wages and benefits were pitifully low. Rauschenbusch believed that the Christian church had a special responsibility to challenge the system to provide more equitable wages and better working and living conditions for laborers. Two of his books, *Christianity and the Social Crisis*[15] and *A Theology for the Social Gospel*,[16] were landmarks of social idealism, and for a long time served as the principal inspiration for the social gospel movement. Under Rauschenbusch, who exhibited a strong sense of mission, Johnson was imbued with a deeper sense than ever before of the social implications of Christianity. His commitment to these ideals informed his sense of mission in all of his public activity in subsequent years.

Johnson was an outstanding student at Rochester. He led his class in grade averages during the three years there and graduated as valedictorian. During those years, he kept up a steady correspondence with his college mentor, President John Hope of Morehouse, informing Hope of his scholastic standing at the seminary.

While at the seminary, Johnson served as pastor of the Second Baptist Church in Mumford, New York, a small community a few miles from Rochester. He enjoyed his duties there, which he assumed in January 1914. During the summers he lived on a farm some two miles from the village, where he could have "plenty of quiet for rest and study and where I shall have all the good greens and vegetables and fruits to eat." He continued:

> Here I shall gain a much-needed discipline in adaptation of mind and soul to the needs and affections of plain people and, incidentally, I shall have the opportunity of studying first hand the problems of the rural church. I am persuaded that here in this field of the rural church lies one of the largest opportunities for religious work that can be found among our people.[17]

At Second Baptist, Johnson developed his talents as a preacher and administrator, and was able to practice the professional skills he was learning at the seminary.

As his theological studies progressed, Johnson constantly wrestled with the problem of what direction his life should take. However, he had a definite sense of mission. He was greatly inspired by his studies during his first year at the seminary and expressed a keen desire to get on with whatever he was called to do. In fervid language he stated:

> Sometimes I get very impatient at my studies. I long to be in the thick of the fight! Religion is going to be a great factor in the new adjustment. There never was such a reformation as we are now on the verge of. *This religion reemphasized with new aspects to suit the modern needs will bring forth great moral and spiritual engineers. God grant that I may be one of these among my own people!*[18] [emphasis added]

During his senior year at the seminary, Johnson had several promising offers for positions. Some of his professors urged him to continue his studies on the graduate level, assuring him of adequate financial assistance should he choose further study. But he had "a passion to preach" and decided to enter the pastorate for the time being. He also had a desire for further study. But this aspiration, as he wrote to John Hope, was

> . . . not merely for the sake of standing among men with high degrees. My interest in knowledge grows out of my interest in life, and it is my desire that such further studies as I may pursue will

contribute directly to my knowledge about the life and problems of today and all time and to my larger usefulness in a specific sphere.[19]

Johnson's words in this letter were partly in reply to an offer from Hope to teach at Morehouse College. For several years after his graduation from Rochester, both Hope and Samuel Archer continued to offer Johnson teaching positions at Morehouse. Throughout his time at the seminary, Johnson maintained a close relationship with his former colleagues at Morehouse. Out of his meager student resources, from time to time he made financial contributions to the college.

Rochester Theological Seminary, as was the practice in certain other theological schools, made a distinction between graduating a student and conferring the Bachelor of Divinity degree. According to the school regulations in effect then, the seminary offered this degree "for the purpose of encouraging the higher learning and its bestowal is intended to be a distinct recognition of scholarship." The degree, however, was not conferred until some time following graduation and after the graduate had presented an acceptable thesis "of at least six thousand words on some theological subject."[20] The seminary held that the preparation of a thesis during the student's senior year would interfere with regular course work. The school held that by not allowing the student to do the thesis in his senior year, "the continuance of scholarly work in the early years of the pastorate will be encouraged and a higher standard for the thesis may be demanded."[21] Hence, although Johnson was graduated in 1916, his Bachelor of Divinity degree was not conferred until four years later.[22]

During his three years at Rochester, Johnson kept up a serious and regular correspondence with his new love, Anna Ethelyn Gardner. After graduating from Spelman in May 1914, she embarked on a teaching career at Alabama A and M College in Normal. Rochester was a long way from Tuscaloosa, but that did not diminish the strength of their relationship. Apparently Johnson was convinced that Anna Ethelyn, indeed, was the one with whom he would be profoundly happy for the rest of his life. Accordingly, in the summer of 1915, he traveled to Normal and made his formal marriage proposal, "with all of its humorous and serious connections."[23] For both of them, life took on new significance. Shortly after he graduated from Rochester, Johnson was ordained as a Baptist minister on June 27 at the Second Baptist Church in Mumford, New York, where he had been serving as a student pastor. Thirty-five ministerial delegates from the surrounding communities participated. Dr. Clarence Barbour, the president of Rochester Theological Seminary, also was present and said the ordination prayer. Dr. Barbour was deeply impressed with Johnson and supported him in all of his future plans.

From time to time during his days at Rochester, Johnson had been invited to speak at student YMCA conferences. These speaking engagements brought him increasing recognition. President John Hope of Morehouse had highly recommended Johnson to Dr. Jesse E. Moorland, secretary of the Colored Men's Department of the International Committee of the YMCA. A native of Ohio, Moorland was one of the most influential African Americans at that time. Educated at Northwestern University and Howard University, he was elected to the Board of Trustees of Howard in 1906 and served for many years. He willed to Howard University his extensive collection of books, pamphlets, artifacts, photographs, and other materials concerning the African and African-American experience. Combined with materials from Joel E. Spingarn, one of the principal leaders of the NAACP, this collection is housed in the Moorland-Spingarn Research Center at Howard.

Moorland was greatly impressed by Johnson's sharp intellect, effective delivery, and imposing presence. Incidentally, Moorland was also Alice Woodson's uncle and had met Johnson years earlier in Alice's home when Johnson was a high school student in Memphis. Moorland invited Johnson to participate in a summer training session sponsored by the YMCA. Moorland was extremely pleased with Johnson's performance. On July 2, 1916, he wrote to President John Hope of Morehouse:

> You will be glad to know that we had a wonderful Summer School. One of your graduates, Mr. M. W. Johnson, was with us, led our Bible classes and proved himself the most remarkable man we have ever had in this particular phase of work. He has, after our urgent request, consented to serve us the coming year, beginning September 1st, as one of our Student Secretaries, looking after Mr. (Max) Yergan's field. . . . I cannot express to you how rejoiced I am at having the services of this splendid man for the coming year.[24]

Johnson welcomed his appointment as student secretary of the International Committee of the YMCA. Assigned to the Southwest Region, Johnson enthusiastically immersed himself in the work of the YMCA. Shortly after assuming office, he conducted a survey of the African-American colleges in the Southwest, a study that resulted in the reorganization of the Student Conference of the YMCA's Southwest Region.

The position gave Johnson the chance to travel widely and to use his analytical skills in assessing the YMCA and other religious programs in the various schools and colleges served, or perhaps to be served, by the YMCA. It was also an opportunity for him to gain challenging experience as a speaker and to get to know important national leaders who would recognize his talents and potential. The demand for his future leadership was assured.

Not the least important consideration for the new position was that his steady income enabled Johnson to set a date for his marriage: Christmas Day, 1916. He chose Kemper Harreld, professor of music at Morehouse College, to be his best man.[25] Mordecai and Anna Ethelyn were officially united as husband and wife in Augusta, Georgia.

During his tenure as president of Morehouse College, John Hope invited Johnson to participate in a conference on "Moral and Religious Education" in connection with the observance of the fiftieth anniversary of the founding of that institution. In his letter of acceptance, dated January 23, 1917, Johnson asked Hope to clarify the focus of the presentation he was to make: ". . . the general tone of the conference, and the personnel and subjects of the speakers as may help me to orient myself." In his invitation to Johnson, President Hope must have commented on Johnson's recent marriage, for Johnson closed his letter by saying, "I thank you for what you say about my marriage. A month after the event I am still happy."[26]

Although Johnson enjoyed his position with the YMCA, an incident occurred that dispelled his enthusiasm for the organization. He had expected the YMCA to take a bold stand against American racism, but there was no evidence of this occurring. While attending an important conference of YMCA staff members in Atlantic City, the planning officials yielded to some blatantly discriminatory arrangements. As was common at that time, the African Americans in the group were not allowed to have rooms or eat in the hotel where the meetings were held and where the white attendees stayed.[27] Johnson was always acutely sensitive to racial prejudice and discrimination. He had matched wits with whites at the theological seminary, outranking them scholastically in each of his three years there. For this reason and because he differed little from them in physical appearance, he deeply resented the racial discrimination in which the YMCA colluded. He could not tolerate this violation of the basic Christian principle of brotherhood by a nominally Christian organization. He immediately resigned in protest. He had served less than a year.

This was the time for a new beginning, not only for Johnson's career, but also, even more significantly, for him and Anna Ethelyn. She was three months pregnant.

4

The Charleston Pastorate

*J*ohnson showed moral courage and fortitude when he
resigned suddenly from the YMCA, especially because he
had no immediate job prospects. His action indicated not only
a strong resentment against racial discrimination, but also a
profound faith in himself and his future. His strong academic
foundation, his having turned down several job offers a year
earlier, and his experience as a college teacher and as a student
pastor gave him confidence. Moreover, the brief stint as a
YMCA secretary had provided him with national exposure as a
talented young leader. He never considered the risk of
extended unemployment.

The times, however, were uncertain. For three years the
nations of Europe had been in the throes of World War I, and
the possibility of America's involvement was increasing.
German submarines began attacking ocean shipping. After
they sank the British luxury liner, the *Lusitania,* with the loss
of 1,000 lives (including 128 Americans); a British passenger
ship, *Sussex;* and a third ship, the *Artica,* that possibility
became reality. On April 6, 1917, President Woodrow Wilson
led the nation into the conflict. Except for some exemptions,
the government began calling all able-bodied men between the
ages of eighteen and thirty-five into military service. Ordained
clergymen were exempted. Johnson accepted his exemption, as
a "Duly Ordained Minister of Religion," and devoted himself
to examining the primary issues of the conflict from religious
and moral perspectives. The American slogan for the war, "To
Make the World Safe for Democracy," appealed to him as it

did to other idealists. He, like them, looked forward to a new day for democracy whenever the war ended.

By this time, Johnson's reputation as a well-trained clergyman and compelling speaker resulted in several job opportunities. The one that appealed to him most was with the First Baptist Church in Charleston, West Virginia, the outstanding church for African Americans in the state. Located in the Kanawha River Valley, Charleston then was a prosperous industrial center with approximately 35,000 inhabitants. Of this number, some 5,000 were African Americans. The headquarters of the booming coal-mining and gas industries were located there, and the Kanawha River provided excellent facilities for the thriving chemical plants.

Charleston, the state capital, has an unusual history. Originally a part of the state of Virginia, the counties that now make up West Virginia consisted of Virginia residents whose interests and concerns differed from those of the people in the eastern part of the state. Many inhabitants had migrated from that area to the western counties to find adequate means of subsistence: a search made necessary because of the system of slavery in the eastern counties that deprived many whites of opportunities for gainful employment. This and certain other factors, including the feeling of being neglected by the state government, led these western counties to secede from the rest of Virginia. The counties were admitted to the Union as the thirty-fifth state on June 20, 1863.

Between 1912 and the early 1920s, the conditions of economic life in West Virginia resulted in strife between capital and labor. Demonstrations and violence sometimes required the intervention of the National Guard and other units of the U.S. military. At that time, the state was a crucible in which one could test proposed solutions to social problems related to economics. Such issues, including those of the war, would be a concern for any minister committed to a social gospel.

On September 1, 1917, Johnson began his ministry at the First Baptist Church. At long last the time had come for him to begin the pursuit of his cherished career objective: to be a "moral and spiritual engineer," which he would do as the pastor of a well-established congregation in a strategically located community. Organized in 1868 by a Council of Founders led by the Reverend Lewis Rice, the First Baptist Church had become the state's leading congregation of African-American Baptists. As early as 1852, in what was then western Virginia, African-American Baptists, along with some Methodists, had begun to hold worship services.[1] In 1865 the Reverend Rice gave the use of his home as a meeting place for the group. In the same year he spearheaded the efforts to secure permission to build a house of worship on a lot owned by a man with extensive property holdings. Three years later, the members formally organized the First Baptist Church and had it incorporated under the name of the First Regular Baptist Church of Charleston. In time, the congregation built a new and larger edifice. Following frequent changes of pastors through the years, the Reverend John W. Bullock became minister and contributed significantly to the church's stability.[2]

With much anticipation, Johnson and Anna Ethelyn packed their belongings and moved to the capital city of West Virginia. By now, he was twenty-seven years old and more determined than ever to make a significant contribution in his ministry. He and Anna Ethelyn were eager to get settled in the parsonage. Furthermore, the pastorate would not require as much travel as had the YMCA position. Because they were soon to become first-time parents, Anna Ethelyn needed to have the sense of security provided by her husband's close companionship. For his part, Johnson was ecstatic at the prospect of becoming a father. Two months after he assumed the pastorate, their daughter was born. She was a source of pride and joy to both parents. The membership of the First Baptist Church was also proud, especially the women of the church, who had been a source of special support to the young expectant mother. Johnson and Anna Ethelyn chose to name the baby Carolyn Elizabeth in honor of and to perpetuate the first names of the baby's paternal and maternal grandmothers.

First Baptist included in its membership most of the professional African Americans in the city, along with a large representation of ordinary citizens. Members included Anderson Brown, real estate investor and chairman of the board of trustees; and T. G. Nutter, outstanding attorney, Howard University graduate, and prominent spokesman for the African-American community. All of the professions were represented among the First Baptist members.

Johnson made friends easily with all types of people in the community. He conversed with those at the lowest economic and social levels with the same empathy and ease he showed when talking with professionals, even those whose religious views differed from his. For example, one of the leading African-American lawyers in the city was Clayton E. Kimbrough Sr., also an alumnus of Howard University and an outspoken agnostic. Johnson and Kimbrough held lively discussions on various topics, including religion. Kimbrough's wife was a prominent member of First Baptist Church. Her grandfather was the Reverend Lewis Rice, who helped found the church. Kimbrough would challenge biblical claims, and Johnson would counter calmly and amicably in providing logical interpretations. Each man maintained respect for the other's intellect and integrity, although Johnson never swayed Kimbrough's thinking.[3]

In 1919 Johnson's long-time friend and college roommate, John W. Davis, was elected president of West Virginia State College at nearby Institute, West Virginia. Like several other state-supported institutions at that time, West Virginia State was a political hotbed and political machinations were quite prevalent. In fact, politics was the dominant factor in determining the leadership and progress of the college. A few months after Johnson assumed the pastorate of First Baptist, Davis had been asked to become a candidate for the presidency of West Virginia State. He wanted no part of becoming involved in a secular and politically embroiled institution. The most recent president, Byrd Prillerman, had been badly mistreated by the political establishment, much to the dismay of his friends.

Johnson was pleased, however, when he learned that his friend and former college roommate was being considered for the presidency. Davis knew about the situation with Prillerman and refused to accept the position until Prillerman urged him to do so. By temperament and experience Davis was better suited for the position than Prillerman had been.

From 1914 to 1917 Davis had served as registrar at Morehouse College. He then moved to Washington, D.C., where he was executive secretary of the 12th Street YMCA. Both Johnson and Davis were delighted over their close proximity, and for the next seven years they and their families enjoyed a pleasant relationship.

Throughout World War I, which extended through the first eighteen months of his pastorate, Johnson never hesitated to call attention to the basic issues involved. He cited discrimination and segregation in the armed forces and in governmental agencies in the nation's capital. In his sermons and addresses he denounced the blatant racism prevalent in a nation fighting to preserve democracy. Meanwhile, Johnson showed a profound concern for the welfare of the citizens of the state, especially those who worked in the coal fields, West Virginia's principal industry. He traveled widely and provided counsel wherever he could.

After the first nine months of his pastorate, Johnson took the summer off and returned to the University of Chicago. There he did research toward completing the requirements for the Bachelor of Divinity degree.[4] This primary activity and research was preparation of the thesis that the Rochester Theological Seminary required for the degree. He submitted the thesis to the seminary on March 1, 1920, and received the degree on May 1, 1920.

The topic Johnson chose for his thesis was "The Templars," more fully designated as "The Order of Knights Templars."[5] As described by Johnson, this order was "an organization founded at Jerusalem by two French knights, Hugh de Payens and Geoffrey de St. Omer" in 1118 C.E. These two men along with seven companions appeared before the Patriarch of Jerusalem and, naming their group "the poor soldiers of Jesus Christ," took the monastic vow of chastity and obedience. They pledged themselves "to fight in defense of the holy places and to keep the roads free and safe for pilgrims."[6] Johnson set forth the history of the order "from the socio-psychological point of view." He gave an account of how this order of dedicated men trained themselves for both religious devotion and military expertise, then used these disciplines to defend the holy places in Palestine from non-Christian invaders.

Johnson described the initial success of the Templars, including how they acquired prestige and won military victories. These successes were followed by defeat at the hands of the Muslims in Palestine, then the achievement of tremendous wealth, power, and influence in Europe. Later, jealous of their eminence and covetous of their wealth, some princes of Europe persecuted and finally destroyed the order.

Throughout his thesis Johnson lauds the Templars for their courage in battle, commitment to their ideals, and acumen in the financial marketplace. Perhaps these qualities were what motivated him to do research on the organization.

Johnson was not content with merely a preaching ministry. He tried to put into practice some economic principles he had studied and taught at Morehouse and to implement the social gospel that he learned as he sat in Walter Rauschenbusch's classroom. As a young idealist, he wanted to make a meaningful contribution to helping resolve social issues. Because food was essential for every household, he asked himself why not carry out a plan by which not only the members of First Baptist, but also the entire community, could purchase their groceries at significant savings?

At Rochester, the study of the cooperative movement that began in Europe during the first half of the nineteenth century intrigued Johnson. Central to the philosophy of this movement were control by the membership, freedom from religious or political discrimination, service at cost, and the education of members in improving their total well being. The principal proponent of this ideal was a group founded in England in 1837, known as the Rochdale Cooperative. With these principles in mind, Johnson organized the Rochdale Cash Grocery Cooperative, with members of his church forming the nucleus of the association. Although this organization did not endure for many years because of the lack of trained people to carry on its operations, it nevertheless raised the consciousness of those involved regarding the importance of understanding the economic forces affecting their security.

Conscious of the effects of racial discrimination on his people, Johnson recognized the need for a Charleston branch of the NAACP, and he spear-headed the organization of a branch there. In working out the details, he corresponded with Walter White, the executive secretary of the national organization. The African-American community in Charleston responded whole-heartedly. The local NAACP membership grew to as many as 1,000. This branch played an effective role in alleviating some discriminatory policies adversely affecting African Americans in that community.

First Baptist Church made progress on several fronts during Johnson's ministry there. One of his first acts was to install a budget system for systematic, regular giving, which resulted in more efficient financial operations. The church was able to buy land for constructing a new edifice in the future, made necessary by the threefold increase in the membership.

Johnson instituted other innovations during his pastorate, including the creation of a church library for collecting and preserving historical and other materials about the African-American community. He established a department of social services to better meet the needs of the underprivileged. In addition, he modernized the educational work of the church following the basic principles of religious education. He also began a weekly bulletin to keep the membership informed of all aspects of the church program.

Johnson gave himself unstintingly to carrying out the social gospel, not only in his parish but also throughout the state. Through his wide travel, he became aware of the many problems of working people. The difficulties of the coal miners were of special concern to him. Frequently, he was in demand to speak at colleges, especially during religious emphases weeks. For four years, he kept up the brisk pace of an active pastorate along with other activities, getting little rest or relaxation. As a result his health suffered. Being conscious of his situation, his congregation granted him a leave of absence for one year.

Johnson was interested in continuing his academic development, which he had indicated when he graduated from the seminary and had been offered a scholarship for further study. However, his immediate interest then was the pastorate. Now, after four years at First Baptist, he was ready for a change and to reapply himself to rigorous academic pursuit. He wanted to broaden his scholarship in the philosophy of religion and to secure further academic credentials from the most prestigious university in the country. He boldly asked President Clarence Barbour of the seminary whether the fellowship it was offering could be granted for his study at Harvard. The seminary faculty agreed. Harvard approved his application and he was accepted to work toward the degree of Master of Sacred Theology.

But Johnson first had to work out some problems. The need for a supply pastor was met when the church engaged the Reverend Charles H. Haynes to serve in Johnson's absence. By now little Carolyn was four years old, and Anna Ethelyn and Johnson were expecting their second child. He did not want the family to be separated for nearly a year. Fortunately he was able to secure suitable accommodations in Cambridge, not far from the university, so that the family could be together during his time of study and renewal. In September 1921, Johnson enrolled in the Harvard Divinity School.

During the 1920s the moral and theological intellectual climate in America and in some parts of Europe was in turmoil. Science and scientific methods had made rapid strides. Darwin's evolutionary hypothesis had undermined some cherished religious beliefs. The deeply felt conflict between science and religion had led to a sometimes bitter controversy between religious fundamentalists and liberals.

More than any other theological school at the time, the Harvard Divinity School was a center of modernist thought regarding religion. As early as 1805, the corporation there had named a Unitarian minister as Professor of Theology. From the time of its formation in 1816, forty years before it became an integral part of the university, the Divinity School was dominated by the modernist Unitarian theological perspective.[7] Generally the professors accepted the claims of modern science; the Darwinian evolutionary hypothesis posed no serious problem to them. In addition, the recent trends in biblical criticism and the objective study of the scriptures were an essential part of the Divinity School program. While other seminaries prepared students for the pastorate, Harvard was noted for preparing scholars. While many other seminaries were conservative theologically, Harvard was the epitome of theological liberalism. Its embrace of the social gospel reinforced Johnson's intellectual heritage from Walter Rauschenbusch. He cherished that atmosphere.

At Harvard, Johnson met a distinguished group of scholars, among them George Foot Moore, an outstanding interpreter of religion of his time; and George La Piana, Moore's close friend, who was professor of church history. La Piana, a "Catholic Modernist," represented the theological climate at Harvard. It was said of him that

> He saw religious and political conservatism as interrelated; and, with his strong passion for social justice, he inveighed against the machinations and ruses of American plutocracy and rejoiced in the breakthrough of the social gospel among the younger ministers.[8]

Johnson reveled in the scholarly climate at Harvard. His academic year went very well. Studying with such professors as Moore and La Piana, he was able to delve into some crucial issues in the philosophy of religion, church history, and the relation between religion and society. At the same time, he demonstrated a sharp intellect in both his classroom performance and in informal academic contacts. In later years, the Harvard chapter of Phi Beta Kappa elected him an honorary member.

Two events of vital importance occurred two months before his graduation. First, in April 1922, Johnson's father died. Wyatt was somewhere between 85 and 100 years old. He had been ill for a long time and had been faithfully cared for by his daughter, Sallie, from his first marriage. Johnson rushed to Paris to attend the funeral and to help settle his father's estate. He prepared the eulogy for the funeral, in which he praised his father's virtues (some of which he failed to recognize as a youth). He said this about his father:

> Wyatt Johnson was an industrious [and] frugal man, deeply appreciative of the least kindness. He was of stern opinion and few words.
>
> He was born a slave [but] he died a free man. Abraham Lincoln freed him from slavery, the love of Christ freed him from sin. By his own ambition, he freed himself from illiteracy. By his own hard labor, he freed himself from economic dependency. By his behavior, he freed himself from all restrictions in his intercourse with men and became respected and trusted by all. Now, by the grace of God, he is freed from the bonds of the flesh, freed to move about in that land where there is no old age, no death, where all who have loved the Lord always behold the faith of our Father who is in Heaven.[9]

After the funeral Johnson returned to Cambridge for the impending birth of a son that same month. He and Anna Ethelyn proudly named him Mordecai Wyatt Johnson Jr. As a role model for his son, Johnson now had a new inspiration and determination to maintain his high academic standards in completing that semester.

At the end of that school year he was awarded a Master of Sacred Theology degree. Harvard annually chose, on the basis of competition, one graduating senior from each of the three divisions of the university as commencement speakers. The dean and the Divinity School faculty nominated Johnson to enter the competition to represent all the graduate schools. Johnson won and was chosen to represent the graduate school at the commencement exercises. He could hardly have realized then that this event set the stage for the conditions that were to vitally affect the rest of his life.

A Harvard commencement is always a dramatic event. Founded in 1636 and chartered for the education of ministers, Harvard is the oldest institution of higher learning in the United States. Because of its prestige and the prominence of many of its alumni, the closing exercises of the academic year attract much attention, which was especially the case in 1922 among members of the African-American community, who were proud to learn that one of their number was to give a commencement presentation. Other African Americans had earned degrees from Harvard, but for one to be chosen as a presenter at a commencement exercise was significant recognition—as it had been when W. E. B. Du Bois was chosen to speak at his graduation from Harvard in June 1890.

Representing all the graduate schools, Johnson chose "The Faith of the American Negro" as his subject. The format of the program appeared, in part, as follows:

Orators Hoc Ordain Sunt
Dissertation Latina
Benjamin Franklin Jones, *dum omnes qui adsunt salutat*
de orbis terrarum restituenda
Clyde Guiliemus Phelps—*Disquisitio*—"America's Russian Policy"
Mordecai Wyatt Johnson, A.B., B.D., *Candidatus Theologae,*
"The Faith of the American Negro"[10]

[Translation: *The Speakers in Order Are*
Latin Dissertation
Benjamin Franklin Jones, *Now All Who Are Here Wait*
Upon the Restoration of the World
Clyde Guiliemus Phelps—*Discussion*—"America's Russian Policy"
Mordecai Wyatt Johnson, A.B., B.D., *Theological Candidate,*
"The Faith of the American Negro"]

In his address, Johnson called attention to the simple faith that African Americans had before World War I—a faith that God is loving and just and that the practice of the principles of democracy would eventually result in their being treated fairly. Blacks believed, he said, that "as they grew in intelligence, wealth, and self-respect, they would win the confidence and esteem of their fellow white Americans, and should gradually find the privileges and responsibilities of full American citizenship."[11] Yet, he said, in the years immediately preceding and following World War I, three factors had eroded this faith. First was the stark brutality perpetuated against African Americans, especially that directed against the returning African-American soldiers and carried on by whites who feared that those who fought "to make the world safe for democracy" would try to enjoy some of it at home. Second, the erosion of faith had roots in young African Americans who had lost their confidence in capitalism, which they felt had "no fundamental good will for Negroes or any sort of laborers." Third, a larger group, he said, believed "in religion and the principles of democracy, but not in the white man's religion or the white man's democracy."

Johnson pointed out that while most blacks did not share the preceding sentiments, they were nevertheless "completely disillusioned." Moreover, he continued,

> They see themselves surrounded on every hand by a sentiment of antagonism which does not intend to be fair. They see themselves partly reduced to peonage, shut out from labor unions, forced to an inferior status before the courts, made subjects of public contempt, lynched and mobbed with impunity, and deprived of the ballot, their only means of social defense. . . . And now they are no longer able to believe with Booker T. Washington, or with any other man, that their own efforts after intelligence, wealth, and self-respect can in any wise avail to deliver them from these conditions unless they have the protection of a just and beneficent public policy in keeping with American ideals.[12]

The impact of this address played a significant role in Johnson's future. Judge Julian Mack, a member of the Harvard Board of Overseers, was seated on the platform. He was deeply impressed by the speech. Immediately after the ceremonies, he sought out Johnson and gave him warm compliments. Among other things, Judge Mack said that he was "proud of Harvard today," because the speeches given by students made him feel that Harvard had "returned to the spirit of leadership of liberal American thought." He added that Johnson's speech made him feel that "the spirit of the great old Harvard is alive and on the march again." Judge Mack continued, "Young man, you know what I am going to do for you? I am going to tell Mr. Julius Rosenwald about you. It will be good for you to have him know you."[13]

Less than twenty-four hours later, Johnson received a telegram from Rosenwald in Chicago inviting Johnson to meet him in Scarsdale, New York, at the home of his son-in-law. After the meeting, Johnson and Rosenwald adjourned to the home of Nathan Strauss, a prominent philanthropist, in Mamaroneck, New York, where Judge Mack had already arrived. Following lunch, Judge Mack gave an appreciative account of the Harvard commencement, especially Johnson's address, and asked Johnson about his career plans. Johnson replied that he was on leave from his church in West Virginia and that he planned to return as promised from his leave of absence. (Although unknown to Judge Mack, Johnson had received an attractive offer from George Foot Moore, professor of the history of religion at Harvard, to make an in-depth study of African religion. Under Moore's direction, Johnson would earn the Ph.D. degree. Johnson was not free to accept Professor Moore's offer either until he had fulfilled his pledge to return to his church in Charleston.)

Nevertheless, Judge Mack, speaking for the other three men present, urged Johnson "to choose a career of speaking and writing." Mack stated that the Harvard address demonstrated that Johnson was the person to make a needed contribution to race relations through a public forum. Mr. Rosenwald seconded Mack's sentiments and promised to give Johnson his financial support should he accept the offer to change careers.

Johnson expressed his appreciation for this unusual offer, but respectfully declined it. First, he was committed to returning to Charleston following his leave of absence. Second, his becoming "a professional writer and speaker so early in his life might lead him . . . to become a propagandist of a growingly shallow kind, without spiritual depth and without true intellectual power."[14]

Judge Mack, Rosenwald, and Strauss expressed keen disappointment at Johnson's refusal of their offer, but respected his right to choose other endeavors. They added that they hoped that in time Johnson's career would "offer them another opportunity to help him."

Obviously, Johnson was still committed to the pastorate. As yet no other area or context within which he could be a "moral and spiritual engineer" had seriously attracted him.

The effect of Johnson's commencement address was also significant at a national level. In commenting on the speech, Benjamin Brawley, one of Johnson's former teachers, said that it made an indelible impression on the

American public. Brawley felt that the speech destined Johnson for distinction and that not since Booker T. Washington's speech at the Atlanta Exposition in 1895 had such a significant address been given.[15]

Following the commencement exercises at Harvard and the conference with the three distinguished philanthropists, Johnson returned to Charleston and to his congregation with renewed vigor and determination to carry forward a dynamic preaching ministry. Meanwhile, he had numerous requests for speaking engagements all over the country. For example, he continued to conduct the annual religious weeks at Howard University. The following year, Howard conferred on him the honorary degree of Doctor of Divinity, making him one of the youngest persons, at age thirty-three, ever to be so honored by that institution.

In his sermons at his church in Charleston, Johnson was more profoundly provocative and effective in his messages than ever before. The year at Harvard had given him a noteworthy stimulus. Soon some members of his congregation were so impressed that they employed a court stenographer for two months to record his sermons in shorthand. Because Johnson rarely spoke from a manuscript, these verbatim recordings of sermons from his early years give insight into his theological perspective, especially about his idea of God, his social and personal ethics, his conception of Jesus of Nazareth, and his ideas about responsibility for social change.[16] The subjects of the recorded sermons include "The Blindness of Obsession"; "The Social Consequences of Sin"; "The Responsibility of Privilege"; "Work, Business, and Religion"; "The Radical Claims of the Gospel"; and "The Responsibility of the Chosen." These sermons represent important aspects of his philosophy of religion.

The idea of God is a challenging problem area of religious philosophy. An examination of these sermons shows that Johnson's idea of God is consonant with the classical cosmological and teleological proofs of God's existence. The cosmological proof is based on the understanding of the universe as a rational, ordered whole: an orderliness that can be explained only in terms of a "divine Orderer."

In these sermons, as well in his later public addresses, Johnson often refers to what God had in mind "from the foundation of the world," thus suggesting an orderliness in the creation process. Also, his idea of God represents the teleological argument for God's existence: God had a purpose in creating the universe, and He has a purpose for each person to fulfill in the world. For Johnson, God is a creator who has a definite purpose for all his creatures. God "has a big job on his hands that He intends to get done and has intended before the foundation of the world." For Johnson, God is not a "patient, indulgent grandmother," who helps us carry out our plans whatever they are and is always ready to say, "Bless your heart; come sit on my knee." On the contrary, God is the one who set the stars and planets in their orderly courses. "This universe," Johnson says, "stands together in harmony, rolls swiftly on singing its song and doing that because it recognizes the power of an Invincible Purpose, and a powerful hand that has set it going and keeps it alive waiting for the fulfillment of the purposes of God." God's purpose is seen, not only in the vastness of the heavens, but also in the smallest living cell. "The whole creation is a wonderful plan awaiting finally for the Son of God, the man with the crowning face of the eternal God—a plan that there should one day stand on top of the universe beings who would converse with him with understanding and knowledge."

In the 1920s, when Johnson delivered these sermons, the persistent problem for Christian theologians was the relation of science and religion. Science was advancing dramatically, and some scientific claims were a direct challenge to certain biblical teachings. Darwin's theory of evolution was of particular concern to theologians. If Darwin's theory was sound, what happens to the account in Genesis that God created the world in six days? Moreover, the biblical chronology dates the creation as occurring in the year 4004 B.C., while modern scientists discuss the origin of the universe in terms of many millions of years.

For some "Bible Belt" states, the issue of evolution was so controversial that some state legislatures enacted laws prohibiting teaching the theory in public schools. The controversy drew national attention when John T. Scopes, a Tennessee public school teacher, challenged the law and included the theory of evolution in his biology course. This challenge precipitated the famous Scopes trial (often called "the monkey trial") of 1925, during which the religious fundamentalist orator, William Jennings Bryan, and the agnostic lawyer, Clarence Darrow, were locked in a heated debate. Scopes was found guilty but the judge gave him a nominal fine.

The modern theologian can either flatly deny the probability of the theory of evolution or attempt to show that God himself is behind the evolutionary process. Johnson took the latter position and addressed the problem squarely in one of his sermons. He viewed creation as a gradual process of evolution. It was God's purpose, he felt, that the higher forms of life would evolve from the lower forms. He maintained that "God has been working through the ages to create spiritual beings who would think and live like him, be righteous like him, and be full of compassion and kindness like him."

Another crucial issue in the philosophy of religion is the problem of evil, expressed by this question: If God is all good, all loving, just, all knowing and all powerful, why does evil exist? To answer this question, the theologian must make a distinction between natural evil (such as earthquakes, storms, floods, and pestilence) and moral evil (man's inhumanity to man). He must show that either (1) what we call evil is not really so—it just happens that we do not understand God's total purpose, (2) God purposely allows evil to show his goodness, or (3) God has given man free will and does not interfere with this freedom even when man acts destructively. This latter view implies that in giving man free will, God thereby limits himself, and that when man disobeys divine laws, or is the victim of misfortunes, God suffers too.

In responding to this issue, Johnson proposed the idea of a limited God, one who deliberately limited himself when he gave man free will. "He has so fixed it that He cannot force his own will on His own creatures, but must await their cooperation," without which God cannot carry out his purposes. When man fails to cooperate with God, God suffers: "He is continually crucified."

A modified form of the idea of God's foreknowledge and of election is seen in one of Johnson's sermons. There he maintained that God "not only has a picture of you now, but has a picture of you as you will look when Christ Jesus controls your spirit and makes you an angelic creature. But that spirit will never be realized unless God gets hold of your will and mine." In addition, he maintains that "Very few people have been chosen by God to help him carry out his purpose which he had before the foundation of the world." He summarizes the Apostle Paul's view that some persons are unable to hear God's voice under any circumstances. Moreover, he cites the story of God's choosing Abraham for a special mission, and choosing other Hebrews such as Joseph, son of Jacob; Moses; Elijah; the great prophets of the eighth century—in short, a handful of selected ones from the "chosen people"—to carry out his purpose.

One may easily surmise from Johnson's emphasis on being chosen that he felt he himself had a special mission from God. Two quotations from one of his sermons suggest this. At one point he says, "I want you to understand that you ought to rejoice because God has laid his hands on you for the carrying out of his purpose." And again, "Whenever a man, or woman, comes to the place where he is mightily gripped by the moral and spiritual things of the world, he may know, not merely that he has faith in God, but that God has chosen him and is using him as an instrument for the carrying out of His purpose, which he had before the foundation of the world."[17]

Johnson was in the position of continually having to turn down offers for positions. A few weeks before his graduation from Harvard, President J. Stanley Durkee of Howard University offered him a professorship in the Divinity School. Dr. Jesse Moorland implored Johnson to accept the offer: "You must heed the call. I have done my best. God wants you here. . . . You come to Nineveh—Howard is moving forward."[18] President Durkee had offered Johnson a position "as a full Baptist professor in the School of Religion, as pastor of the Baptist students, and as college preacher . . . at a salary of $2,000 and a house." Johnson replied to Moorland's plea as follows:

> I have written him [Durkee] that the offer is very attractive to me with two exceptions: (1) that I should not care to accept the official status of Baptist professor and pastor of the Baptist students and (2) that I should find it necessary to request that he make a decided advance in the salary. . . .[19]

When Dr. Moorland's retirement from the position of senior secretary of the Colored Men's Department of the YMCA was observed at Storer College, Harpers Ferry, West Virginia, in July 1923, Johnson was invited to participate. The general arrangements committee comprised practically all of the outstanding blacks in the nation. A partial list included Robert R. Moton, principal of Tuskegee Institute; John W. Davis of West Virginia State College; Bishops John A. Gregg and R. R. Wright of the AME Church; Henry Allen Boyd of the National Baptist Convention; and Emmett J. Scott of Howard University. The speakers included President John Hope of Morehouse; Channing H. Tobias, who succeeded Jesse Moorland in the YMCA position; and Johnson, who spoke on the topic, "Dr. Moorland's Contribution to the Negro Race."

Johnson's appearance on this program as a young man with many older, influential African Americans had the effect of making his talents widely known. It was inevitable that with his intellect, educational background, platform presence, demonstrated leadership, and moral commitment, he would be tapped for larger responsibilities than the pastorate of the First Baptist Church in Charleston could provide. Such an opportunity was soon to come from Washington, D.C.

5

Howard University Presidency— The Early Years

*H*oward University owes much of its beginning to Civil War Major General Oliver Otis Howard, whose name it bears and who was responsible for the first major funding of the school. He even served as its third president. In many respects Howard is unique among higher educational institutions in the country. Located in the nation's capital, it is one of three institutions of higher learning (except for the military academies operated by the federal government) whose principal source of income is from congressional appropriations. Moreover, with its ten professional schools, Howard is the only comprehensive university in the country with a primarily African-American enrollment. It therefore has the largest contingent of black scholars. Sometimes called the "Capstone of Negro Education," Howard is an important part of the history of African-American higher education.

At the close of the Civil War in 1865, the central social question was how to prepare more than 4 million freedmen for constructive citizenship. The primary answer was to establish schools for the preparation of leaders such as preachers and teachers. Before 1865, educational opportunities for blacks were scarce. Although some free blacks had been admitted to colleges in the North and had shown academic competence, emancipation clearly required establishing schools on a broad scale to meet the needs of the freedmen.

The federal government established the Bureau of Refugees, Freedmen, and Abandoned Lands, commonly known as the Freedmen's Bureau, to resolve some problems growing out of the new situation. Abraham Lincoln appointed General Howard to head this agency. Howard's responsibilities included not only establishing schools and hospitals, but also providing food and shelter for the homeless. A native of Maine, General Howard was noted not only for his military accomplishments, but also for his piety and social concerns.

The decision to create what became known as Howard University was made in a prayer meeting at the First Congregational Church in Washington, D.C., on November 20, 1866. The plan called for a school to train "preachers (colored) with a view to service among the freedmen." Soon after, the organizers, in recognition of General Howard's major role, proposed that the school be named "The Howard Normal and Theological Institute for the Education of Teachers and Preachers."[1] This title was not satisfactory, however. On March 2, 1867, the school was chartered under the name of Howard University. It is striking that the primary motive for establishing Howard was the same as for founding all early colleges in the nation, including Harvard and Yale. The primary emphasis of the nine colleges that predate the Revolution and that survive today was on the training of preachers and other leaders.[2] Howard's first students were four white girls, the children of teachers. The school was situated on a hilltop, the site of a former slave plantation. Its initial grant was $150,000. The Freedmen's Bureau funded it until the federal government abolished the bureau in 1872. That development, along with the panic of 1873, created a financial crisis for the institution. The federal government came to Howard's rescue in 1879, and, except for the period 1872 to 1878, continued to support it on an annual basis. Each year, the institution had to lobby for that support, and for a long time the continued appropriations were not guaranteed.

In the fifty-eight years from the founding of Howard in 1867 to the beginning of Johnson's tenure in 1926, ten men had served as president of the institution.[3] Of these, all were white ministers. The school continued to grow, but by 1926 it was far from being a first-rate university. During this period, the mid-1920s, the nation had almost recovered from World War I and economic life was moving ahead, albeit to an unanticipated depression. Republican politics dominated. Calvin Coolidge was in the White House, and the general tenor of the country was optimistic, but not with respect to race relations. Segregation and racial discrimination were rampant in the South, where lynching of blacks was commonplace. Discrimination existed on a more subtle basis in the North. Blacks, however, continued to migrate in large numbers to the North for better job opportunities and upward mobility.

During "the Roaring Twenties," many people emphasized new dance tunes, illegal alcohol, and good times. African Americans were forging new paths in literature and art. Based primarily in Harlem, they were producing significant and prolific works in all the arts, giving rise to what was called the "Harlem Renaissance." Alain Locke chronicled this movement in his landmark work, *The New Negro*, an edited volume,[4] followed some years later by *The Negro Caravan*, edited by Sterling Brown, Arthur Paul Davis, and Ulysses Lee.[5] In poetry, novels, plays, short stories, and music, African-American intellectuals gave expression to the deep longings, and the joys, of their race. A new racial consciousness was abroad, and African Americans became increasingly committed to education, realizing that it was the key to survival.

The Reverend J. Stanley Durkee became president of Howard in 1918 and served until 1926. Before his appointment, sentiment had been expressed from time to time that Howard should have an African-American president. Alumni and some supporters of the university did not welcome Durkee's appointment. He discouraged studies in African-American history, which Carter G. Woodson felt was a basic necessity for black students. Woodson, an outstanding Ph.D. graduate in history from Harvard, was the primary authority on African-American history. He recognized the paucity of reliable information about African Americans and diligently sought to fill that need. In 1915 he published *The Education of the Negro Before 1861*,[6] and in 1916 he founded and edited the *Journal of Negro History*. He became dean of Howard in 1919, but soon resigned when the administration would not allow him to teach a course in African-American history. Earlier, Durkee had denied Alain Locke's request to teach a course in race relations. Locke, a Phi Beta Kappa graduate of Harvard and a Rhodes scholar, with a Ph.D. in philosophy, had joined the Howard faculty in 1916. He, Kelly Miller, and others insisted that education at Howard should focus some attention on African-American achievements. They also held that the university should modify its curriculum to this end. Miller, a graduate of Howard, had joined the faculty in 1890 (the year of Johnson's birth) as a teacher of mathematics and later became dean of the College of Arts and Sciences. He wrote and lectured extensively on problems in race relations.

President Durkee alienated the faculty by centralizing authority and by greatly reducing the power of three prominent deans, Kelly Miller, George C. Cook, and Lewis Baxter Moore, sometimes called "the Triumvirate."[7] Cook had graduated from Howard and had joined the faculty as early as 1881. Later he was principal and then dean of the English department. In 1903 he became dean of the commercial department and professor of civics and commerce. Moore, a graduate of Fisk University, joined the faculty in 1895 and first taught in the preparatory department. Later he taught Latin and pedagogy, and eventually became dean of the Teachers College, an outgrowth of the department of pedagogy. For some time these men exercised complete control over their areas of the curriculum, including the disbursement of funds. Durkee felt that this arrangement created too much power for the deans. Accordingly, he instituted a centralized rather than decentralized administrative policy.

During the periods of unrest in Durkee's administration, Alain Locke became the spokesman for the faculty, one of whose basic complaints centered on salary inequities. In 1925, Durkee recommended assigning Kelly Miller to public relations, retiring Dean George Cook, and dismissing Alain Locke and three other dissident professors. In protest the students went on an eight-day strike.[8]

Eventually, after much publicity of the complaints against the administration, the alumni drew up a list of charges against President Durkee. Although forty-seven professors testified before the Board of Trustees, the Board gave him a vote of confidence. The local Howard alumni formed a committee to help resolve the strike. By acknowledging the logic of some of their complaints, they appeased the students, who ended their protest.[9]

By this time, President Durkee had become convinced that his effectiveness as president was at an end. He announced in March that he would resign effective June 30, 1926. Most of the Board of Trustees recognized that the time had come to elect an African-American president, and the search for a new administration began.

The Triumvirate—Miller, Cook, and Moore—were all viable candidates because of academic experience and prominence in the university. If any two of them had dropped out of consideration, the other probably would have been elected. None, however, chose to do so.[10]

Meanwhile Johnson's reputation continued to spread beyond the African-American community. Sherwood Eddy, a prominent YMCA activist, was among those instrumental in bringing Johnson to the attention of prominent national figures. Eddy had worked for fifteen years as a YMCA secretary in India and later had worked with students in other Asian countries. He had met Johnson when the latter was working as a student secretary of the YMCA. Eddy, like Johnson, was a strong proponent of the social gospel and had spoken and written voluminously on the subject. Knowing of Johnson's interest in world problems, Eddy invited him to participate in Eddy's seminar in Europe. Johnson enthusiastically accepted the offer. The First Baptist Church was sympathetic to his desire to have this experience and underwrote his expenses for the trip.

Meanwhile some influential persons connected with the university felt that Mordecai Johnson would be the ideal leader for the institution. He had a sharp intellect, was an eloquent communicator, and had moral integrity. Furthermore, Johnson already was well known at Howard. As stated earlier, the university had granted him the honorary degree of Doctor of Divinity in 1923. For five years he had been visiting Howard annually to speak at the Day of Prayer and to conduct a series of lectures during the week of that observance. He had impressed both students and faculty on those occasions. Often there was standing room only when he spoke.

During his visits to Howard, Johnson on occasion had conversations with President J. Stanley Durkee, who was experiencing some serious public relations difficulties. Durkee had once said to Johnson: ". . . if I were not a man who knew how to stay on my knees [in prayer], I think I would have a long time ago gone insane here. In all my life, I have never been so much misunderstood as at Howard University."[11]

In April 1926, after Johnson had given his annual series of religious lectures, Emmett J. Scott, the secretary of the university, wrote asking Johnson to meet with a small group to talk about the situation at Howard. He also asked whether Johnson would consider having his name offered as a candidate to succeed Durkee.[12] Although surprised, Johnson agreed to meet with the small group, which consisted of Scott, an outstanding member of the faculty, and a member of the Board of Trustees. At that time the situation, not only at Howard but also at other African-American universities headed by white presidents, was volatile. This situation was exacerbated by conditions following World War I. African-American soldiers returning from that conflict felt that the democracy for which they had been prepared to give their lives was still a long way off. Blacks across the land had a growing spirit of self-determination.

Despite his high regard for President Durkee (after all, it was under his administration that Johnson was awarded an honorary degree and that Durkee had offered him a faculty position at Howard), Johnson agreed that the time had come for Howard University to have an African-American president. As to his becoming a candidate, Johnson declined. He cited the fact that two able men were on the faculty, each of whom was a logical nominee for the presidency. These two were Dwight O. W. Holmes, dean of the Graduate School, and Charles H. Wesley, a distinguished professor of history. Johnson did not want to compete with these two men.

Johnson did, however, express his deep concern for the status of higher education among African-American youths. Because Howard University enrolled almost half of the total number of African-American college students, he recognized that Howard was in a strategic position to provide significant educational leadership and opportunities for young African Americans. Johnson emphatically insisted that he would not be an active candidate for president of Howard and persuaded the group never to consider or mention his name in that connection.[13]

On June 6, 1926, the Board of Trustees elected Bishop John A. Gregg as president. An outstanding prelate of the AME Church, Gregg was a native of Kansas, a graduate of Kansas State University, and a veteran of the Spanish-American War. After being a missionary in South Africa, he had served terms as president of Edward Waters College in Jacksonville, Florida, and of Wilberforce University in Xenia, Ohio.[14] Although Bishop Gregg had informed the nominating committee that he was not available for the position, they elected him anyway, perhaps thinking that the prestige of the presidency of Howard University would take precedence over leading an episcopal district in South Africa. (The AME Church had a deep interest in South Africa and was in the process of building up a significant program there. Bishop Gregg was important and committed to that effort.)

Johnson knew Bishop Gregg well, had a high regard for him, had heard him speak on several occasions, and felt that Gregg was the man for the position. Upon hearing of Gregg's election, Johnson sent a telegram congratulating the Board of Trustees on their choice. They, however, were uncertain at the outset as to whether Gregg would accept the presidency. His election was considered "a holding action."[15] For the next few weeks, an increasingly active movement emerged encouraging the Board of Trustees to elect Johnson. Upon hearing of the pending vacancy at Howard, Judge Julian Mack wrote several strong letters on Johnson's behalf and encouraged Julius Rosenwald to use his influence also. Trustee Jesse E. Moorland made a forceful plea emphasizing Johnson's outstanding intellectual, leadership, and moral qualities.

In a letter dated June 14, 1926, Emmett Scott wrote Johnson that the chairmen of the Board of Trustees and the nominating committee wanted to have a conference with Johnson. Scott assured Johnson that "You have not been a candidate. . . . You will not be asked to be a candidate. . . . You will simply be drafted." Johnson replied that whatever the decision, "You may depend on me to remember that it is the cause of Negro education which is at stake, and to give my heartiest support to Dr. Gregg or to whatever man becomes the first colored president of Howard University." Johnson advised Scott that he would be in New York in time to sail for Europe with the Sherwood Eddy party on June 23.[16]

Johnson met members of the nominating committee in New York at the Hotel Martinique on June 23, the day of his sailing. They talked with him about matters pertaining to the presidency, and about the possibility that Bishop Gregg would decline the offer. They asked about his experience, if any, with handling large sums of money. He answered, "None." He mentioned the budget of his church and the $25,000 that he would collect and transmit to an officer of the West Virginia Baptist State Convention. They laughed. Johnson agreed to allow his name to be presented.[17]

Later that morning Johnson sailed for Europe. The group consisted of national leaders going to London, Paris, Berlin, and some other places seeking a "peaceful and constructive settlement of Europe" after World War I.

In declining the presidency, Bishop Gregg issued a statement saying, "I told Colonel Theodore Roosevelt and General J. H. Sherman from the beginning that, due to a promise made to the people of South Africa, I would return there and assist them in the establishment of the AME Church, and that I could not accept the presidency. They conferred it upon me nevertheless, but I am still bound by my prior promise."[18] Moreover, having already served as president of two institutions, Bishop Gregg was not especially flattered to be asked to take on another one, especially at that stage of Howard's history.

At the meeting on June 30, 1926, the Board of Trustees, by a written ballot, elected Johnson as president. According to one report, the vote was twelve to two.[19] The minutes, however, do not show a distribution of the balloting. The official report was that the vote was unanimous. According to university historian Rayford W. Logan, Charles H. Wesley and Johnson were the finalists.[20]

By this time Johnson was in Europe. He was in a group session in a lecture room once used by the philosopher Henri Bergson at the College de France in Paris when the results of the vote were cabled to him. The cablegram announced that the Board of Trustees had elected him president of Howard by a unanimous vote. Despite the uncertainty of Bishop Gregg's acceptance, Johnson was shocked at the news and telephoned his wife about it. She told him she believed that such an important decision should be made by him alone after the most careful consideration and that she would support him in whatever decision he made. He cabled this reply: "Thanks. Unanimous vote constrains me to accept."[21]

Sherwood Eddy tried to dissuade Johnson from accepting the position. Eddy very much wanted Johnson to continue with his seminar—traveling to Russia, China, and other countries—and to return to America with him and engage in a partnership of programs of "social evangelism." This plan was not in accordance with Johnson's perception of his major purpose in life.

Johnson viewed the presidency of Howard as a calling, a challenge, and a duty. He felt that any African American who assumed the position was bound to experience tremendous difficulty and suffering, primarily because of the deep divisions in the Howard constituency. Johnson stated that "Any able and honorable colored man in the United States (elected to the position) had a bounden duty to the Negro people and to the cause of higher education to accept this position at Howard University and to bear whatever suffering he was called upon to bear to clear up the internal difficulty which threatened the life of the institution.[22] The presidency of Howard University provided him, in a very real sense, the opportunity to become a highly visible "moral and spiritual engineer." He felt deeply that this was a calling. He had not sought the position, rather he was drafted for it. Because of the overall situation, he was convinced that this was the arena in which he was destined to carry forward his mission: the struggle on behalf of the disfranchised and dispossessed members of the African-American community.

Upon returning from Europe, Johnson went to Washington for a conference with members of the Board of Trustees and the principal administrators of the university. Later he returned to Charleston, tendered his resignation to the First Baptist Church, and prepared to move his family to Washington. He assumed the office of president of Howard University on September 1, 1926. He was the eleventh chief administrator of the institution and the first African American. The church and other citizens in the community regretted that he was leaving. They recognized, however, that his intellectual stature and reputation inevitably would result in his being called to a wider sphere of activity than the Charleston pastorate offered.

Several factors contributed to Johnson's election. Among those was the influence of the powerful philanthropist, Julius Rosenwald, exercised through Judge Julian Mack. Colonel Theodore Roosevelt, chairman of the nominating committee, revealed an important factor in why Johnson was chosen over Wesley: "on account of the internal troubles that have been rife in Howard University, it was the belief of the trustees that it would be to the interest of all to select some outside man."[23]

The African-American community generally was well pleased with Johnson's appointment. The *Washington Post* expressed its sentiment as follows: "Negro at Last Heads Howard University. . . . New President Is Well Equipped for the Task Confronting Him."[24] Members of the African-American community applauded the fact that at last one of their own was head administrator for Howard. Dr. J. Garland Penn, one of the secretaries for Negro Schools and Colleges of the Board of Education of the Methodist Church, declared that if the best educational results for Negroes were to be achieved, the philanthropists had to work through Negroes as presidents, teachers, and workers. He believed that economic issues were at stake. "Thousands of Negroes are being educated and have nowhere to work except among our own people," he said.[25] As a whole, the Howard faculty took the appointment in stride. As for the students, they were quite proud.

Yet, some faculty members were not happy with Johnson's selection and showed their displeasure in several ways throughout the first half of his administration. Nevertheless, the decision was final. In due course, Johnson, his wife, and his three children were ensconced in the president's home on the campus.

Johnson was no stranger to Howard University. As discussed earlier, for five consecutive years he had been the principal speaker during the annual Week of Prayer at the university, an observance that many colleges sponsored in that era. Moreover, many in the campus community remembered that three years earlier the university had conferred on him an honorary Doctor of Divinity.

When Johnson took office, the university comprised eight schools and colleges, of which only two were fully accredited. The faculty consisted of about 200 teachers; the student body numbered less than 2,000. Howard's annual operating budget was only $700,000, and the physical plant had a value of less than $2 million.

Johnson had a broad vision for Howard's future. He wanted facilities and a faculty that would compare favorably with any liberal arts university in America. Young black men and women needed a viable institution where they could be trained for effective service throughout the country. He was convinced that a liberal education was central to developing the individual, and that Howard was the ideal place for setting the standards in the various disciplines of learning.

On June 10, 1927, at the first commencement exercises after Johnson took office, he was formally inducted as the eleventh—and first African-American—president of the university. In his inaugural address, he set forth his vision for the university.[26] After tracing the development of the institution from its founding in 1867, he pointed out its current status, showing how it had grown in academic programs, in physical facilities, and in student enrollment. He described Howard University as "the first mature university organization to come to pass among Negroes in the modern civilized world. Its growth from the humblest beginnings is one of the great romances of American education."[27]

Howard University, he stated, is "a monument to the capacity of the Negro himself. . . . The human mind," he continued, "whatever its color, and under whatever serious embarrassment it may have worked, is essentially a dignified thing. . . . All that Christianity and other great religions have dared to believe about it can possibly be true."[28] He maintained that the university existed primarily so that ordinary people, given what they needed, could make their lives happy and productive. Emphasizing the importance of the schools of medicine and law, he expressed the need to have African Americans serve in local and national legislatures and to provide adequate health care to communities in need. Concerning the School of Law, he avowed Howard University's intention to provide lawyers "who are competent, living up to the high standards of the legal profession." Regarding the teaching profession, he emphasized the need for teachers who were competent in their fields, who were aware of the nuances of the African-American mind and of the economic and other problems encountered by institutions of learning, and who would work not according to the clock but because of their love for the people.

As to religion, Johnson pointed out that the 47,000 African-American churches in the United States, representing the most powerful and constructive organizations among this group, required an educated ministry that the graduate School of Religion could provide. That school would have the responsibility of "endeavoring to deliver the people from superstition and from uncharitable sectarianism, binding them into a stable cooperation, clarifying the vision, and releasing their energies for constructive services to the common good."[29]

Johnson set forth his world vision with respect to how a university could contribute to solving common problems. He saw Howard University as making special contributions in this area. Specifically, he referred to the disciplines of sociology, economics, social philosophy, history, biology, anthropology, and religion as sources of information that would provide the intellectual resources by which African Americans and the nation as a whole could be advanced.

In speaking about the destiny of the Negro, Johnson expressed the hope that the race would be freed completely "from every form of public servitude" and that this accomplishment would be achieved not by amalgamation, but by the moral will. He added, "I want my country to conquer all of the inhibitions connected with blackness and all of the fears connected with blackness, but I want the original blackness there, and I want this blackness to be unashamed and unafraid." This statement was more than forty years before the revolution of the 1960s and 1970s when Stokely Carmichael and others coined and popularized the slogans "Black Is Beautiful" and "Black Power."

Johnson closed his inaugural address, as he usually did in subsequent baccalaureate addresses, by urging graduating students to be prepared to work hard and diligently, not for their own self-aggrandizement, but for the public good. He exhorted them to be mindful of their educational heritage and of those persons who in the early post-emancipation years made sacrifices to bring truth in the freedmen. He urged them to be prepared to understand the blindness of prejudice and to comprehend the causes and results of prejudging people of other races. Finally, he urged the graduates to live in a way that would reflect credit on the university that had prepared them for the world.

In an inaugural address, the president must be sensitive to all of his or her publics. The speaker should give attention first to those who founded and maintained the institution. The primary mission should be set forth, including the president's concept of how the mission may be achieved and enhanced. In addition, the address should indicate what financial resources, faculty, curricula, and student services are needed. In short, the president must show the basic reason for the existence of the institution with respect to training its graduates to meet the needs of the people. An analysis of Johnson's inaugural address shows that he met these criteria. The speech conveyed the message that he felt he had a special mission to carry out the realization of the goals set forth.

Much pomp and high expectation characterized the inauguration exercises. The president and the university received greetings from leading institutions of learning, not only in the United States but also from overseas. Among the latter were Oxford; St. Andrew's; the universities of London, Madrid, Amsterdam, Edinburgh, Geneva, Louvain, and Zurich; and Trinity College in Dublin. In addition, the heads of all major religious, fraternal, and educational organizations in the United States sent greetings.

Johnson realized the need for sufficient funds to carry forward his plans. Until he took office, the appropriations from the federal government were not guaranteed. Beginning in 1879, they amounted $10,000 annually.

Each year the university had to appeal to Congress for a subsidy. By 1926 the amount given annually had increased to $200,000. These grants were never adequate to enable the school to operate at a level commensurate with the standards of a full-fledged university. In the absence of statutory authority for the appropriations, the fiscal health of the university would remain tenuous unless the situation changed.

Realizing this critically important need, Johnson vigorously attacked the task of securing the legislation needed to substantiate the congressional appropriations. He appealed for statutory authority for the annual appropriations on several compelling grounds, among which was the moral argument that the federal government had a special responsibility to its largest minority. He cited the fact that the seventeen southern states where most African Americans lived had no university where members of this minority could receive a comprehensive professional education. Almost all the medical and dental schools denied admission to black applicants. The two exceptions were Howard University and the historically black Meharry Medical College, founded in 1876 in Nashville, Tennessee. Johnson argued that, given the necessary funding for improved facilities and faculties, Howard would be able to train a large corps of well-prepared graduates to serve the nation.

Substantial funds were needed to bring the university to the desired level of academic excellence and to provide adequate physical facilities. Johnson's first task in this connection was to raise money so that the school could claim a challenge grant offered by the General Education Board.[30] The Medical School needed $500,000 for a new building and endowment, specifically for upgrading the facilities and personnel of the preclinical branches of its program. During former-President Durkee's administration, the General Education Board had pledged to give one-half of that amount, provided the university raised the other $250,000. Before his resignation, Durkee had raised $125,000, but by the time he resigned, the campaign had fallen apart. Durkee had appointed Emory Smith, a local Congregational minister, as the alumni secretary, a move that the alumni resented because of their suspicion that the appointment was a ploy by the president to exercise some dominance over them. Because of this negative attitude toward Smith, alumni members refused to honor their pledges to the university.

The deadline for completing the campaign was June 30, 1927. By February the goal was not in sight. As he was seeking ways to reach it, Johnson received a telephone call from Julius Rosenwald, with whom he had had no contact since he declined Rosenwald's offer four years earlier to underwrite his becoming a national lecturer and writer in the cause for better race relations following his graduation from Harvard.

Rosenwald telephoned Johnson to say that he was in Washington on business in connection with Herbert Hoover's presidential campaign and wanted to visit Johnson. Johnson was "moved with gladness" at this message. According to his memoirs, the conversation went like this:

Rosenwald: "Well, Dr. Johnson, what on earth made you accept this position? Don't you know that Howard University is one of the worst places to spend your life in the whole of the United States?"

Johnson: "Yes, sir, I know that."

Rosenwald: "What on earth made you do it?"

Johnson: "I thought, sir, that I had resources that would enable me to bring about a constructive change in the heavy conditions prevailing in the later part of Dr. Durkee's administration, and I was determined to do my best to make that change."

Rosenwald: "Very well, if that is your purpose and you are willing to try it, I am willing to help you. I am told that you have got to raise $500,000 by June 30. This is a very heavy task for a young man like you to undertake; already this is February. How in the world you expect to raise this money I don't know."

Johnson explained that the remaining amount he had to raise was $125,000 not $500,000.

Rosenwald: "How in the world do you expect to raise $125,000 between this month of February and June 30?"

Johnson: "Sir, I have got it to do. And I am going to do everything in my power to raise it."

Rosenwald: "I will make you a proposition. I will raise the $25,000 and you will raise the $100,000, and I will tell you what I will do. I will go from this office to the treasurer of Howard University and put down my check for $25,000. And this is not all I will do. If you succeed in raising this money, I will give you help from time to time as you get your plans ready for the leadership of Howard University."[31]

Greatly inspired by this unexpected development, Johnson devised a plan to overcome, at least in part, the alumni's opposition by organizing a group of twenty-five women alumnae living in Washington who would pledge to raise money in the city. He then had the Board of Trustees agree to reassign Emory Smith to the position of financial agent of the university. He and Smith toured the country contacting those alumni who had made $1,000 pledges and reclaimed their support. Members of the Medical School's faculty would sometimes stand on the street soliciting contributions from passersby. The women alumnae raised $25,000. As a result of all the efforts, the $125,000 was raised. About a month before commencement, Johnson notified the General Education Board that Howard University had raised the $250,000 and could match the challenge grant.

Johnson, however, faced another immediate problem. The $500,000 was needed to equip the new building. The federal government had appropriated $370,000 with the understanding that the university would raise $130,000. The General Education Board had promised $80,000 of that amount. The university was to raise $50,000 and had been promised that amount by a foundation. A month before commencement, that expectation collapsed.

Hearing that the university had been successful in raising the $250,000 required for the challenge grant, Abraham Flexner, chairman of the General Education Board, telephoned Johnson just before the commencement day ceremonies expressing the Board of Trustee's pleasure in the accomplishment. He said that the members had heard of the disappointment in getting the additional $50,000 to complete the $130,000 needed to equip the Medical School's building. Flexner wanted Johnson to announce at the commencement exercises that the General Education Board was so pleased at Howard's raising the $250,000 that the foundation not only would give the $80,000 initially pledged for equipment, but also would give the $50,000 balance.[32]

This development enabled Johnson to announce at his first commencement exercises not only that the $500,000 was available for the new Medical School building, but also that the $130,000 for equipment was ensured.

Johnson relied heavily on the friendliness of the General Education Board, established by the John D. Rockefeller family and managed by Abraham Flexner, and the Julius Rosenwald Fund, managed by Edwin R. Embree, for meeting some of the university's critical needs.

On March 17, 1928, Flexner wrote to Embree that Johnson had been doing "extraordinarily well" and needed $500,000 to increase the endowment of the Medical School. "I wish you would turn it over and see whether between us we cannot agree to recommend to our respective boards cooperation in securing this sum," Flexner stated.[33]

Later that year Johnson sent a lengthy letter to Richard W. Pearce, director of the Division of Medical Education of the Rockefeller Foundation, appealing for aid for the Medical School. He cited the need for securing competent leadership to train students in medicine and dentistry, for urgently needed increases in the number of full-time teachers, and for salary increases to attract the best available teachers for full-time service in the schools. When Johnson took office, many teachers in the Medical School taught only part time.

Johnson stated the need to find adequate replacements for the retiring dean of the Medical School and the vice dean of the School of Dentistry. He set high standards for the type of Medical School dean he wanted:

> For the Dean of the College of Medicine we hope to secure a man able to lead in the entire medical program. We should prefer, of course, a man thoroughly acquainted with the best educational programs and curricula now obtained in medicine and who would be competent to bring our own medical school swiftly up to the best standards. We should prefer a man, who, while uncompromisingly thorough in his efforts to meet prevailing standards, will be alert and eager in the study of problems in the field of medical education, capably weighing the proposed lines of advance and willing responsibly to undertake such departures here as our situation may demand and as may, in time, serve to make our school a creative center of medical thought and activity. . . .[34]

Johnson kept in communication with Jacob Billikopf, a trustee of Howard and president of the Federation of Jewish Charities, setting forth the status and needs of the university. Billikopf exercised considerable influence to further the interests of the university, coordinating his efforts with those of the heads of other philanthropic agencies.

Fortunately, as early as two years before Johnson was elected president, two congressmen (Representatives Louis C. Cramton of Michigan, chairman of the Subcommittee on Appropriations of the Department of the Interior, and Daniel A. Reed of New York) showed serious interest in and dedication to promoting crucial congressional legislation undergirding Howard. On June 3 and December 10, 1924, Congressman Cramton introduced bills authorizing annual appropriations to the university. On January 27, 1926, Congressman Reed introduced a bill duplicating the one Cramton had presented in December 1924. The desire to restructure the composition of the subcommittee and election procedures required a delay of action on these bills.[35] Johnson worked closely with Congressman Cramton. Each wrote to influential people in and out of Congress asking them to use their influence in getting the bill passed.

Several other representatives on Cramton's committee were sympathetic to Howard's needs and worked with him on the appropriations project. Along with Cramton, according to historian Clifford Muse, they served as virtually "the Board of Regents of the University."[36]

In his testimony at the hearings on the proposed legislation, Johnson called attention to the gross disparities between the allocation of funds to African-American schools and the others. He pointed out that the burden of providing higher education in those states that maintained a segregated system was assumed entirely by African-American institutions, whose per capita allocations annually were considerably less than those for the other institutions.

Johnson wrote to Julius Rosenwald asking him to support the annual appropriations bill for Howard. Rosenwald met with Roy O. West, secretary of the Department of the Interior, to urge his support of the bill. As a result of the efforts spearheaded by Representative Cramton, Congress passed the legislation on December 13, 1928, guaranteeing that Howard would receive annual appropriations for its operations. The law read in part,

> Annual appropriations are hereby authorized to aid in the construction, development, improvement, and maintenance of the university, no part of which shall be used for religious instruction. The university shall at all times be open for inspection by the Bureau of Education and shall be inspected by the said Bureau at least once a year. An annual report making a full exhibit of the affairs of the University shall be presented to Congress each year in the report of the Bureau of Education.[37]

Shortly after this legislation passed, Johnson received some significant honors. Gammon Theological Seminary conferred on him the degree of Doctor of Divinity. The NAACP gave him its highest award, the Spingarn Medal, "in honor of his successful administration as the first Negro President of the nation's leading Negro university, and for his achievement during the last year of obtaining legislation by which Howard University becomes a recognized institution of the Government of the United States." In 1929 Rabbi Stephen S. Wise chose him as one of the ten greatest religious leaders in the country.

Following the passage of the Cramton bill, Secretary West called a conference of the principal governmental agencies and leaders of philanthropic organizations whose interests had a bearing on the future of the university. Now that the federal government was formally committed to supporting Howard, the objective was to decide in what ways, including collective efforts, Howard University could be established as a first-class institution. This resolve required (1) a thorough examination of the entire program of the university; (2) as stated by Johnson in a memorandum to the Board of Trustees, a clear-cut understanding as to the amount of income required to develop the university into such a first-class service; and (3) a clear-cut understanding with the federal government as to the percentage of support the government would give to the program, both in the matter of current expenses and in the matter of buildings."[38] The commitments growing out of this conference established the bases on which Johnson could appeal to Congress and private philanthropies for needed capital and operating expenses. Both the federal government and private philanthropies began to response to these resolutions.

After leading the efforts in Congress on behalf of Howard University, Representative Cramton maintained his interest in Howard University during the remainder of his tenure in Congress. He kept Rosenwald informed of Howard's development and was active in securing an appropriation from Congress for the purchase of land Howard greatly needed. In a letter to Embree, Cramton wrote that to the extent Congress gave increasing support to Howard, foundations and individuals would be motivated to increase their gifts also. In turn, he felt that the support foundations and individuals gave to Howard would serve as a basis for Congress to increase its support.[39]

In 1931 Howard University sponsored a testimonial banquet to honor Representative Cramton as he was retiring from Congress. Attending were 350 guests, including alumni from thirty-six states along with faculty members and trustees. On that occasion, Cramton declared that "Appropriations to Howard University indicate that Congress has come to the conclusion that no matter what the color, religion, or social position of our citizens may be, it is best for the commonwealth that they be educated." He added that the legislation showed that Congress had concluded that Howard University should assume the educational leadership of colored people, and that his success in spearheading the appropriate legislation was the most important achievement of his congressional career.[40]

Commenting on Cramton's contributions, Johnson stated,

> He initiated and carried through the House of Representatives the substantive law which both houses of Congress passed and which the President of the United States signed on December 13, 1928, giving legal authority for "annual appropriations to aid in the construction, development, improvement, and maintenance

of the University." Before that time all appropriations were gratuities, rested on no substantive legal authorizations, and were subject to challenge at any time. The existence of the University was imperiled. The new legislation was a tremendous development in the history of the institution.[41]

As a further expression of appreciation for Congressman Cramton's efforts on behalf of Howard, the university named its new auditorium in his honor. Nevertheless, historian Clifford Muse found that after Cramton's retirement, "Howard's ability to benefit from strong and persistent congressional lobbying on its behalf was seriously diminished."[42]

Because of the formation of ten-year and twenty-year plans for Howard following the passage of the appropriation laws of 1928, Johnson pushed for progress toward the accreditation of all of the schools of the university. In addition to strengthening the Medical School, one of his basic concerns was the development of a first-class School of Law. When he took office, he became acutely aware of the limitations of the School of Law, which was unaccredited. He asked the dean to apply for accreditation. Johnson was distressed to learn that the subsequent appraisal revealed that radical reorganization and reformation were required before the school could meet the standards for accreditation.

Johnson thought of Associate Justice Louis D. Brandeis of the U.S. Supreme Court. Johnson knew that the son of one of his most revered teachers had married Brandeis's daughter, and he suspected that Brandeis and Johnson's teacher had similar commitments. He telephoned and was given an appointment to see Brandeis. After the usual preliminaries, Johnson asked, "If you were President of Howard University, Mr. Justice, in what way would you proceed to build up a first-class law school?" Brandeis told Johnson that he was glad that he had come to see him, and that he was aware of the Howard School of Law and some of its graduates. He felt, however, that the School of Law's only objective was to prepare a quantity of students to pass the bar. He insisted that the school's emphasis should be on the quality of its graduates rather than on the quantity. Because African Americans as a minority people had not yet secured their fundamental civic and constitutional rights, the simple objective of just producing students who could pass the bar was not enough. In answer to Johnson's inquiry, Brandeis stated that he would "select a few of the ablest men he could find, and train them [in] how to proceed in the courts of law to secure civil and constitutional rights for my people."

Brandeis then said that he would share something important if Johnson pledged not to quote him until after his death. Johnson agreed. Brandeis pointed out that during his tenure on the Supreme Court a number of cases involving civil and constitutional rights had come before it. Most of these cases, he said, were poorly prepared, whether by black or white lawyers. Consequently, the cases had to be thrown out or were decided against the minority. "No greater tragedy" said he, "could happen to a young and struggling people such as the minority to which you belong. . . . Your civil rights are in that Constitution."

Brandeis advised Johnson to recruit a few able men, to train them in how to identify a good case involving civil and constitutional rights, and to nurture those cases until they came before the Supreme Court, "with the constitutional issue so clear that the justices of the Supreme Court will be obliged to rule upon the constitutional issue itself." Brandeis concluded that if this were done, the minority people, "one by one," would recover their constitutional rights.[43]

Certainly this was sage counsel from Associate Justice Brandeis, who served twenty-three years (1916–1936) on the high court. Born in Louisville, Kentucky, to an immigrant but cultivated family, Brandeis graduated from Harvard Law School in 1887 as valedictorian of his class. During his practice of law in St. Louis and Boston, he showed a genuine interest in the concerns of ordinary people. He was said to have had "a passion for public service." As a Jew and the first of his religion appointed to the Supreme Court, he was acutely aware of racial prejudice and discrimination, an awareness heightened by the fact that when President Woodrow Wilson nominated him, Brandeis was approved only after intense resistance from some of the most influential members of the American Bar Association.[44]

Clearly, Johnson impressed Brandeis by his aspiring for an excellent law school and by recognizing the need of African Americans for effective counsel to carry forward litigation that would eliminate crippling social injustices. Brandeis and Johnson maintained a close relationship for many years. Not until 1966—twenty-five years after the death of Associate Justice Brandeis—at the fiftieth anniversary of the Convocations of the School of Religion, did Johnson reveal publicly who had given him this advice.[45]

The afternoon and evening classes of the Howard School of Law in 1926 made it possible for students to hold jobs during the day while studying for a law degree at night. Although some successful lawyers were produced, this arrangement was limited in several ways. The work schedules of the students prevented them from having the advantages of extended fellowship with other law students, adequate hours in the library, and frequent contact with teachers that full-time study in a day law program allows. Moreover, the American Bar Association and the American Association of Law Schools would not grant accreditation to a night law school.

Johnson was much impressed by Charles Hamilton Houston, who had been teaching part time in the School of Law since 1924. Born in 1895 and exhibiting high standards of scholarship throughout his life, Houston was a Phi Beta Kappa graduate and valedictorian of his class at Amherst College. He held LL.B. and S.J.D. degrees from Harvard Law School, where he was in the upper 5 percent of his class. Because of his outstanding scholarship, Houston was awarded the coveted Sheldon Traveling Fellowship, which enabled him to study at the University of Madrid and to travel to other parts of Europe. When he began teaching in the School of Law, he was also working with his father in their joint law firm.

Johnson appreciated Houston's zeal to develop a top-flight law school. Eventually, in spite of some objections, the Board of Trustees voted to transform the night program into a regular daytime School of Law. When the then-dean, Fenton Booth, was appointed Chief Justice of the U.S. Court of Appeals in 1929, the Board of Trustees named Houston as resident vice dean.[46]

Houston had the strong support of two of his former teachers at Harvard, Felix Frankfurter and Joseph H. Beale, as well as that of Roscoe Pound, dean of the Harvard Law School. Frankfurter and Beale were frequent lecturers at Howard School of Law.

Demanding the best from his students, Houston tolerated nothing slipshod or shoddy. If a student failed to meet the academic requirements, he was expelled. Thurgood Marshall, an alumnus who was to become the first African American appointed to the Supreme Court, once said that only eight of the thirty first-year students who entered with him completed the course.[47]

Houston believed that African-American lawyers should develop skills and devote their talents primarily to resolving some crucial civil rights problems of black people. In his words, black lawyers should become "social engineers." By this term he meant that black lawyers must have a thorough knowledge of the U.S. Constitution and must use that knowledge to drive constructive changes in the social status of the underprivileged. In her definitive study of Charles Hamilton Houston, Genna Rae McNeil points out that he held that the duty of the social engineer is to "guide . . . antagonistic and group forces into channels where they will not clash" and to make certain that "the course of change is . . . orderly with a minimum human loss and suffering." Houston said that "A lawyer's either to be a social engineer or a parasite on society."[48]

Among the other lawyers recruited to teach at the School of Law were Leon A. Ransom, who had distinguished himself at the Ohio State Law School, and James M. Nabrit Jr., a graduate of Morehouse College and of the Northwestern University Law School. Nabrit taught Howard School of Law's first course in Civil Rights Law. It was also the first such course in the nation. Later he became secretary to the university and eventually succeeded Johnson as its president. By the 1930–1931 school year, the School of Law, with a full-time, highly qualified faculty, had demonstrated such effectiveness that the American Association of Law Schools and the American Bar Association gave it full accreditation.[49]

When Houston resigned in 1935 to become chief counsel for the NAACP, Johnson appointed William H. Hastie, a distant cousin of Houston and a former governor of the Virgin Islands, to be the dean. Houston and Hastie shared a common devotion to academic excellence. Like Houston, Hastie went to Amherst where he excelled in both academics and athletics. He was elected to Phi Beta Kappa and won several prestigious prizes. Later he went to Harvard Law School and, like Houston before him, edited the *Harvard Law Review*.[50]

A number of promising students were drawn to the Howard School of Law. Besides Thurgood Marshall, whose career included serving as chief counsel to the NAACP and as Solicitor General of the United States before being named Associate Justice of U.S. Supreme Court, the school attracted Oliver W. Hill, civil rights lawyer, along with Spottswood Robinson III, Robert Carter, Scovel Richardson, and William B. Bryant, all of whom became federal judges.

The School of Law soon became the primary institution of legal training for African Americans. It was the catalyst for some of the most significant decisions affecting the civil rights of the black community, including the landmark *Brown* vs. *Board of Education* decision in 1954. Argued before the Supreme Court by Thurgood Marshall, the case resulted in outlawing segregation in public education. Intensive research was done for each civil rights case undertaken. During one of the moot court sessions while preparing for the *Brown* case, someone playing the role of a Supreme Court Justice raised a crucial question that the counsels had not considered. They researched the issue, and indeed, during the argument before the Supreme Court, an Associate Justice raised that very question. The NAACP lawyers were well prepared.

These contributions of Howard's School of Law prompted the activist Federal Judge A. Leon Higginbotham to ask, in his famous open letter to

Clarence Thomas after Thomas was appointed to the Supreme Court, ". . . What would have happened to you if there had never been a Charles Hamilton Houston, a William H. Hastie, and a Thurgood Marshall, and that small cadre of other lawyers associated with them, who laid the groundwork for success in the twentieth-century racial civil rights cases?"[51] Another observer, A. L. Higgs, stated, "This generation does not face any task as formidable and as awesome as those that faced William Hastie, Charles Hamilton Houston, and Thurgood Marshall."[52]

Johnson was justifiably proud of the School of Law. He shared the opinion of Associate Justice Brandeis that the African-American community needed able black lawyers. He saw the school as the training ground for well-prepared advocates who would break down some of the walls of segregation and discrimination against which he himself fought constantly. It is significant, as Johnson points out in his memoirs, that "of the five cases involving segregation in the schools [that] were being heard before the Supreme Court, nine of the ten lawyers representing the Negro people in these cases, under the leadership of Thurgood Marshall, were either graduates of Howard University Law School or members of the faculty of the School of Law." Johnson often referred to the School of Law as "my law school," a claim he did not make of other schools in the university.[53]

Johnson built up each of the other schools that were unaccredited when he took office. He wrote to deans of certain outstanding graduate schools requesting recommendations for faculty positions. New buildings were constantly under construction, and the student body increased steadily.

Johnson was particularly concerned about the university's finances and often personally checked the accuracy of figures, including those concerning enrollment. One example of his administrative style is recorded by Benjamin Mays, who cites an experience while he was dean of the Howard University School of Religion. A friend told Mays about an extensive theological library containing books representing rich resources that the School of Religion needed. The collection was valued in many thousands of dollars, but Howard could purchase it for $10,000. Contrary to May's expectation, Johnson did not jump at the offer. Instead, he had two other experts evaluate the collection before he approved the purchase.

Meanwhile, Johnson continued to cultivate the interest of Julius Rosenwald, as well as other philanthropists, and of Congress. The financial underpinning of the university grew through appeals to Congress and to foundations, such as the General Education Board and the Laura Spelman

Rockefeller Memorial Fund. Whenever there was a need, Johnson did not hesitate to call on these sources of support.[54]

During his tenure, Johnson appointed several nationally known scholars. As we have seen, Ernest E. Just, the internationally known cell-biologist, and Alain Locke, the Harvard-trained philosopher and the first African American named a Rhodes scholar, were already on the faculty when Johnson took office. Benjamin Brawley, a notable English scholar, was also at Howard when Johnson came. Besides the outstanding law professors were Percy Julian, a skilled chemist; Charles Drew, a specialist in hematology who perfected the process of storing blood by converting it to blood plasma and who worked with the American Red Cross and the British Army on blood plasma projects; and Ralph Bunche, who taught political science and who later was awarded the Nobel Peace Prize for serving as a United Nations mediator for Palestine. Others in this group included E. Franklin Frazier, a sociologist elected president of the American Sociological Society in 1948; Rayford W. Logan, a Harvard-trained historian whose specialty was Latin-American Negro history and who served on the U.S. National Commission of the United Nations Educational, Scientific, and Cultural Organization (UNESCO); and John Hope Franklin, an internationally recognized historian whose book *From Slavery to Freedom* became a classic.[55] Not to be excluded were William Leo Hansberry, an authority on African history and culture; and Merz Tate, an outstanding scholar in history and anthropology. The field of literature was enriched by Arthur Paul Davis; Sterling A. Brown; and Frank M. Snowden, a classicist. Contributing to the sciences were David Blackwell, an outstanding mathematician, along with Herman Branson and Halson V. Eagleson in physics. No other institution boasted so many African-American scholars.

A dramatic change Johnson made during the first part of his administration was to limit the emphasis on athletics. Football was one of the major interests of students, alumni, and many people in the wider community as well. Before Johnson took office, Howard University, as well as many other institutions, provided special dining tables and a special menu for the football team. Howard granted free room and board for football players. Johnson ordered that these practices be discontinued, much to the dissatisfaction of many people, especially students and alumni. Johnson took the position that he had signed an Amateur Agreement with other institutions not to subsidize individual athletes. The students became belligerent and threatened to strike. In a session with them in Rankin Chapel, Johnson outlined his commitment to academic integrity, pointing out that if he compromised this commitment, they would in the long run lose respect for the institution. Johnson enjoyed athletics, having actively participated during his college years in football, basketball, and baseball, He did not object to football as a co-curricular activity. Actually, on occasion, he could be seen watching the football team practice. In time, students and others saw the wisdom of Johnson's position on athletics. They took pride in the fact that Howard was more than what was represented by a good football team.

Obviously, Johnson viewed Howard's mission as providing a sound liberal education that prepared leaders who would make positive changes in society. His quest for top-flight faculty; his persistent campaign for financial resources for capital expansion, curriculum improvements, and operating funds; and his "hands-on" type of administration showed a strong commitment to establishing a first-rate university. But this was not to be achieved without considerable controversy.

6

Howard University—Confrontations, Criticisms, and Recognition

*U*ntil now, a continuous barrage of criticism from those who resented his appointment had failed to interfere with Johnson's accomplishments. Criticisms began soon after Johnson was elected and prompted letters of support and encouragement from close friends. For example, President John Hope, Johnson's mentor at Morehouse, wrote him a long letter expressing sympathy and support. Because of the confidential nature of the communication, Hope included it in a letter to Johnson's wife, with the request that she hand it to him personally. Hope included the consoling words, "What you folks are going through may be difficult, but it is the day's work on a tremendously big job." In a communication dated August 12, 1928, Hope wrote:

> Dear Friend: . . . I regretted to leave [Washington] without an opportunity to talk fully with you about some of the problems and difficulties that are with you now. When I think of your work and my work and our mutual interests, there comes to me that line from the *Iliad*, "But Menelaus came because he knew how his brother toiled in battle." You may feel assured that I am ready to be of assistance to you. . . . If there is anything weighing heavily on you now that a word from me might help you to handle, feel perfectly free to write to me personally.
>
> There may be some things that you will have to do that will be unpleasant to do. They may be so

unpleasant to do that you may find yourself attempting to accomplish them on impulse. I warn you against impulses. You will have to use the greatest calmness in the handling of some situations that might almost crush you to go through with. All of that goes with the job, my friend. This will have to be your guide and assurance: the welfare of Howard University as Howard is to administer in the best possible way to the group to which it is especially committed, namely Negroes. And this purpose of Howard University has to be considered also with reference to the relations of Negroes to white people and those better relations that you and I would have come to pass. . . .

In all of this you must be careful, not only of what you do, but what you say. And when I say "what you say," I am thinking about your conversations and your public utterances. For there are some already quite willing to take your honest public statements to embarrass you. In fact, if I may be bold enough to make the suggestion (I would not be at all hurt if you did not accept it), I would suggest that you do little or no public speaking for the next few months. Dig in at Howard University and keep quiet. You may surprise and discomfit some people if you do that. I would advise you to be on the job at Howard all seven days of the week; and if you can find an eighth day, use it. . . .

Will all good wishes and with the highest confidence in your ability to handle the situation . . . I am

Your friend,
s/ John Hope[1]

The most remarkable advice John Hope gave to Johnson in this letter was that he should sharply curtail his public speaking, an implication that Hope himself was disturbed by some of Johnson's utterances. Apparently, Hope did not realize the depth of Johnson's determination, for Johnson was not the type of person to withdraw from controversy.

Johnson expressed appreciation for Hope's "good letter of counsel," which he had "read with great profit." But he flatly rejected the suggestion that he curtail his public speaking activities, stating that he had already obligated himself for several important occasions. He added that to defend himself against misinterpretations, he had begun the practice of handing out brief summaries of his remarks to the press.[2]

Certain faculty members with terminal degrees who had served at the university for some time had difficulty accepting the naming of a Baptist preacher, who had not even earned a doctorate, to head the "Capstone of Negro Education." Indeed, Johnson's employment experience in higher education was limited to two years of teaching at Morehouse College following his graduation with a Bachelor of Arts degree. For one of these years he was acting dean. Some felt that his lack of experience as a college administrator would hinder the progress of the university. Some older members of the faculty, notably "the Triumvirate," had been at the university even before Johnson was born.

Others took advantage of Johnson's penchant for criticizing the short-comings of capitalism and lauding certain goals of Russian communism, and attempted to discredit him on these grounds. Most of this fault-finding came from sources outside the university. However, some from the university community were concerned about Johnson's public statements, in view of the possible effect on outsiders, especially federal officials.

Among the problems that Johnson had to face were those involving direct conflicts with personnel on the faculty and staff. A serious breach occurred between Johnson and Dr. Ernest E. Just, the noted biologist. A graduate of Dartmouth College and the University of Chicago, he had joined the Howard faculty in 1907. At first, Just was enthusiastic about Johnson's appointment to the presidency of Howard. Apparently he felt that an African-American president would be sympathetic to his professional ambitions. In fact, Johnson was supportive of Just. Just had gained recognition from a number of outstanding educators and foundation executives, particularly from Edwin R. Embree of the Julius Rosenwald Fund.[3] Because of Embree's admiration for Just, the Rosenwald Fund had pledged $15,000 a year for five years to build up the biology department at Howard.

Embree wrote to Rosenwald assuring him that he had received high praise for Just from Dr. Frank R. Lillie, chairman of Chicago's department of zoology and director of the Marine Biological Laboratory at Woods Hole, Massachusetts. It was under Lillie's direction that Just had completed his Ph.D. The recommendation from Lillie, according to Embree, "was about as strong a statement as one scientist can make of another."[4]

Johnson earlier had written Embree urging support of Just's application for a grant to strengthen the biology department at Howard.[5] In a second letter, Johnson expressed his appreciation to the Rosenwald Fund for receipt of the grant and described how the money would be used. He also called

Embree's attention to an important article that Just had published in an international journal devoted to biological research. In his letter to Embree, Johnson said,

> I am deeply indebted to you for your thoughtful attention to the needs of this deserving scholar. You are about to come to his assistance at a critical time in his career and just at the point when this assistance may cause his work to blossom and bear rich immediate fruits. As in prospect, I look at the free and glad self-expression which may come to him through your office, and at the joy which you and Mr. Rosenwald will have in knowing you have made such an expression possible. I am very happy.[6]

Just misunderstood the terms of the Rosenwald grant, which resulted in an escalating difference of opinion between him and Johnson. Just felt that the grant was for his personal use, independent of the concerns of the university administration. However, in giving the grant to Howard, the foundation had stipulated that the money was for the department of biology and not specifically for Just. The resolutions for the grant read as follows:

> Resolved that the sum of fifteen thousand dollars ($15,000) be and it is hereby appropriated for the Department of Biology of Howard University, under the leadership of Dr. E. E. Just, for the year 1928–1929.
>
> Resolved that the Julius Rosenwald Fund pledge itself to appropriate fifteen thousand dollars ($15,000) during each of the four years of 1929 to 1933 for the Department of Biology of Howard University if Dr. Just continues to direct that department and to pursue scientific research and graduate instruction substantially in accordance with the program outlined on the statement above.
>
> Resolved that the sum of five thousand dollars ($5,000) be and it is hereby appropriated, of which so much as may be needed shall be used in the purchase of scientific equipment, including books and journals, for Dr. Just's Department during the five-year period, 1928–1933.[7]

To get a full understanding of Just's position, Embree wrote to Dr. Lillie at Woods Hole to get his opinion about Just. Embree stated that "naturally because of his own work and his prolonged absences from Washington, Dr. Just has not been able to give much attention to this side of his work [working with students at Howard]. I fear he is not really interested in it. Maybe he is the kind of man who does brilliant work himself, but finds it difficult to teach others, even advanced students."[8]

For his part, Just wrote to Dr. Guy B. Johnson, a member of the Board of Trustees, saying that the Rosenwald grant was given to him as an individual.[9] Guy Johnson asked Embree about the stipulation of the grant, saying that Just had written to him.[10] Embree replied to Guy Johnson in a confidential letter:

> Dr. Just has been one of the most difficult persons with whom I or this Fund has ever tried to work. We made what seems to me an unusually generous grant to him and his work and have received nothing but complaints and recriminations. . . . The appropriations of the Julius Rosenwald Fund . . . were to Howard University for the development of . . . teaching in biology. It was understood between us and the authorities of Howard University that this grant was made because of our admiration for the work Dr. Just was doing, but the grant was definitely to Howard. . . . I am convinced that Dr. Just has been treated with unusual generosity both by Howard University and by outside donors. I am equally convinced that nothing will persuade Dr. Just that he is not a scientific martyr constantly hampered and discriminated against by University authorities, fellow scientists, and patrons of science.[11]

In a letter dated October 5, 1932, Embree replied to a complaint from Just:

> I think it is very important that all of us understand clearly the terms of our appropriations. As I have been careful to point out in my letters to you and to President Johnson, our contribution has never been to you personally, but to Howard University for the support of the department you are directing. It seems to me as important from your standpoint as from ours to have this relationship clear. . . .
>
> We are trying simply to strengthen the University and, specifically in this instance, the Department of Biology under your leadership.[12]

The main problem Johnson had was that Just neglected the development of the biology department. Just was frequently absent, promoting his personal advancement at the expense of the department. At the same time, Johnson expected complete commitment to the university by faculty and staff. Such a commitment, of course, served to enhance the reputation of the university and its programs. According to Dr. Herman Branson, former professor of physics at Howard, most of the faculty sided with Johnson in his dispute with Just.[13]

Johnson was embroiled in controversies with two other faculty members: James A. Cobb, vice dean of the School of Law, and Arnold Donowa, dean of the Dental School. In June 1930, Johnson recommended to the Board of Trustees that the office of vice dean, which Cobb held, be abolished. From the records of the Board of Trustees, the reason for this administrative change is not clear.[14]

In any event, Johnson's action created considerable enmity on the part of Cobb's friends.

Dean Donowa was dismissed because of the university's dissatisfaction with a proposal he put forth concerning the autonomy of the Dental and Medical Schools and, more specifically, for his having "insubordinated himself to the established regulations of the Board of Trustees . . ." and having "written and circulated letters which injuriously interfere with the public relations of the University."[15]

Other prominent faculty members with whom Johnson had notable differences were Abram Harris in economics, Alain Locke in philosophy, E. Franklin Frazier in sociology, and Percy Julian in chemistry. Harris, a standout in his field, received a job offer at the University of Chicago. For some reason Johnson made no effort to retain him at Howard. Harris told a friend that he would have stayed if he had been made to feel wanted there.[16] Unfortunately, Harris's position at Chicago was of a lesser rank than the one he held at Howard. According to one report, Johnson and Locke hated each other. Nevertheless, at a Board of Trustees dinner, Johnson had called on Locke to give a response for the graduate school. In introducing Locke, Johnson had said, "and we love him." One faculty member attributed Johnson's success as president to this kind of willingness to overcome differences.[17]

The basis of Johnson's dispute with Percy Julian was never publicly stated. Julian left Howard and used his knowledge of chemistry to become highly successful in the commercial world.

As an administrator, Johnson showed a broad familiarity with all segments of the university. At meetings of the deans of the several schools, he showed a remarkable knowledge of every aspect of each school's operations. He had a clear understanding of the direction he envisioned for the university. One senior faculty member said that he brought a vision of greatness to the university.

Yet his determination caused some of his critics to label him as autocratic or dictatorial. Rayford Logan recalls the soubriquet, "the Messiah." Embree referred to him as "the Lord High Chancellor." Some faculty members, including Just and Frazier, were infuriated at what they perceived as Johnson's imperious and ecclesiastical posture. Just called him "a Psalm-singing S.O.B." Frazier opined that Johnson's manner "masked a deep incompetence in piloting a modern university."[18]

Harsh criticisms also came from certain other faculty members. Among these was a small group from the social sciences, including (besides Frazier) economist Abram Harris, political scientist Ralph Bunche, Harold Lewis, and two or three others. This group would meet on Saturday nights at Bunche's home to trade critiques of Johnson and his administration. They complained that he was a preacher and not an academician, that he appeared to have a "Messianic complex," that he was heavy handed in dealing with the faculty, and that it was difficult for those opposed to him to make him persona non grata to the trustees of the university. Johnson's critics found the latter concern particularly frustrating.[19]

Not all faculty members shared these negative opinions. Otherwise, Johnson could hardly have survived as president. Some recognized that a strong administrative hand was essential in guiding an institution such as Howard during that period. In fact a strong administrative stance was characteristic of most presidents of African-American institutions of higher education in those years.

At one point, the pressures of administration, the controversies with some staff members, and the time and energy required in raising funds for the expansion of the university, along with major public speaking engagements, began to affect Johnson's health. While he tenaciously retained his vision for Howard's future, the plethora of problems eventually took a toll, and the strain was evident. In a letter dated December 20, 1930, Embree proposed to Johnson that he take a six-week vacation in the company of George Arthur, an officer of the Julius Rosenwald Fund, who also needed a rest. Embree said, "While I realize how difficult it would be for you to take away from Washington for six weeks, I think you would find the leisure and the recuperation and perspective that comes from it worth more than detailed work 'on the job,' however important these details seem, day by day." Embree said that, moreover, the Fund would "consider it an honor" to bear the expenses of the trip, which would be given as a fellowship.[20]

Johnson replied that he was grateful for the offer and felt that the proposed trip "would be helpful to me and my work here." But certain transactions vital to the university prevented him from making the trip at the time originally scheduled. Later, however, it did become feasible for him to leave the campus for an extended rest period. Several years later, at another time when his physical condition dictated a rest, he planned a trip to Bermuda with his beloved wife. Before leaving, he had a thorough physical examination. At first he was thought to have myocardial degeneration or a swelling of the heart. Further examination revealed that his heart was all right and that the condition was caused by the tremendous pressure of his office. He and Mrs. Johnson went to Bermuda for several weeks, getting complete rest and relaxation. Their supporters welcomed them warmly on their return.

In the early 1930s two situations were sources of frustration for Johnson: his modest salary and his unhappy relations with the secretary-treasurer of the university, Dr. Emmett J. Scott. On the first point, the expenses involved in entertaining visiting dignitaries in his home were substantial, particularly because discrimination against African Americans by the hotels in Washington required that he entertain prominent black visitors to the university in his home. This situation, along with the needs of a growing family, created serious financial strains. He confided about this problem to one of his trustees, John H. Sherburne. Others, also, were aware of his concern. For example, Embree wrote to Billikopf, one of Howard's trustees, of the inadequacy of Johnson's salary: "I think he should have a salary that will enable him to live in some comfort and to travel when he needs to and meet the heavy costs of entertainment which falls these days upon a university president. It seems to me that his total income should not be less than $10,000–$12,000." Billikopf replied that raising Johnson's salary from $7,000 to $8,000 with an allowance of $500 for entertainment and travel was "wholly inadequate."

Billikopf inferred from Embree's letter that Johnson was unhappy with his salary, and, accordingly, he wrote "a strong letter" to trustee Sherburne requesting that the salary question be reopened. Embree wrote to Sherburne urging an increase in Johnson's salary. For one reason, said Embree, "In Mordecai Johnson, Howard University has not only the outstanding president of any Negro institution, but one of the ten or twelve really distinguished, capable presidents of any of the American universities." Embree proposed a salary of not less than $10,000 to $12,000.[21] Later, Sherburne informed Embree that Johnson had discussed the matter of salary with him and that the salary had been increased by $1,500. Sherburne added this significant paragraph: "If he is put on a level far above the other members of his race in similar employment, he is going to create a jealousy and an envy among his own people which will eventually destroy much of his usefulness and power if he goes on the payroll at a salary of $10,000 a year, which I entirely agree with you is not as much as he is worth."[22]

Although Sherburne admitted that a salary of $10,000 a year was "not as much as he [Johnson] was worth," the reason for his reluctance to approve that salary is striking. Why would such a salary deprive Johnson of much of his usefulness to other African Americans? And if the presidency were held by a white American at that time, would Sherburne have objected to the salary figure? Fairness would demand that any president should receive a salary commensurate with his value.

The second major cause of Johnson's frustration was his relationship with Dr. Emmett J. Scott, whom former president J. Stanley Durkee had appointed to the new position of secretary-treasurer of the university in 1919. Scott had come to Washington with a glowing reputation. A native of Houston, Texas, he held honorary doctorates from Wiley College and Wilberforce University. He had served as secretary of the Negro Business League, as a member of the American Commission to Liberia, and as confidential secretary to Booker T. Washington of Tuskegee Institute. During World War I he served as special assistant to the Secretary of War, advising on affairs affecting black soldiers and civilians. From 1924 to 1933, he held high political positions, including membership on the Republican National Committee and the Campaign Committee of the Republican Party.[23]

Despite Scott's reputation, Johnson was unhappy with his performance as secretary-treasurer of the university. He expressed to Embree his dissatisfaction with Scott. In March 1931, Embree related to Billikopf a recent conversation with Johnson during which Johnson poured out his heart. Embree said that Johnson was "quite discouraged and dispirited—so much so that he had virtually made up his mind to submit his resignation at the April meeting of the Board of Trustees." (Johnson had been in office only four and a half years.) Embree had talked Johnson out of resigning and speculated that Johnson was dissatisfied with Scott's performance because he considered Scott's methods slovenly. (Johnson had said that Scott's financial reports were rarely satisfactory and showed carelessness and inefficiency.) Embree suggested Scott felt that Johnson was prejudiced toward him.[24]

To exacerbate this situation, Johnson was reluctant to complain to the trustees about Scott because of the high esteem the trustees and the public had for Scott. The executive committee had given Scott accolades for his services in 1928, and since then had disregarded Johnson's negative appraisal of him. Therefore, rather than continue to complain about Scott, Johnson proposed to the trustees that he "engage the services of a budget officer who would relieve Scott of essential work and allow him to function as treasurer." The executive committee of the Board of Trustees, however, rejected this suggestion, which created an intolerable situation for Johnson and led to his depression and his thoughts of resigning.

The trustees eventually retired Scott, however, in response to Johnson's position and despite Scott's plea that he be retained beyond the compulsory retirement age of sixty-five.[25]

An additional source of frustration grew out of some land purchases the university made. The General Education Board and the Julius Rosenwald Fund had made large grants for the purchase of land near the university. Word of the projected purchases must have leaked out, because the asking prices for the properties were almost doubled from the estimated value. Apparently Johnson felt that some trustees had used their positions to negotiate deals unfair to the university, either directly or indirectly, and had sold properties to the university at exorbitant prices. Johnson was outspoken in his suspicions regarding the land purchase; he felt that the executive committee of the board had failed to handle the matter discreetly. In addition, he believed that the architect and certain members of the executive committee had colluded on the purchase of two other properties (for $150,000 and $50,000) not included in the original plan. The architect and the executive committee put pressure on Johnson to agree to these purchases. He refused, saying that if they insisted on the plan, he would put the matter before the entire Board of Trustees and explain his objections. The matter was dropped, but not without bitter feelings against Johnson.[26]

Criticism of Johnson continued. After a meeting of the executive committee in April 1931, Billikopf wrote to Embree that several members of the U.S. Senate and House of Representatives had spoken to trustee Sherburne saying that Johnson must go. Billikopf commented on Johnson's allegedly having spoken sharply to the members of the executive committee, one of whom was so indignant that he threatened to resign within seventy-two hours unless Johnson apologized. (Johnson did not.) No record exists as to whether that trustee carried out his threat to resign.

As mentioned earlier, Johnson's outspoken criticism of certain failures of capitalism and his sometimes favorable comments regarding some features of Russian communism resulted in charges of communist leanings against him and some faculty members. Congressman Arthur W. Mitchell of Illinois proposed a congressional investigation of the faculty to determine the basis of the charges. In addition, Dean Kelly Miller persuaded Senator Millard E. Tydings of Maryland to demand an investigation of Johnson and the university by the Department of the Interior, under whose auspices appropriations to the university were authorized.

The House Committee on Un-American Activities, headed by Representative Martin Dies, sponsored several investigations of Johnson and the university to determine whether communist teachings were being fostered there. This was an obvious attempt not only to embarrass Johnson, but also to intimidate certain members of the faculty. Federal investigators visited the library to request copies of programs on which certain professors had spoken, but found nothing subversive. Meanwhile, Representative Oscar De Priest, Republican of Illinois, came to the Johnson's defense based on his own investigation. De Priest argued against the request for a sweeping investigation of the university. He declared that the faculty "turmoil" was caused by a small clique and that no maladministration had occurred.

When questioned by a congressional committee on the spurious charge, Johnson said,

> I am not a communist. I am always on my guard against any dogmatic panacea for the settlement of the complex difficulties which confront us in the modern world. On the other hand, I am not in accord with those who believe that the best way to deal with communism is to persecute those who believe in it. I am not of the opinion that patriotism requires any thoughtful man to subscribe to the doctrine that there is nothing good in the Russian experiment. The determination of the leaders of this movement to make use of modern scientific and technical resources to emancipate the masses of people from poverty and its ills, including the disease of acquisitiveness, is a commanding undertaking which no modern nation can ignore.[27]

A representative of the Julius Rosenwald Fund wrote to Robert R. Moton, principal of Tuskegee Institute, requesting some confidential facts about Johnson in relation to the accusations against him. Moton replied: "Johnson is a great president, an earnest, honest, high-minded, Christian leader who is unselfishly dedicated to the task of making Howard University a creditable and efficient educational institution." Moton said that Johnson's friends agreed that he "has not always been tactful in dealing with opposition and with error, which at times resulted in a distorted perspective concerning many things that may not have been to his liking." Moton added that certain members on the staff at Howard were "much more concerned to discredit President Johnson than to advance the interests of the University."[28]

Meanwhile, the attacks on Johnson continued. For some time, an anonymous "Special Reporter," alleged by some to have been former Dean Kelly Miller, sent weekly articles bitterly critical of Johnson to the *Afro-American* newspapers. A typical criticism was that Johnson lacked preparation for the job. One release stated, "It is neither a secret nor an insinuation that the president of Howard University has had no intensive training for his position. His selection to such a position was a terrible slap at the trained educator. It was sheer folly to expect such a novice to begin a career with the most intricate and expensive type of machinery. . . . Only luck of the most fortuitous nature can guarantee success to a person conspicuously untrained for his job."[29]

In an effort to secure congressional support for Johnson, Billikopf wrote to Senator William E. Borah to solicit his advocacy for Johnson with respect to the claim that he held communist leanings and was a detriment to the university. Billikopf expressed his belief that

> . . . Howard is doing wonderful work and that its president, Dr. Mordecai W. Johnson, is unquestionably one of the three or four greatest Negro leaders produced in America within the past generation or two. It is largely because Dr. Mordecai Johnson enjoys such a remarkable reputation, because he possesses great integrity of character and lofty ideas that the Julius Rosenwald Fund, the Rockefeller Foundation, and kindred organizations in recent years have invested hundreds of thousands of dollars to make Howard an ever-increasing force in the life of Negroes in America.[30]

Billikopf explained to Borah the nature of the criticisms made against Johnson and added that the Board of Trustees had always sustained the president. He said that some dissatisfied individuals had enlisted the sympathy of certain members of Congress, who in turn had introduced a bitterly phrased resolution in the House of Representatives demanding an investigation of Johnson's administration and conduct. Finally, he asked Borah to grant Johnson an interview and added that Supreme Court Justice Louis D. Brandeis was well acquainted with the affairs of Howard and would confirm in every detail Billikopf's high esteem of Dr. Johnson's character and ability as an administrator.[31]

Early in 1931 the criticisms mounted steadily in some quarters. The Board of Trustees held a special meeting to consider the charges. Students and faculty were unsure of the outcome. Before the meeting, students had posted signs around the campus. Some read, "Johnson for Howard, Howard for Johnson." Others simply read, "Justice." The students threatened to go on strike if the trustees acted unfavorably toward their president.

Many students waited in the library for the outcome of the meeting, which began at 11:00 A.M. and continued until 7:30 P.M. Upon hearing the announcement that the trustees had acted favorably regarding Johnson, the students clapped their hands in jubilation and lit a bonfire on the campus that caused someone to turn in a fire alarm. When the firefighters came and saw the students' festive mood, they decided to let the fire burn itself out. Meanwhile, students went into Andrew Rankin Memorial Chapel and had the organ played loud enough for the music to be heard across campus.

That same night the Baptist Ministers Conference of Washington and other Johnson supporters met at the Garnett Patterson School to protest any negative action that the trustees might take against Johnson. Prominent individuals from across the country sent telegrams of support. Following the announcement of the trustees' decision, the meeting turned into celebration.

The trustees' unanimous decision, announced by General John H. Sherburne, president of the board, included the following words: "The President of Howard University, in the five years he has filled the position, has shown a vision and a quality of leadership which cannot be excelled. The Trustees believe they have found in him a man capable of bringing Howard University to its goals: an institution of learning, second to none, dedicated to the mental and spiritual advancement of Negro Americans." The trustees said that they unhesitatingly affirmed their "faith in our president's loyalty to the American government and to the principles on which it is founded. . . ."[32]

The criticisms, nevertheless, continued. The alumni sent out releases maintaining that the university was in shambles and that Johnson should be removed immediately. At one annual Charter Day observance, some alumni distributed brochures titled "The Case Against Mordecai Wyatt Johnson" to the 300 attendees.[33] Included was a resolution demanding his resignation. The brochures, dated October 10, 1937, were prepared by the executive committee of the General Alumni Association and contained several complaints. The brochures claimed that Johnson had resisted the development of a strong, aggressive alumni association and had fostered dissension among members, fearing "that some well-grounded criticisms of his administration might cause a well-organized body of alumni to rise in righteous ire at the rape of their Alma Mater."

Regarding students, the primary charge was that widespread unrest had been caused by the rise in costs for tuition and rooms. As for faculty, the protesters claimed that morale was poor because of "favoritism, dictatorial methods, insecurity of tenure, discriminatory salaries, and petty and personal vindictiveness." Moreover, they accused Johnson of maladministration, represented by the loss of several key faculty members to other institutions, the investigation of the university by the Department of the Interior, and the alleged protest by Howard Medical School graduates across the country against the proposed placing of Freedmen's Hospital under Howard University, an action that they felt was a good idea, but not under Johnson's administration.

In the catalog of complaints, the executive committee of the alumni association specified other charges that *Time Magazine* published in an extended article titled "Trials of a President." The article detailed three main charges: (1) that while Lucy D. Slowe, dean of women for fifteen years, lay on her deathbed, President Johnson had sent a message announcing his intention to appoint her successor within twenty-four hours; (2) that Public Works Administration (PWA) money had been misappropriated; and (3) that Johnson had refused to withdraw charges against a fired laboratory assistant who accused a Howard University professor of seducing his young wife. The article continued, "Last week when university trustees investigated the charges, President Johnson . . . declared that the general alumni association includes only 253 of the 8,000 living Howard alumni and that it employs tactics almost equivalent to gangsters."[34]

Regarding the first charge, Johnson said that he had asked Dean Slowe to suggest an acting dean and had sent her a note expressing the hope that she would soon be back. Concerning the second charge that PWA money had been misappropriated, Secretary Harold Ickes of the Department of the Interior revealed that he had found "no improprieties" regarding the handling of PWA money. Regarding the third charge, Johnson said that the laboratory assistant had failed to produce any evidence of seduction.[35]

One serious accusation about Johnson related to the misuse of funds. Secretary Ickes impounded $100,000 that the Department of the Interior had appropriated in 1934 toward building the library at Howard. The problem arose over the charge that part of the appropriation for the library was used for the new chemistry building. A special meeting of the Board of Trustees was called in New York. Some were convinced that Johnson would be fired for misuse of funds and Johnson's detractors, including Just, looked forward to this happening. The matter was covered widely in the press, but after a thorough investigation, Johnson was cleared and the public was assured that no dishonesty was involved. Nevertheless, one man close to the financial matters of the university maintained that some funds designated for the library had actually been used for the chemistry building.[36]

Secretary Ickes was one of Johnson's most important supporters. Speaking at a dinner sponsored by the Assistant Secretary of the Interior for the officers and faculty of the various colleges of the university, their wives, and several white friends, Ickes said,

> I am for President Johnson. He is doing an excellent job under very difficult conditions. He is deserving of our gratitude.... One of the first groups which called on me when I assumed office as Secretary of the Interior Department ... was a committee which came to talk to me about President Johnson. This committee described him as a quite terrible man who was pursuing a policy they complained would tear Howard down. I told the members of the committee to bring in their specifications. They have not produced them yet.... I think that we ought to be grateful that Howard University has a president of the caliber of Mordecai Johnson. I bespeak for him your devoted and unqualified support.[37]

One alleged criticism that aggravated Johnson considerably was an editorial that appeared in the *Chicago Defender* in which Edwin Embree of the Rosenwald Fund, with whom he had enjoyed pleasant relations, was quoted as having said, "Of the four major Negro colleges, Howard University, the wealthiest of them all, has not made the best use of its opportunities. Its influence has been lessened and powers dimmed by administrative incompetence."[38] When Johnson read this, he was furious and fired off a telegram to Embree quoting the editorial verbatim and asking: "Please advise by wire collect if you are quoted correctly." Embree's first reply was not satisfactory to Johnson, who sent another telegram requesting full clarification. Embree replied, "Editorial you quote from *Defender* is not correct statement of my remarks at International House. I mentioned, as I often do, the four university centers which to my mind are most important to the Negro group and made some general analysis of each. I made no reference whatsoever to administrative officers except to make some pleasant remarks about President Jones, the guest of honor. Warm personal regards."[39]

The seriousness of the charge in the *Chicago Defender* elicited reactions from several Johnson supporters who came to his defense.

Dr. Benjamin E. Mays, dean of Howard's School of Religion, sent a long letter to Embree. Mays wrote, "If you are correctly quoted, I would like to know the criteria used by you in judging Howard less competent and more mediocre than some other institution." Mays maintained that some people unsympathetic to the university were happy to use any opportunity to embarrass the institution.[40]

Several other national leaders including William Lloyd Garrison questioned Embree about the statement in the *Defender*. In responding to Garrison's query regarding the accuracy of the quotation, Embree said that his remarks to the Fisk alumni had been so misrepresented that he had issued a press release correcting the misstatements. Embree continued,

> The best answer I can give to your general question is to enclose this statement.
>
> I have high admiration for President Johnson. Howard is the only Negro university with the professional departments, law and medicine, and the only one which is doing a large amount of graduate instruction. Increasingly, the race will have to look to Howard for advanced education in the professions and in scholarship and science. It seems to me that President Johnson has done a fine job both in obtaining increasing support from Congress and in building up something approaching a real university. Of course neither he nor the university is perfect. One continues to hear charges of dictatorship and tactlessness but as you say, "These are common charges against university presidents." I do not know where this university could look for a better president.
>
> I have no sympathy whatever with captious and partisan criticism. I suppose a university situated in the national capital will always have more than its share of politics and dissension, but the actions of various groups in this case seem to me inexcusable. I hope the trustees will stand firmly behind Howard and its president.[41]

Embree's statement that being dictatorial is a common charge against university presidents was quite true, as we have seen, especially during the period of Johnson's presidency. To provide stability to all segments of their institutions, leaders required a firm hand. This was indeed the case at Howard University when Johnson took office. Administrative procedures had to be revised. Various factions among the faculty and staff were trying to protect their turf, unmindful of the good of the whole. Because of the scholarly attainments of certain faculty members—sometimes far surpassing those of most faculty members in historically black institutions—some teachers at Howard held themselves in lofty esteem and did not like challenges to their egos. There had been some turmoil at Howard before Johnson arrived. Thus, Johnson must have sensed the need for strong leadership to harness all its resources and to guide the university as a whole toward its potential goal, even if in the process some egos were bruised.

Although Howard was established primarily to serve African Americans, it was a national institution, so the administration had to deal with the problem of racial balance. This was particularly true regarding the Medical School. Aspiring doctors have competed vigorously for admission to medical schools, and during Johnson's tenure, many white applicants sought entrance to Howard's Medical School. Because the institutions from which most African-American applicants came did not possess all the facilities to prepare students for medical schools that many of the predominantly white institutions had, the African-American scores on medical aptitude tests ranked lower than those of whites. Therefore, Johnson was reluctant to favor admitting white and African-American applicants to the Medical School on the same basis. On the basis of their medical aptitude test scores, the white applicants would have taken up most of the spaces intended for first-year pre-med students, thus putting a great burden on African Americans whose opportunities to enroll in northern universities were seriously limited. Incidentally, some of Johnson's critics referred to this policy in an attempt to discredit him by charging racism.

In 1949, African-American educators complained about the quota system then used by many northern universities in admitting black students to their graduate schools. At a meeting of the Association of American Colleges that year, the black administrators caucused and resolved to bring up the matter during a plenary session of the association. The group named Johnson to present the complaint. Just as the black administrators were leaving the caucus room, one member said to Johnson, "But you use a quota system at the Howard University Medical School, don't you?" Johnson answered, "Yes, but that's different."[42]

And, of course, the "difference" was that because institutionalized racism placed serious limitations on African-American students in getting a medical education, as well as on those seeking a wide range of other graduate studies, students who wanted a medical education needed every opportunity to reach their goals. Moreover, the value of some standardized tests in assessing the potential of students is controversial. Certainly the graduates of the Howard University Medical School and the Meharry Medical College have proved competent in their professions. In view of the overall social climate, the admission policy of Howard Medical School was the only way to produce a more adequate supply of physicians and dentists to serve the black community.

In time the harsh criticisms of Johnson and his administration abated. No matter how vicious the attacks against him, Johnson remained silent and never rebutted them publicly. A friend once asked him, "How do you manage to remain resolute and with outward calm in the midst of the criticisms against you?"

Johnson replied, "I have the faith that in due course the truth will be revealed."[43] Once he responded to a similar question, saying that he had built a retreat in Maryland near the confluence of the Potomac and Shenandoah Rivers about sixty-five miles from Washington, D.C., where he would go on certain weekends to relax in the quiet countryside. He had no telephone in the house, but arranged with a neighbor to receive any emergency calls from Washington.[44] In responding to the question of why attacks were made against him, he said, "People have reasons for doing things, and sometimes we are not the best judges of other people's reasons."[45] Some who knew him well said that he rarely spoke unkindly about anyone.

Despite his dignity, Johnson had a sense of humor. Sometimes one asked, "How are you, Mr. President?" He would reply, "For a man of my age and wickedness, I am doing very well." Some faculty members would imitate Johnson in giving this answer to inquiries made of them. Others tried to emulate Johnson's speaking style, which was sometimes oratorical and pompous.[46]

In March 1941 on the fifteenth anniversary of Johnson's presidency, university officials planned the seventeenth annual Howard University Charter Day as a testimonial to him. The Charter Day program contained a salute from "the students, faculties and employees, alumni and trustees of Howard University," who expressed gratitude to him for all his accomplishments and paid special tribute to his "great record of constructive achievements" as president of Howard University over the past fifteen years.

The program detailed six areas of special appreciation for Johnson's contributions:

1. You have revolutionized the physical plant of the University.
2. You have placed the University on a sound financial basis.
3. You have improved the quality of the teaching staff and the conditions for teaching.

4. You have been in the vanguard of Negro education in advancing security and tenure of teachers.

5. You have increasingly insisted on high standards of scholarship.

6. You have consistently promoted the highest academic standards in all branches of the University.

Under each of the six categories the committee listed the major achievements Johnson had made during his administration.

The list ended with the following words:

> But in our judgment, the greatest achievements which you have made at Howard University have been these:
>
>   You have instituted and developed democratic practices in the internal administration of the affairs of the university, and in the face of criticism and pressure and at great personal sacrifice, you have at Howard University maintained academic freedom— the very life blood of a university in a democracy.[47]

Modernizing the physical plant included constructing a building for the College of Medicine at a cost of $500,000 and securing an endowment of $500,000 for it. In addition, three new dormitories for women students were completed at a cost of $660,000. A new chemistry building was built at a cost of $636,300; a new classroom building at $461,200; a new library at $1,120,811; a new heat, light, and power plant at $555,557; and a new men's dormitory at $626,200. The underground mains of the Howard University water system were also reconstructed. The total cost of the buildings alone was $5,180,088. During the remainder of Johnson's administration, more buildings would be constructed.

Putting the university on a sound financial basis included development of the Twenty-Year Plan, during which congressional appropriations and grants from philanthropies greatly increased (gifts from the latter totaling more than $2 million). In addition, since Congress had passed the substantive law in 1928 making Howard University a permanent beneficiary of annual appropriations, the capital assets increased threefold, the library's book collection doubled, and its equipment trebled.

Regarding the faculty, the full-time teaching staff was doubled, teaching loads were reduced, and average teachers' salaries were doubled since Johnson took office. The report also pointed out that tenure regulations and an attractive retirement plan had been developed.

The faculty's high standards of scholarship were shown by the fact that during Johnson' administration more than "686 scholarly publications, including 62 books and monographs, 531 articles and papers, and 93 other creative contributions such as poetry, paintings, etc., have been produced by the faculty." Also the *Journal of Negro Education,* a high-quality informative periodical, was established during his administration.

In detailing Johnson's promotion of the highest academic standards in all branches of the university, the report called attention to the reorganization and accreditation of the College of Dentistry, the School of Law, the School of Religion, and the College of Pharmacy. The Division of Social Work of the graduate school was admitted to membership in the American Association of Social Work, and the enrollment of the graduate school increased from 46 in 1926–1927 to 407 in 1938–1939.

This tribute to Johnson was a climax to fifteen years of struggle. The university's continuous progress under his administration was a measure of his leadership. The list of achievements printed on the Charter Day program represented accomplishments despite many attempts to discredit him. Johnson weathered them all.

Johnson himself summarized his achievements in a "Special Memorandum" to the trustees outlining matters regarding future financial aid to the university and presaging what should be done during the next ten-year period. He pointed out that as of the academic year 1940–1941, the federal appropriations to the university amounted to 65.5 percent of the total budget and that a "renewal of understanding" with the government must be in place for the future.[48] Other accomplishments mentioned in this memorandum were the "wholesome relations maintained with the federal government and the preservation of academic freedom throughout the university."[49] The latter included not only freedom of teaching but also "maintenance of complete freedom of expression by the student body, including freedom of speech, freedom of assembly, freedom of petition, freedom of protest, with a resulting complete relaxation of tension between students and the administrative side, which characterized the institution in its former years, and a great increase in esprit de corps and loyal cooperation by the student body throughout the university."

In a memorandum to Embree, Johnson stressed

. . . establishment at Howard of democratic faculty-administration processes as affecting all major matters of policy and procedure at the university, facilitating discussion, criticisms, and initiative from below upwards, as touching appointments, budget, educational policy, and all matters fundamentally affecting the university.[50]

With regard to freedom of thought in academe, Johnson's strongest statement was made in an address he gave at the conference on "Academic Freedom in the University," to which reference has already been made. Speaking on the subject "The Social Responsibility of the Administrator," Johnson describes at length his confrontations with certain individual members of Congress and of congressional committees that attempted to stifle freedom of thought at Howard. These individuals and groups particularly objected to communists or communist sympathizers appearing on campus programs. Johnson vigorously resisted those efforts. At that conference Johnson declared, among other things, that Howard University should close its doors rather than submit to the suppression of research and honest expression of thought.[51]

These assertions and actions belie the view that Johnson was a dictator. Certainly he had strong convictions that he stoutly defended, and this stance led some to feel that he was a dictator at heart. Doubtless his strong beliefs made him impatient with those who did not share his ideas, as is often the case with such individuals. Also, a characteristic of persons with sharp minds is to think that others should see things as they do. Johnson's primary concern evidently was to achieve his goals for the university—come what may. Clearly his idea of administration did not coincide with the ideas of some of his critics. That all elements of the university did not view him as a dictator is indicated in the sentiments expressed in the seventeenth Charter Day program, quoted above, that praised Johnson for having "instituted and developed democratic practices in the internal administration of the university."

Following the tribute paid to Johnson at the Charter Day observance, opposition to him declined. Some opponents had grown weary of fruitless efforts. By now, new generations of students had become alumni. The latter did not share the opinions of some who were at the school when Johnson took office. The Board of Trustees consistently supported him. It is difficult to argue against success, especially when such success is achieved "against the odds," to use the title of Embree's biographical essays. The remainder of Johnson's tenure was what university historian Logan refers to as "the golden years."

7

Howard University—
The Later Years

*D*uring the remaining years of his administration, Johnson continued to initiate and implement plans to construct new buildings and to enhance the instructional facilities. These included a new School of Engineering and Architecture building in 1952; a new Biology Department building, a new Dental College building, and a new College of Pharmacy building in 1955; a new Law School building in 1956; a new Administration building in 1957; and a new College of Education building in 1958. Such an extensive building program had not been undertaken in any previous period in Howard University's history. Such growth is all the more remarkable because it was done in spite of nagging controversies, including unfounded accusations against Johnson and some faculty members of communist subversion.[1]

Johnson worked with the faculty in promoting new curriculum programs. An African Studies curriculum was installed in 1954, chaired by Professors Rayford Logan and William L. Hansberry. In the same year, an African Language and Area Center was created.

One index to the quality of instruction and programs in an educational institution is the type and number of national honor societies chartered on the campus. During 1941–1960, thirteen national honor societies were chartered at Howard University. Principal among these was Phi Beta Kappa, the most prestigious collegiate honor society in the nation. Others were Epsilon Sigma Theta (classics), Pi Sigma Alpha (government), Psi Chi (psychology), Omicron Kappa Epsilon (dentistry), and Beta Kappa Chi (natural sciences).

The establishment of a Ph.D. program was another of Johnson's objectives. The viability of a doctoral program depended on the quality of the undergraduate instruction in general and of the subject matter area in particular. Johnson worked closely with trustees and faculty to build a Ph.D. program. After considering and working toward this goal over some five years, the decision was made. A Ph.D. program in chemistry was authorized in 1955, and three years later the first candidates were graduated. In 1958, a Ph.D. program in physics was initiated.

In 1955, Johnson reached Howard University's mandatory retirement age of sixty-five. He had completed twenty-nine years of service and was still physically vigorous and intellectually strong. The university was in the midst of its greatest expansion period ever, both regarding its physical plant and the development of curricula. The trustees were not prepared to entertain the notion of his retirement, nor was he eager to leave his post. To comply with the regulations, the trustees voted formally to retire him as of June 30, 1955. Immediately, however, they voted to reappoint him for a five-year period. Because the regulations did not prohibit rehiring an individual, the action of the trustees was in order. Obviously, this action underscored their high regard for the contributions Johnson had made to the university, despite the stormy periods that characterized most of the first half of his administration.

Johnson maintained a high regard for the students at the university. His office was in the campus library, and students saw him frequently. Some said that he always spoke as he passed them on the campus and would address them as "Son," "Daughter," or "Young Man." From time to time, one could see him talking to groups of students. One blind graduate student tells with warm remembrance how, whenever Johnson happened to be driving by as the student was about to cross a campus road, Johnson would order his driver to stop immediately until the student was safely on the other side.[2]

Five children were born to Mordecai and Anna Ethelyn Johnson. In order of birth they were Carolyn Elizabeth, Mordecai Wyatt Jr., Archer Clement, William Howard, and Anna Faith. The last two were born after Johnson became president of Howard. His children characterize Johnson as a loving father who was always available to his children.[3] They admired him, but were never in awe of him. They recognized that he was a great man, but enjoyed him for his sense of humor. Johnson and the children read plays and books together and enjoyed playing games. When he was not called away by official duties, the family ate every meal together. Sometimes the family gathered around the piano, and while Anna Ethelyn played, he sang. He had a rich baritone voice. His favorite song was "To a Wild Rose."

Johnson took pains to see that his children got answers to all their questions. If the question related to some aspect of philosophy, religion, or economics, Johnson usually answered it immediately. If he did not have the answer, he would find it and give it to his child the next day.

One day, one of his adolescent sons asked him, "Dad, just what is my mission in life? What must I do with my life?" The son had often heard his father talk to students and others about assuming social responsibilities. He was at a point in life when he was beginning to consider several options for his career, and he wanted to get some wise direction from his father, whom he trusted implicitly. After a moment of studied reflection, Johnson said, "Son, your mission in life, whatever may be your chosen profession, is to endeavor to bring the Kingdom of God on earth." Johnson taught his children never to fear anything and to be prepared always to do what was right.

Johnson loved poetry, especially that of Paul Laurence Dunbar. He also loved the Uncle Remus stories written by Joel Chandler Harris. Among his favorite writings were works by Rabindranath Tagore and the Mahatma Gandhi. Every night before retiring, Johnson would go to his study to read from his favorite sources. Sundays were special occasions for the family. Before breakfast, the family would meet in the living room for prayer. Then followed a discussion of family affairs and of whatever problems one of the children may have had. He inquired of each child how he or she was doing in school and tried to resolve any problems. Johnson would also ask each child to recite a verse of scripture.

After breakfast on Sundays, the family would go to the Shiloh Baptist Church on the corner of 9th and P Streets, N.W., where the Reverend Earl L. Harrison was the pastor. All of the Johnson children were enrolled in Sunday School. Some Sundays the family would attend services at the Andrew Rankin Memorial Chapel on campus. There, the family would always sit together on the right.

The Johnson household was always busy and frequently visited by important personalities. Johnson would tell the children about the background of these people and provide opportunities for the children to talk to them. Visitors included members of the Board of Trustees; Eleanor Roosevelt, the wife of the President of the United States; and the presidents of other institutions, including John Hope of Morehouse, David Jones of Bennett College, and John W. Davis of West Virginia State College. The latter three were Johnson's closest friends. In addition, Howard Thurman, dean of the Andrew Ranklin Memorial Chapel, would often visit and play with the children.

Johnson and his wife invited her mother, Mrs. Elizabeth C. Gardner, to live with them for some years before she died. This still-beautiful, dignified lady from Augusta, Georgia, was a joy to the household. The love between her and her grandchildren was mutual. They enjoyed hearing her wonderful stories, and she enjoyed their vivacity and the promise in their young faces. In due course, the shadows of her long life lengthened, and she died in April 1937. At her funeral in Rankin Chapel, Johnson's brilliant young executive assistant, Richard Hurst Hill, officiated and comforted the family with fitting encomiums.

In summary, Johnson showed great love for his family and provided "quality time" to his children. He deeply loved his wife, who, according to one staff member, was one of the most beautiful and eloquent women she had ever seen and one of the best dressed. Once in his preliminary remarks before giving a commencement address at Spelman College, Johnson told the graduates, "Here at Spelman I met the two most inspiring women I have ever known. One of these I carried away with me to be my helpmate and the great inspiration of my life."

The firstborn in the Mordecai Johnson family, Carolyn Elizabeth, is married to Dr. Beverly Graves, a Philadelphia physician. Mordecai Wyatt Jr. practiced dentistry in Texas and the District of Columbia, and is now deceased. Archer studied theology and medicine, once served as Director of Psychiatry at the Lorton Penitentiary, and now practices psychiatry in Puerto Rico, where he and his family make their home. William Howard trained as an engineer and worked with the National Aeronautics and Space Administration (NASA) until his retirement. The youngest, Anna Faith, lives in Boston, Massachusetts, and is associated with a public service agency.

From the time of his statutory retirement in 1955, when the trustees immediately rehired him, Johnson was gratified at how the university was moving toward the goals he had envisioned for its academic and physical development. As new buildings were being constructed and academic programs were achieving national recognition, he began to enjoy the satisfaction that comes with accomplishments made and dreams realized.

At the same time, Johnson was getting not only national but also international recognition. The Republic of Panama conferred on him the Order of Varco Vinez de Balboa, its highest award to a private citizen. The Kingdom of Ethiopia awarded the Order of the Star of Honor, with Grand Cordon. The Republic of Liberia gave him the Medal of Commander of the Star of Africa, an honor bestowed at the same time on his former college roommate and close friend, John W. Davis. The Chapel of the Four

Chaplains gave him the Brotherhood Citation, and the Jewish Theological Seminary of America gave him the Universal Brotherhood Award. Ten institutions of learning, including Temple University, Michigan State University, Morehouse College, and the University of Liberia, conferred honorary degrees on him, including the titles of D.D., LL.D., L.H.D., and D.C.L. As stated earlier, one of these honors was conferred by Howard University before he became president.

Notwithstanding the honors he received, it is striking that during his thirty-four-year tenure as president of Howard only nine educational institutions conferred honorary degrees on Johnson. In light of his national prominence and in view of the many such honors that others in similar positions received, one would have expected his receiving more awards. Possibly he did not accept all that were offered to him or had conflicts with his own commencement programs. Perhaps college or university officials were wary of his controversial reputation.

In 1956, Johnson attended the second general conference of the International Association of Universities in Istanbul, Turkey. That same year he was the guest of the government of Liberia at the inauguration ceremonies of President William V. S. Tubman in Monrovia, and later he toured Sierra Leone and the Gold Coast (Ghana). The following year he was the guest of the government of Ghana at its Independence Celebration. He also attended a meeting of the International Association of Universities in Nice, France, where he was elected an alternate member of the administrative board. After that meeting he traveled to the Middle East, including Lebanon, Syria, Jordan, and Israel.

Perhaps the most significant of Johnson's international presentations was the address he delivered at the First Atlantic Congress sponsored by the Parliamentarians Conference of the North Atlantic Treaty Organization that met in London, England. He was a member of the board of directors of the U.S. delegation and of the Free World Committee of the Congress. As one of the five plenary speakers, he addressed the Congress on the subject, "The Need for a Program of International Economic Aid."[4]

Johnson's professional affiliations included membership on the Advisory Council of the Virgin Islands, National Advisory Council on Education, National Advisory Board of the India League of America, National Association for Mental Health, Medical Educational and Scientific Advisory Council of the National Fund for Medical Education, Committee on Pre-Professional Education of the American Association of Colleges, Advisory Committee of the International Development Placement

Association, and General Executive Board of the National Religion and Labor Foundation.

In addition, he was a member of the Board of Directors, National Council of the United Negro College Fund; Vice Chairman, National Council for the Prevention of War; member of the Board of Directors, National Council of Christians and Jews; and member of the Board of Directors, American Civil Liberties Union (ACLU).

Johnson's acceptance of membership on all these boards is an indication of his broad concerns. Although Howard University was not a member of the United Negro College Fund because of its primary funding by the federal government, Johnson was much concerned with the higher education of African Americans. Hence, his counsel on the fund's board was welcomed. His desire for interracial understanding was represented by his serving on the National Council of Christians and Jews. He had a strong interest in the program of the ACLU, an organization that often championed the rights of defenseless people. This interest led to his awarding an honorary degree to Patrick Malin, then chairman of the ACLU, who was an effective advocate of civil rights.

Well before the end of the academic year 1958–1959, Johnson indicated to the trustees that he would retire on June 30, 1960. In due course, the trustees passed appropriate motions praising him for the outstanding service he had rendered to the university for thirty-four years. They also provided a life pension, a house, health benefits, and secretarial service. In addition, they conferred on him the title President Emeritus.

In a farewell speech given on the last day of his active service, Johnson stated,

> I am not troubled at all at the prospect of retiring. The fact is that I have sought retirement. In the first place, I think that an institution which has lived under the steady influence of one president for thirty-four years needs a breathing spell and the touch of a fresh and more youthful hand in its affairs. When I expressed my desire to retire to the Board of Trustees some fourteen months ago, I told them that nothing would delight me more than to see a vigorous and wise successor take hold of my work.[5]

At the time he was seventy years old.

When asked what he planned to do when he retired, Johnson replied that it was his intention to spend the next year just *thinking*." He said that he would do some speaking, but hardly as much as he had done during his active career. The subjects about which he wanted to speak were global in scope. He said,

> I want to think about America and the Negro's role in our great country. I want to think about America and the West and their relations with the Soviet Union. I also want to think about the underdeveloped and oppressed people of the world, and how we can bring them to a decent standard of living and the right for them to determine their own futures. And even after this period of thinking, who knows, I might embark upon a new career.[6]

The trustees appointed a committee of distinguished persons to plan a testimonial dinner to recognize Johnson's contributions and to commemorate his retirement. That dinner, held on November 21, 1960, at the Park Sheraton Hotel, attracted 1,250 guests, including notables from various branches of the federal government, representatives from foreign countries, educational leaders from across the nation, alumni, faculty, and students. The planning committee was composed of forty distinguished individuals, including Mrs. Eleanor Roosevelt and Lorimer D. Milton, chairman of the Board of Trustees. Others included Ralph Bunche, United Nations Under-Secretary; Associate Supreme Court Justice Felix Frankfurter; baseball great Jackie Robinson; Herbert Lehman, former governor of New York; Roy Wilkins of the NAACP; and Congressmen Cooper of Kentucky and Bowles of Connecticut.[7]

Five speakers paid tribute to Johnson's leadership and achievements: Arthur S. Fleming, secretary of Health, Education, and Welfare; Benjamin Elijah Mays, president of Morehouse College; Eric Johnston, president of the Motion Picture Association of America and chairman of the Committee for International Economic Growth; Harry I. Wood, president of the General Alumni Association; and Dr. Herman Branson, professor of physics. Dr. James M. Nabrit, who succeeded Johnson as president of Howard, introduced him to the group and presented him with a sterling silver tea set and a fitting plaque.

President-elect John F. Kennedy, then a senator, sent a telegram praising Johnson for his leadership in higher education and said that "Howard University has grown into one of America's most distinguished institutions of higher learning." President Dwight David Eisenhower sent a message describing Johnson as "a great humanitarian . . . and an inspiring example to all."[8]

Johnson was pleased that so many people recognized his efforts of thirty-four years. Still sound of mind and body at seventy years of age, he looked forward to the future.

Clearly during his career as president of Howard University, Johnson met and overcame many obstacles, including the resentment of some faculty members and alumni when the trustees looked beyond the campus and appointed a Baptist preacher—with little experience in academic administration—to preside over the nation's most prominent university for African Americans. This resentment was exacerbated by Johnson's refusal to respond publicly to their criticisms. He was even resented for his success in securing funds from philanthropic individuals and organizations and support from the federal government, even though the result was the constant upgrading of the university. All the strategies devised to deprecate him and relieve him of the presidency failed. Even the serious charges of his misappropriating funds and of his having communist sympathies and encouraging communist teachings at the university could not be proved.

Johnson was resolute in his commitment to raise Howard University to an academic level commensurate with that of any institution of higher learning in the United States. Sometime this effort entailed confrontations with faculty and staff members whom he felt compromised the basic integrity of the university. Johnson felt "called" to strengthen and maintain that integrity as part of his overall mission in life. A person who lacked his keen intelligence and strength of spirit could not have succeeded so well against the odds he faced. Johnson justified the faith that the trustees of Howard placed in him when they elected him to the presidency in 1926. As a further demonstration of their appreciation and admiration, in 1973 they named the newly constructed administration building the Mordecai Wyatt Johnson Administration Building.

8

The Incisive Orator

*B*ecause of his strategic position and his exceptional gifts as a public speaker, Johnson was constantly in demand to deliver addresses throughout his career. He traveled 25,000 miles a year responding to invitations, and he had standing speaking engagements with several organizations. For instance, he spoke at the Ford Hall Forum in Boston annually. He also was the speaker on Educational Night at the yearly sessions of the National Baptist Convention, USA, Inc., the largest ecclesiastical body among African Americans.

Part of Johnson's success as a speaker can be traced to his early training in the sixth grade, when his teacher, Benjamin Sampson, drilled students in the fundamentals of effective public address. Johnson read widely, stayed abreast of and analyzed issues, and demonstrated a remarkable perspective regarding crucial problems. He carefully prepared what he had to say, but always spoke without a manuscript. For special occasions his preparation would extend well beyond midnight. On the days he was to deliver a major address, he never ate a substantial meal before his presentation.[1]

One of the striking things about Johnson was that, even while under the pressures of administrative responsibilities and some persistent criticisms, he could make outstanding addresses on numerous subjects in various parts of the country. Because he gave practically all of his speeches with few, if any, notes and because much of what he said in public was not recorded but was excerpted in the press, some of his valuable ideas and insights have been lost. But thanks to the African-

American press routinely covering the occasions at which he spoke, we have the essence of many of Johnson's presentations on special occasions.

In his speeches Johnson expressed deep conviction, and sometimes his listeners gained the impression that he possessed the final truth on his subject. Some felt that if only the world would take notice and give heed to what he said, then society could find solutions to its most difficult problems.

Possessed of a phenomenal memory, he could quote reams of statistics without notes. He was famous for the length of his speeches. He rarely spoke for less than an hour (often longer), but he held his audiences spellbound. At times after speaking for forty-five minutes, he would look at his watch and exclaim, "My, I've just got through the introduction!" He was known to say, "The Lord told me to speak, but he didn't tell me when to stop." He always had a packed audience whenever he gave an address. Occasionally, in his later years, while describing the religious faith of African Americans, he illustrated his point by singing in his rich baritone voice.

He used his voice as an instrument, with cadences ranging from a booming volume to a soft whisper. His gestures were polished and impressive. He varied his posture, sometimes rocking back on his heels, at other times leaning over the lectern. His English was impeccable.

The following are two examples of how some listeners reacted to his speaking:

> He opened his mouth, and I yielded myself to the charm of the deep, mellow voice that is the Negro's heritage. With psychological skill in handling his audience, he prefaced his remarks by counting up the points of unity between himself and the Quakers; then he traced the difficulty between our races back to its economic sources. He was saying things in a new way, eyes met in pleased surprise. These were new pastures—pencils scribbled busily. Presently, tears came, were dashed away to clear my gaze on this protean speaker, and yet kept coming; I strove to keep from visibly shaking.
>
> Puzzled by my unusual emotion, I interrupted my fascinated gaze to turn appraising eyes on the row behind me: one met my eyes in sympathetic smile, all the other eyes were fixed on the speaker and on their faces was a stricken, convicted look. *Convicted* seems a strong word, yet that word was used the next morning by a comfortable, white-haired veteran from a southern city who recorded that he had been cut to the heart.

Presently, that rich voice, sometimes booming in, sometimes denunciation, sometimes persuading in softest sympathy, ceased, and a vibrant silence covered us.[2]

On hearing Johnson give a speech in Philadelphia, one lady asked rhetorically:

Why did this man get under all defenses and so wring your heart that little else seemed to matter? This is not the first time we have had our souls hung before us and the thin slices and smudges pointed out, but never before with such sincerity of comprehension of the struggle involved, with such sympathy for the weakness of the honest, striving soul. It is another demonstration of the compelling power of love, which shells us out of our pitiful armor of evasion and leaves us sobbing, face to face with our stark selves.[3]

Johnson's speaking style exhibited the use of all the major elements of effective speaking: abundant use of imagery and metaphor, imaginative language, factual illustrations and statistics, personal pronouns, communion or identification, allegory, specific names, collective nouns, imperative superlatives, repetition, rhetorical questions, and movement from low volume to crescendo.[4] To this list can be added "humor." Someone once asked Johnson whether he believed in intermarriage. He replied:

Oh, yes. I believe the human race is one race. I believe in it. But now, personally, if you're asking what my program is, I want to say to you that I did not marry the little brown skin woman that I married because she is colored. I married her after meeting two or three million women in the world, and because I think she is the most beautiful, sweetest, and most gracious creature the Lord ever made. If she should ever throw me over, I know 10 other colored women by name in the United States I'd like to speak to privately. And, since I have been to India, I raise that up to 100.[5]

In using those methods, Johnson never failed to capture the attention of his listeners. He told a story, or, put another way, he put his materials in concrete rather than abstract form. He made good use of illustrations and kept his audience focused on where his discourse was leading. Often, some listeners would figuratively, if not literally, be sitting on the edges of their seats—fascinated by his thinking, his delivery, and his platform presence.

Because he did not write out his speeches for publication, many of the actual words and nuances in Johnson's speeches were lost. In 1940, Colgate Rochester Theological Seminary, which had merged with Rochester by this time, invited Johnson to give the Annual Rauschenbusch Lectures. The lectures had been established in 1931 in honor of the late Walter Rauschenbusch, who was one of Johnson's teachers at the seminary. Johnson gave four lectures on the theme "Christianity's World Opportunity in America." Although, according to stipulation, those lectures were to be published, Johnson never got around to preparing his for publication. This absence was much to the disappointment of the seminary, of those who heard him, and of those who wanted a record of his message during this important series.

A look at the headlines of some news accounts of his presentations over the years shows his emphases: "Johnson says 'Segregation Saps the Nation's Strength' "; "God Hates U.S. Hypocrisy"; "South Is Doomed by Slavery"; "The World Significance of Abraham Lincoln"; "H.U. Prexy Predicts a New World Order"; "Churches Aid to Negro Is Inadequate"; "Johnson Warns Clerics of Trouble"; "Howard President Says, 'Walls of Jericho Are Falling Down' "; "The Negro and the World Crisis"; and "The Colored Americans' Attitude Toward the Catholic Church."

Johnson chafed at the results of the evils of slavery and was acutely conscious of the false sense of superiority that some whites felt toward African Americans. He could see the economic basis of racism, and he recognized how racial prejudice adversely affected not only African Americans but also whites. He said that the white man needed to be emancipated from the prejudice that enslaved him and pointed out that he pitied some white leaders because they did not realize what slavery had done to them.

One of the most striking characteristics of Johnson's personality was his willingness—whatever the audience or the people who had invited him—to speak his mind freely. He relished the opportunity to challenge the stereotypical views of race, religion, and society. He enjoyed making people "uncomfortable with their prejudices."[6] Once when he gave an address at Storer College in West Virginia, an unreconstructed member of the platform group became so disgusted with Johnson's scathing condemnation of racism that he ceremoniously snatched out his hearing aid.

Speaking at a convention of Jesuits on the subject "The Colored Americans' Attitude Toward the Catholic Church," Johnson stated:

> As far as educated colored Americans are concerned, you fail to exist. . . . In view of your tremendous power, you have been disappointing. . . . You have only 300,000 colored Catholics.

Why? Because you operate too much on the motive of pity and benevolence. You have appealed to the colored Americans too little with the voice of Ezekiel, "Son, stand upon thy feet." Your message has been a kind one, but a condescending one. You have failed to encourage the colored Americans to rise to your own stature. You have not developed a Catholic priesthood. . . . You are the one church that has had the most influence in the Latin countries, and in every one of these there has been no race problem. You have behind you the finest of organizations and the example of noble devotion. But, for the majority of the educated Negroes, you do not exist. You have not more than a handful of colored Americans in all your colleges. That's not an accident; it's a policy.[7]

During World War II, Johnson sat on a panel with other dignitaries to make a nationwide radio presentation. This was the first broadcast under the auspices of the Office of War Information over Washington station WOL telling of the role African Americans were playing in the war effort. The other speakers included Fred D. Patterson of Tuskegee Institute, Frank Graham of the University of North Carolina, and Mrs. Eleanor Roosevelt. The participants had presented the substance of their remarks in advance for review. Johnson's came back red-penciled, whereupon he quickly restored his original thoughts that had been censored and discussed them on the air. He stated, "I could not conscientiously say some things which were given me to say."[8]

Johnson delivered a commencement address in Kentucky in which he called Great Britain a "cold-blooded exploiter of colonial people." In reporting the speech, a Louisville newspaper called him "a lunatic." On his return to Washington, Johnson called Rayford Logan to tell him about Johnson's criticism of Great Britain and to ask what he thought of it, because Johnson planned to make the same accusation in three or four other commencement addresses that were scheduled. Logan replied that he would be glad to document the statement, an offer that Johnson gladly accepted.[9]

During World War II, Johnson inveighed against segregation in the armed forces and said that white America's proclaiming the "Four Freedoms" represented gross hypocrisy. Continuing, he said, "God must respect the Germans who boldly state their principles, and are fighting unitedly for them; God must respect Russians who have marshaled all their forces to fight for their ideals. White America with one hand upholds the Four Freedoms and, with the other, holds down twelve million colored Americans, and says by acts and deeds that these freedoms are not for them." While World War II was in progress, Johnson had occasion to share the platform with a navy lieutenant. In his address, Johnson was highly critical of the racial policies of the navy. He maintained that segregation affected African Americans in various branches of the armed forces and resulted in "tragically low" morale among them. "The navy," he said, "is perfectly in accord with Hitler's concept of race and will not have colored Americans around except in menial positions." Johnson added that the air force's recently formed unit of African-American pilots was nothing more than a token effort to train colored men.[10]

Johnson declared that World War II represented "a Civil War within the whole of western civilization," during which democratic governments, whose preservation was of utmost importance, were in jeopardy. "In our deepest moments," he said, "we know that one great determinative power in democracy is the moving, religiously undergirded, realistic, and active reverence which human beings actually have in our hearts and wills toward other human beings, toward every human being, and toward every individual human being as such."[11]

Johnson believed that World War II would spawn a new world order, either through love or violence. "Progress by persuasion is the best method," he stated, "but, if persuasion fails, progress will take its place anyway." In the same address, he called attention to Russia's achievements: "By reaching an understanding that there will be enough for all and protection for all, Russia has welded an ignorant people together and has become a world power."[12]

During an address on "The Negro and Our National Destiny" at the Ford Hall Forum in Boston in May 1944, Johnson proclaimed that "the Negro has received his nastiest treatment during the past five years." As he saw it, the morale of the Negro was at its worst since emancipation. Because of this, Johnson said that "The Negro soldier was fighting the war with guns, but not with his soul."[13]

Johnson was prophetic with regard to the breakdown of segregation in public education. In 1946, speaking at the inauguration of Charles S. Johnson as president of Fisk University, Johnson proclaimed:

> The walls of segregation are falling and you (southern whites) cannot prevent it. . . . I will tell you why. Because you will not be able to pay the cost. For the first time in history, you are going to realize the real cost of segregation. The walls are falling because they are going to be destroyed within and without. . . .

Did I say that the walls are falling? . . . I amend that! They
have already fallen. I predict that the Walls of Jericho (segregation) will fall. . . . White women and white men, colored
women and colored men, students and teachers will walk hand in
hand upon the college campuses in the South.[14]

Within twenty-five years his prediction became a reality, but students
and teachers were not always walking "hand in hand."

A news reporter for the *Baltimore Afro-American* gave the following
account of some reactions to Johnson's prediction:

I looked around at southern white folks and southern colored
folks. President F. D. Patterson, Tuskegee, was leaning forward on
the edge of his seat; a white person whose name I did not get sat
on the front seat, laughing approvingly. Dr. Charles S. Johnson,
who was being inducted as president of Fisk University, sat with
his right hand to his jaw and his face expressionless; President E.
C. Peters, white, Paine College, Augusta, Georgia, sat tense. Dr.
Johnson just stood there and stared at them as if reading them,
weighing them.

There was a burst of applause. Other speakers on the
platform seemed concerned, uneasy. Harvie Branscomb, white,
chancellor, Vanderbilt University and native of Alabama,
presided. He seemed restless. Later, when he summarized remarks
of the speakers on the panel, he quoted every speaker except Dr.
Johnson. W. C. Jackson, white, chancellor, the Women's College
of the University of North Carolina, [who] spoke mostly on the
democracy of Thomas Jefferson, twisted and turned in his seat.
His facial expression was one of astonishment and concern.[15]

Johnson never failed to pay homage to the northern white missionaries
who came south at the close of the Civil War and established schools for the
freedmen. He appreciated the fact that they were prepared to endure insults
and other forms of hostility from some southern whites who resented their
teaching the freedmen and living with them on the basis of social equality. In
one address Johnson said:

At the close of the Civil War, the Christian religion came to our
rescue. A group of people who respected us as children of God
came down here from the North and took up residence, suffered
ostracism that they might teach us the truth, that the truth might

set us free. These early white educators who are responsible for many of the Negro colleges in the South came because they were compelled by the love of Christ.[16]

In his 1946 address at Fisk University, Johnson praised those missionaries who came south immediately after the Civil War "when the personality of black people was at a great discount, when this southern area was greatly troubled and suffering by reason of its recent experiences, and when there were very few to be found who believed that the Negro people would ever be able to stand erect and to grow into full self-respecting and highly esteemed citizenship." He continued:

> Themselves being white, they could have taken great pride in that fact and could have lived distinguished careers without ever touching these humble people. But they thought not a thing to be grasped after to be white, but humbled themselves and came here and made themselves obedient to the needs of slaves and the children of slaves. They saw all the deficiencies, and warpings, [sic] and shortcomings that the people in this region saw in us, but they saw what the people of this region have not yet come to see: that underneath rude personalities, bruised and aborted by the slave system, there was the unrevealed and essential dignity of human nature endowed by its creator with unlimited possibilities.[17]

Johnson touched on a similar theme in a Founders' Day address on Howard's campus, during which he praised the philosophy behind the establishment of the university:

> We are here celebrating something that is far more important to this country than an additional appropriation to the Army, namely, a heroic example of the truly great American democratic spirit establishing nonsegregated education in the nation's capital.
>   The greatest enemy to our system of democratic life is not the enemy which is confronting us from the outside, but that enemy which is corroding democracy within—namely, the extent to which segregation has enfeebled our faith in and our loyalty to our democratic institutions. . . . Democracy's strength lies in the worth of the particular individual without allowing any group mark or identification—such as race, color, creed, or national origin—to operate against him.[18]

Johnson had a high regard for Abraham Lincoln. In a radio address in February 1941 on "The World Significant Soul of Abraham Lincoln," Johnson said that "Abraham Lincoln died too soon, that his work is not completed, and that the wounds of the nation made in the Civil War have not been healed." He asserted that because of segregation, the United States was unfit for world leadership: "This is a world crisis. . . . If we cannot do away with segregation in Washington and in the public schools in the nation, if we cannot establish fair employment in industry, we are not fit for world leadership." Concerning Russia, Johnson stated, "That country offers bread at the expense of liberty; we must give bread with liberty." He condemned colonialism and called on the United States to urge our allies to cease this policy. He said that the colonial powers of Europe have "ruthlessly conquered more territory and have done more discriminating or segregating than any other country in the world."[19] He opined that America, with its productive superiority, could put an end to colonialism over the next ten years merely by refusing to support those countries that practiced it.

In 1963, with an uncanny foresight of what actually happened after the assassination of Martin Luther King Jr. in 1967, Johnson told a Baptist Ministers Conference in Washington that "One of these days the people are going to break down and can't stand it any longer, if you don't get to them and show them how to win. They need work and the daily necessity of their children. They need work for the boy who needs to help his mother with the other children. . . ." He asked, "What is the matter with the capital of this nation that we can't do these things?"[20]

Twice a year, Johnson spoke at the Andrew Rankin Memorial Chapel on campus, and he always addressed the university and Divinity School convocations. Each time he was scheduled to speak on campus, the chapel or auditorium was filled, not only with students and faculty, but also with citizens in the community. His basic theme on those occasions was that educated African Americans had a tremendous responsibility to those less fortunate. At commencement exercises he would urge the graduates to go to "Brazzos Bottom," down in Mississippi, and raise the quality of life of the black people there. The citations that Howard gave to those receiving honorary degrees show that he emphasized the contributions the recipients had made to people in need. To Martin Luther King Jr., he said, ". . . you came to be that leader and you have led your people on a victorious pathway seldom tried in human life. You have shown them how to overcome humiliation and abuse without violence and without hatred in deed or words. . . . You have taught them the spirit of Jesus of Nazareth, to love their enemies and to pray without ceasing for those who [spitefully] use them."[21]

To Pearl Buck, Johnson said, "There are no words to express the joy which we feel in the Negro minority, when we behold you, a southern woman, after years of devoted service to the people of China, returning to our country and speaking about our lives and the things that are precious to us, with a heart that is utterly free from race prejudice which has so long injured our people and has so deeply, if not fatally, wounded our nation."

In the citation given to Patrick Murphy Malin of the ACLU, Johnson lauded him for ". . . standing there, sensitive and watchful for every public practice that would weaken our belief in the inherent dignity and high possibilities of human life; and we see you steadily working to sustain and to advance the equality of the individual before the law."[22] In a citation to Jack R. ("Jackie") Robinson, Johnson praised him because, among other things, his remarkable ability and self-control "made possible the effective beginning of a major revolution in American baseball—a revolution which has popularized and strengthened beyond measure our deepest American faith: our faith in the open door of opportunity for every human being, whatever his race or color, religion or national origin."[23]

Johnson influenced many lives through his speeches. One notable example is his influence on Martin Luther King Jr. During King's student days at Crozer Theological Seminary, Johnson spoke there shortly after returning from India where he had conferred with Mahatma Gandhi. In that address, Johnson described Gandhi's philosophy of nonviolence. King was deeply impressed and set about learning how Gandhi's philosophy and methods might be the basis for transforming race relations in America. King's successful use of that philosophy changed the course of race relations in this country and catapulted him to world prominence. Eventually, Johnson offered King the position of dean of the School of Religion at Howard. King refused, citing his desire to continue his work with the civil rights movement.[24] One wonders how the status of race relations in America would have been affected if King had accepted Johnson's offer.

Through the power of the spoken word, Johnson helped to shape the thinking of thousands who heard him over the years. The quotations in this chapter show a well-informed person, addressing a variety of concerns and having the courage of his convictions. They also show that his primary emphasis was on revolutionizing thinking and practice in race relations in America. Johnson sought to educate white Americans as to equal justice and opportunity for the underprivileged. He called attention to inequities and raised the consciousness of many people regarding the status of human relations.

Johnson's concerns were not limited to this country. He recognized the plight of the millions of third-world people who, during his time, were under colonial domination; and he challenged the colonial powers to raise the standard of living and the political involvement of those under their aegis.

Measuring the total influence of exceptional personalities is difficult. It is safe to say, however, that innumerable people have been challenged, inspired, or influenced, either directly or indirectly, by Mordecai Johnson— the man and his message.

9

Another Beginning

*J*une 1960, the effective date of his retirement, represented an end and a beginning for Johnson. Besides the subjects that—in his farewell speech—he said he "wanted to think about," he could reflect on how his world had changed since his graduation from the Rochester Theological Seminary. The primary social issue upon which he focused was justice in human relations.

The world of 1960 was quite different in many ways from the world of 1916, when he took his first professional job as a student secretary of the YMCA, then abruptly resigned in protest against the racial discrimination he encountered in that organization. As pastor of the First Baptist Church in Charleston, West Virginia, he had preached and worked against the social inequities of that city and state. He had had a part in making 1960 quite different from 1926.

Now, he had completed the most significant thirty-four years of his life. Much had been accomplished during his years as an educator and national spokesman for human dignity and freedom. For one thing, in 1960 the nation was in the midst of the most unprecedented social revolution since the Civil War. Through the years, the NAACP had spearheaded the attack on racial discrimination in its many forms. President Harry S Truman had taken bold steps to eradicate certain forms of racial discrimination and to implement some democratic ideals. For example, on July 26, 1948, he had issued an executive order calling for the end of racial segregation in the armed forces. By appointing commissions to study and bring back recommendations on civil rights problems, Truman had put the force of the federal government squarely behind the efforts to abolish the evils of racist policies.

The Supreme Court's 1954 decision in *Brown* v. *Board of Education*, a landmark case, had dealt a lethal blow to segregation in public education. Although yet to be realized fully, that decision was the foundation for breaking down racial barriers not only in public education, but also in other areas of American life. Rosa Parks's refusal in 1955 to move to the back of a bus in Montgomery, Alabama, had resulted in a successful bus boycott movement there and also in certain other southern cities. The drive toward a more egalitarian society was well under way. Segregation was beginning to break down in various areas of the nation: in hotel accommodations, in eating establishments, in public recreation parks, and in public transportation. Moreover, African Americans were gaining increased political power. In several elections they represented the balance of power in key areas. An increasing number of African Americans began to aspire to public office and were being elected.

Johnson could look with satisfaction at the fact that "his Law School" had played an indispensable role in developing cases for litigation and in producing competent, highly skilled attorneys to argue successfully before the federal courts, including the Supreme Court.

Johnson played a role in all these developments, and he could take pride in them. Improvements in human relations by 1960 represented a realization of what he had fought for as an educator and national spokesman for civil rights. His endeavors had advanced human rights and changed the thinking of some of the hostile, the ignorant, the indifferent, or the naive supporters of discrimination and segregation in American society. Despite the reactionary forces that sought to impede progress in racial justice, the nation was moving toward a more just society. Still, complete justice in human relations was yet to be achieved. Although the millennium had not come, at the start of his retirement Johnson could look backward with some modicum of satisfaction and look forward to what the future might bring. It was indeed a new beginning.

Two years after his retirement, Johnson was appointed to a three-year term on the District of Columbia School Board, comprising ten members— seven whites and three African Americans. With his long background in higher education, he felt that he could make a meaningful contribution to public education in the District. He accepted the appointment with some anticipation. In 1962, in those schools affected by the historic Supreme

Court decision of 1954, public education was undergoing a transition from a segregated to an integrated system. The school situation in the District of Columbia was better than in most of the southern states, but it was not ideal.

Johnson had some reservations regarding certain School Board policies, and he never hesitated to express them forcibly. The principal policies to which he objected were (1) the track system, (2) the hiring of temporary teachers who he felt were unqualified, and (3) his belief that the board was given incomplete information regarding certain budget expenses.[1] The School Board's policy at the time was to separate pupils according to their test results. This separation involved creating a track system that often placed minority pupils in the lowest track, thereby depriving them of the opportunity to be uplifted by the performance of their peers who scored at higher levels. The track system could result in teachers not putting forth special efforts to raise the level of aspirations of students in the lower levels and in creating a sense of inferiority and frustration for those students. At one point, the board approved setting up special evening classes for pupils who were in the seven to sixteen age group and who were judged as uncontrollable in the regular classroom.

Johnson resented the track system because it represented discrimination against African-American students. In an address to a Baptist Ministers Conference in the District of Columbia, he said that they must take some action regarding the schools "and the four-track program in which colored children have been dumped by the thousands in the hands of temporary teachers." He continued,

> It is so easy for a middle-class civilization to say that John Jones across the tracks can't profit from an education. . . . I'm not to be assimilated into an appraisal that poorer class children are impossible. How do we know what they are capable of learning? I am not prepared to help us do less than our best for the children in the city.[2]

During a board meeting on this issue, one member suggested that they were dealing with a "practical problem." Johnson replied that "There were four and one-half million whites in the South who didn't own slaves. The middle-class slave masters gave them a name. They gave them the name poor white trash!"[3]

Johnson vehemently opposed the hiring of twenty-seven temporary teachers. At a special meeting of the board, he urged that it go into executive session to discuss the matter. His request was overruled by the District

Superintendent of Schools on the ground that since charges had not been made against the superintendent, the discussion should be open to the public. Johnson argued that a section of a report relating to temporary teachers be revoked because, in his opinion, it was illegal. The board did not agree.[4] Johnson felt that teachers were hired not on merit, but on politics.[5]

Moreover, in Johnson's view, financial reports given to the board were inadequate and monies were appropriated "on an unequal basis, harming predominantly Negro schools."[6] This type of discrimination was totally unacceptable to Johnson, and he inveighed against it.

In his insistence on more opportunities in the system for competent and available African Americans, Johnson opposed the appointment of a white candidate as head of the elementary schools in the District. He was not opposed to the appointee *as a person*. Indeed, he described her as a "distinguished lady." He felt, however, that the appointment implied that— throughout the nation—no African American could be found who was adequately prepared for the position. Moreover, the appointment would delay the progress of integration, for it meant that all of the eight top positions in the school system would be filled by Caucasians.[7]

Johnson had negative views regarding Superintendent of Schools Carl F. Hansen. He thought the superintendent was "a dangerous man," and he strongly opposed Hansen's reappointment. He was so vocal in his opposition that six Board members were successful in having a motion passed that Johnson be censured for "intemperate language."[8]

Johnson's persistent protests against what he perceived as inequities in certain School Board policies made some people consider him too controversial, thus creating an uncomfortable atmosphere within the board. Accordingly, the District Court judges refused to reappoint him at the expiration of his three-year term, even though many citizens and civil rights groups made a strong effort on behalf of the African-American community for Johnson's reappointment. The judges gave no reason for their action. At the meeting when the board announced the termination of his service, Johnson declared, "I thank God that He has relieved me of the responsibility of being a part of you."[9]

Not long after, a visitor said to him, "Dr. Johnson, I suppose that by now, having had some time to relax from your administrative duties, you will do some writing."

Johnson replied, "I had planned to do some writing after one or two years of retirement, but when I got ready to do so, I sent a request to the university for my files. They told me that they could not find them. This made it impossible for me to do the kind of writing to which I had looked forward."[10] Johnson was disappointed that he did not have the opportunity to prepare a written record of his career using his extensive presidential files. Those records covered not only his thirty-four years as president of Howard, but also his significant role in critically evaluating national and international policies.

That the extensive files covering Johnson's years at Howard were lost or misplaced is highly unlikely. The most likely reason for the university's not sending the presidential files to him was that they were the property of the university and an invaluable record of thirty-four of the most significant years in the institution's history. The university has the right to make sure that its records are kept intact and are not lost.

Anyway, Johnson was deeply disappointed at this development. His inability to have access to his presidential files so he could write his memoirs represented a great historical loss.

Several people urged Johnson to write his autobiography. Benjamin E. Mays pleaded with him, saying that Johnson owed it to present and future generations. Fortunately, Johnson did take time to dictate or write about significant experiences covering his youth and leading up to his adulthood and presidency of Howard. Apparently this effort was to prepare for an extended autobiography or for the use of a future biographer. These disjointed documents are valuable sources of insights into Johnson's thinking and the ways in which he approached crucial problems and issues. It is not clear at what point in his later life these brief memoranda were prepared.[11]

If and when the university makes Johnson's presidential files available to researchers, the accounts of his interactions with members of Congress, philanthropists and philanthropic organizations, trustees, faculty and staff, alumni, national and international leaders will illuminate an important era in American education and social history.

Johnson's most constant source of support through the years was his beloved wife, Anna Ethelyn, who combined her duties as a wife and mother with community service.

While in Charleston, she organized a drama department in the church, she was active in the Sunday School and the adult organizations of the church, and she formed a club for young girls. On coming to Howard, she led the organization of faculty wives, who held her in high esteem. She was concerned with civic matters and sought the cooperation of the White House and District of Columbia officials in promoting certain community programs.[12]

In March 1969, Anna Ethelyn became ill. During her illness Johnson often would sit by her bed and softly sing the songs both loved. These were moments of remembrance of hopes and dreams, of serious problems overcome, and of shared joys and sorrows.[13] His expression of love, sealed by a marriage spanning fifty-three years, cheered Anna Ethelyn profoundly. Nature, however, was not to be denied, and she died on February 28, 1969, at seventy-seven years of age.

At her funeral, conducted on March 4 by Dr. Evans Crawford, dean of the university's Andrew Rankin Memorial Chapel, present and former officials of the university paid glowing tributes to Anna Ethelyn. Eulogies were spoken by G. Frederick Stanton, secretary of the university; Miss Madeline Coleman, retired professor in the School of Music; Dr. W. Stuart Nelson, retired vice president of the university; Dr. Daniel Hill, former dean of the School of Religion; the Reverend Jerry Moore, pastor of the Nineteenth Street Baptist Church; and Mrs. Ruth Norman of the First Baptist Church in Charleston, West Virginia.[14] All of the speakers expressed appreciation for her life and contributions and offered remembrances of her great dignity. Anna Ethelyn's children were all there, recalling the myriad ways in which their mother expressed her love for each one. In facing the awesome reality and finality of her death, some bravely held back tears; others wept silently. After the service, Anna Ethelyn was entombed in Washington's Lincoln Cemetery.

Johnson grieved for some time over the loss of his beloved wife. She had been a grand lady, the object of his deepest affection, the loving mother of their five children, and his devoted companion in a marriage that lasted more than half a century. Adjusting to the void in his life was difficult. The memories of all the significant moments and events that they had shared served to sustain him.

Time, however, is the great healer. While on a speaking engagement in Memphis, Tennessee, a few months following Anna Ethelyn's death, Johnson had a long conversation with an old friend, Fred Hutchins, whom he had known as a youth when attending Howe Institute there. Both were members of the Primrose Club for young people. Hutchins had grown up with Alice Woodson. He knew the story of Johnson's first love and had kept in touch with Alice through the years. After talking about the old days, Johnson asked him, "By the way, whatever happened to that very pretty little girl, 'Sweet Alice,' I was supposed to marry?"

Hutchins answered, "She is a widow now, living in Austin, Texas, and operating a very prosperous funeral establishment. I have her address and telephone number."

Johnson said, "Give it to me right now."[15]

Johnson had neither seen nor communicated with Alice Woodson since her college days at Fisk University. After graduating from Fisk in 1912, she had returned to Memphis, where she was employed as a teacher. The shattering of her dreams to marry Johnson had been devastating, but Alice had resolved to go on with her life, although she could not entirely forget the handsome and brilliant "Monty" who first ignited in her the spark of love. She had often thought of that disappointing night when she and Johnson were to have become formally engaged.

For Alice, returning to Memphis to teach school was an opportunity to ignore the past and concentrate on her future. She was attractive, well educated, and socially in demand. Eventually, John Q. Taylor, a young physician who had recently settled in Memphis, began showing a more than casual interest in her. He was suave, handsome, and very personable. Alice was surprised to learn that John was a 1911 graduate of Meharry Medical College. He had been a student there during part of the time she was at neighboring Fisk University, but they never knew each other. In Memphis, their relationship became increasingly strong, and in 1916 they were married (the same year in which Johnson married Anna Ethelyn).

Ironically, somehow Johnson heard of Alice's marriage to a graduate of Meharry, and at first this confirmed his erroneous suspicion that she had been courting a Meharry student during her days at Fisk. Also, because he thought she had betrayed him, he was never inclined to contact her in later years. Not until some time after they had married others did Alice and Mordecai learn through mutual friends that the matron at Fisk, for reasons they never understood, had deceived them when Johnson journeyed to Nashville to propose to her in 1912.

Alice and John Q. Taylor had had a happy marriage. Three children were born to them: a daughter, Alice, called "Baby Alice"; a daughter, Edwina; and a son, John Q. Taylor Jr. Baby Alice died of food poisoning in 1920, shortly after Edwina was born. When World War I came, Taylor volunteered for service and saw action with the 366th Infantry Regiment in France. During an enemy attack he was severely gassed. For years after his return he was in and out of the Veterans Hospital and suffered a series of strokes. Meanwhile Alice, with two young children to care for, had to find employment. She sought another teaching position in the public schools, but the school board had a policy of not employing married women as teachers. However, because she was the wife of a disabled war veteran, was responsible for rearing two children, and had previously demonstrated her efficiency in the system, the board gave her special permission to teach. John Q. Taylor's physical condition continued to decline, and he died in 1931.

Later, Alice met and married Charles B. King, a graduate of Wilberforce University. He was an insurance man with the reputation of being an excellent salesman. Eventually, they moved to Austin, Texas, where he established a funeral business. Alice's son, John Q. Taylor Jr., adopted his stepfather's last name, and became known as John Q. Taylor King. The elder King and Alice made a very successful team until his death in 1941.

After her husband's passing, Alice Woodson King took over and expanded the mortuary. Her two children, John and Edwina, and her daughter-in-law, Marcet King, took the required courses to qualify as licensed funeral directors. The business thrived. At the same time, Alice participated in a wide range of community affairs. She was an active member of the Wesley United Methodist Church, the United Methodist Women, the Top Ladies of Distinction, the Alpha Kappa Alpha Sorority Inc., and several other civic organizations.

When they were old enough to understand, Alice told her children about her first love and his notable achievements, and about the deception that shattered their romance. One day her son, John, then a student at Fisk University, attended a chapel service where Johnson spoke. After the service John introduced himself to Johnson and explained who he was. Johnson expressed interest in John and asked to be remembered to his mother.

John Q. Taylor King had a distinguished career both in the military and in education. He entered the U.S. army as a private, rose to the rank of captain, and retired as a major general. He served in army installations in Asia, Europe, and the United States, and was selected to complete courses at several senior service schools. After he received many military awards and decorations, Governor Mark White appointed him a lieutenant general in the Texas State Guard in 1985. His educational odyssey included degrees from Fisk University, Huston-Tillotson College, and DePaul University. He received a Ph.D. from the University of Texas at Austin. After many years as an instructor and administrator, he was elected president of Huston-Tillotson College in 1965, a position he held until his retirement in 1988. A recipient of many honors and awards, including Phi Beta Kappa, General King compiled a record of which his mother was quite proud.

Earlier, during the 1950s, when he was an army officer, John Q. Taylor King happened to be in Washington for a meeting and went to see Johnson at Howard. When he asked the secretary if Dr. Johnson was in, she replied, "No, he's not, but I expect him shortly. Would you like to wait?"

He said, "Yes, I would." She asked him to sit in a waiting room next to the office. Soon, King heard Johnson, who had come into his office through a side entrance, speaking to his secretary, who reminded him that he had an appointment at that hour. Johnson began to leave for his appointment.

Realizing that he was about to miss seeing Johnson, King reminded the secretary that he was waiting. Johnson saw and spoke to him, "Sir, are you waiting for me?"

"Yes, I am," King replied.

"Do you have an appointment?"

"No, I don't. I just happened to be in the area. I came by to see you and bring greetings from one of your childhood friends."

"Yes, who is that?"

" 'Sweet Alice' Woodson. 'Sweet Alice' Woodson is my mother."

Johnson expressed keen interest and invited King into his office, telling his secretary to inform the people with whom he had an appointment that he would be late. He and King talked for forty-five minutes. He asked about King's career, and King recounted what he had done in the military and as a teacher. He informed Johnson that his mother had been widowed for the second time. As they parted, Johnson said, "Any time you are here, feel free to come by and see me."

Before leaving for this appointment, Johnson told his secretary, "Now, any time this young man or any members of his family come here looking for me, you find me and let me know they are here, and keep them here until I come. These are real friends. This is the son of a pretty girl with whom I grew up. I always want to see him or any member of his family when they are in Washington or on campus." Clearly he had not forgotten his first love.

Following his return from Memphis in the fall of 1969 and the renewal of his acquaintance with his long-time friend, Fred Hutchins, Johnson lost little time before telephoning Alice in Austin, Texas. One day when Alice's son, John, then president of Huston-Tillotson College, went to his mother's home for a brief visit, the telephone was ringing just as he entered. Alice became engaged in an animated conversation. The dialog continued for more than thirty minutes, by which time King signaled that he had to leave. His mother waved goodbye and continued talking. When he next visited, he said, "Mother, do you realize that when I was here last, that was the first time ever you shooed me away? That must have been a very important call. Who in the world were you talking to."

She said, "That was Monty" (her nickname for Johnson). It was their first conversation in fifty-eight years.

King understood, for after Anna Ethelyn had died, he had quietly entertained the idea of his mother and Johnson getting together. He asked his mother when Johnson would be coming for a visit. She replied, "We didn't talk about that. We just decided to keep in touch."

Johnson and Alice talked regularly by telephone and exchanged letters. He called every night at nine o'clock. It became clear that they might be considering marriage when Johnson announced that he was coming to Austin to visit.

King and his mother went to the airport to meet Johnson. With much anticipation they waited for him to deplane. He stepped off the plane with his cane in hand and hat cocked to the side. After Johnson came down the gangway, King and his mother walked up to him, and as he approached them, Johnson tipped his hat and said, "Madam, how are you?"

"Sir, how are you?" she replied. They stood looking at each other.

"Aren't you going to embrace?" King asked.

"Oh, yes, yes," said Johnson. They embraced, and a thousand memories were replayed in their minds.

"Let's go to my house," King said. "We are having a faculty meeting there and some of Dr. Johnson's former students will want to greet him."

The faculty members were pleased to see Johnson. King asked him to say a few words, "but not to talk for an hour and twenty minutes!" Johnson talked for forty-five minutes and had everyone spellbound. He returned to Washington, but made three subsequent visits to Austin that year.

After the third visit, Johnson called John King to arrange another visit so he could talk with Alice's children about the prospect of his marrying their mother. Upon his arrival, Johnson asked King where he could talk with him and his sister in private. In a downstairs activity room Johnson told King and his sister, Edwina, the story of how he had met a pretty little girl who lived across the street from his boarding house when he was studying at Howe Institute in Memphis. He told of making the trip to Nashville in 1912 to propose to Alice, and of being misled by the dormitory matron. He recounted the events and expectations leading up to that visit, and the crushing disappointment. But now, after fifty-eight years, the two of them had a second chance to get married and would like the consent of Alice's children.

"Well, Dr. Johnson," King said, "I think you realize that you and mother are over twenty-one, and you really don't need the consent of anyone besides the two of you to get married. But I appreciate your asking us for our advice. I only have two questions to ask of you, Dr. Johnson. Have you discussed this with your children, and what is their attitude about their father getting married?"

"Yes, I have talked with all of my children and they said that if that's what I want to do, that's fine," Johnson replied.

"You know your age and you know mother's age and both of you are in good health now. Have you given any thought concerning what you would do if you should become ill or mother should become ill or, even more important, both of you became ill at the same time?" King asked.

"Yes, we've discussed that several times. We decided that we would cross that bridge when we got to it," Johnson answered.

"Fine, as long as you have thought about it. That's great," said King.

Following these exchanges, Johnson looked at Edwina and said, "Madam, do you have any questions?" She was on the verge of tears at the prospect of her mother's leaving Austin and was tempted to express her objections, but King quietly signaled her not to speak. Whereupon King said, "Well, let's go upstairs and make the great announcement to the rest of the family."

Two of King's three sons were enthusiastic about the proposed marriage. His youngest son and his daughter, however, were opposed, primarily because they had lived near their grandmother all their lives. She had always been there for them, and they did not like the idea of losing her companionship.

Johnson returned to Washington with an enthusiasm and a renewal of spirit he had not experienced for some time. A faculty member at Howard University met Johnson shortly after he deplaned from his trip to Austin. Johnson was aglow with happiness and told his listener about his impending marriage. Johnson exclaimed, "And she has never loved any man but me!"[16]

The date was set for the wedding, which was planned by John King and his wife. King wrote a special ceremony for the couple, reasoning that, as mature as Johnson and his mother were, they did not require the wording of the traditional ritual. Mordecai was eighty years old, and Alice was seventy-eight. The pastor of Alice's church, Wesley United Methodist Church, was of the old school and was not pleased about using a nontraditional marriage service. The couple invited another clergyman, a Baptist minister and friend of the family, to join her pastor. On April 12, 1970, the ceremony was held in Alice's son's home with the two ministers officiating. All of her grand-children were there, as were three of Johnson's children. Not present were Johnson's daughter, Anna, who was living in Boston, and his son, Archer, a psychiatrist, who was living in Puerto Rico. Following the wedding, the family released an announcement and held a reception in Austin. More than 500 people attended. Some simply wanted to see this man who was going to marry Mrs. King, an independent widow for twenty-nine years. Others who had known Johnson wanted to be part of the marriage celebration.

It was fitting that Mordecai and Alice should honeymoon in Memphis, the site of their first love. They enjoyed visiting with the friends who still resided there. Later, they set up housekeeping at his home on Buchanan Street in Washington.

On one of Johnson's visits to Austin after he and Alice were married, he informed John King that he understood that a Caucasian man related to him had moved from Paris, Tennessee, to a town in Texas. He gave the name to King, who did some research and found that a descendant of the person whose name Johnson had given him did have a relative operating a drug store in that town. Johnson, his new wife, and the Kings drove to the town and found the drugstore. As they entered the place, they were all struck by the close resemblance between the druggist and Johnson. They looked like brothers, with the same type of physique, facial features, and baldness. King kept quietly prodding Johnson to tell the druggist who he was, but Johnson refused to divulge his identity. His only interest was in visiting and seeing the man. Johnson made small talk with him about the drugstore and how business was in the community. Johnson apparently had subscribed regularly to his hometown newspaper, the *Paris Post-Intelligencer*, which was how he could keep up with people who had the same ancestry.

Johnson must have given much thought to his racial heritage. He must have been acutely aware of the mentality of the white establishment, that "one drop" of Negro blood was sufficient to classify an individual as a Negro. Those in power maintained this stance for political and economic reasons. They tried to place the stigma of inferiority on everyone with a trace of African ancestry and implied that even the slightest amount of Negro blood was powerful enough to override all other racial strains.[17] As the dominant group classifies all such persons this way, it is easier to keep them in subjection, and at the same time, it undergirds their sense of superiority.

Johnson's light complexion made it possible for him, if he desired, to pass as white. During his time in the history of race relations in America, his light skin could be an advantage, particularly when he was traveling and wanted comfortable accommodations on trains and in hotels and restaurants. No doubt he and other light-skinned African-American leaders—such as John Hope of Morehouse, who was blond with blue eyes—whose professions required travel, sometimes chose this option.

People such as Johnson and Hope could move freely in two worlds. Thus, they could understand the psychology and attitudes of whites as well as blacks. Among whites who did not know them, they could choose to conceal their identities. From Johnson's easy access to the white world and his own biological background, he knew that the claims of racial inferiority and white superiority had no basis in fact, but were used to suppress the minority.

Like John Hope, Johnson, as Benjamin E. Mays put it, was a "voluntary Negro," choosing to retain the identity of his birth. In situations where he was aware that people in the audience might view him as white, he made his racial background clear. This revelation heightened the impact of his message.

During a question period following an address Johnson had given to a white audience in Memphis, Tennessee, the first query was "Are you a colored man?" Johnson replied, "My mother was about my color and my father was a dark man." He continued by saying that he attended Howe Institute in Memphis, which all present knew was a school for African-American youths.

Despite the above observations, some statements attributed to Johnson require consideration. Writing in his book, *Adventures of a Bystander*, Peter F. Drucker quotes Johnson as saying in a speech to a student-faculty assembly at Sarah Lawrence College in Bronxville, New York, that African Americans' "greatest problem" is their failure to recognize that their African forebears engaged in the slave trade. He went on to say that this fact imposes on African Americans a guilt that must be resolved if they are to become "truly free." What made this slave trading worse, he is quoted as saying, is that, unlike the Greeks, who sold Greek slaves only to other Greeks, the Africans sold members of their own race to slave traders of other races. Drucker cites this to illustrate what he calls the "integrity" of African-American scholars of the New Deal era of the 1930s and 1940s.[18]

If this account is accurate, the statement is in stark contrast with all the other reports of Johnson's addresses to black and white audiences. As perceptive as his analyses of social issues were, how he reached this conclusion is difficult to understand. First, few African Americans have been aware that Africans themselves engaged in slave trading, and it is doubtful that this knowledge is a condition of their becoming "truly free." Moreover, for the Akans of the Gold Coast (now Ghana), who were active in slave trading, selling their war captives was an alternative to killing them as other conquering people did. Furthermore, the Akans apparently put little emphasis on racial differences. Even in Ghana today, a white man, formerly an official of the British government who chose to remain after Ghana achieved independence, enjoys the title of "Chief."

From our perspective, the only logical explanation for Johnson to have made this statement is that he may have been asserting that American whites, too, must share a sense of guilt for their ancestors having accepted slavery as a justifiable economic system.

Drucker reports another remark by Johnson that arouses curiosity. According to him, Johnson used the term "nigger" in a matter-of-fact way in casual conversation with him. In speaking about how technology has served to change attitudes, Drucker quotes Johnson as saying that technology has been a factor in freeing African Americans from a certain fear of whites. He quotes Johnson: "The American Negro was free the day one of them realized that a white man is just as dead if run over by a nigger as by . . . a white." Why Johnson used the term in this context is problematic. As most people know, blacks and Jews sometimes use epithets applied to them in conversations among themselves, but not with persons outside their ethnic groups. Does Johnson's alleged use of this term in conversation with a white man suggest he was merely using the word that a white person would use in that situation? Or had he subconsciously identified with Caucasians and thought of African Americans objectively or of himself as separate from African Americans? Indeed, when addressing African-American audiences, Johnson sometimes used the term "you people." In any case, other African Americans would strongly disapprove of Johnson's use of the "n" word in such a situation as reported.

Two years after his remarriage, Johnson and Alice were invited to return to the place of his birth, Paris, Tennessee, to be honored by the community. Johnson was one of five people in the field of education who were born or raised in Paris and who were singled out for recognition during the Annual World's Biggest Fish Fry observance. He was delighted with the invitation and elected to stay at the home of his boyhood friend, Robert Woodson, while he and Alice were in Paris. In replying to the invitation, Johnson stated, "We look forward with eagerness to see once more the people and the grounds made so precious to me in my boyhood." The others honored on that occasion were Dr. Thomas D. Jarrett, president of Atlanta University; Dr. Cecil C. Humphreys, president of Memphis State University; Dr. Joe Morgan, president of Austin Peay University; and Dr. Larry T. McGhee, chancellor of the University of Tennessee at Martin.[19]

During his latter years, Johnson experienced some health problems. In 1975 he was admitted to the Howard University Hospital for treatment of a cardiovascular illness. While he was there, physicians installed a pacemaker. His health gradually declined, however, and at 6:00 A.M. on Friday, September 10, 1976, he died in his sleep. He was eighty-six.

Johnson's funeral was held in the Andrew Rankin Memorial Chapel at Howard University on September 14, 1976. The body lay in state there the preceding day. Because the Rankin Chapel could not accommodate all the local and out-of-town mourners who wanted to share in the service, it was televised by closed circuit to several hundred people in the Cramton auditorium.

Dr. Benjamin E. Mays, a long-time friend, former dean of the Howard School of Religion, former president of Morehouse College, and then president of the Atlanta School Board, delivered the eulogy. Among those who paid tribute were Johnson's college roommate, John W. Davis; Howard Thurman, former dean of the Rankin Chapel at Howard (a recorded message); Dr. Dorothy B. Ferabee, president of the Women's Institute at the American University; and James E. Cheek, president of Howard University.

Because of his sympathy for the ordinary person, Johnson had requested that some of the men who worked around the campus buildings and grounds be included among his pallbearers. Their inclusion in the service was a symbol and testimony of his concern for people at all social levels. The funeral cortege carried his body to the Lincoln Cemetery, where, as proprieties dictated, he was entombed beside Anna Ethelyn.

Newspaper editorials paid glowing tributes to Johnson following his death. The editor of the *Washington Post* stated:

> It was not mere coincidence that the growth of Howard University from a weak unaccredited secondary school/college into a recognized center of learning occurred during the presidency of Mordecai Wyatt Johnson. Dr. Johnson . . . had the vision, determination, and administrative skills to bring about this transformation, which at times involved bitter struggles just to keep Howard alive. Though this achievement would have been enough to gain him worldwide recognition as an educator, it was by no means the full measure of his greatness. Mordecai Johnson's most important contribution to America and to the Negro was that he provided the climate in which was forged the instruments that overthrew Jim Crow.[20]

The *Washington Star* wrote:

> Mordecai W. Johnson saw far and saw clearly. The embodiment, but not the horizon, for his vision was the transformation of Howard University in thirty-four years, under his leadership, from an educational gesture to a mature and vigorous institution. The influence of Dr. Johnson . . . permeated the long march of Black Americans toward a full sharing in the nation's ideals. . . .

There was in his philosophy no passivity, no acceptance of the image to which racism and ignorance consigned generations of Black Americans. Rather, Dr. Johnson challenged, fought tenaciously, and at risk, for the ideals of racial equality.[21]

A commentary by Wallace Terry read during a telecast over WTOP/ TV 9 stated, "Mordecai Johnson was a strong patriarch and a remarkable visionary, a kind of Biblical cross between Abraham and Isaiah. However much he struggled alone, his faith in himself and in his beliefs never wavered. It stood as strong as the buildings he raised up and the students who marched forth."

An editorial in the campus publication, *The Hilltop*, stated:

Dr. Johnson was a scholar among scholars, a president among presidents, a man among men—but even more important, he was his own man. He was not slow to criticize slovenly standards, racism, imperialism, or any species of intolerance or injustice. He held up to withering scrutiny black as well as white leadership in civic, religious, and economic life. Dr. Johnson rejected the view that the University ought to avoid critical analysis of social and economic issues.[22]

Following Johnson's death, the Paris (Tennessee) Civic League donated $500 to the courthouse lawn beautification project as a memorial to Johnson. A black civic group in Paris named a recreational park in his honor.

After a short while in Washington, Alice Woodson Johnson returned to her home in Austin, Texas, where she was comfortable with her children, grandchildren, and many friends. Hers had been a beautiful and significant life, even though punctuated by the disappointment of her first love, by the untimely passing of two fine men to whom she had pledged her fealty, and by twenty-nine years of widowhood. The ultimate beauty was when, at long last, she shared six romantic years with her first love, "Monty." In 1984, eight years after Johnson passed away, she died at age ninety-one.

Possessed of a powerful mind and, in some instances, radical ideas, Johnson was masterfully skilled at conveying his thoughts effectively to all types of audiences, while keeping his focus clear and showing "grace under pressure." Mordecai Wyatt Johnson's contributions were not merely parochial, but national and international in scope. The overall influence of his life can hardly be adequately measured. He was a man with an overriding purpose, a man with a mission.

Mordecai's journey was long from the little town of Paris, Tennessee, "Home of the World's Biggest Fish Fry," to the president's mansion and the administration suite of an outstanding university in the nation's capital. The road was long from the unpretentious home of an ex-slave father to the Great Hall in London, England, where Johnson challenged world leaders of the North Atlantic Treaty Organization to implement standards of social justice for people in underdeveloped countries of the world. To quote Robert Frost, Mordecai Wyatt Johnson traveled the "road less traveled." Along the way, he used leadership and forensic skills to advance the cause of human dignity and justice among the oppressed peoples of the world. In the process he was sometimes maligned by those with conflicting interests. Yet he prevailed over all efforts to disparage him. He labored for thirty-four years to build a great center of learning where young men and women could acquire the knowledge, skills, and inspiration to prepare them to make a difference in the world.

We can truly say of the modern-day Mordecai as was said of the ancient Mordecai in the book of Esther: "He was a great man . . . for he sought the good of his people and promoted the welfare of all their descendants."

Bibliographical Notes

*M*ordecai Wyatt Johnson left very few written documents. However, we are fortunate to have some valuable unpublished memoirs that he occasionally wrote about certain aspects of his life or that he dictated, transcribed, and edited. These are on file at the Moorland-Spingarn Research Center at Howard University, Washington, D.C. This material has provided valuable insights into Johnson's thinking and personality. Several sermons and significant addresses are included in the appendixes.

Certain repositories have been of indispensable significance as I compiled this biography. The "Julius Rosenwald Papers, Re: Mordecai W. Johnson" on file in the Amistad Research Center at Tulane University contain important correspondence between Johnson and Edwin R. Embree, between Embree and directors of other foundations, and between Mordecai and those above. The controversy between Johnson and Professor Ernest E. Just and between Just and the Rosenwald Fund is detailed here, clarifying some misconceptions regarding this matter. While Kenneth R. Manning's biographical work, *Black Apollo of Science: The Life of Ernest Everett Just* (New York: Oxford University Press, 1988), is comprehensive, his interpretation of the conflict between Just and Johnson differs with the correspondence on file in the Rosenwald Fund Papers. Those files contain considerable correspondence pertaining to the contributions by philanthropic foundations to the development of the university during the first half of Johnson's tenure.

Primary data regarding Johnson's early years as a student in Atlanta are available in the archives of the Robert W. Woodruff Library at Atlanta University in Atlanta, Georgia. The correspondence between Johnson and President John Hope is illuminating.

The Moorland-Spingarn Research Center at Howard University contains files that were especially useful for this study. These include several boxes of materials: a large volume of news clippings, reports of Johnson's speeches, accounts of events at Howard, and other matters pertaining to Johnson's tenure. The African-American press covered Johnson's speeches regularly, and the Washington daily papers carried news about Johnson and Howard University. The center holds the memoirs of certain persons who interacted with Johnson, such as the papers of Dean Lucy D. Slowe.

On January 12, 1990, the Moorland-Spingarn Research Center sponsored a symposium celebrating the 100th anniversary of Johnson's birth. Speakers included some former teachers and administrators who served during his administration, as well as his daughter, Mrs. Carolyn Graves. The videotape of this event illuminates Johnson's personal and administrative characteristics.

Edward A. Jones's *A Candle in the Dark: The History of Morehouse College* (Valley Forge, Penn.: Judson Press, 1967) and Frank L. Forbes, *The Story of Athletics at Morehouse College, 1890–1967* (Atlanta: Morehouse College, 1967) are definitive histories of Johnson's later high school and college years. Moreover, an address titled "The Founding of Atlanta Baptist College" by the Reverend William J. White, one of the founders of what later became Morehouse College, gives a firsthand account of the beginnings of that institution (typescript, in the Moorland-Spingarn Research Center). Materials regarding Johnson's student days are available in the catalogs of Atlanta Baptist College, 1907–1911, and the *General Catalog* of the Rochester Theological Seminary.

The local newspaper of Johnson's birthplace, the *Paris Post-Intelligencer*, the publication *Henry County (Tenn.) Sesquicentennial, 1923–1973*, by Barbara Baggett and David Cooper, (Paris, Tenn., Sesquicentennial Committee 1975); "The History of the Mt. Zion Baptist Church" (of Paris, typescript, n.d.); and Thomas O. Fuller's *History of Negro Baptists in West Tennessee* (Memphis: Thomas O. Fuller, 1936) provide useful details about Johnson's geographical origins and religious heritage. Edwin J. Cashin's two volumes, *The Story of Augusta*, (Augusta, Ga.: Richmond County Board of Education, 1980), and *The Quest: A History of Public Education in Richmond County, Georgia* (Augusta, Ga.: Richmond County Board of Education,

1983) provide information on the family background of Anna Ethelyn Johnson.

The story of the rise and development of the First Baptist Church in Charleston, West Virginia, and Johnson's contributions to the church during his nine-year pastorate there is told in Richard H. Hill's *History of the First Baptist Church of Charleston, West Virginia* (Charleston, W.Va.: privately printed, 1934).

Two histories of Howard University are significant: Walter Dyson's *Howard University: The Capstone of Negro Education, A History, 1867–1940* (Washington, D.C.: Howard University, 1941), and Rayford W. Logan's *Howard University: The First 100 Years, 1867–1967* (New York: New York University Press, 1969). Logan's book has the advantage of his having had access to the minutes of the university's Board of Trustees. A book by Michael R. Winston (ed.), *Education for Freedom—The Leadership of Mordecai Wyatt Johnson, Howard University, 1926–1960: A Documentary Tribute to Celebrate the Fiftieth Anniversary of the Election of Mordecai Wyatt Johnson as President of Howard University* (Washington, D.C.: Howard University Archives, Moorland-Spingarn Research Center, May 5, 1976), is well edited and packed with significant information about Johnson and his tenure at Howard.

Edwin R. Embree's book, *Thirteen Against the Odds* (Port Washington, N.Y.: Kennikat Press, 1944), and Mary White Ovington's book, *Portraits in Color* (New York: Viking Press, 1944), contain reports of interviews in which Johnson gave accounts of some of his important personal experiences.

Genna Rae McNeil's definitive work, *Groundwork: Charles Hamilton Houston and the Struggle for Civil Rights* (Philadelphia: University of Pennsylvania Press, 1983), and Gilbert Ware's *William Hastie: Grace Under Pressure* (New York: Oxford University Press, 1984), contain excellent details of the development of the Howard University School of Law under Johnson's leadership.

Benjamin E. Mays's autobiography, *Born to Rebel* (New York: Charles Scribner's Sons, 1971), and Howard Thurman's autobiography, *With Head and Heart: The Autobiography of Howard Thurman* (New York: Harcourt Brace Jovanovich, 1979), are rich accounts of the experiences of those outstanding personalities with respect to the times in which Johnson lived and of their tenures at Howard University during his presidency.

Two doctoral dissertations are of significant value: Jenifer Bailey Butler, "An Analysis of the Oral Rhetoric of Mordecai Wyatt Johnson: A Study of the Concept of Presence" (Ph.D. dissertation, Ohio State University, 1977), and Clifford L. Muse Jr., "An Educational Stepchild: Howard University and the New Deal" (Ph.D. dissertation, Howard University, 1989), contain excellent materials about Johnson's speaking style and about Howard University during the Franklin D. Roosevelt era.

Also useful is the typescript *Mordecai Wyatt Johnson: A Bibliography of His Years at Howard University, 1926–1960*, prepared by James P. Johnson, Nanette Simms, and Gail A. Kostunko and on file at the Moorland-Spingarn Research Center.

Bibliography

Primary Sources

Johnson, Mordecai Wyatt. Unpublished memoirs on file at the Moorland-Spingarn Research Center at Howard University, Washington, D.C. These are in disjunctive form and written on special topics. Also miscellaneous correspondence and other items of Johnson's are among his papers at this depository.

Johnson, Mordecai Wyatt. Unpublished sermons.

Johnson, Mordecai Wyatt. Published addresses.

Johnson, Mordecai Wyatt. "The Autobiography of Mordecai Wyatt Johnson." Howard University, Moorland-Spingarn Research Center. Typescript, n.d.

Johnson, Mordecai Wyatt. "The Contributions of the Honorable Louis Convers Cramton to the Development of Howard University." Howard University, Moorland-Spingarn Research Center. Typescript, n.d.

Johnson, Mordecai Wyatt. "The Faith of the American Negro." In Michael R. Winston, *Education for Freedom. The Leadership of Mordecai Wyatt Johnson, 1926–1960.* Washington, D.C.: Howard University, Moorland-Spingarn Research Center, 1976.

Johnson, Mordecai Wyatt. "The Financial Support of Howard University During the Next Ten Years." A special memorandum for the Board of Trustees, 1941. Microfilm copy of selected items in the Amistad Research Center from the originals at Fisk University.

Johnson, Mordecai Wyatt. "The Future Outlook of American Negroes." Last in a series of lectures on Negro education and race relation problems held under the auspices of Teachers College, Columbia University, during the spring of 1930. Supported by the Julius Rosenwald Fund.

Johnson, Mordecai Wyatt. "Prophets of Unsegregated Institutions." An address delivered at the inauguration of Charles S. Johnson as president of Fisk University. Pamphlet, 1948.

Johnson, Mordecai Wyatt. "Significant Items in the Development of Howard University During the Period from July 1, 1926, to June 30, 1942." A memorandum from Johnson to Edwin R. Embree, 1942. Microfilm copy of selected items in the Julius Rosenwald Fund archives in the Amistad Research Center from the originals at Fisk University.

Johnson, Mordecai Wyatt. "The Social Responsibility of the Administrator." In *Academic Freedom in the United States.* Papers contributed in the Fifteenth Annual Spring Conference of the Division of the Social Sciences, March 22, 23, and 24, 1953, Gustave Auzenne, ed. Washington, D.C.: Howard University, 1953.

Johnson, Mordecai Wyatt. "The Templars." Bachelor of Divinity thesis, Rochester Theological Seminary, 1920.

Hope, John and Eugenia. The John and Eugenia Hope Papers. Alfred Hornsby, ed. On file at the Robert W. Woodruff Library at Atlanta University.

Logan, Rayford W. The Diary of Rayford Logan. Manuscript Division, Library of Congress.

Rosenwald, Julius. The Julius Rosenwald Papers re: Mordecai Wyatt Johnson. Amistad Research Center, Tulane University.

White, Rev. William J., D.D. "The Founding of Atlanta Baptist College." An address by the founder. Typescript, May 13, 1907.

Atlanta Baptist College. *Catalogs*, 1906, 1907, 1908.

Rochester Theological Seminary. *Catalog*, 1916.

Rochester Theological Seminary. *General Catalog*, 1850–1920.

Books

Baggett, Barbara, and David Cooper. *Henry County (Tenn.) Sesquicentennial (1823–1973) Brochure.* Paris, Tenn. Sesquicentennial Committee, 1975.

Bardolph, Richard. *The Negro Vanguard.* New York: Reinhart, 1959.

Bartlett, Robert M. *They Work for Tomorrow.* New York: Association Press, 1943.

Boulware, Marcus H. *The Oratory of Negro Leaders: 1900–1968.* Westport, Conn.: Negro Universities Press, 1969.

Brawley, Benjamin. *History of Morehouse College.* Atlanta: Morehouse College, 1917.

Brawley, Benjamin. *Negro Builders and Heroes.* Chapel Hill, N.C.: University of North Carolina Press, 1937.

Brawley, Benjamin. *A Short History of the American Negro.* New York: Macmillan Co., 1931.

Brody, Fawn. *Thomas Jefferson, An Intimate Biography.* New York: Norton & Co., 1974.

Bullock, Ralph W. *In Spite of Handicaps: Brief Biographical Sketches with Discussion of Outlines of Outstanding Negroes Now Living Who Are Achieving Distinction in Various Lines of Endeavor.* Foreword by Channing H. Tobias. New York: Association Press, 1927.

Carpenter, John H. *Sword and Olive Branch: Oliver Otis Howard.* Pittsburgh: University of Pittsburgh Press, 1964.

Cashin, Edwin J. *The Story of Augusta.* Augusta, Ga: Richmond County Board of Education, 1980.

Cashin, Edwin J. *The Quest: A History of Public Education in Richmond County, Georgia.* Augusta, Ga.: Richmond County Board of Education, 1983.

Davis, James F. *Who Is Black?* University Park: Pennsylvania State University Press, 1989.

Davis, Michael D., and Hunter R. Clark. *Thurgood Marshall: Warrior at the Bar, Rebel on the Bench.* New York: Carol Publishing Co., 1992.

Drucker, Peter. *Adventures of a Bystander.* New York: Harper & Brothers, 1979.

Dyson, Walter P. *Howard University: Capstone of Negro Education, A History, 1867–1940.* Washington, D.C.: Howard University Graduate School, 1941.

Embree, Edwin R. *Thirteen Against the Odds.* Port Washington, N.Y.: Kennikat Press, 1944.

Encyclopedia Britannica. 1965 ed. Vol. 4.

Forbes, Frank L. *The History of Athletics at Morehouse College, 1890–1966.* Atlanta: Morehouse College, 1967.

Franklin, John Hope. *From Slavery to Freedom.* New York: A. A. Knopf, 1947.

Fuller, Thomas O. *History of the Negro Baptists in Western Tennessee.* Memphis, Tenn.: Thomas O. Fuller, 1936.

Garrow, David. *Bearing the Cross—Martin Luther King, Jr., and the Southern Christian Leadership Conference.* New York: William J. Morrow and Co., 1986.

Hill, Richard H. *History of the First Baptist Church of Charleston, West Virginia.* Charleston, W.Va.: Privately Published, 1934.

Jones, Edward A. *A Candle in the Dark: The History of Morehouse College.* Philadelphia: Judson Press, 1967.

Kluger, Richard. *Simple Justice: The History of* Brown v. Board of Education *and Black America's Struggle for Equality,* New York: Knopf, 1976.

Logan, Rayford W. *Howard University: The First 100 Years, 1867–1967.* New York: New York University, 1969.

Logan, Rayford W., and Michael Winston. *Dictionary of American Biography.* New York: W. W. Norton and Co., 1982.

Manning, Kenneth R. *Black Apollo of Science: The Life of Ernest Everett Just.* New York: Oxford University Press, 1988.

Mays, Benjamin Elijah. *Born to Rebel.* New York: Charles Scribner's Sons, 1971.

McFeely, William S. *Yankee Stepfather: General O. O. Howard and the Freedmen.* New Haven, Conn.: Yale University Press, 1968.

McGuire, Phillip. *He, Too, Spoke for Democracy: Judge William Hastie, World War II, and the Black Soldier.* New York: Greenwood Press, 1988.

McNeil, Genna Rae. *Groundwork: Charles Hamilton Houston and the Struggle for Civil Rights.* Philadelphia: University of Pennsylvania Press, 1983.

Minus, Paul. *Walter Rauschenbush: An American Reformer.* New York: MacMillan, 1988.

Muse, Clifford L. Jr., ed. *Mordecai Johnson Souvenir Booklet Prepared in Observance of the Centennial of His Birth, with a Biographical Sketch and Photographs. January 12, 1990.* Washington, D.C.: Howard University, Moorland-Spingarn Research Center, 1990.

Ovington, Mary White. *Portraits in Color.* New York: Viking Press, 1927.

Read, Florence M. *The Story of Spelman College.* Atlanta: Spelman College, 1961.

Richardson, Ben Albert. *Great American Negroes.* A review by William A. Fodery. New York: Crowell Press, 1956.

Robinson, Donald B. *The Day I Was Proudest to Be an American.* Garden City, N.Y.: Doubleday, 1958.

Rosenberg, Stuart. *A Humane Society.* Toronto: University of Toronto Press, 1962.

Tewksbury, Donald. *The Founding of American Colleges and Universities Before the Civil War.* New York: Bureau of Publications, Teachers College, Columbia University, 1932.

Thurman, Howard. *With Head and Heart: The Autobiography of Howard Thurman.* New York: Harcourt Brace Janovich, 1979.

Torrence, Ridgely. *The Story of John Hope.* New York: Macmillan Co., 1948.

Ware, Gilbert. *William Hastie: Grace Under Pressure.* New York: Oxford University Press, 1984.

Who's Who in Colored America, 1933–1937. 4th ed. Thomas Yenser, ed. Brooklyn, N.Y.: Thomas Yenser, 1939.

Winston, Michael R., ed. *Education for Freedom—The Leadership of Mordecai Wyatt Johnson: A Documentary Tribute to Celebrate the Fiftieth Anniversary of the Election of Mordecai W. Johnson as President of Howard University.* Washington, D.C.: Howard University, Moorland-Spingarn Research Center, 1976.

Wolters, Raymond. *The New Negro on Campus: Black College Rebellions in the 1920s.* Princeton, N.J.: Princeton University Press, 1975.

Woodhouse, F. C. *The Military and Religious Orders of the Middle Ages.* New York: Pott, Young and Co., 1879, 208.

Pamphlets/Brochures

Anonymous. "History of the Mt. Zion Baptist Missionary Church, Paris, Tennessee." Typescript, n.d.

Davis, John W. "Mordecai Wyatt Johnson—Potentially God's Other Self." An address delivered at the Third Annual Mordecai Wyatt Johnson Lecture Series, Howard University, January 25, 1980.

Johnson, James P.; Nanette Simms; and Gail K. Kostunko, eds. "Mordecai Wyatt Johnson—A Bibliography of His Years at Howard University, 1926–1960." Typescript. Washington, D.C.: Howard University, Moorland-Spingarn Research Center, 1976.

Mays, Benjamin Elijah. "The Relevance of Mordecai Wyatt Johnson for Our Times." Inaugural Address in the Mordecai Wyatt Johnson Lecture Series at Howard University, January 27, 1978.

Muse, Clifford L. Jr., ed. *Mordecai W. Johnson.* A souvenir brochure prepared in connection with the observance of the 100th anniversary of his birth. Washington, D.C.: Howard University, Moorland-Spingarn Research Center, January 12, 1990. Biographical sketch, photographs.

Doctoral Dissertations

Butler, Jenifer Bailey. "An Analysis of the Oral Rhetoric of Mordecai W. Johnson: A Study of the Concept of Presence." Ph.D. dissertation, Ohio State University, 1977.

Muse, Clifford L. Jr. "An Educational Stepchild: Howard University and the New Deal." Ph.D. dissertation, Howard University, 1989.

Articles

Carlson, Beverly C. "Pursuit of the Promise: An Overview." *American Baptist Quarterly* 9, no. 4 (December 1992): 282–89.
Editorial. "Mordecai Wyatt Johnson at Howard University: Review and an Assessment of His Years at Howard." Washington: *New Directions, The Howard University Magazine*, January 1977.
Donnelly, Shirley. "Genesis of Baptists in West Virginia." *American Baptist Historical Society Chronicle* 13, no. 1 (January 1950): 2–3.
Higginbothem, A. Leon. "An Open Letter to Clarence Thomas." *University of Pennsylvania Law Review* 140, no. 3 (January 1992): 1015.
Higgs, A. L. "A Tribute to Thurgood Marshall." *Harvard Law Review* 105, no. 1 (November 1991): 65.
Stirling, Ann Biddle. *Opportunity Magazine* 5, no. 3 (March 1927): 81.
Williams, George H. "Professor George La Piana (1878–1971), Catholic Modernist at Harvard (1915–1947)." *Harvard Library Bulletin* 21, no. 2 (November 1973): 64.

Journals and Newspapers

Atlanta World.
Baltimore Afro-American.
Chicago Defender.
Washington Afro-American.
Washington Post.
Washington Star.
Washington Times.
Washington Times Herald.
Time Magazine.
Jet 88, no. 2 (May 22, 1995): 54–58.

Interviews

William A. Brown, August 25, 1992.
John W. Davis, September 14, 1976.
Everett C. Herrick, October 1931.
Mordecai Wyatt Johnson, June 1972.
William H. Johnson, October 25, 1991.
Mrs. Clayton E. Kimbrough Sr., May 19, 1979.
Dr. John Q. Taylor King, September 11, 1987.
Josephine Herreld Love, February 1996.
The Reverend Oliver W. Willis, July 14, 1992.
Mrs. Robert Woodson, August 10, 1989.

Notes

1

The Early Years

1. Comments from *New York Post* on file at the Moorland-Spingarn Research Center (hereinafter MSRC) at Howard University in Box, Biographies, Mordecai W. Johnson.

2. Quoted in Barbara Baggett and David Cooper, *Henry County (Tenn.) Sesquicentennial (1823–1973) Brochure* (Paris, Tenn.: 1975), 2.

3. Beverly C. Carlson, "Pursuit of the Promise: An Overview," *American Baptist Quarterly* 9, no. 4 (December 1992): 283.

4. National Association for Equal Opportunity in Higher Education, pamphlet, n.d.

5. "Carolyn Freeman" is the name Mordecai gives as that of his mother in his typescript, "Autobiography of Mordecai W. Johnson, President Emeritus of Howard University." In the obituary he wrote for his father in April 1922, he used the name "Callie Allen" (MSRC, Mordecai Wyatt Johnson Papers, Box 178–8, Folder 14). Certain biographical accounts, notably Walter P. Dyson's *Howard University: Capstone of Negro Education, A History, 1867–1940,* p. 398, and Benjamin Brawley's *Negro Builders and Heroes,* p. 221, give Mordecai's mother's name as Carolyn Freeman Johnson. A possible explanation is that "Callie" was a nickname for "Carolyn" and that her middle name was Allen. Thus she was probably known in the community as Callie Allen. In any case, Mordecai named his first daughter Carolyn Elizabeth in recognition of the first names of her paternal and maternal grandmothers, respectively.

6. Cf., "History of the Mt. Zion Missionary Baptist Church, Paris, Tennessee" manuscript by the church historian, n.d.

7. MSRC, Box 178–8, Folder 14.

8. Mrs. Robert Woodson to Richard I. McKinney, August 10, 1989.

9. "History of Mt. Zion Missionary Baptist Church," op. cit.

10. Edwin R. Embree, *Thirteen Against the Odds* (Port Washington, N.Y.: Kennikat Press, 1944), 177.

11. Quoted in Embree, op. cit.

12. MSRC, Box 178–14, Folder 30.

13. Loc. cit.

14. MSRC, Box 178–14, Folder 18.

15. Thomas O. Fuller, *History of Negro Baptists in Western Tennessee* (Memphis, Tenn.: Thomas O. Fuller, 1936), 117.

16. MSRC, Box 178–15, Folder 14.

17. This and most of the accounts in this book relating to Alice Woodson are from a taped interview with her son from her first marriage, Dr. John Q. Taylor King, in Austin, Texas, September 11, 1987. The name "Clinton" is in honor of General Clinton B. Fisk, one of the founders of Fisk University.

18. Fawn Brody, *Thomas Jefferson, An Intimate Biography* (New York: Norton & Co., 1974), passim. Cf. also, *JET Magazine* 88, no. 2 (May 22, 1995): 54–58.

19. MSRC, Box 178–14, Folder 30.

2

Formative Years in Atlanta

1. Ridgely Torrence, *The Story of John Hope* (New York: Macmillan Co., 1948), 31ff.

2. Loc. cit.

3. William J. Harvey III, the son of William J. Harvey Jr., to Richard I. McKinney, 1995.

4. The John and Eugenia Hope Papers, Robert W. Wooduff Library at Atlanta University.

5. Atlanta Baptist College, *Catalogs*, 1906, 1907, 1908.

6. Quoted in Edward A. Jones, *A Candle in the Dark: The History of Morehouse College* (Valley Forge, Penn.: Judson Press, 1967), 149–50.

7. Atlanta Baptist College, *Annual Catalog, 1907–1908*, 24.

8. Frank L. Forbes, *The History of Athletics at Morehouse College, 1890–1966* (Atlanta: Morehouse College, 1967), 37.

9. John W. Davis to Richard I. McKinney, September 14, 1976.

10. Forbes, op. cit., 37.

11. John Q. Taylor King, op. cit.

3

Graduate School and Marriage

1. Quoted in an address on "The Social Responsibility of the Administrator," in *Academic Freedom in the United States. Papers contributed in the Fifteenth Annual*

Spring Conference of the Division of the Social Sciences, March 22, 23, 24, 1953, ed. Gustave Auzenne (Washington, D.C.: Howard University Press, 1953), 128–29.

2. William H. Johnson, son of Mordecai, to Richard I. McKinney, September 14, 1991.

3. William A. Brown, a relative of the Gardners, to Richard I. McKinney, August 25, 1992.

4. Edwin J. Cashin, *The Quest: A History of Public Education in Richmond County, Georgia,* (Augusta, Ga.: Richmond County Board of Education 1983), 74.

5. Ibid., 75.

6. Edwin J. Cashin. *The Story of Augusta.* (Augusta, Ga.: Richmond County Board of Education, 1980), 184.

7. From the archives of the Registrar's Office, Spelman College.

8. MSRC, Box 178–14, Folder 30.

9. Quoted from Mary White Ovington, *Portraits in Color* (New York: Viking Press, 1927), in Robert M. Bartlett, *They Work for Tomorrow* (New York: Association Press), 61.

10. Everett C. Herrick, president of Andover Newton, to Richard I. McKinney, October 1931.

11. Benjamin E. Mays, *Born to Rebel* (New York: Charles Scribner's Sons, 1971), 61.

12. Howard Thurman, *With Head and Heart: The Autobiography of Howard Thurman* (New York: Harcourt Brace Janovich, 1979), 45.

13. In 1925 with the election of the Reverend Everett Carlton Herrick as president, Newton abandoned its policy of racial discrimination and admitted all students on the basis of ability, academic preparation, and promise. Meanwhile, a year later, Newton Theological Institute and Andover Theological Seminary, founded in 1808 under the auspices of the Congregational Church, merged on the Newton campus and became what has since been known as the Andover Newton Theological School.

14. Rochester Theological Seminary, *General Catalog,* 1850–1920.

15. Walter Rauschenbusch, *Christianity and the Social Crisis* (New York: Macmillan Co., 1907).

16. Walter Rauschenbusch, *A Theology for the Social Gospel* (New York: Macmillan Co., 1917).

17. Mordecai W. Johnson to John Hope, June 3, 1914, MSRC, Box 178–6, Folder 1.

18. Mordecai W. Johnson to John Hope, March 29, 1914, ibid.

19. Mordecai W. Johnson to John Hope, November 4, 1914.

20. Rochester Theological School, *Catalog,* 1916, 26.

21. Loc. cit.

22. Rochester Theological Seminary, op. cit., 315.

23. MSRC, Box 178–14, Folder 1.

24. The John and Eugenia Hope Papers.

25. Josephine Harreld Love, the granddaughter of the Reverend Mr. William J. White, to Richard I. McKinney, 1995.

26. The John and Eugenia Hope Papers.

27. Embree, op. cit., 186–87.

4

The Charleston Pastorate

1. Richard H. Hill, *History of the First Baptist Church of Charleston, West Virginia* (Charleston, W.Va.: Privately published, 1934), 5, 6.
2. Ibid., 8, 9.
3. Mrs. Clayton E. Kimbrough Sr., to Richard I. McKinney, May 19, 1979.
4. Letter from the Registrar of the University of Chicago to Richard I. McKinney, March 25, 1990.
5. Mordecai W. Johnson, "The Templars," Bachelor of Divinity thesis, presented to the faculty of Rochester Theological Seminary, March 1, 1920.
6. Quoted in ibid., 1, from F. C. Wodehouse, *The Military and Religious Orders of the Middle Ages* (New York: Pott, Young and Co., 1879), 208.
7. *Encyclopedia Britannica*, Chicago, Vol. 22, 703.
8. George H. Williams, "Professor George La Piana (1878–1971), Catholic Modernist at Harvard (1915–1947)," *Harvard Library Bulletin* 21, no. 2 (November 1973): 64.
9. MSRC, Box 178-2, Folder 8.
10. Quoted in Marcus H. Bouleware, *The Oratory of Negro Leaders,* (Westport, Conn.: Negro Universities Press, 1964), 75.
11. Quoted in Michael A. Winston, ed., *Education for Freedom: A Documentary Tribute to Celebrate the Fiftieth Anniversary of the Election of Mordecai W. Johnson as President of Howard University* (Washington, D.C.: MSRC, 1976), 44–69. Also printed in full in the Appendix of this volume.
12. Ibid., 48.
13. MSRC, Box 178–14, Folder 31.
14. Ibid.
15. Benjamin Brawley, *Negro Builders and Heroes,* MSRC, Box 170–15, Folder 2.
16. These sermons are in Appendix A of this volume.
17. From the sermon on "Being Chosen," ibid.
18. Jesse Moorland to Mordecai W. Johnson, June 7, 1922.
19. Mordecai W. Johnson to Jesse Moorland, June 10, 1922.

5

Howard University Presidency—The Early Years

1. Rayford W. Logan, *Howard University: The First 100 Years, 1867–1967* (New York: New York University, 1969).
2. Cf., Donald Tewksbury, *The Founding of American Colleges and Universities Before the Civil War* (New York: Bureau of Publications, Teachers College, Columbia University, 1932), 55ff.
3. George Whipple, secretary of the American Missionary Society, was elected in late spring 1926, but declined to serve. Bishop John A. Gregg of the African Methodist Episcopal Church was elected June 8, 1926, but also declined to serve.

Cf., Walter P. Dyson, *History of Howard University, Capstone of Negro Education, 1867–1940* (Washington, D.C.: Howard University Graduate School, 1941), 384, 398.

4. Alain Locke, *The New Negro* (New York: Boni, 1925).

5. Sterling Brown, Arthur Paul Davis, and Ulysses Lee, *The Negro Caravan* (New York: Dryden, 1941).

6. Carter G. Woodson, *The Education of the Negro Before 1861* (New York: B. P. Putnam's Sons, 1915).

7. Dyson, op. cit., 363ff.

8. Raymond Wolters, *The New Negro on Campus: Black College Rebellions of the 1920s* (Princeton, N.J.: Princeton University Press, 1975), 112–18.

9. Dyson. op. cit., 375.

10. Loc. cit.

11. MSRC, Box 178–15, Folder 13.

12. Ibid.

13. Ibid.

14. *Who's Who in Colored America, 1933–1937,* 4th ed., Thomas Yenser, ed. (Brooklyn, N.Y.: Thomas Yenser, 1937).

15. MSRC, Box 178–14, Folder 15.

16. Ibid.

17. Ibid.

18. *Baltimore Afro-American,* July 3, 1926.

19. Ibid.

20. Logan, op. cit., 143.

21. MSRC, Box 178–15, Folder 17.

22. Ibid.

23. *Baltimore Afro-American,* July 31, 1926.

24. *Washington Post,* August 1, 1926.

25. *Baltimore Afro-American,* July 3, 1926.

26. The complete text of Johnson's Inaugural Address is included in the Appendix of this volume and also in Winston, op. cit., 20–32.

27. Winston, op. cit., 21.

28. Ibid., 22.

29. Ibid., 24.

30. MSRC, Box 178–14, Folder 30.

31. MSRC, Box 178–14, Folder 31.

32. Ibid., Box 178–14, Folder 30.

33. Microfilm copy of selected items in the Julius Rosenwald Fund archives in the Amistad Research Center from the originals at Fisk University (hereinafter JRF).

34. JRF.

35. JRF.

36. Clifford L. Muse Jr., "An Educational Stepchild: Howard University and the New Deal," Ph.D. dissertation, Howard University, 1989, 21.

37. JRF Papers, Box 247, Folder 13.

38. JRF Papers, Box 177, Folder 12.

39. JRF Papers, Box 247, Folder 13.

40. *Baltimore Afro-American,* April 4, 1931.

41. MSRC, Box 178–14, Folder 4.

42. Muse, op. cit., 388.

43. MSRC, Box 178–15, Folder 4.

44. *Encyclopedia Britannica,* 1965 ed., Vol. 4, 96–97. Also interview with General John Q. Taylor King, March 7, 1987.

45. MSRC, Box 178–15, Folder 4.

46. Genna Rae McNeil. *Groundwork: Charles Hamilton Houston and the Struggle for Civil Rights* (Philadelphia: University of Pennsylvania Press, 1983), 69–70; also Logan, op. cit., 266–67.

47. Michael D. Davis and Hunter R. Clark, *Thurgood Marshall: Warrior at the Bar, Rebel on the Bench* (New York: Carol Publishing Co., 1992), 55.

48. McNeil, op. cit., 84–85.

49. Logan, op. cit., 267–68.

50. Gilbert Ware, *William Hastie: Grace Under Pressure* (New York: Oxford University Press, 1984), 16–20.

51. A. Leon Higginbotham, "An Open Letter to Clarence Thomas," *University of Pennsylvania Law Review* 140, no. 3 (January 1992): 1015.

52. A. L. Higgs, "A Tribute to Thurgood Marshall," *Harvard Law Review* 105, no. 1 (November 1991): 65.

53. Dr. Herman Branson, speaking at the observance of the 100th anniversary of the birth of Mordecai W. Johnson, sponsored by the MSRC, January 12, 1990.

54. Muse, op. cit., 32.

55. John Hope Franklin, *From Slavery to Freedom* (New York: A. A. Knopf, first published in 1947, followed by a number of editions through the 1980s). As of early 1993, over a million copies of this text had been sold.

6

Howard University—Confrontations, Criticisms, and Recognition

1. The John and Eugenia Hope Papers.

2. Ibid.

3. Kenneth R. Manning, *Black Apollo of Science: The Life of Ernest Everett Just* (New York: Oxford University Press, 1988), 155–57.

4. JRF Papers, Box 248, Folder 1.

5. Ibid.

6. Ibid.

7. Ibid.

8. Ibid.

9. Ibid., Box 247, Folder 8.

10. Ibid., Box 247, Folder 9.

11. Ibid., Box 247, Folder 8.

12. Ibid., Box 248, Folder 6.

13. From a videotaped address on the administration of Mordecai W. Johnson at a symposium in honor of the 100th anniversary of his birth, in the MSRC archives, Howard University, January 12, 1990.

14. Logan, op. cit., 284–85.
15. Quoted in ibid., 286.
16. Cf., Rayford W. Logan, "The Diary of Rayford Logan," Library of Congress, Manuscript Division, 1943.
17. Ibid.
18. Ibid.
19. Harold Lewis, from an address given during the symposium celebrating the 100th anniversary of the birth of Mordecai Wyatt Johnson, videotape, MSRC, Howard University, January 12, 1990.
20. JRF Papers, Box 247, Folder 4.
21. JRF Papers, Box 247, Folder 5.
22. Ibid.
23. From *Who's Who in Colored America, 1933–1937,* 4th ed. (Brooklyn, N.Y.: Thomas Yenser, 1937), 460–61.
24. JRF Papers, Box 247, Folder 5.
25. Logan, op. cit., 340–41.
26. JRF Papers, Box 246, Folder 5.
27. Quoted by Dyson, op. cit., 437.
28. JRF Papers, Box 247, Folder 5.
29. *Baltimore Afro-American,* December 1, 1934.
30. JRF Papers, Box 247, Folder 6.
31. JRF Papers, Box 247, Folder 6.
32. From the archives of the MSRC, Howard University.
33. Ibid.
34. "The Trials of a President," *Time Magazine,* March 20, 1938.
35. Ibid.
36. Logan, "Diary," op. cit.
37. Reported in *The Atlanta World,* March 22, 1935.
38. *Chicago Defender,* March 19, 1938. Also JFR Papers, Box 247, Folder 8.
39. Ibid.
40. Ibid.
41. JRF Papers, op. cit.
42. Mordecai W. Johnson to Richard I. McKinney, January 1949.
43. Benjamin E. Mays, "The Relevance of Mordecai Wyatt Johnson," Inaugural Address of the Mordecai Wyatt Johnson Lecture Series, Howard University, January 27, 1978.
44. Mordecai W. Johnson to Richard I. McKinney, June 1972.
45. Mordecai W. Johnson to John Q. Taylor King, quoted in taped interview with Richard I. McKinney, November 11, 1987.
46. Logan, "Diary," op. cit.
47. The 17th Annual Charter Day dinner program on file at the MSRC.
48. Mordecai Wyatt Johnson, "Significant Items in the Development of Howard University During the Period from July 1, 1926, to June 30, 1942." A memorandum from Mordecai W. Johnson to Edwin Embree, JRF Papers, Book 247, Folder 13.
49. Ibid.
50. Ibid.

51. Quoted in an address on "The Social Responsibility of the Administrator," in *Academic Freedom in the United States: Papers contributed in the Fifteenth Annual Spring Conference of the Division of the Social Sciences, March 22, 23, 24, 1953* (Washington, D.C.: Howard University Press, 1953).

7

Howard University—The Later Years

1. Logan, op. cit., 423.
2. The Reverend Oliver W. Willis to Richard I. McKinney, July 14, 1992.
3. These accounts of the Johnson's family life are from a taped interview with one of his sons, William H. Johnson (October 25, 1991), and from remarks by his older daughter, Carolyn Johnson Graves, during the observance of the 100th anniversary of his birth, January 12, 1990.
4. See the full text of this address in the Appendix.
5. Quoted in *New Directions, The Howard University Magazine,* January 1977, 19.
6. Ibid.
7. *Washington Sunday Star,* November 20, 1960.
8. Ibid.

8

The Incisive Orator

1. Mordecai W. Johnson to Richard I. McKinney, October 1949.
2. Ann Biddle Stirling, *Opportunity Magazine* 5, no. 3 (March 1927): 81.
3. Quoted in Benjamin Brawley, op. cit., MSRC, Box 170–1, Folder 2.
4. Jenifer Bailey Butler, "An Analysis of the Oral Rhetoric of Mordecai W. Johnson: A Study of the Concept of Presence," Ph.D. dissertation, Ohio State University, 1977.
5. In an address titled "Platform for Freedom," *Baltimore Afro-American,* January 15, 1954.
6. Rosalyn Carter, wife of President Jimmy Carter, is quoted as saying that President Ronald Reagan made people "comfortable with their prejudices."
7. *Washington Afro-American,* January 6, 1945.
8. *Washington Afro-American,* January 30, 1943.
9. Logan, "Diary," op. cit.
10. *Washington Afro-American,* May 9, 1942.
11. A radio address, February 12, 1941, typescript on file at MSRC, 12.
12. *Washington Afro-American,* December 11, 1943.
13. *Pittsburgh Courier,* May 26, 1943.
14. *Washington Afro-American,* November 27, 1947.
15. Douglas Hall in *Baltimore Afro-American Magazine,* November 27, 1947.

16. *Norfolk Journal and Guide,* November 10, 1940.

17. Mordecai W. Johnson, "Prophets of Unsegregated Institutions," an address delivered at the inauguration of Charles S. Johnson as president of Fisk University, pamphlet, 1948.

18. *Washington Evening Star,* March 4, 1952.

19. *Washington Times Herald,* December 16, 1957.

20. *Washington Afro-American,* March 23, 1963.

21. Quoted in Michael R. Winston, op. cit., 36.

22. Ibid., 40.

23. Ibid., 43.

24. David Garrow, *Bearing the Cross—Martin Luther King, Jr., and the Southern Christian Leadership Conference* (New York: William J. Morrow and Co., 1986), 96.

9

Another Beginning

1. *Washington Afro-American,* March 23, 1963.

2. Ibid.

3. *Washington Afro-American,* October 19, 1965.

4. *Washington Evening Star,* June 23, 1965.

5. Ibid.

6. *Washington Post,* June 24, 1965.

7. *Washington Evening Star,* July 23, 1965.

8. *Washington Post,* June 24, 1925.

9. Ibid.

10. Mordecai W. Johnson to Richard I. McKinney, May 1966.

11. Memoirs on file at the MSRC, Mordecai Wyatt Johnson Papers, Boxes 178–14.

12. *Washington Star,* March 3, 1969.

13. The Reverend Evans Crawford, dean of the Andrew Rankin Memorial Chapel, Howard University, to Richard I. McKinney, October 1992.

14. Program on file in the MSRC, Howard University.

15. From the taped interview with Dr. John Q. Taylor King, op. cit.

16. Dr. Theophilus E. McKinney Jr. to Richard I. McKinney, September 1991.

17. Alvin Pouissaint, "Black Children: Coping in a Racist Society," *Vital Issues* 1, no. 2 (Winter 1992): 2.

18. Peter F. Drucker, *Adventures of a Bystander* (New York: Harper & Brothers, 1979), 10.

19. *Paris (Tenn.) Post-Intelligencer,* April 27, 1972.

20. *Washington Post,* September 17, 1976.

21. *Washington Star,* September 15, 1976.

22. *The Hilltop*, September 17, 1976.

Mordecai Wyatt Johnson　　　　　　　　　Moorland-Spingarn Research Center, Howard University

Alice Woodson as a young woman   Moorland-Spingarn Research Center, Howard University

Mordecai W. Johnson as a young man   Moorland-Spingarn Research Center, Howard University

Alice Woodson King Johnson Moorland-Spingarn Research Center, Howard University

The Primrose Club, Memphis, Tennessee. Mordecai Johnson and Alice Woodson second row from the back, fourth and fifth from the left, respectively.

Moorland-Spingarn Research Center, Howard University

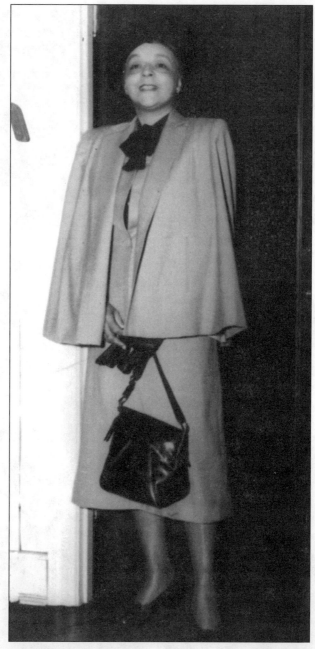

Mrs. Anna Ethelyn Johnson

Moorland-Spingarn Research Center,
Howard University

The extended Johnson family.

Moorland-Spingarn Research Center, Howard University

Left to right: Dr. Mordecai Johnson and Dr. John W. Davis receiving honors in Monrovia, Liberia

Left to right: Dr. and Mrs. James Nabrit and Dr. and Mrs. Mordecai W. Johnson at the retirement banquet.   Moorland-Spingarn Research Center, Howard University

Mordecai W. Johnson, the orator.   Moorland-Spingarn Research Center, Howard University

A. *Sermons from the Early Years*

A. *Sermons from the Early Years*

Charleston, West Virginia
July and August 1924

At age thirty-four, only two years after his study at Harvard, Mordecai Johnson was a more impressive speaker than ever. Thus, some members of his church in Charleston felt that his sermons should be recorded. Accordingly, they employed the services of a court stenographer to come to the church on six Sundays during July and August 1924 to take down his sermons in shorthand. A typescript of these sermons is reproduced in this appendix. As you read the transcription, you should be able to hear the voice and message of Mordecai.

1. The Blindness of Obsession

In this sermon, Mordecai Johnson calls attention, especially that of young people, to various obsessions that render people blind to the crucial issues of life. Among the obsessions he names are the struggle for riches; the denigration of certain types of honest labor; and the belief that the acquisition of book learning by itself, of getting into the "right" social group, of developing an industrialized society, or of following the crowd will bring fullness of life.

Mordecai urges young people to be wary of all attempts to obtain their blind allegiance, as well as to critically analyze and evaluate all things and to "learn to keep their eyes open."

THE BLINDNESS OF OBSESSION[1]

TEXT: Matthew 20:33—"Lord, that our eyes may be opened."

Two blind men were sitting on the roadside from Jericho. They were no doubt very unconscious, at the moment, of their blindness. No doubt they had been blind for a long time and they had sought out one another's companionship. And no doubt they were sitting on the side of the road listening to what sounds they could hear as they conversed with one another, quite unconscious of their infirmity because they were used to it. But in a few moments they heard the tramping of a mighty multitude coming down the road from Jericho, and somebody in the vanguard of that multitude let out the word that Jesus of Nazareth was passing by. Immediately those two men became acutely conscious of their blindness.

I do not know all the hundreds of reasons that might be given for those men becoming acutely conscious of their blindness at this time, but among all the reasons that had been given hitherto, certainly there was one new one. They had no doubt heard of Jesus, the Son of David. They had heard of the cures he had worked, the immediate effect that he had had upon the minds and bodies and the souls of other men, and—well, he was passing by for the only time in the world that they might get a chance to see him. They became acutely conscious of the fact that the only thing they wanted to do, they could not do, and that was to see his face. Not only did these men become acutely conscious of their blindness, but also their consciousness was a hopeful consciousness. When they heard about this Jesus, immediately they felt that there was some hope that they might see him. So they began to cry, "Jesus, Son of David, have mercy on us." It was the cry of men acutely conscious of their needs and men hopeful in the presence of a mighty personality that they might find healing for their blindness.

It is strange that they very disciples of Jesus were those who began to discourage the men. They did what we call "shooing them off." They said to the men, "Don't make so much noise. Don't bother the Master." I don't know what was in their minds, but put it down to something like this: "You are just two blind men, and the world is full of blind men. There are hundreds of blind men who never have seen from their birth, and thousands have wanted to get cured just as you do, but they have died still blind. The chances that you can be cured of your blindness are so very few, why raise all this raucous and disturb the Master?"

---

[1]July 13, 1924.

Others there probably had in their minds the idea that the Master was interested in a large political or social question that he called the "Kingdom of God" and did not think he should be bothered with two ordinary and perhaps ragged blind men sitting on the side of the road crying. So they insisted that these two men stop calling and let the Master pass by. But the two men could not be stopped. The fact that Jesus of Nazareth with his God-illumined face was going by made them want to see him, made them feel that it was a terrible thing to be blind when Jesus of Nazareth was passing by. And they continued to cry because they could not help themselves, "Jesus, the Son of David, have mercy on us!" And they continued to cry, because they felt that all of the things that they had felt about Jesus were not mistakes, not lies, not misunderstandings. It made no difference how far away he might be, there was a man with a heart and with power to give sight to their eyes if he could only be made to hear.

Now, young people are often asking in these days why it is that we can keep on talking about this Jesus who lived and died 1900 years ago. Why is it that we are interested in our particular present-day problems, some of which Jesus himself never had to face? Why is it that we have institutions like the church and individuals like so-called Christians who continually go around the world and say, "Have you seen Jesus?" or "Have you come to Jesus?" or "Have you made it right with God?" And there are times when our young men and our sophisticated men of brains out in the world fall almost over when we keep on saying to them, "Come to Jesus." "Have you seen Jesus?" "Have you got right with Jesus?"

And if you ask me one of the reasons we keep on presenting Jesus to you, you will find it right here in the experience of these blind men. When Jesus lived and came near people, he made those people acutely conscious of their needs, and he filled them with a hope that somehow they might overcome their troubles and their blindnesses and their weaknesses and see and be new creatures. That is why we keep on telling you about Jesus. Jesus fills men with an acute and hopeful feeling that there is something the matter with you and that he can make it all right. And when he was alive, not only did he do that to people who were sick in their bodies, but also he did it to people who were sick in their minds and in their souls. One reason Jesus is continually interesting and challenging to this modern world is the things that he troubled men about when he was on earth in his day are the same things that he will trouble men about today if they will listen to him. While he did not face our problems in just the way that we are facing them, he faced the fundamental principles of them. If we will come near to Jesus today in any walk of life, he will make us acutely and hopefully conscious of our weaknesses and our needs, and at the same time make us feel that he is the one to guide us to a way of salvation.

I want to call your attention this morning to some of the blind spots that Jesus discussed in his days. Men in all ages have been made blind by certain obsessions, certain things that consume their minds and make them unable to see. One of the obsessions that seized upon the minds of men in Jesus' day was the obsession that riches, in themselves, are able to satisfy the deepest hunger of a man's life. And that is true today. In all ages, there have been multitudes of people who have felt that "if I could just get my hands on enough money, I would be perfectly happy." They are divided into all kinds of groups. There are some who feel that they must get it honestly, and there are some who feel that they must get it anyhow. But in all ages of the world, there have been multitudes of men and women, and especially in their youth, who have felt that if they could get their hands on enough money, they would be perfectly happy.

Now I want to carry you back to a day when a young man who had gotten his hands on enough money met Jesus. I don't want to pick out a rich man who had gotten his money wrongfully; I want to pick out a clean, upright young man. You remember where the New Testament says the rich young ruler came to Jesus. He was a rich man and a ruler and a decent man, because he said he had kept all the commandments from his youth up. And when Jesus looked upon the honest riches and upon the honest, dignified ruler's stature, and saw that he was a clean man who had gotten everything that he had honestly, the Scripture says Jesus "loved him."

But what happened to that young man? Just as soon as he saw Jesus, he began to feel just like the blind men on the roadside: "There is something the matter with me. I can't tell just exactly what it is. I have felt it before, but I have never felt it as strongly as I feel it today as I look into the face of this man Jesus. As I look at this man who is standing here with his simple garments on, with no place to lay his head, with no high position in society, and with no bank account or no great investment, and as I hear him talking and see the light that beams from his eyes, there is something in my heart that tells me there is something the matter with me and I don't know what it is."

And the rich young ruler ran up to Jesus and said, "Lord, what shall I do to inherit eternal life?" My friends, I am not talking a fallacy. I am not talking the theories of any man. I am telling you about a rich young man who had plenty of money and not only had plenty of money but also had a high position in the world. Not only did he have plenty of money and a high position, but also he was a good man who had kept the ten commandments from his youth. When he looked into the face of Jesus, he felt that he had missed the main thing for which a man ought to live. At that moment he said, "Lord, what shall I do to have eternal life?" And one of the reasons why I stand in this pulpit and continually talk to young people about Jesus is I know that today some obsession is in your minds. It is in the minds of the young people of the city of Charleston. There are hundreds of young people today whose minds are filled with the conviction that if they could just get their hands on enough money, everything would be all right. Some boys are trampling over their mothers, are wounding the hearts of their sisters and brothers, and are doing things that will make us sorry as long as we live.

I want to call your attention to the fact that you young men are like this young ruler. After he had gotten it all—and after you have gotten your high position in the world—one of these days you, like the young ruler, are going to face Jesus. When you face him, you are going to know that you have missed what life was meant for. You have missed the substance of life, and you will have to come at last to Jesus and say, "Lord, what shall *I* do to have eternal life?"

There is another obsession that men have been under in all ages of life. It is so closely connected that I want to speak of it now: the obsession that when a fellow is doing a piece of work, if it isn't acceptable to us, why, he can't be any account. Really, he just may be rich, but he can't be right.

Now there was a whole class of people among the Jews called Publicans. The Publicans were making their living in a way that was not satisfactory to the Jews. They were tax collectors for the Roman government. The Roman government had taken the political independence away from the Jews and collected taxes from them. The Publicans were the men who saw that the taxes were collected, and many of the Publicans no doubt used their position for graft. Because the Publicans were, in general, grafters, and because the work they were doing was generally reprehensible to the Jews, there came to be a general feeling among the Jews of Palestine, especially the Jews of the higher class, that no man could be a Publican and a gentlemen.

We feel an obsession today, for example, for politics. We have so much corruption in our politics—so many men have used the offices of the people to get graft for themselves—that we have almost come to the conclusion, as many religious people have, that a man can't be a successful politician and get a nice home for himself, and so forth, unless he is a grafter.

Well, now, Zacchaeus was a man who was hurt by that obsession of the people of that day. Zacchaeus used to say to his people, "I am an honest man. I am a Publican, but I am an honest man. I get my living honestly."

But the people said, "You are a Publican. No man can be honest and be a Publican." But way down in Zacchaeus' heart, he knew that although he occupied a place that was reprehensible in the sight of his fellow men, he was conducting himself in a way that was pleasing to the God of Abraham. And when he—one of the most pathetic figures in the New Testament—heard that Jesus was coming along, he climbed up in a sycamore tree. He climbed way up there in order that he might look at Jesus' face. As he saw Jesus coming by, the eagerness with which he fastened his eyes upon Jesus made him feel that there was a man with something that he wanted.

Now, what was Zacchaeus wanting? He wanted to know what this little secret thing was that there had been so much talk about—if a man could be a Publican and a honest man. Is this little secret thing right, or must I accept the general judgment of my fellow citizens? And they went to Zacchaeus' house. And these people wondered when Jesus went to Zacchaeus' house if Zacchaeus would bring out his pile of money and tell Jesus how much he had. Zacchaeus reached down in the secret place of his heart and said, "Master, there is one thing I have kept down in my heart. Half of my goods I give to the poor, and if I have taken anything from any man wrongly, I will come back and give it to him fourfold."

Jesus looked at him and said, "You who are a son of Abraham, you have got an unclean job; live like a son of Abraham under hard circumstances. Blessed is your house."

My friends, the world of politics has become so corrupt in American life today that even when a man of good sense goes into it, people are willing to say that there is something wrong about him somehow. If you will just search him, you will find that there is something right in that man somewhere. But, my friends, if politics in America are going to be clean, some clean men must go into them. Those men must bear all that the people have to say about them.

Another obsession that men have labored under from time immemorial and that young people are going after today with tooth and club is the obsession that a certain amount of book learning—if you just get enough of it—is a sure road to happiness: "If I just get a certain amount of book learning, I am just certain to be happy." And so we look up at our colleges and our universities, and we see the degrees of Bachelor of Arts, Bachelor of Science, Bachelor of Philosophy, Master of Arts, and Master of Sciences. Above all, we look up at that sweet degree of Doctor of Philosophy and we say to ourselves, "If I could just manage by any means to get hold of one of those degrees, why, happiness is right in my hands. I will just have it. I will be certain about it."

Well, there were undoubtedly men like that in Jesus' day. There was the Sanhedrin, for example, that was composed of men of learning and dignity—men who had political wisdom, economic wisdom, and religious wisdom. They sat there in Jerusalem to be the guides and leaders of the Jewish people. Among them was a man named Nicodemus. He knew, undoubtedly, that he had political wisdom, economic wisdom, and religious wisdom sufficient to be the leader of his people for several years. One day he was passing by a crowd of men, and he looked over into a little place and saw the clean, clear eye of the Lord Jesus. As soon as he saw that, he became discontented with his place in the Sanhedrin with all its economic and political wisdom. Away in the hours of midnight when nobody could see him, he slipped over to the place where Jesus lived and said, "Master, no man can do these things that thou doest except God be with him. Master, give me the secret and the help that you have." Now, that is just what I am talking about, my friends—the very sight of Jesus and the very hearing of Jesus are sufficient to make a man discontented with himself.

On another day, pressing this same point, two men from Greece came to the little place where Jesus was staying, and they saw one of his disciples standing there. They said to one of his disciples, "Sir, we would see Jesus." Now, who were the Greeks? Any historian will tell you that they were the most learned and wonderful people in this world, were the Greeks. They were men of wisdom. They were the foundation of modern science. They had temples and palaces of art and things of beauty and an intelligence that surpassed any of the ancient nations that surrounded them. But when these Greeks got a little bit of the word of Jesus that drifted out, perhaps, from the mouth of some Jew who had slipped out from Jerusalem, they became discontented with all the wisdom of Greece and went to Jerusalem searching out this man, even this man who understood a wisdom deeper than that which came from the schools of philosophy. And when they got to Jerusalem, they cried out, "Sirs, we would see Jesus"—pressing the same point.

My friends, there was another man who was trained in the best wisdom of the Jewish schools—trained at the feet of Gamaliel, the leading teacher of his time. Not only was he trained in Hebrew, but also he could quote Greek poetry and was acquainted with all of the learning of his time. When he went outside his own land over into Greece, he could stand up there at Athens and at Corinth, the most learned places in the whole Grecian world, and talk to the Greeks, quoting their poets, concerning the spiritual realities of life. But when Paul on the road to Damascus caught a vision of Jesus of Nazareth, it blinded him for a time, but it ruined for him the fame of this world. After he got up from that vision of Jesus Christ, he said, "All things that I have ever known, I cast them away as dung if I might know this man Jesus and come into the fellowship of his wisdom."

And I say to you that no people, no man, could call me a disparager of the wisdom of this world. I have spent twenty-six or thirty years of my life seeking it. I know its value. I know how necessary it is to know economics. I know how necessary it is to know sociology. I know how necessary it is to study biology and master mathematics and chemistry, but I know also that all these things may be separated from the childlike wisdom that comes from the simple and lowly home of Jesus of Nazareth. It is only those who know the wisdom of Jesus of Nazareth who are ever going to be able to do any good in this world or ever be able to be happy.

There is another obsession that has taken hold of men of all times and that is the obsession that the man who is busy is the man who is our benefactor. Show me a man who is continually busy, and I will show you the world's benefactor. Now, Jesus knew that type, and God knows we have got that type today. We have exalted the man who is at his office every morning at 8:00 o'clock and leaves at 5:00 and has spent his whole day buying peanuts at twenty cents a gallon and selling them at fifty cents a gallon. We have those in this age who are disposed to think that we have made great progress because a man devotes all of his time from 8:00 o'clock in the morning until 5:00 o'clock in the secret of the universe.

Jesus came in contact with that type of belief in his day, for in his day he went to the home of Mary and Martha one day, you remember, and Martha got busy with her domestic science and she and Mary went out in the kitchen. I can see them right now. Martha went to picking a chicken, and Mary went into the dining room to get a fork. And while she was in there, Jesus said, "Mary, I want to say a word to you." And Mary forgot all about the fork, and Jesus' conversation became so interesting that she laid down the fork and sat down at his feet.

And Martha was picking the chicken, fixing dinner, and after a while missed Mary. Then she came out and said, "Master, make my sister come out and help me in the kitchen so we can fix this dinner."

And Jesus said to her, "Martha, thou art careful and troubled about many things. But one thing is needful."

What was Mary doing, my friends? There was something that Jesus said to her while she had the fork in her hand that raised a question about the meaning of all this activity, and that is one of the glorious things that Jesus does for busy people. Here you have got yourself fixing dinner, ordering flowers, buying fine linen, and putting nice things on your table, and so busy. Then comes the word of Jesus, who says, "What is the meaning of all this? Is life more than meat, or is it just meat? Does life consist of beautiful apparel, or is there something deeper than beautiful apparel? Is life being able to reach all men everywhere, or is life being able to understand and penetrate into deeper mysteries of things after you get there?"

Oh, my friends, if you and I could listen to Jesus today. If you and I could just do that today. We are all just as busy as we can be selling our lives and our souls for what? Jesus asks you the question, "For what? For what are you doing all this activity? For what are you piling up all this energy? They also serve who only stand and wait." They also serve who lay down the hammer and the plow and the mallet and go into some house of God and bow down with humble men and pray. They also serve who shut themselves in their closets and think hours and hours and hours, because those are the people who are trying to understand what the meaning of all this is. They are likely to come out and give us a pathway of action that will be salvation to our souls and our homes.

There is another obsession, and it is just here that we Americans have a sophisticated asininity. We think that because we have more smoke coming out of our smokestacks and more express going down the road and more railroad trains running than anybody else that we have got the proudest civilization on earth and have made all the great advances in the world. But if we walk over to China, into that civilization that has been in existence for 6,000 years, and where the courtesy that is manifested between a daughter and her mother is something we Americans can hardly dream of, if we go over there, with all our trains and our automobiles, we are conscious then that they may have more than any civilization. Why, we are just sophisticated fools. Those men have been walking on their soles for 6,000 years, and the dignity and beauty and loveliness that prevail in a Chinese home where the mother is respected as though she were the daughter of God is amazing to us Americans. And every day, before men go out to their labor, they look at the tablets of their ancestors and bow down and swear that "This day I will live in honor; I will live in dignity; I will live in purity. And when I come back home from my labor this day, I will not lay a strain on the altars of my fathers."

And Jesus comes among us and raises questions about all this vigorous activity that we are going through. We need more calm. We need to be quiet. We need more prayer. We need more thoughtfulness. We need more people who have the courage to be led to sit down and think over the meaning of life.

Another obsession that has always taken possession of the men of the world is that if you can only belong to the right group, you can be happy; if you can only belong to the right group, you can be happy. It is not sufficient for you to do this or that, but you must be careful and belong to the right group. We have about 215 denominations in America. You be sure that you know all about these denominations and choose carefully the right one, or else you can be off.

Now, there are several social classes in Charleston. Be careful, you young lady coming in here. Don't fall in with the wrong group. If you get with the wrong group, you are just wrong, just wrong, just wrong. There are several races in America, and for God's sake don't get tangled up with the wrong race. If you can't be an Anglo-Saxon, why then be a Spaniard. For God's sake don't be a Negro, for you have to belong to the right group in order to be happy.

Now, my friends, not only did that obsess the people of other days but also it obsesses us. You can hear it right around in Charleston today: "If you only get in the right group, you will be all right." A little morality, supposed morality, in this world today is just a thick coat of varnish that people put over themselves in order to keep themselves respectable in a group that they have no business in whatsoever. But Jesus struck at that. He was going along one day, passing along the borders of Sychar. On entering the city, he said to his disciples, "I see a well by the way here, and I am thirsty and will take a drink of water. If you will go over and buy me something to eat, I will wait here for you."

While they were sitting at the well, there came a woman up with a pitcher, with her head high and the pitcher sitting on her shoulder and dressed in lovely garments. She was a Samaritan, and the Samaritans and the Jews had been hating one another for 500 years. They hated one another so badly that if a Jew was getting married and a Samaritan happened to be present and his Samaritan eyes fell upon the marriage certificate, it was illegal and had to be thrown into the trash basket and a new certificate issued. They would not sit down and eat with one another and would not read out of the same Bible. They would not worship along the same lines.

And this Samaritan woman came along and saw this Jew sitting there. Then Jesus said, "I am thirsty. Will you give me a drink?"

No doubt a great lump came up in her heart and she said, "What do you mean? I am a Samaritan woman come to draw water. The Jews and Samaritans don't have any dealings with one another. I have a mind and belief that if your friends had not gone off yonder, you would not ask me for a drink of water—me, a Samaritan woman; but now you are willing to ask a Samaritan woman whom you hate for a drink of water. No! Got no drink of water! Have no dealings with one another." There she was. She was showing Jesus how the Samaritans actually hated a Jew. "We worship God in this mountain, and you worship in Jerusalem. Both of us can't be right. If I am right, you must be wrong, and if you are right, I can't be right."

"Listen," Jesus said to the woman, "if you knew who it was that speaks to you, and if you knew what I had to give you, you would forget all about this pitcher and you would say to me, 'Master, let me have some of that water that you have in your heart.' For I tell you, woman, that the time will come when you shall neither worship in this mountain nor at Jerusalem; for God is a Spirit, and they that worship him must worship him in spirit and in truth."

And the woman was so discouraged at what Jesus had said to her that she forgot all about the water, threw the pitcher down on the ground, went back to the city, and said, "Come and see this man who has told me about the meaning of life."

And twenty years from that day, reflecting on what Jesus had said to that woman, it was Paul who burst out and said, "In Christ Jesus there is neither Jew nor Greek, neither bond nor free, neither male nor female; for in Christ Jesus all men are made of one blood."

Oh, if we just had that today! If the Christian churches would just have that! If we could just get it out of our minds that if we get in the right group, we will be all right.

Another obsession that belongs to the other side is "If I have fallen out of the right group and the right group has put its foot on me and despises me, well then I might as well stay where I am." Oh, don't we have that today? "If I have committed adultery and my family has denied me and my social group have cast me out, then I might as well go on down, for life does not mean anything more to me." "I have stolen something or been put in jail and have got the disgrace and stigma of it on me. Life is not worth living."

Jesus met that group. There was a whole group of people in that day called sinners, and sinners were those who didn't have anything to do with the orthodox religion. They had done something against the law—committed adultery or stolen or had been cast out—and the Pharisees despised the sinners. While Jesus went along one day, a group of sinners invited him to dinner, and he went and sat down. A woman was there who had been taken in adultery, and this woman had done something kind today. Somebody spoke about it, and Jesus fastened his eyes on her and said, "Daughter, what a beautiful deed. If the world could be filled with what you have done today, the Kingdom of Heaven would have come in."

The woman got up from the table, went back to the place where she lived, looked at the bed, looked at her companions, and she could be contented no more, no more. She could sell that body of hers no more. She could talk wild talk no more. There was a pure, clean man that had looked into her eyes and said, "Daughter, you have got lovable qualities in you; you have got lovable qualities." She nursed that in her bosom and day by day became a new creature until one night she saw Jesus sitting down at supper. She ran into the room, washed his feet with the tears from her eyes, and wiped them with her hair.

Jesus disturbs folks. He comes into your presence and makes you feel the wicked world is about you. "I can look way down in you and see something that is precious to the living God. If you will just let that grow and be sweet and strong, you can redeem the world." I don't blame that woman. I don't blame her.

The obsession that you are in the wrong class has nothing to do with the victory and beauty and glory of your life if you have once seen Jesus. You know a lily can grow in a mud pond as well as in the vegetable kingdom.

Now the last obsession that I want to talk about is one that is peculiarly characteristic of people who live in a democracy like our government, and that obsession is this: When the majority of people are going this way, it stands to reason that happiness is in that direction.

Now you just consider our mind processes. How often a daughter comes home today and says, "Mamma, I want to go to such and such a place."

And her mother says, "Daughter, I think it would be better for you to go to such and such a place."

But the daughter is used to arguments, and she says to her, "Mother, the rest of the girls are going to this place, and I don't see why I can't go. It stands to reason that if the majority of people are going in this direction that it must be right, and the people who stand off from this majority must be wrong, must be wrong."

You hear that everywhere today. "The majority of people are looking out for themselves. Why shouldn't I look out for myself?"

Jesus met that type in his day. He came with a message of salvation for his people, but they followed the majority. And one of the saddest things in the world is to stand up and see a great man like Woodrow Wilson with a mind fifty years ahead of his generation having to submit to the puny votes of a group of men who have no conception of what he is thinking about and no conception of his vision for the salvation of the people. Jesus met that type in his day.

My friends, listen: If you are going to do anything in this world, you must stand off. That is what Woodrow Wilson said. That is what Theodore Roosevelt said. That is what Abraham Lincoln said. Once when there was just a little handful of men sitting by his side, Jesus looked at them and said, "Will you too leave me?"

And Simon Peter, who had come out from the majority, looked up at him and said, "Master, where shall we go? Will you tell us? Thou hast the words of eternal life."

And the obsession of the majority is the obsession of men's minds. The virtue of the world has never resided in the majority. God's great leaders have always been crucified. God's great leaders have always stood up before the people and said, "If any man will be my disciple, let him take up his cross and follow me." When the multitudes have seen the cross, they have always run. Only a few who have caught sight of the vision have followed it and caught the words of eternal life.

That reminds me of one more obsession, and then I am through. An obsession has gotten into the minds of men that where there is suffering, there is unhappiness. If you want to be happy, avoid all suffering.

Now, my friends, Jesus met that in his day. You know his answer to that man. He said, "If any man will be my disciple, he must deny his mother and his father and leave his houses and his lands and be wherever I am. I say unto you if any man will be my disciple, let him take up his cross and follow me." In the Garden of Gethsemane, after he had spoken to his soul and prayed to God, Jesus said to his disciples, "Come on. The Son of Man is betrayed and must be crucified for the redemption of many."

Paul through his suffering had come to feel that in some deep sense, the deepest happiness is connected with the deepest suffering, for he says, "I have not yet apprehended, but this thing I want to do: I want to enter into fellowship with his sufferings and be partaker in his death." Paul discovered that the way to happiness is the way to the cross. The suffering man is the man who lays hold on the realities of life, and the one who runs from the cross runs from life.

But let's come back to the blind men for about five minutes. When Jesus had come and these blind men in their trouble cried out, it was the very disciples of Jesus who tried to stop them. Mark you that, my friends. The very disciples of Jesus were the ones who tried to stop the blind men. Don't you know that today the greatest reason the hungry young man, who wants to understand life as it is, can't get to Jesus is Jesus' disciples are in his way—in his way. For year and years and years, the disciples of Jesus have been holding up to the young men the theological Christ: the pre-existent Son of God who came down in trails of glory and was born at Bethlehem and endowed with miraculous power of overcoming all things before him and ascended into heaven—who met the tribulations of men face to face, met all problems squarely, looked all men in the face, and challenged all men to come to him because he had eternal life.

When I preach Jesus today, my friends, I am not preaching the theological Christ who came down in trailing clouds of glory from some miraculous and material heaven up yonder. I am preaching the spirit of the love of God that walked in the consciousness of a man like you and me. And, bless you, when you have looked into his face, you will never be satisfied in this world anymore until you learn that God is love.

Another way that the disciples of Jesus have gotten in his way of men's understanding is that we have got too many denominations. In former years, we have spent the greater portion of our time talking about "my church," "my way of serving the sacraments," "my way of opening church," "my way of fixing up the window glass." We have become so busy quarreling over the kind of house in which Jesus shall be worshipped and the kind of ceremony with which we shall worship Jesus that the hungering minds of young people have run from us—because they want to know how to live the higher life, because they can get houses for themselves. Any intelligent young man can get along. But he wants to know and understand life, and he wants us to quit disputing about denominationalism and forms and ceremonies, and tell him what he must do to live a life in Jesus and to have some of that life in him.

There is another way in which the disciples of Jesus have gotten in the way of young men's understanding of him. Why, right here in Charleston we have group distinctions in the Christian religion, one race worshipping God over there on Quarrier Street with ushers standing like sentinels at every door to keep other races out; another race over here talking about "This is a colored church"; another one talking about "This is a High Church" and "This is a Low Church," making God the God of a race, when he is the God of the human race. And no man has the right to come between young men and young women in that way.

If you will read the newspapers of Japan, you will see that the leaders are saying to the young Japanese Christians and to the Japanese missionaries, they are saying, "If you come with the spirit of Jesus, we will listen to you; but if you come talking of your racial superiority and materialistic civilization, stay at home. We want to see Jesus; we want to see him; we don't want to see you."

That is the trouble today. I say to you young men and young women, don't let any church, however much it may insist upon the glory of its denominationalism, keep you from seeing Jesus for yourselves. Don't you let any form or ceremony keep you from seeing Jesus for yourselves. Jesus says, "I am the way, the truth, and the life." Don't you let the sectarianism that divides the church arise to keep you from getting into line with those who are in the vanguard of universal brotherhood.

In conclusion, let me say that in spite of all the disciples of Jesus, Jesus heard the blind men; Jesus heard the blind men. And when he heard them, he said he had compassion on them and touched their eyes and their eyes saw. I can see today that miracle that he did, for I know that he did heal them and that since that day the compassion of Jesus for blind men has raised up men all over the world who look with compassion on blind men's eyes and makes them say, "I will search until the day of death comes upon me, until I learn how to open your eyes—learn how to open your eyes." And there are other men who have lost the belief that some eyes can see, but, like the teacher of Helen Keller, have gained an intimate knowledge of the blind girl and have been eyes for her. They have made her see through their eyes.

The compassion of Jesus has fixed it so that blind men can see. And do you know the reason? I can never believe that the cutting of my body with a knife or the putting of a dose of some medicine in my stomach is the only way that I can be saved from death. Men never will believe that, but they will continue to believe what Doctor Jones said from this pulpit one night: "There is some underlying connection between what is known as my soul and my body. And it makes no difference how many men may work on my body or how many doses of medicine may go into my stomach, I shall never be perfectly healthy until my mind is right with my God."

Every physician knows that the number of cases that he can't prescribe for are just about as many as the number that he can prescribe for, because the world today is full of psychoneurotics—people who have stomachache and spinal trouble and backache—people who have all sorts of things. But when the physician comes, he sees that everything is in proper condition. What is the matter? The patient thinks he is sick because he knows that his spiritual life is wrong. He does not feel that he can be right unless his soul is correct. He must get in a better state of mind and believe in God, and trust God and try to do right, and then all his toothache and stomachache and backache and a thousand other things will leave him. There will be very few things for the doctor to take care of with his medicine.

When Jesus fully comes into the world, we will still have our doctors to take care of our bodies, but those same physicians with the clear eyes of Jesus will look into your eyes, my friends, and say to you, "Here, I give you this prescription. Take it over to the Gem Pharmacy and have it filled; but after you have taken this prescription, retire into your closet and talk with your God and get right with Him."

Jesus heard the blind men. And, young men, Jesus is hearing the men who are discontented about life today, too. There is many a young man who is going to launch out in the world today where he can give his life to create something in this world. And there is many a man trying to get his little A.B. who after he gets it will stick it down in his pocket and try to put his understanding of life at the disposal of the human race to heal its diseases. And when Jesus comes into this world, the eyes of many a man are going to be opened, and the brotherhoods of right and love are going to come in.

Let me conclude by saying, "Are you seeing today or are you blind?" Are you blind? You can't look Jesus in the eyes with your selfish heart and your crass life. You have got to face him sometime or other. Why not face him now? Just as sure as he made the blind man discontented, just as sure as he made the blind man hopeful, and just as sure as he opened the blind man's eyes, just so sure can he make you discontented, just so sure can he fill you with hope, and just so sure this same Jesus is able to open your eyes.

May God bless you and keep you.

2. On Giving and Receiving

The theme of this sermon is the responsibility of the privileged. Here Mordecai Johnson points out the stagnation of selfishness, and he shows how some committed philanthropic individuals and institutions have contributed to the education and well-being of the privileged of his time. Those who have received, he urges, have the responsibility of sharing their gifts with others.

ON GIVING AND RECEIVING[2]

TEXT: Matthew 10:8—"Freely ye have received; freely give."

A certain man took a mustard seed and planted it in the ground. The mustard seed took unto itself the strength of the soil and all the richness thereof. It grew and sprouted above the ground and took unto itself the nourishment of the atmosphere and the light of the sun. It grew into a healthy, normal, beautiful, and nourishing plant. But that mustard seed and the mustard plant were not satisfied with growing into a normal, healthy, and nourishing plant. No sooner had the mustard plant come to its maturity than it shot up from itself strong offshoots, and on top of them it crystalized a bunch of seeds in order that it might carry on all the potencies and beauties and nourishments of the whole mustard race.

Now the mustard seed, in the first place, had with it all the achievements of the mustard race. When it went into the ground, it added to all the achievements of the mustard race all of the strength and nourishment and richness of the earth. It was not satisfied merely to grow up into a mature and nourishing plant itself, but it wanted to project itself into the future, so that out of its own achievements a new and better mustard race might be born.

Now when Jesus says to his disciples, "Freely ye have received; freely give," it is put in the form of a commandment. But if you will observe this about the commandments of Jesus, it will be an enlightenment and a strength to your mind: The commandments of Jesus are also statements of fact. They are always invitations. In other words, Jesus never commands a man to do what is unnatural for him to do, but the commandments of Jesus represent the law of our nature. "Freely," he might have said to the mustard seed, "freely give," and so it be.

So Jesus said to his disciples as he sent them out on his mission, "Freely ye have received; freely give."

If you had the privilege this morning of searching into all the history of all the living things upon the earth, you would find that everything—every living thing upon the earth—is moved by a compulsion to give itself away. There is no living thing on the earth that does not gather unto itself all the potencies of the past in a concrete living reality and then projects all that has passed through itself into the whole race of living things in the future. The tendency of reproduction is a necessity in the world of life, and no living thing outside of the human race ever tries to interrupt it. But of all God's

---

[2]First Baptist Church, July 20, 1924.

creatures, the highest alone is the one that tries to stop the natural law of nature and to get everything out of the past and out of God's world and put nothing into it. This generation in which we live is filled with young women and young men who have no intention whatsoever of gathering up the potencies of life in themselves and projecting them into the future. This generation is full of childless homes that are not childless by accident but childless by intention.

And then you will find men today who have gathered into themselves all the intellectual heritage of the past, have sat down in institutions that have cost the human race millions of dollars and energy untold, and have arrogated unto themselves the privilege of receiving all of these things. Then they have come into a community and sat upon them like a leech, sucking the blood of that community and giving nothing to it of their own intellect. You will find other human beings nowadays who have received all of the spiritual sustenance that has come down through the human race from time immemorial, who rejoice in all the spiritual productions of the past, but who have no intention whatsoever of giving themselves in any unselfish and productive and creative way to the human race.

The unselfishness of individual men is the profoundest and most marked exception in the world I know to this law of "Freely ye have received; freely give." And do you know, my beloved, I believe it is because men do not think deeply enough. I think that one of the things that we need most in this age is not more activity but more meditation. I think that the life of our cities, the life of our race and our nation, and the life of the whole world would be deeply enriched this morning if men would sit down just for a few moments and think what they have received from the human race and from nature.

I want to put before you, for just a few moments, some of the things that we have received.

The first thing that I will speak of that is familiar to every human being is the name of mother. Have you ever thought, my beloved, have you ever just sat down and thought what your mother put into your life. I don't care what kind of mother she is, how ignorant she may have been, or how many crude mistakes she may have made. Has it ever occurred to you how and why your life is so sweet today—this life that you are scrambling around with and that you enjoy so much when the wind blows and the sun shines? Where did you get it? Did you get it from a selfish source?

Ah, you got that life of yours because some woman dared to do what tens of thousands of women today have sworn that they will never do. You got that life from the bosom of a woman who went down into the valley of the shadow of death and sweated in agony and in blood, and moaned and groaned and looked death in the face anywhere from one hour to one and two days in order that that body of yours might be brought to life. In the midst of her suffering, her agony, and her blood, when she looked down and saw your little face, she drew your little body to her and cried with great joy because she had through blood brought forth your body.

How did it happen to be that you are healthy and strong and have come out here today to the house of God to sit down and worship instead of being decrepit and thin and anemic, lying off in some hospital somewhere? It was the eternal vigilance of that same woman who watched over your meals day by day to see that you ate this and did not eat that. Who kept her ears open to your cries even when she was asleep and when the least little movement that you might make, day or night, would arouse her from asleep, and she would get up and tuck the coverlets about you, or lay a little warm cloth on your head, and do it for anywhere from one to five and six and seven and ten and twelve and fifteen years? Why, where did all this nourishment that you got into your body come from during those fourteen or fifteen or twenty years when you were doing no productive labor? There were two human beings who made themselves slaves for your sake.

There are many men and women today who will not bring forth children into the world and will say, "I do not propose to make myself a slave to any little old child." That is not what happened in your early years, in the fourteen or fifteen or sixteen years when two human beings gave up their freedom and made themselves slaves in order that you might have something to eat and something to wear and a house to live in. Had you ever thought about that?

Then how does it happen today that you are not disgraced and abused and despised and rejected by the world down in some worthless district of some far-off and rude city, or behind the jail bars, or in the pen, or even with your neck broken from your body in the grave? How is it? Is it because you had all the wisdom and knowledge and education to keep yourself from degrading morally? No. It was because that same woman, that same father, watched over you with eagle eye day by day and in the night when you were sleeping complacently, and in some corner in the darkness weeping tears of agony, lifting up her voice into the heavens crying, "O my God, my God, I have brought forth a child, and he has come to be fifteen years of age and now is going down in the world. Make him to be a clean and upright man!" That is how you came to be here. Have you ever thought of these things? Have you ever thought of these things?

And what does the selfish man say? He says to himself, "All of these things I received. For none of these things will I be grateful. I was not responsible for any of them." And he dismisses entirely from his mind the fact that he has been produced and nourished and sustained in this world by the unselfish stagnation of a mother and father who have made themselves slaves for his life.

Just one or two more things. Had you ever thought about this universe that you live in and get along so well in? Had you ever thought how every morning that you awaken, there is a fresh supply of good air waiting there for you to breathe? Had you ever thought that this mighty universe with all of its physical bodies so much larger than you is always very careful to give you a fresh supply of air and good, clean water every morning? And had it ever occurred to you that the whole universe in which you live is so constructed and sustained that you can breathe fresh, living air and drink fresh, living water every day? And had you ever thought that every dollar's worth that you eat in the world—these little nickels and dimes and quarters that you put down in the grocery stores—would not be worth one scintilla if way down in the very bowels of the earth, there were not some mysterious powers continuously producing cabbage, mysteriously producing wheat, and profusely producing all of those things, those living things none of which you are responsible for, things that not a single human being in the world could produce, things that all the human beings in the world could not produce, if that mysterious producing power were not somewhere hidden there continually looking out for your welfare? "Freely ye have received." Freely you have received from your own human mother. Freely you have received from the great, unselfish mother that surrounds you. Surely, some great and invisible power is looking after your welfare.

And then again every single one of us in here today is economically free to work where he pleases. You can go and sell your labor to anybody that you choose. Do you realize that sixty-odd years ago your own fathers and mothers were absolutely bound and their wills were bound so they could not sell their own labor? Many of them had to get up before daylight and work until the sun went clear down without receiving any compensation whatsoever, except bread and meat and a rough place to put their poor backs. Here you are today sitting in a land absolutely free to sell your labor to whom you please. You can work when you please, and you can walk away from work if you please. You can do practically as you please with your body, mind, and soul. Did you work this out yourselves, or have you freely received?

Just a little reflection will tell you that every single Negro in this world—in this land today—who is free is made free by the blood of men who have gone out on the battlefield and died. Our liberty is washed in blood! Washed in blood this day! Washed in blood! Washed in the blood of men who have died on the battlefield, in the blood of men who have been dragged and beaten and bruised for speaking about the name of liberty in order to make you free. Freely ye have received. Freely ye have received.

Here we are today, both white and black, in a country that calls itself a democracy. Why, you don't have to be ruled over by any man unless you give him your consent. You vote for him. Why, our governmental institution is placed partially under your control. Why, the whole organized life of the people is under the control of the people. How does that come to pass? Did this generation create it? Was anybody here responsible for it? I tell you that the very state and government under which we live was produced by the labor and the sweat and the blood of ten thousand upon ten thousand human beings through years and years of strife. And I sit here this morning and breathe the air of liberty made possible by the sacrifices of thousands and thousands of lives! Freely ye have received! Freely ye have received!

How did it happen that you are living here in this fertile and productive and beautiful country with its wide stretches of land? Why are we here? Were you and I—with all of our individualistic ideas and selfishness—responsible for the opening up of this great and free land to human beings so we can live without restrictions, live with perfect freedom, move out on a farm, or live in a city? How was it made possible? It was made possible by a handful of pilgrims who became discontented with the way men were made to worship God in a foreign land; who, in order to worship God according to the dictates of their own consciences, came across the mighty deep with all of its dangers; and who, after the trials and tribulations of a pioneer people living out in that wilderness, gave us a government of the people for the people and by the people. We have received it all. Freely we have received. Freely we have received. Freely we have received.

And how does it happen, my beloved, that this land is maintained today? How does it happen? Suppose you were not a man of faith; you didn't believe in anything—didn't believe in God. If you don't believe in God, you don't believe in men. If you don't believe in God, you don't believe in men. You don't believe in anything but your own welfare. Let's see. But even so, your very existence is made possible by men of faith. The most selfish man in the United States today lives off of the faith of other men. The very society in which you live—the one that makes it possible for you to be successful and unselfish—is itself maintained by men of faith. The only society in which any man can be successful—unselfish for any considerable period—must be a society maintained by men who are essentially different from what he is; because if a society did not have a great deal of unselfish elements in it, there would not be anything for him to take away from it and draw into himself. If every man were like unto himself, his own existence would be curtailed. Every adulterer is responsible for the joy that he takes: the faith and the purity of womanhood. If nobody believed in the purity of womanhood, if nobody believed in the sanctity of the home, then all the rejoicing in the ignominious liberty that he has would be nothing. Every man would be in that same state, and he would be a selfish parasite just like everybody else.

Every selfish businessman who does not give as much as he receives from society cannot be successful, because he is sitting on top of a society maintained by a faith in which men are giving and taking upon an equality, and he himself is a parasite. Freely you have received! Freely you have received!

I can't enumerate all, but I have enumerated those things that we have received from our mothers, from the very character of the universe itself, from Abraham Lincoln, from those men who gave up their lives that we might be free, from those pioneer pilgrims who came across the waters and planted this land of liberty, and from all the men of faith who have sustained this land of liberty as it is today and upon whom all free men are living parasites.

One more thing I want to mention: There is hardly one of us in here under thirty-five years of age who has not come into possession of some degree of education. Freely ye have received. Had it ever occurred to you how absolutely impossible it would be for you to create and maintain the instruments necessary to the education of your own mind, this educational system of the schools to which you send your children and to which you yourselves have gone, but for the unselfish labors of thousands upon thousands of human beings generation after generation—this educational system which now stands here at your doorsteps to educate your mind and the minds of your children? Freely ye have received! Freely ye have received!

Now, my beloved, the first lesson I want to draw from this so that you can understand it yourselves and go and meditate upon it is this—and you can extend it into domain after domain: You will finally say there is absolutely nothing that is worthwhile in your life that you have not received, that you have not received.

There is written somewhere in the Scriptures this pregnant question: "What has thou that thou hast not received?"

What is there in your life today that is worth anything at all that has not come to you through the stream of the human race? It is as if each individual were a pond into which all of the noble achievements of the human race were poured like a mighty rivulet. Into the pond of your physical life and your mental life and your spiritual life, all the achievements and potencies of the human race have been poured. You have received all that the human race has given and all that God has given up to this present time.

Now the first thing that is perfectly manifest is that a selfish human being is a monstrosity, is a monstrosity. Any human being who lives for himself and himself only is a monstrous creature. The very foundation of his life is the basest of all human qualities—ingratitude. For a man to be selfish in such a world as this, he must shut his eyes and his mind and his heart to all the great things that he has received from the human race. He must close the windows of his soul to all the potencies and beauties that have flowed unto him from the past. A selfish man is, at rock-bottom foundation, an ungrateful human creature. He is lower than a pig who receives slop and groans his approval, because everything that he has received has come from the hands of other human beings or God. And he receives it all without a grunt of gratitude and goes clamoring into the trough for more. A selfish man is a monstrosity. And the more intelligent he is, the greater the monstrosity.

A selfish man with a Bachelor of Arts degree, or with any degree whatsoever received from organized private institutions of learning, is an egregious monstrosity, because the most expensive education in the world is the college of professional education. It could not be maintained except thousands of dollars were poured into it that were never expected to be restored, and unless thousands of lives of scientists and philosophers and historians, who must live off very small salaries, were given in order that everyone who came to those institutions might have some learning. Thus an intelligent man who has been to an institution of learning and received a degree—and, above all, the man who has been prepared for professional proficiency—is an egregious monstrosity, because he has tapped all the sources of humanity, tapped all the sources of the human race, taken them to himself, taken the best that they had to give, and turned his head away in ingratitude and given nothing back. He is a monstrosity! He is an egregious monstrosity!

And, above all, an educated Negro—my God, what a monstrosity! Some day it will appear that of all the human beings of God's living earth, an educated Negro is an egregious monstrosity, an egregious and hellish monstrosity, because there is hardly a Negro alive in this world today who has received a smattering of education above the high school who has not received it through the agony and pain of someone who has sacrificed his very life in order to give it to him. Until recent years, every higher educational institution in this land for Negroes was maintained by people who had offered up their lives upon the altar of the Christian religion and said to Jesus, "Wherever you want me, I will go." And they went down into Virginia, went down into Georgia, went down into Louisiana, and suffered all manner of ostracism in order that you might receive an education. Then you take it all and come to the city of Charleston and set yourselves up like a mighty leech sucking the blood out of it. Why I tell you, hell is too good a place for you! Too good a place for you! An educated Negro who is selfish is an egregious, hellish monstrosity. Why, if I had one for my daddy, and I was named after him, I would change my name. How can a man think? How can he think? How can he even breathe below his own stomach band without realizing that he is in debt so deeply to the human race for all he has in the world. If he does not, he is a base ingrate and scoundrel.

The second thing I want to say is that such a man is bound to be unhappy and a failure—bound to be unhappy and a failure. He can accumulate all the wealth he pleases. He can have as nice a house as he pleases, have all the entertainments he pleases, gather together all the fine silverware he pleases, and move in an exclusive society, but the selfish man cannot be happy. It is not just merely because Jesus says so. You just can't be happy. It is not in you. If the capacity for happiness is gone, you will be discontented as long as you live. You will get hold of $50; and you will find after you get that, you will want a thousand. And when you get a thousand, you will find that you will be anxious to get $5,000 and that you will almost commit murder to get it. And when you get that, you will want $10,000; and you will commit all sorts of monstrosities against your race and against your country, against your nation. You will never be satisfied, and you will go into hell with that burning fire of dissatisfaction in your heart, because the life has been killed in you.

I am not talking theories now. When I was a little boy, I was baptized in a lake. The water was clear and sparkling and living fish were there. That lake received all sorts of living streams unto itself. I used to go and stand there and see the sparkling waters come down into that lake, and yet they did not overflow the lake. But after a while, I noticed that down in the bottom of the lake, people had placed some outlet pipes and fresh water flowed out into a little branch. That little branch went on down through the land watering the fields and plants down to the river.

I went back home the other day to that same lake where I was baptized. Instead of a fresh and sparkling stream with living fish in it, it was dead things with green scum on the top of it. No living fish there. No living fish there. The fish had all died, and those things that create disease—mosquitoes and other pests—were skimming over the surface of the water. I felt afraid to venture near it because of the rank growth that had come up on the side. And I knew that poisonous vipers would be likely to be in the weeds. What had happened to it? Only one thing. Just one thing had happened. The owner of the place had gone away, and he left the outlet pipes to be clogged. Into that place came fresh water, but it kept coming and it didn't go out. It kept coming and it didn't go out, until finally the fresh water turned itself aside and went around, and the stagnant water choked up the live fish and killed all living things and covered all with a green scum.

So it is with a selfish man. You set a human being down in the cavalcade of humanity. Behind him are the unselfish lives of all the teachers, all the prophets, all the priests, all the martyrs. If you let it flow out through you into humanity, you can have life. If you stop the outgo, God himself will stagnate you and you can't be happy as long as you live. You can't be happy. You can't be happy. You can't be happy. Happiness is impossible to a stagnant selfishness, and I am so glad. I am go glad.

Why is it impossible, my friends? Why is it impossible for a selfish man to be happy? It is impossible for a selfish man to be happy for the same reason that a self-giving man is a normal man and a selfish man is an abnormal monstrosity—just as I told you before. The normal thing for any lake to do is to receive the lovely living and beautiful waters and pass them through its bosom on down to the lesser streams that water the lovely earth. And the natural thing for a human being to do is to recognize that you are an agent of the human race—that all that has come into you has come in order that you may concentrate it and put it out from you better than you received it. Not only ought a man to give it out for himself, but also he ought to give out from himself something besides what he has received. Every man who has sucked at the vital bosom of this earth ought to give out from himself stronger milk than that which he received. That is the law of life. That is the law of life, and I have taught it in my ministry.

I have watched those who have cultivated the capacity to give, and I have seen them in their poverty smile as they gave of their week's wages. I have so often brought to you my personal, intimate knowledge of a member of this race of ours who at one time was in possession of several hundred thousands dollars, but when she got a hold of that money, she was so moved by her human associations that she kept on lending it and giving it away. She finally lost all that she had by lending and giving so freely—too freely was what they said—too freely, as if she knew what too freely meant. I attended her during the last two or three months that she was alive, and I noticed that the instinct of giving was so strong that she could not restrain it. I have gone out when she was so crippled that she could hardly stand up beside her ironing board. There she was, a woman who had been worth $100,000, standing up at the ironing board, ironing clothes for a dollar and a half a week. I have gone in there when she was sitting down figuring out how she could give it away—how she could give it away. As she was scrambling around under her old pillow once, trying to find her pocketbook in which there was a bank account that she had put in her own name, she murmured that she had given it all away but that money, and she wanted to give that to one little human child. And she smiled and laid back on her pillow and went to meet Jesus.

Freely ye have received; freely give.

Now I want to call your attention to what is beautiful about Jesus. I said that this life that I am speaking of is a normal life. The life that gives is a normal life. Not only does that life give money but also it gives time, gives away its intellect, gives away its spirit.

But just before I go to Jesus, there is one thing I have forgotten. The reason the giving life is a normal life and the receiving life that does not give is an abnormal life is the life that does not give does not truly receive.

Let me advance that point for a moment for your consideration.

You and I this morning are the beneficiaries of Abraham Lincoln's statesmanship, but we haven't received all that Abraham Lincoln had to give. What did Abraham Lincoln have to give to his country? He gave his country union. He gave his country freedom of the slave. But was that all? Was that all? The human race has been prone to think that was all. Every now and then, we go and lay a wreath on the tomb of Lincoln and on the tombs of our martyrs because we have received the benefits of their labors. But there is one other thing that Abraham Lincoln had to give. Abraham Lincoln gave his country his spirit, didn't he? Didn't he give to his country an undivided and noble and unselfish devotion to the highest things? Did he not give that to us? And is it not just as much an obligation to every man who receives the benefits of union and of liberty to receive the spirit of Lincoln along with it? And how is ever a man to receive what Lincoln has to give when that man is a selfish, base ingrate? I tell you there are many men alive today who honor the name of Abraham Lincoln and shed tears at his memory whom he would kick off of his front doorstep if those men came to call. That is a hard statement, isn't it? There are many Negroes alive today who shed tears when they think of Abraham Lincoln, and teach their children to revere his name, that in truth—either physically or spiritually—he would kick off his doorstep if they came to call on him. Why? Because, although you have been the beneficiary of what he had to give you, you have refused to take his spirit into your heart. Oh, that I might emphasize that today!

One of the greatest tragedies in the world today is the aggregation of intelligent Negro minds in cities like New York, Chicago, and Boston. If I were living in Chicago or Boston or New York and if I were one intelligent Negro, I would be wanting to say my prayers three times a day. What right have we—fifty years after slavery—when we can see down in Louisiana and Mississippi and in the coal fields of West Virginia where Negroes are suffering for education; where they have only a four-month school or a six-month school; where they have a teacher who has accidentally passed the eighth grade; where white men and white women from the North and the West and the East have year after year gone down from those civilized centers that we are now seeking; and where they have given up their culture, given up their fellowship there, and have gone down in those places and given up almost life itself to teach these little black children?

And just as soon as one of us Negroes gets sufficient education here, we run off to New York or Boston or Chicago where we won't have to offer anything. And we stay up there and take from our ignorant, poor, benighted people down in Georgia. I hope too many of them won't come up here to take our money. They are the basest ingrates that God ever brought from the bowels of the earth. We may talk about the Negro race growing big and powerful, but unless God Almighty exercises more mercy toward this race than he has ever exercised toward any race in the world, we will produce the biggest bunch of base ingrates that ever cluttered up God's green earth. Then can you wonder why a man of spiritual insight does not take off his hat and bow his head at every bank account and every degree that he sees? The Spirit of God says to me, as He said to those in ancient times, "The harvest is truly great, but the laborers are few." And those who ought to be laborers are running away from the harvest field.

So I say that he who does not give has not truly received. Jesus so said. Didn't he tell his own race that they were having their organized meetings every night as to how they were going to set the Jewish race free from their enemies; how they would go out with their torchlight processions to honor some prophet whom they afterwards killed; how they sang, "Glory be to Zachariah," "Glory be to Isaiah," "Glory be to Elisha," and "God bless his holy name"? And they afterwards killed him. And if that same prophet were to appear among you today, you would kill him, too. You say that you worship the prophets because of what they did for you, but you have no intention of receiving that prophet's spirit in your heart. That is what Jesus said. He said the Kingdom of Heaven is within you. No man has a right to talk about the Kingdom of God who is not willing to bow his own neck and receive the Kingdom of God in his own heart. These are hard sayings but they are true, and men live by tough meat as well as they do by milk.

Now, the final thing that I want to say is—and I am just now coming to the Gospel: How beautiful it is to look at Jesus of Nazareth! How beautiful it is to look at Jesus of Nazareth! How beautiful it is to look at him! Somewhere in the Scriptures there is written this word. "In the fullness of time God sent his own son." And, as I said to you the other night, my beloved, from this pulpit, Jesus of Nazareth gathers up unto himself the full and total significance of the Old Testament. What do I mean by that? I mean to say that Jesus Christ drew unto himself all the deepest and purest and sweetest essence of the entire history of his race, so that when Jesus came and lived and died, it may have been truly said that the Jewish race had come to its flower. It had bloomed, and the sweet fragrance and savor of all of its years of agony have come to be spread abroad in the world.

For Jesus, as it were, reached back to Abraham and drew out all the faith that Abraham had in his bosom and took it into his own bosom. Jesus turned back to Elijah and other prophets and drew from them all of the courage and sincerity and truth that they had in their hearts and took it into his. He reached back to Isaiah and took all of his magnificent vision of the Kingdom of God and buried that in his bosom. He reached back to the wonderful Psalms and drew out of them their sweetest essence and distilled them like dew in his own heart. When Jesus walked out of the plains of Galilee and looked out, a humble man, and said, "I am the Way, the Truth, and the Life," he meant to say, "I have received unto myself all that the human race has to give. I know it is in me. It is concentrated and beautiful and true. If any man would live, let him come unto me and drink of the Water of Life."

How beautiful it is to look upon Jesus when you see not only that he freely received but also that he freely gave. How much did he give away? Look at him, you lustful and covetous eyes who are spending all your lives pilling up stuff for yourselves, piling up stuff for yourselves! Look at him. He lived thirty-three years without accumulating a place to lay his head. Look at him all you who glory in your degrees that you have buried under a pile of selfishness and arrogated unto yourselves social position and power. He not only gave himself away but also sat down and ate with the poor and the degraded and despised and rejected. He sat at the feet of the humble rabbis. Not only did he give away his energy and social position and high standing in society, but also when they came to take him to Calvary to be crucified and have his blood spilled upon that awful place, he gave up his life. Freely he had received; freely he gave away. He received everything; he gave everything away. Oh, how beautiful it is to talk about Jesus. He received everything and gave everything away.

Now, my beloved, I am through. I am through. If any man alive can think these thoughts—and almost any man can think them as well as I, and many of you better than I—if any man can think these thoughts and then continue to glory in his bank account, to glory in his house, or to glory in his social standing, or to glory in anything that he possesses, except he gives himself away, I don't see how he can be straight, for everyone of us stands at the very end of human advancement. All that is true and beautiful in the human race has been poured out into our lives. If we don't give it away, it is because we have put a stopper in our own outlet pipes, and we are becoming stagnant every day, every hour. And that is why I am here preaching, telling you if you want to find life, come to Jesus. Come to Jesus. If you want to find life, come to Jesus. Come to Jesus. He teaches you how to receive and how to give.

Oh, how I covet for you this morning the desire and the activity of giving! Oh, how I long this morning that you might begin to pour out yourselves unto the blood. Oh, I know that there are some of you who are so poor that you haven't got any money, but give away, just give away what you have. Give away some of your time. Get up and go down to the jail, and there find some mother's child who is lonely, dejected, and separated from his loved ones. If you haven't got any money to carry to him, take him a few apples that you bought for your own table. If there is a woman in need of a little help, give her a little of your time. Go over there and sweep her room. Wash her clothes. Do something for her. Do something to pour out your life into the human race. If you have got an intellect that has been trained by long years of arduous toil, don't prostitute that holy possession by using it continuously for your own selfish ends, but put it to work for the Gospel of Jesus Christ—for the betterment of the human race. Go out and make it do something for the advancement of mankind. If you have got a heart in you that was received from somebody who was filled with passion for the Glory of God—if you have got a spirit in you that has been regenerated by the Holy Spirit of Jesus Christ, then the highest thing that you can do is to find some soul who is being deranged and broken and beaten by sin and to teach that soul to receive the Spirit of that same Jesus Christ.

I want to close by saying, as I have so often said before, that the greatest gift that you can receive from the human race is its spirit. The greatest gift you can receive from Abraham Lincoln is the spirit of Abraham Lincoln. The greatest gift you can receive from Jesus is the spirit of Jesus. The greatest gift you can give to another human being is the spirit of Jesus Christ. If you have nothing else to give, give that.

Dean Charles R. Brown of Yale University recently wrote a sermon for the magazine *World's Work*. The *World's Work* offered a prize of $500 to the man who would submit the best sermon, and Dean Brown wrote a sermon on this text—and I commend this text to all the poor and to all who have not much of this world's goods: "Silver and gold have I none, but such as I have give I unto you. Arise, take up that bed and walk." You remember the story. A blind man was sitting on the wayside toward the temple. He heard these two disciples of Jesus Christ coming. He knew that they had tender and compassionate hearts. He reached up and said to them, "Sirs, give me alms, for I am blind and I cannot see, and need food and clothes. Give me alms!" And Peter looked down on him with compassion and remembered that Jesus gave him the power to heal the wounded spirit and the blind eye. And he said to him, "Sir, silver and gold have I none, but such as I have give I unto you. Arise, take up thy bed, and walk."

Give your silver and gold if you have it, but if you have no silver and gold, give the things that you have. Covet that great gift that comes to one man when he can look into another man's eyes and say, "I can give you not of this world's goods, but if you will listen to me a while, I will let the Spirit of the Living God into your heart. I will give you strength and peace that passeth all human understanding."

3. The Social Consequences of Sin

In this sermon, Mordecai Johnson maintains that the consequences of wrongdoing are not primarily experienced in an afterlife, but in the society in which it occurs. Not only individual sins, but also institutionalized evils pollute the social stream, and what is done in one generation redounds to good or evil in later years. "The sins of the fathers transmit their evil effects on the institutions of the race," and on the minds of their children.

Johnson maintains that the redeeming factor in all this is that Jesus of Nazareth has been the source of much that is god and pure in the world. He has shown humanity that the power of God helps people to transform their lives so that they will not be contributors to the pollution of society.

THE SOCIAL CONSEQUENCES OF SIN[3]

TEXT: Jeremiah 6:8—"As a fountain casteth out her waters,
so she casteth out her wickedness."

I want to speak with you this morning about the social consequences of sin.

I was riding several days ago on the New York Central Railway, looking down into a river that was a fairly clear stream. As I looked into this river, the train passed a small bridge. Under that bridge was a sewer, and that sewer spouted into the river a stream of ugly, polluted water. Some little children [who] were near me called attention to the fact that the stream of ugly polluted water was traceable in that river for yards and yards and yards and yards.

Now the human race is like a continuous flowing river reaching from the day that the first man begot the first child down to the end of the ages and the end of the human race. And every sinner who sins—whatever his sin may be—turns loose into the human race a stream of pollution that hurts, that harms, and that oft-times damns hundreds of human beings.

It is very difficult for us to understand this without quiet prolonged reflection, because the whole temper of our American mind is against this real understanding of the nature of sin. The whole democratic movement in the world places emphasis upon individuality—upon the sacredness and the freedom as well as the responsibility of the individual. The vast majority of men never receive the democratic doctrine as a whole. They receive only the part of it that says, "I am a free individual and can do as I please, and nobody has a right to say to me what I shall do and what I shall not do." Too much of the preaching of the world has been addressed to that individual without showing him his underlying grievous mistake. Too much of our preaching has been saying to the individual, "If you do wrong, God will make a record of it, and when you die, you will go to Hell." And many an individual sinner has answered back in his heart, "If you will just give me about fifty years of this time that I am having now, I will be willing to run the risk of going to Hell when I die."

---

[3]July 12, 1924.

But the consequences of sin are not confined to what may happen to the individual when he dies. They concern the whole human race. I want to repeat that whenever an individual commits sin of any kind, he lets loose into the human race a stream of pollution that hurts and oft-times damns hundreds of human beings.

This is not a theory, but a proposition to be proved by the citation of scientific facts. You take the simple sin and the common sin that grows out of lust—adultery, lechery, and all of the sins that are connected with sex. It is amusing to find that grown men who have given over their lives to the indulgence of these sins will talk about them with such a degree of pride that their own children, especially their boys, standing around on the street corners in their little gangs, have come to conceive that one of the chief glories of a man is to take a "scalp" from the opposite sex. And young men today in their group life actually—if you could come upon them when they are not conscious of the adults present—look forward to the day when they may come back to that group with some immoral innuendo or actually tell the story indicating that "I have at last come to that state of manhood that I have heard my father talking about when bragging to other men." The reason this father has been able to brag about this thing is either because he has an incorrigible vanity or because he has no true conception of the ills that have already come into the human race because of the indulgent licentiousness of man.

Every intelligent man knows today, for example, that the world is now full of children with scrofula, children with blind eyes, and that insane hospitals are filled with children born feeble-minded from the day they came into this world because of the indiscriminate indulgence of men and women of the human race. No sensible man can stand up complacently and look upon the objects that his own sin has caused to come into this world, an individual who will never see and who is feeble-minded, and who, if he reproduces his kind, will produce a brood of feeble-minded people. But that is exactly what has come into the human race from sexual indulgence and the licentiousness of men and women. And this is only a suggestion of it. Wherever in any particular community sexual license is turned loose and the sin of adultery is made light of, that community is filled soon with disease easily discernible by the records of the hospitals where multitudes of women have to be operated upon for diseases they never would have except their own husbands indulged in the awful license and lust. Then many a woman's husband goes down to her bedside today to pray about her delivery from the operation which that woman has undergone as a result of the selfish indulgence of her husband's own luxury loving and ungodly life.

I want to indicate to you also how the sins of the individual tend to institutionalize themselves. Every reader of history with any knowledge of the Greeks will tell you that among the Greeks dancing was a thing of beauty and that among many people dancing has been a thing of innocent and delightful beauty. You can go in certain European countries today and observe the folkdances of the people there, just as clean, just as beautiful, and just as innocent of any debauchery or licentiousness as they can be. I stood for a half an hour in one of our Western states—in Arizona—and watched a group of Indians dance for an hour and a half. They had the most delightful joy. They showed all sorts of forms and ceremonies connected with war, of forms and ceremonies connected with worship, and they had a splendid time, with no suggestion of evil in it whatsoever. But you take a fifty-cent ticket and go to any one of our dance halls tomorrow night, and you will see that dancing has been so degraded in our modern life that there is not a woman inside who would allow her picture to be taken on the street in the attitude in which she finds herself within that dance hall. And if she would come out on Washington Street and stand in front of this church and have her picture taken in the attitude that she finds herself using in the K & P Hall, she would be arrested and put in jail for destroying public morality.

Now what has happened? Our sexual license, our disregard of the sin of adultery, our low estimate of the moral sacredness of the character of women—these have degraded one of the most beautiful and lovable institutions of the human race into a thing that is indecent and low. People can hardly dance in modern civilized life unless they do it accompanied by music low enough to stir up their sexual passions.

The great cry that the pulpit and all decent humanity have against dancing today is not the response of the feet to music, but it is the degraded and low character of the stuff that is indulged in and that goes by the dignified name of dancing. The dance hall is dominated by an erotic sex instinct, and no man can stand and look upon it for half an hour without his seeing that the dominant factor is the relationship of the sexes, which is a sign of the degradation of the modern civilized life.

A few years ago in Virginia and Georgia a group of lazy, but not very vicious, men had some crops that they wanted to tend, and the sun was very hot. They wanted the fruits of the crop, but they didn't want to work and so they started to take the native Indians and make those Indians do the work. They were Christian people—supposedly. They came over here on a Christian mission, but their laziness caused them to develop the habit of using Indians for the forced work. But the Indian was a proud and wild fellow, and he didn't work very well in that harness. He caused so much trouble that these ambitious and lazy gentlemen decided that they would have to look for a new source of slaves. So a group of our ancestors was brought over here and made slaves.

Now, those men were simply lazy; they simply got away from their Christian principles for a short time. But their laziness exercised a certain suggestibility over the rest of the community, and other people began to buy slaves. Soon we had the laziness of those men institutionalized into the system of slavery in this country. When the Constitution of the United States came to be written, that institution had already had so much effect upon the minds of the men who were engaged in it that one of the fundamental principles of the Constitution had to be modified in order to meet the laziness and moral instability that slavery had produced. In a very few years the system of slavery got to the place where the laziness of those men threatened to divide the Union, and it cost the blood of over a million of the choice sons of America, along with bitterness and hatred that have lasted over sixty years, for this country to get rid of the institutional effects of the laziness of those men who wanted to get the fruits of other men's labor without regarding the sanctity of human freedom. Even today, any sensible man can see that the effects of the institution of slavery are not nearly gone, but in large sections of this country today people whose hearts really want to do right, who really want to carry out the principles of democracy in their hearts, have got hatred and bitterness toward other people in this country—toward the North so strongly that they can hardly have a meeting on any question, whether it is political or religious, without these hatreds coming up and dividing the unity of the nation.

Moreover, during those years of slavery, those few men encouraged other men to think lightly of the personality of black people. Thus they have thought so lightly of the black personality, that now, sixty years after the Civil War, it is impossible for them to conceive of a black man as a human being. In this country, in some ways the most enlightened country in the world, we have the most diabolical crime in the universe of burning and lynching of human beings—all growing from the fruits of the laziness and moral laxity of a group of human beings who wanted to get crops without putting forth the energy to raise those crops.

I want to speak to you about those who say, "What I do nobody is responsible for. You don't have to do what I do. Just let me alone, and if God is going to punish me for what I do, let Him punish me. I will risk it when I die." I say under no circumstances can a man get off in that way. Whenever you sin in any way, you are driving into the human race a stream of pollution that will undermine the vitality and will damn hundreds for years and years and years after you are dead.

For a long time in the civilized world, men drank whiskey with perfect moderation. Thousands of people in the world had their little toddies every morning. I met an old man the other day in good health, ninety years old, and I asked him what was responsible for his health. He said to me, "My wife just gives me a little toddy every morning and gives my children a little toddy every morning." And he said, "It has been all right with me." And he said, "I have no idea of dying yet; I am going to live on six more years. The Lord has assured me that I am going to live six more years."

Here is an example of a type of hundreds of people years ago who used to drink a very little bit in moderation and thought nothing about it. But there was a fellow who would drink a little bit more than his little bit. He got to drinking just a little bit more than was good for him, and the more he drank, the more valuable he became to the organized institution that sold the liquor. The moderate fellow would come in and get a jug occasionally and put it in his basement, but he didn't help the trade much because he didn't swill down so much of it. Not so with the man who had to have a drink at breakfast and on his way to work and on his way back to dinner. The saloon man has his eye on this fellow and says, "This is a valuable customer." He did what he could do to produce that kind of customer. After a while, the immoderate drinking of a few men so increased the cupidity of the sellers of liquor that before we awoke to what we were doing, we had saddled upon us one of the most damnable organizations that the world had ever seen: the organized liquor traffic, which was actually putting alcohol into candy to give to the children before they were two years of age to produce in them the desire for liquor in order that they could become rich when those children grew up. It took years and years of the prayers and tears of women, of preachers in churches, and of political organizations to pass laws against that damnable traffic and take it from the American life, which even today is using millions and millions of dollars to defeat the laws of this country and is today the most powerful group in the United States to destroy the effectiveness of the Constitution. People who sell liquor would overturn the Constitution in order that they may re-establish their damnable institution and feed the children upon enough whiskey to make themselves rich. This shows how the sins of men tend to institutionalize themselves and have a grip upon humanity.

All literature is full of recitations of the cupidity of men. The fellow who stands behind a counter and bargains to give you five pounds of sugar—but sells you four pounds and three-quarters while he is talking to you—takes your money. All literature is full of that. It wasn't very serious as long as it was merely an individual matter, although long before our present time thousands of human beings were hurt by the injustice of merchants and money handlers. But see what has come in our generation. The cupidity of a few individuals who want just a little bit more money than is due them, that is a simple principle. This individual who started out from behind a grocery counter saying, "Now it is none of your business if I have sold four and three-quarter pounds of sugar for five pounds. It is none of your business. It is between me and God. If I get away with it and my customer still likes my sugar, that is all right." And if a preacher should say to him, "You will go to Hell when you die for that," he would reply, "I will risk going to Hell when I die."

See what has become of it. Just a few weeks ago, we discovered that the cupidity had organized itself, that it had three or four members in the cabinet of the President of the United States who had almost captured the machinery of one of our great parties, if not both of them. Such cupidity was actually selling out the whole American people, selling them away, delivering them into the hands of their friends, telling the people constant lies day by day, and filching them not merely of thousands of dollars—one man alone in one department of the government stole $200 million away from the people in one period of office. It institutionalized itself, mind you, and was feeding upon the very vitals of the nation. I am indicating to you how the sins of individual men tend to organize themselves and take a grip upon the very vitals of the human race and to destroy the growing power of humanity.

Now, that wouldn't be too serious itself if sin did not have another effect. It is this third effect about which I am going to spend a little time and on which I would like to put most emphasis: The sinful mind transmits itself; the sinful mind transmits itself, transmits itself. I have read sometimes with a great deal of marvel how many distinguished men have gone from this country to give their lives to be missionaries in Africa, China, India, and all the uncivilized world and the civilized world too. I read that the Southern Baptist Convention had a most marvelous force of missionaries in China. Yet when I go down to the southern states where I was born and reared, it is an awful sight to see that hardly a single white man or woman in any little town has walked out from his family and said, "I am going to give my life to teach these poor, ignorant, young Negro boys and girls running around here without any education."

They have strength enough to send a world of missionaries to China, a world of missionaries to India, and some of them even to Africa. But those little black children right down there by their doors are worse off than tens of thousands in China and yet not a single soul goes out and plans a Sunday School. Not a single soul goes out and builds a little schoolhouse and says, "Mother and Father, I cannot be happy in this home. I must go out here and teach these little Negro children." And if one of those little children taught by the missionary in Africa were to come here dressed up with a clean collar and tie on, and were to walk in the service where the money was being raised to send the missionary to Africa, why, he would almost create a panic in the morning service.

Now why does that happen? Right here in our town, it is the same way. For thirty days, a wonderful individual has been here preaching the gospel of Jesus Christ supposedly to all the people. At the end of his thirty days when the collections have all been made, when the governor stands there, and when a glorious impression has come upon the community, there comes a sudden decision that there is one-quarter or one-seventh of the population that they haven't seen: "Suppose we preach the gospel to them." There comes out from that man and from Brother Pat Withrow—whom we all admire for his life—an invitation for us colored people to go and attend a Jim Crow meeting to hear the gospel of Jesus Christ from a man who wouldn't dare to invite us over there during these other thirty days. It appears that they think you can actually invite a human being to hear the gospel of Jesus Christ and insult him at the same time, and he won't see the insult but will receive the invitation.

This is nothing to laugh at my friends; it is one of the saddest things in the world. Don't you suppose that man wants to preach the gospel to you and to me. If he is a Christian, he cannot help preach the gospel to you and me because there is something in the gospel of Jesus Christ that says, "Go, preach it to every creature." But what is the matter? The sins of the fathers have transmitted their evil effects onto the institutions of the race or have transmitted their evil effects to the minds of their children, so men are afraid to do in the presence of their own compeers what they know their conscience and their God call them to do out of a free heart. In the long run, a man's sins are acquired by his children, and his sins take away from them the delicacy by which they should understand the tender feelings of other human beings. I am indicating this to you not in order that you may go away with an objective ill feeling toward anyone. The same law works right with us, for whosoever commits a sin on his own individual freedom and responsibility and then claims for himself that he alone takes the responsibility on himself is the man whose mind is brutalized. No man can sin and take the consequences and responsibilities of that sin upon himself.

In order to impress that upon you, I want you to do some figuring with your pencil and paper in your hand. Take a list of the businesses of Negro people in the city of Charleston, and you will see that so far as numbers of businesses are concerned, a whole host of business operations in town are drawing their money from sources that contribute nothing to the vitality of the people. In many cases, the businesses are so conducted that every dollar that comes into the till must be paid for by the morality and decency and respect of the race from which the dollar is drawn. The love of money has so possessed even us—who above all people in the United States ought to have moral and spiritual things on our minds—that in the first generation after slavery, we have so far forgotten the laws of life that we are willing to draw into our private coffers money from the degradation of the people. A man who conducts an unsupervised dance hall in order to fill the coffers of his pocket, or a Christian who holds stock in a concern that makes it its constant activity to conduct unsupervised dance halls while lewd positions are taken by the dancers and illicit liquor is being sold, is a criminal in the deepest sense of the word. The times will come when all such men will be excluded from the churches as a danger to the human race. Yet we somehow feel that we can sit quietly in the churches and look at the face of the preacher because he talks about Hell only and the damnation that comes to us after life. I tell you: Your children will arise someday and be taught in their high schools here to take a piece of black chalk and scratch it across the names of our most illustrious citizens because they will see that the citizens made their standing in the community by the degradation of the common people. The man who has invested his money in these places is just as guilty as the man who stands at the door and receives the filthy coin, and he knows it, too. What I am trying to impress upon you is the social consequences of sin, the social consequences of sin.

Now let me take up the fact that the population, which the individual sinner turns loose into the body of the people, is so strong and enduring that the people cannot be saved except there is a continual warfare against its influence on the human race. Not only must your sin be cared for, but also in order for the Negro people of Charleston—let me bring it right home—to come to the place where we have a considerable number of pure clean families unadulterated by immorality, we have got to fight for a continual stream of influence against some of the men who have been strongest and greatest among us. Many of them have been marauders of our homes like banded ruffians coming upon unsuspecting homes and breaking them up and talking about "what a wonderful man I am because so many of the women love me." Unborn generations—my friends, I am terribly serious about this—I am not afraid of destroying a young man's reputation because if I read the scriptures right, it is already destroyed—unborn generations of children have got to come into the world with scrofulous faces, blind eyes, and degenerate and imbecile minds just because some unscrupulous scoundrel talking of his own vanity has violated the virtues of womanhood in order to satisfy his own lusts.

In the first Psalm, there is a very significant passage. I have often thought about it. "The ungodly are not so, but are like the chaff which the wind driveth away. Therefore the ungodly shall not stand in the judgment, nor sinners in the congregation of the righteous. For the Lord knoweth the way of the righteous; but the way of the ungodly shall perish." What does that mean, my friends? It means that when the human race comes to its final consummation, when the plans of God have worked out for the redemption of humanity, there will be many supposedly great names that will be erased from the memory and from the influence of the human race forever. There will be no speck or scintilla there about them. Why? Because it took God so many years to purge the human race of the pollution that people have poured into it, He will rejoice to see the black space opposite their names. How can it be otherwise when humanity has had to struggle so long to redeem itself from that pollution? Charleston will be many a year getting over the pollution and destruction and degradation that have been written on the second floor of that building standing on that corner. The Negro race will be many years getting over the pollution and degradation and awful smelling horror that comes from the back fences and from the front gates of that institution there.

I cannot stop it; you cannot stop it, because the lust for gold has so gotten hold of the souls of men that they are willing to shove it down into their pockets by polluting their people and polluting the children and mothers and sons and daughters for generations yet unborn. So when Jesus stands up before the individual sinner and says, "The kingdom of Heaven is at hand, repent," it is not Jesus alone who stands there. It is the unborn child of every Negro and white family ages upon ages down history standing before you and pleading with you, "Don't squirt the polluted venom of your sins into my face and destroy my life before I am born." The whole human race looks on the face of Jesus and pleads with you saying, "Cease now before it is everlastingly too late. Come away from your sin before it is everlastingly too late."

I don't see how it cannot appeal to a man unless he is a brute. I don't see how. I don't see how. I don't see how. I don't see how. I respect a man who in some sense says, "I will take care of Hell if that is all you have to say to me. I will take care of Hell." But then a man looks upon the moving picture screen of life and sees that he is a parasite like an old fat louse stuck on the back of humanity sucking its blood in order that he may get fat—why, there must be times in the life of every sinner when he looks at himself in the glass and despises the image that he sees. The reason Jesus allowed himself to be crucified upon the cross and hanged up there where you and I could see him is he knew that the salvation of the whole human race was bound up with the actions of the individual. The more prominent that individual was, the more terrible was his sin and its effect upon the human race.

I know that it appeals to men when they see it. But just in that moment when this thing appeals to a man is the moment when he discovers something else, and it is awful for a man to discover. He discovers that he is not free. He discovers that this thing that he is doing, he is doing because something that has come down from the past has laid hold of him. Many a sinner comes to the places where he realizes that he is hurting his own wife, hurting his own family, hurting his own race, and hurting his own community, but he finds himself in the grip of the thing so strong—he finds the thing so prevalent around him—that there is set up a battle in his soul. The forces that are against him are stronger than the forces for him, and he cannot quite overcome his temptations.

I would have you realize the force of the truth I am talking about. It is the sins of the fathers—the sins of men who have died long ago—that have a grip on your life. The redemption of your life, as well as the redemption of the human race to which you belong, means getting yourself free from the sins of the fathers and following some noble figure like Jesus Christ in purity of life.

We are fighting to relieve ourselves from the sins of the fathers that will grip themselves upon this generation and will make parasites of us all unless some mighty spiritual influence like Jesus delivers us from them.

Why do Negro men take stock in concerns that they know are selling the moral life of their people? I will tell you why. Not only were you brought as slaves to this country by white traders but also our black forefathers went and sold us into slavery to white people. Don't you ever forget that. Not only was the man a criminal who brought us here—although his face was white— but also those black captains went into the heart of Africa and chained us and brought us to the coast to sell us. Those also are guilty, and some of those black captains are alive and in Charleston today. They go around roping the feet of Negroes and roping their souls and leading them up to the chopping block to be sold into all kinds of evil in order that they may satisfy their lusts and fill their filthy pockets. One of the first duties of Christians is to go out and take the stocks and bonds that they have invested in things that destroy the human soul and sell them or destroy them. A man cannot sit in heaven and invest in hell. Where your investments are, there your hearts will be also.

How are we going to get rid of the stream of the influence of our fathers? Isn't it wonderful, friends, when you think of it? Knowing these things as you know them—and you know them better than I do because I have only made suggestions—isn't it wonderful that Jesus with all that coming down from his race, isn't it wonderful to see him standing there at the top of history. Isn't it wonderful to see him there, to see the streams of adultery that pass into his life in past generations. There must have been some mighty chemical in his soul, because when it came out, it was all clean and pure. No woman was ever insulted by Jesus. No concern that made money off the destruction of his race ever had the investment of his dollar, but all the filthiness that flowed into his soul from times past was washed out and a powerful chemical that purified it all went into his soul so that nothing came out of Jesus but that which was pure and clean and constructive for the human race. Although all the theologies about Jesus should fail, and all the churches decay and be lost, the solitary fact is that Jesus stood there in the midst of history receiving all the pollution that flowed down the stream of the human race. He cast them off from him and purified them and let them pass from Him as living water. That fact will be a testimony to his moral and spiritual grandeur to the end of time. Remember what he said when he was talking to the woman at the well: "If you knew who it was that speaks to you, instead of hesitating about giving me this water that you draw from this well, you would say, 'Give me of the water that flows from your bosom because it is the water of eternal life.'"

No Hebrew child ever received any pollution from Jesus. Even the women who were degraded and down in the very gutter of life, when they looked to his face and saw how he loved them and how he respected them for what they could be, got up and threw off their robes of filthiness and wept tears at this feet, because the sight of Jesus was a purifying thing. It is beautiful to think that in that man all the impurities and pollutions of the human race were overcome. Do you wonder that—after He had died, when His disciples were in trouble, being bandied and beaten here and there by the opposition—there came a word from Heaven, "In this world ye shall have tribulation, but be of good cheer. I have overcome the world."

The glorious thing and the last thing I want to say to the sinner today is that you gentlemen have to stand in the stream of the pollution of the fathers. Our from the bosom of Jesus there flows another stream: a stream of redeemed humanity, of women who can tell you that before they saw the face of Jesus, they were unclean. But after they saw his face, they became purified and clean and became mothers of clean families. A stream of men will testify that they were grafters and leeches upon humanity until they saw Jesus, and when they saw Him, they turned about and followed Him in newness of life. One of the most glorious opportunities open to any sinner today is to quit associating with the people who glory in the lusts of the flesh, and to live a life that is filled with the love of God and humanity and where men glory, not in what they take away from the human race, but in what they give to the human race in purity and service. That is what the church means.

In conclusion, I can understand the doctrine of the immortality of the soul. I can understand it. The Kanawha River is a living river. I walked down there one day, and I saw coming out of another little spot a sweet, clean, clear piece of water that came from a spring. Don't you know that I noticed that as the Kanawha River flows down—it flows on down and flows on down—and although there are times when there are floods and when all the mud from those mines comes sweeping down into the Kanawha River, if you wait a few days, that little stream will regain the upper hand again. The doctrine of the immortality of the soul means this to me: Every humble life that resists the sins of the human race and allows the love of Jesus to flow out from it is like that stream that flows into the river. As the human race goes down the stream of time, God will see to it that the mud is put on the bottom and the clear little stream will go on flowing into eternity. If my soul tells me anything that is right when I read the life of Jesus, it is this: There is no kind and sweet act, no pure thought that was ever thought, and no constructive social deed that was ever done that will ever be lost. But in the final reckoning when all things are made clear, all these little spoutings that have come out from human hearts and thrown themselves into humanity will be recognized as the faithful ones who have redeemed the human race.

That is why the Gospel is great to me. It means that the faithful men and women—every one of integrity in high office and low place—are not only fighting the battle of their own individual salvation but also fighting against all the pollutions of all the people who have ever lived, who are living now, and who will ever live. Each is fighting with God a battle that can never be lost, and eternity will prove that the victory belongs to him.

Now if I have been talking to anybody today who is not a sinner, you will pardon me, because all that I have had today to say is addressed to sinners. We are all in some sense sinners. That is, all like sheep have strayed and taken our own way. We have all hidden in our bosoms secretly the thought that nobody is responsible for this but me. Nobody will suffer for this but me, and sometime I will make it all right with God. But keep in your mind today, my friend, this picture: Every sin that you commit goes into this stream of pollution that destroys the human race, and the sins that you have already committed have already set up in this world currents of destruction and harm that you cannot stop to save your life. That is why you cannot run ahead of humanity and undo the harm you have already done. You have to go and see God who holds the stream of history in his hand. You have to say, "Father, I have committed wrong, and the one to whom I have done wrong has gone yonder. I know that wrong has gone down into my children and children's children. I know that you have the redeeming love and you have the blood to shed to run away down the stream of history and pick up the wrong I have done and cleanse the human race." My friends, that is the only true and sincere attitude. A man must go to God to wipe out his sin because it takes an omnipotent God and suffering Savior to undo the sins of the individual.

Let us stand.

4. *Work, Business, and Religion*

Mordecai Johnson maintains that a person's work cannot be entirely separated from his or her religion, that work "is the expression of one's religion," and that the spirit of God should be expressed in one's work. He objects to the old saying, "Business is business, and religion is religion." Rather, he sets forth the unity of the individual. The attempt to compartmentalize one's life leads to moral decay. In whatever occupation people find themselves, they should put the spirit of God in the foreground of their lives.

WORK, BUSINESS, AND RELIGION[4]

TEXTS: I Corinthians 6:19—"What? Know ye not that your body
is the temple of the Holy Ghost which is in you,
which ye have of God, and ye are not your own?"
Psalms 90:17—". . . And establish thou the work of our hands
upon us; yea, the work of our hands establish thou it."

I want to read two texts this morning. One of them states a fact in the form of a question, and the other is a prayer.

I Corinthians 6:19: "What? Know ye not that your body is the temple of the Holy Ghost which is in you, which ye have of God, and ye are not your own?" Now the Holy Spirit will immediately indicate to you that what I am going to do is true—that if you put "work" in place of "body," the same thing is true. "What? Know ye not that your work is the temple of the Holy Ghost which is in you, which ye have of God, and ye are not your own?" It might be truly said, "And your work is not your own."

Then the ninetieth Psalm and the seventeenth verse: "And establish thou the work of our hands upon us; yea, the work of our hands establish thou it."

You can see from these two texts the substance of what I want to say this morning. And what I have to say this morning on this subject of work, business, and religion is only introductory because we hope to return to it time and time again.

I hope to say two things that are of the essence of the Gospel and the truth of religion: A man's work is the expression of his religion; the relationship between a man's work and his religion is analogous to the relationship between a man's spirit and his body. The next thing I want to say is, to put it negatively, "No man can establish the validity of his own work." To put it positively, "No work is fit and enduring except God establishes it by his spirit." Or to put it even more positively, "Wherever the spirit of God is expressed in a man's work, that work is holy and is itself a religious act wherein a man is in direct touch with the living God."

Now I want to depart just a moment. I have on my mind a problem that has worried you, and is worrying men today—is worrying the human race today as it has worried the human race in times past.

Down here on Capitol Street, we have retail stores, wholesale stores, banks, and every form of business activity. In those stores, in their gardens, in

---

[4]August 10, 1924.

their offices, all of us human beings are at work. Over here on this spot and in a few other spots, there are churches. Are these business houses and these churches separate and distinct institutions that have nothing to do with one another? When a man is at business or at work, has that nothing to do with his religion? Or is he religious only when he is doing specific religious things like coming to church, praying, giving an offering, or singing or preaching? That is to put it abstractly.

There is a widespread tendency in our times to insist that religion is something distinct from work and business. The United States Steel Trust has recently made a very powerful expression on that point. For years and years, the United States Steel Trust has made money by the degradation of human beings, working them twelve hours a day and oft-times demanding of that same set of men that they come back and work four hours more.

Religious men investigated the United States Steel Trust plants in a certain town in Pennsylvania, and they expressed the conviction that the practices of the United States Steel Trust were against the interests of men and of God and ought to be changed. Whereupon representatives of the United States Steel Trust made this answer, "Religion is religion; business is business. You religious men know your theology, your hymn book, and your Bible, but we know business. We do not propose to be interfered with by your impractical declarations on business." But in spite of the declaration of the United States Steel Trust, the common sentiment of humanity in the United States agreed with the declaration of those ministers, and the United States Steel Trust, in deference to the public opinion created by those courageous men, entered an eight-hour day on a humanitarian basis.

Our two largest newspapers in our city have recently made statements in the same direction. For example, yesterday, I believe, the *Charleston Mail* in making a perfectly legitimate criticism on some minister's words was not satisfied to make the criticism that every public institution has a right to make but went on and said, "Let us remind the gentleman of the cloth that we have division of labor in the United States. We have businessmen and we have preachers, and the preachers are to preach out of the Bible and sing hymns, and the businessmen and the workers are to run the labor unions, the banks, etc., and they are two separate fields of endeavor."

They may be right, but I am just judging their position with that of another very distinguished man. To show you how widespread the opinion is, just a very few days ago Mr. Samuel Gompers, the distinguished and able leader of the American Federation of Labor, saw a report of the Federal Council of Churches that stated Mr. Gompers and the American Federation of Labor had for a long time stood in the way of American labor's getting a proper political expression. I have seen that expression made by laboring men themselves and by labor newspapers time and time again. But when it was made by the churches, Mr. Gompers became supremely indignant. Not only did he criticize the position taken by the Federal Council of Churches, but also he himself (which was his perfect right) went on to defend the thought that the churches must confine themselves to and must be satisfied with spiritual things.

Now among public men of high character, there is a decided tendency to separate and distinguish the fields of religion and business and to work just as clearly as a church building is separated from a bank building, holding that they do not have anything to do with one another and that when one of them offers an opinion on the other, he goes out of his province.

If the matter was simply a matter of Mr. Gompers and the *Charleston Mail*, we humble people, just sixty years removed from slavery, might let it pass. But, do you know, that thing is in us also? There is many a laboring man today who goes to church and who makes a sharp distinction or division between his laboring activities and his religious activities. If you would question him closely, he would say to you, "Now, on Monday I go to work and on Sunday I attend to my religion. For the most of the time, I am attending to my daily bodily needs, but on Sunday I am attending to my spiritual needs." So there are many of us today who feel that when we come to church, pay our church dues, and sing hymns, that is the time when we are really religious, but when we are working or are engaged in our business or profession, we are just attending to business.

Now, is that a true position? Does it stand that way? Are the two fields separate? Oh, there is a lot in human nature that would love for it to be that way. Just see what happens when men make them separate. Look what happens on the business side (I have seen it happen many a time). Then I will tell you what happens on the religious side.

As soon as a certain type of man comes to the conclusion there is a direct and thorough cleavage between business and religion, he begins to think, "Let me see: Six days for most of my working hours I am busy working; getting bread, meat, and clothes; paying rent; or buying my house. I do not need a preacher or anybody else to tell me how necessary that is. That is perfectly manifest. One day a week and two hours on that day I go to church, and the preacher talks to me about things that I cannot see. Sometimes he gets a grip on me but most of the time he does not. Now it looks to me as if this working side of my life, this business side of my life, is overwhelmingly important and absolutely necessary, while this religious side of my life does not matter much. Anyhow, it is just about one-seventh as important as the other side. It is a kind of distant, far-off dream. Here is a man over here who says there is nothing to it. I just conclude there is nothing to it, and I will just attend to my business and carry on my work." That is a legitimate issue and a legitimate conclusion from the separation of religion and business.

See what has happened in the world whenever religion feels it has nothing to do with the bank and politics and with the man who works out in the ditch. Several times in history the world has become decidedly corrupt in its business and in its social and political relationships. Several times in history religious men have felt that the claims of God upon the soul were so strong that in all probability they did not have anything to do with business, with social life, or with politics. So they have withdrawn from the world— those "hermit souls" that you read about. They have gone into the desert places living alone, eating figs off the trees or anything they could pick up, begging from day to day, and withdrawing themselves entirely from business and social relationships and political life. What always happens?

You can read the literature of such a movement as that. As those men began to get on the borderland between insanity and sanity, they began to have a multitude of dreams. They began to be led away by a multitude of visions. Those visions were such a hodgepodge of themselves that those men became impressed with a multitude of things around them, and many of them became absolutely useless to themselves or to the world.

In other words, I am saying to you that, as a matter of history, wherever religion and business and work have consented to a separation, both business and work have suffered on the one hand, and religion has suffered on the other.

Again the first doctrine I want preach to you out of the Gospel of Jesus Christ is that there cannot be any separation between business and work and religion, and for this simple and perfectly commonsense reason: The same man who sits in the pew on Sunday morning and listens to the sermon is the same man who is behind the bank counter yonder, the same man who works in the ditch, the same man who organizes politics, the same man who attends to the labor union yonder. There cannot be any separation between his business and his religion because it is the same man who has both the business and the religion.

That is a perfectly commonsense reason. There is no such thing as a man being a scoundrel in religion and a saint in business. There is no such thing as a man being a saint in religion and a scoundrel in business. It is absolutely impossible.

As I stated to you in the beginning of my remarks, the whole matter is analogous to the relationship between the mind and the body, or, to put it better, the soul and the body. Discussions have gone on in the world with regard to the soul and the body. For years and years some of the most distinguished men and deepest thinkers in the world thought there was a distinct separation between the soul and the body. Just as soon as men agreed on that, look what happened.

St. Paul said that the only way you can be a religious man is to beat down your body, beat it into subjection. Do not engage in anything you do not have to; beat your body and let your soul stand up on it like David did on Goliath, with a stone, and say, "If you do not behave, I will cut your head off."

Epictetus said, "We do not know so much about this soul business in Athens and what a man does after life that you are talking and worrying so much about. We are not so sure about that. But we are absolutely certain about this body. I am absolutely sure about my getting hungry and thirsty. I am absolutely certain of needing a house when it rains. I am absolutely certain I like beautiful flowers around me. So I conclude that the only way for a man to lead a happy life is to pay all attention to his body. Pay attention to it in a nice, decent, gentleman-like fashion, but look after the body."

Paul comes back in one of his noblest moments—not when he was trying to be a philosopher but when the spirit of Jesus Christ had fallen upon him—and says, "Know ye not that your body is the temple of the Holy Ghost." In that one phrase Paul rose and uttered the relationship between the soul and the body. The body is the temple in which the living God takes up His residence.

When you look at Jesus Christ, is that not what you see? You see a human body radiated and made beautiful by the spirit dwelling in it. I imagine the hands of Jesus Christ were beautiful to look at as they touched the blind man's eyes. I imagine the eyes of Jesus Christ were things of sparkling beauty that one would have stood a long time and looked at with delightful affection because out of those eyes there shone the spirit that was from above. I imagine that the feet of Jesus Christ as he trod on to Jerusalem—facing the cross with certainty, dignity, and confidence in the living God—were stronger and more courageous than the feet of each one of those soldiers marching along by that body that was filled with the spirit of the living God.

The Gospel about your body is this: The good news about it is that this body of yours—even in the case of some of us who have been slaves, who have been beaten and whipped and scourged—may shine with the glory of God. God may take hold of this black hand that has slaved and say, "I will use you to bless some little children." God can take these crude lips and bring out of them words that will make men tremble. That is the good news about the body.

The good news about your work is that your work and your business may become God's temple when you take Him along with you in your work. That is the reason Jesus Christ said, "I have come to preach good news to the poor." He meant to us, to the poor men.

You do not have to go to the temple on the mount to worship God; you do not have to go to the temple at Jerusalem to worship God. You can worship God in this ditch were you are working in the slime and mud. You can worship God in this hospital where you stand with your instruments in your hands as an efficient nurse tending some soul at death's door. You can worship God, doctor, by the way you hold your scalpel while helping some soul who begs to live. You can worship God by the way you work in your kitchen and attend to the region of your kitchen so one walking in there and seeing how you work will know that God has made a temple of your kitchen.

That is the Gospel and that is the good news about work. My friends, it is such good news that slaves who have been living under the worst conditions in the world have discovered it, and many of them have been content to suffer in slavery by seeing the glory of hard work.

The other day I buried a woman who was 106 years old and who had been a slave practically all her years. When I buried her, I could not keep from looking at her countenance in that coffin, and the peace that passes human understanding was on that dead face. I stood there trying to preach, and the thought kept continually forcing itself in my mind, "How can this woman, whose back has been beaten so many times, who has been abused so many times, how can she lie in this casket so peacefully? How could she delve and toil and live 100 years and go down to her grave in peace?" The spirit of the Lord said to me, "She discovered that the slave can fall in love with his work the same as a free man. He can so love his work and so address himself to the needs of those who abuse him that the suffering will come off his back as water off the back of a duck. The spirit of God will come into his soul as the spirit that passeth all understanding."

Do you know that one of the greatest philosophers was a slave, Epictetus. The other day I was sitting by a distinguished professor of Harvard who said, "Gentlemen, when I get weary of this world, I turn to old Epictetus who, in his slavery, discovered the spirit of God; and when he speaks to me, my soul is at peace."

There is nothing wrong about common work—the truest end of work and not the accidental end of it—because God made everyday work and business. That is the fundamental reason the religious man must continually cry against all kinds of base work, all kinds of base methods, all kinds of harmful activities in connection with men's work and men's business. The religious man is just as sure to cry out against them as he lives. He cannot help it to save his life. If Mr. Gompers and the whole Federation of Labor should say he could not, yet would he do it. If all the newspapers in the world should say he should not cry against it, yet he has to cry. When he sees his whole vision degraded, he has to cry out.

Old Ahab, the King of Israel, was a businessman and he had a keen wife, Jezebel. He and Jezebel got off a decidedly good business deal in a crooked manner. They rejoiced in it because not only was it good for them but also they thought it was good for the kingdom. They had 300 prophets visiting them and eating at their table. Every one of them was just like the newspapers, telling lies every morning to bolster the kingdom. They told the king and queen that everything they did was all right. But Old Elijah said, "Every one of you is a liar, and the truth is not in you. I know you are prophets and liars, and I dare every one of you to come up to the mountain and try it out between my God and your god."

In the time of another one of the kings of Israel, the nation was so prosperous that the people were singing praises to their God every morning, "Glory be to our God. He has given us such wonderful prosperity. Our houses are builded out of bricks and mortar. We have our summer palaces and our winter palaces. We are receiving our spices from the East. Our temples are bedecked with gold, silver, and precious stones."

The prophets were saying to the king, "Blessings on you; you have saved our nation."

One day a fellow walked into the town who said he was a herdsman. He had been out herding sheep, and he said God bothered him. He said, "He told me to come up here and tell every single one of you that you are liars." He said, "If you think He is pleased by the giving of a little gold and silver in His collection box, you are mightily mistaken. What God wants is justice and righteousness."

They took him off on the side and said, "You are disturbing the business of the community. If you want to talk this way, go on back out there where the sheep are, but do not talk this way at the king's palace where we are having a banquet."

Amos said, "I am not a prophet or the son of a prophet. I do not enjoy this business of cussing out kings, princes, and priests. I would not have done it if God had not bothered me."

It was not out of those 300 prophets (because the name of every one of them has been forgotten), but it was out of Elijah, Amos, Hosea, Micah, and such men who stood up before their generation and told the prophets, princes, and kings, "You are all liars if you think God wants anything but justice, righteousness, and mercy." It was out of that class of men that God raised up His son to rule the world.

It is of the very nature of the wicked and perverse generation not to want to hear the truth about its work and business because it is right there that the issues are. When a man criticizes work and business, a group of men always rises with the cry, "He is fighting business." They know they are liars. He is fighting corrupt and unrighteous business.

There is no conflict among work and business and religion, for the fundamental reason that God himself can dwell in a good man's work and in a good man's business.

Religion is not in this world to sanctify laziness, slothfulness, the possession of nothing, and the want of nothing. Religion is not in this world to sanctify that. Religion is in this world for ability and genius, which are needed in the building of the world. But religion is bound to cry out against all of those parasites and hucksters who would take the whole fabric of work and chuck it to the dogs.

So we have a kind of watchword in our day, and you hear a man speaking of sharp practices in a business transaction with another. You call his attention to the fact that certain things should not be done in connection with business transactions, and he may argue with you for a while until he sees he cannot get out. Then he will hump his shoulders and say, "Oh, it is a matter of business with me."

The answer of religion is that "there are several kinds of business." There are several kinds of business. There is a business in which a man's word is his honor. There is another kind of business in which a man gives his word only to deceive. He agrees to give you oak lumber, and he gives you wallboard. He agrees to give you brass, and he gives you some stuff scrubbed over with brass. He agrees to give you one kind of foundation, and he puts in it something that will send your house down in ruins. He agrees to give you the best kind of carpentry and hires a "jackleg" and instructs him to swindle you.

That kind of business has no right to exist. When people realize their rights, that man will suffer worse than would a horse thief in the West. When men's laws were not so well developed and a man in the West stole a horse, he was hanged. Now a man will sell a poorly constructed house, beat his neighbor out of money by doing it, and go about "nigger-rich." When men were strong, hanging would not have been too good. Yet such men call on the present generation to worship them as gods. I would rather be a man feeding on rancid hot dogs, the lowest of any race, or any race, than dependent upon that kind of crookedness.

So let the issue be made clear. What the church is after is not a world in which there is no business, no toil, no money, no wealth, no leisure, no beauty, but it is after a world in which money, toil, work, and business will be sanctified because the men who toil and work and conduct business will do it by putting the spirit of God in the foreground. They are bound to express God in their business.

It is a comfort, and I want to make it reach the majority of us that there are only three things, my beloved, that, in the case of ordinary people like you and like me, will keep our business from being religious.

The first of them is that the business itself is destructive of the higher human values. If it is, God cannot and will not come into it. Can you imagine the Lord God running a bootlegging establishment in this age and time, when the whole United States of America is trying to keep the Eighteenth Amendment and to support the Constitution? Can you imagine the Lord God fitting up a gambling den and inviting your sons and daughters to enter and play for the glory of God and the advancement of the human race? Can you imagine the Lord God running a filthy, cheap amusement place; smiling at one old hoary-headed prostitute and another; and inviting them to come there and dance together at $1.50? What you need, brothers and sisters, is commonsense. Could you imagine the Lord God, even though He would not go there and do that Himself, being so enamored and delighted with the profits of it and saying, "While I cannot precisely sit at the door and take tickets, yet I will get a rake-off on the dice and when you get the profits, give me 12 percent"? Can you imagine Him doing that? Just use good common sense. Could you imagine that?

What is the matter with the minds of men that they could expect that the house of God would be a place in which that thing would be sanctified and hold and in which the men who do it would be elected to the deacons' board and put up as high men of the church? It is preposterous. All we need is commonsense. The first thing that faces men's work is that God cannot have anything to do with it, whatever its nature, if it hurts the human race or keeps the human race from growing toward God. In the very nature of the case, no Christian man with a conscience can engage in it. He will leave it as a child leaves hot stuff when he first puts his hand on it. The first endeavor of every Christian man and woman will be to engage in the kind of work and in the kind of business that is in itself connected with the fundamental needs of the human race.

The second thing that vitiates good work—even though the work be good itself—is the way you do it. You run the love of God out of your hearts. You may be a school teacher—which is a high calling—and you may do that work so slovenly and so lazily and so neglectfully that God would delight in nothing so much in the world as to see you put off the faculty. He might plead with you a long time and work on a superintendent a long time to give you one more chance. But in the very nature of the case, however holy work may be in itself, when you do it slovenly or so lazily or so neglectfully or in any manner whatsoever as to hide defects and not to bring out excellence, then your work is degrading and discouraging to others.

Whatever kind of work you are in, if it is decent work, put your best intelligence and mind into it; put your honor into it. A man may be in the workshop and God himself is there. He honors and loves you and calls you His children. You can lay down your wrench and say, "God has fixed this automobile. Blessed be His name." If I carry an automobile to a man's shop and there is something the matter with it that I do not know, the man comes and with his intelligence divines the situation, conceals nothing from me, and puts everything in right and says, "Here is the car. My honor is in that. If it is not straight, then bring it back to me." I feel like saying to that man, "I thank you for discovering a man who fixes automobiles with his soul as well as with his hands."

The third and last thing that degrades work is the use of the proceeds therefrom for purposes destructive of human life and its powers. For example, here is a man who may do perfectly noble work and who may do it well and excellently, but when he gets his money in his hand, he puts it to no constructive use whatever. He patronizes cheap amusements, buys whiskey for himself and others, and uses it to carry people where it is not good for them to be. Or he uses it to maintain a home that is not constructed for welfare. He has then spoiled all the effects of his labor by putting the money to a bad use.

Conversely, the one who will dignify his work is the one who will take the proceeds of it and put the money into something his soul approves of.

I want to sum this all up by taking an everyday working man who has a wife and two children. He goes out and works with his pick and his shovel. He has a job digging a main for a sewer for the city. It is a dirty job, but it is an interesting job and absolutely necessary and noble. He goes down into that dirty hole, and his superintendent is off somewhere yonder. He sees the opportunity to get by down there. His head is below the surface. He can kill time and can throw a big old stone down in the hole and throw a little dirt over it and give the impression that he has been working there for hours. He has all that temptation but, just as if God Himself were looking down on him, he works steadily and fills that hole as it ought to be filled, tramples it down, and does what I have seen thousands of those workmen do and what I love for them to do while the boss is off yonder—sing, "Blessed be the name of God." Then he comes up out of that dirty, grimy place and carries home in his pocket a yellow envelope on Saturday night to the wife, who comes to the door with her sleeves rolled up after the children are in bed. He says "Honey, here are my week's wages. Go up and pay the milkman, pay the woman who helped us with the laundry, get the children some shoes, and if you have anything left after the necessities, give a little to the House of God and lay a little aside for the children who will have to be educated by and by." Let him rest in peace. God is in that house. The time will come when there will be no temples. There will be no synagogues but God will dwell in the home of the honest workingmen who do an honest day's work with an honest purpose and who worship God around the fireside because they love His name.

Beloved, you may say what you please, but the spirit of God tells me that every legitimate human business is capable of being conducted just like that workingman's business, just like he conducts his life. Every legitimate human business is capable of being a straight-out, honest, and above-board business that will offer itself for the inspection of any man.

Every legitimate business is a business that can be done with honor. There are no circumstances in this world that will justify a Christian man in doing any business with dishonor. Every legitimate business in this world is capable of bringing a man such proceeds that he can use those proceeds for the development of some high spiritual quality. Every legitimate business is like that.

As I said just now, the time will come when every business on this earth will be shot through with an invisible dignity and religion, and men will not have to go to church and say to the preacher, "Tell us about God," for every man will know God himself.

I wish I had the time to take this matter up in connection with labor unions and capital and the future of the Negro race, the future of our country. Every labor union leader knows more about labor unionism than I do. Every capitalist knows more about capital than I do. But not a solitary man of them living knows more about the inner workings of a human soul than Jesus Christ did.

There is no occupation in the world in which God is not at work, in which people do not have an influence that, expressed, will reach the heart of common humanity. The Church will never be able to work out the technique of the real estate business. The Church will never be able to work out the technique of a bank. It will never be able to work out the technique of the medical profession. It will never be able to work out the technique of cooking. But the Church is always here to tell men that it has the final word on the morality of all businesses and that it will never cease—until its presence has been made unnecessary by the living presence of God Himself—to speak to each man's individual soul.

May the Lord bless you and make His face to shine upon you—make it shine in that kitchen, that grocery store, that real estate business, that banking business, that dentist's office, that house where you are painting. Whenever you go, may men somehow be made to feel that "God Almighty has something to do with this work that I have done in this place."

5. *The Radical Commitment*

Here Mordecai Johnson focuses on the rigorous requirements for a full commitment to a life of Christian integrity. He maintains that Jesus said that when one chooses to follow Him, one must be prepared to make that commitment the primary loyalty in his life. Obedience to high principles may require separation from certain people, even your closest relatives, including your parents, sisters, and brothers—if they are allied with a destructive principle, group, or way of life. Johnson maintains that following the crowd will always be easy. To keep a challenging commitment, however, requires determination and courage, which are needed if one is to develop and maintain a life of Christian wholeness.

The Radical Commitment[5]

TEXT: Luke 14:26— "If any man come to me and hate not his father, and
mother, and wife, and children, and brethren, and sisters, yea, and
his own life also, he cannot be my disciple."

That is an amazing statement, a most amazing statement. Here is a simple, homely, Galilean peasant preacher. His words have attracted great multitudes. He is an eager preacher, earnest preacher, saying good things and hard things. His soul undoubtedly thrills as he looks at this large multitude hanging on his words, and yet he is afraid of that multitude. He desires way down in the bottom of his heart to have a multitude of followers just like that, but when he sees the multitude of followers there, he becomes afraid. I invite you to look in your New Testament to see how Jesus feared the multitude of those who followed him and praised him. One day, turning to this multitude, he made to them this amazing statement: "If any man come to me and hate not his father, and mother, and wife, and children, and brethren, and sisters, yea, and his own life also, he cannot [not he may not] be my disciple."

That is the hardest possible word that one man could utter to another on the question of leadership and following, isn't it? Jesus has picked out the holiest ties of this earth. Look there: he has named that sacred word, "father," and that holy word, "mother." The Ten Commandments say, "Honor thy father and mother, that thy days may be long upon the land which the Lord thy God giveth thee." And Jesus says, "If you hate not your father and your mother, you cannot be my disciple."

He mentions that blessed word, "wife," that has come to be so precious. Will not a man leave his mother and father and strike out in the world and spend half of his lifetime getting a home properly built and furnished for a wife? And will not a man—well, haven't many men gone to the death chair and to the gallows in defense of the honor and the person of their wives? And doesn't Jesus himself say that when a man or a woman are married, they become one flesh, and "What God hath joined together, let no man put asunder"? But it is that same Jesus who says, "If a man hate not his wife, he cannot be my disciple."

He mentions that blessed word, "children." Children! They are so precious to us and form the little gems around which our home is securely built: the foundation and the rock and strength and power of many a home

---

[5]August 17, 1924.

of this land. Didn't Jesus himself place a little child in the midst, and did he not say that whosoever did the least service unto one of these little ones had done it unto him? Did he not say, "Suffer the little children to come unto me and forbid them not, for of such is the Kingdom of Heaven"? And it is this same Jesus who says, "If a man hate not his own child, he cannot be my disciple."

Then to complete the whole thing, Jesus puts down "brethren" and "sisters," by which he undoubtedly means not only those who are closely kin to us in our immediate family, but also all who claim kinship to us by blood or by race or by nationality. Surely he would not stop at race or nationality if he told a man to hate his father and his mother and his wife—would he? Thus, in order to complete this hard saying, he says if a man hate not his brothers and sisters—including the kinship of race and national kinship— not he *may not*, but he *cannot* be his disciple.

Now, my beloved, I want to ask you a question. Has a man good sense who makes a statement like that? Can he be in his right mind? Suppose a man were to make that statement today on a street corner. He would be suspected of a mild degree of insanity, wouldn't he? And that is exactly what happened to Jesus when he made that statement and similar statements. Some of his own kin people came and sent word unto him to tell him to come out and not disgrace the family. "He is a little off. Tell him to come on." But, my friends, Jesus means this thing. He is not crazy. He is in a perfectly balanced state of mind, and he is a man who loves his mother. You can tell that, can't you? He loved his mother. The Scriptures say he was obedient unto his mother and his father; and among the last words on the cross were words telling a man to look after his mother, weren't they? He says it with perfect sanity, perfect balance of mind. The reason I know he means it is he repeats it in the New Testament several times—repeats it in different ways. Jesus tells them, "If you want to be a true disciple of mine, you must hate your father, hate your mother, hate your wife, hate your brother, hate your sister, hate the members of your own race, hate the citizens of your country, and even hate your own life."

And do you know, my beloved, that is one of the reasons men have admired Jesus since the time that he came upon the earth. Don't you know I just love him for that statement. And there are men without number who worship Jesus today because of his statements like that.

Now what is he saying to that multitude? This is, in substance, what he is saying: "If you are following me for any other reason in the world than because you believe this thing that I am teaching is supremely important—

above every other earthly consideration—you might just as well leave me now, because under no conditions can you be my disciple." Now, mark you. Here is a man in the early part of his ministry seeking followers—actually going to men and talking to them one by one, saying, "Come and follow me." Isn't he? But as soon as he gets a man close to him, he turns around on him and says, "If you are going to follow me through, you must hate your mother, hate your father, hate your wife, hate your children, hate your brother and your sister, hate your own life. If you don't, you cannot be my disciple." Do you wonder, my beloved, that over there in the sixth chapter of John it is said, "Many of his disciples went back and walked no more with him"? Do you wonder?

A brother came running one day and said, "Master, I will follow you wherever you will go."

Jesus said, "Now, brother, just wait. Just get calm; cool." He said, "I haven't any place to lay my head. Sit down and count the cost right now. If you are not willing to undergo all the hardships that I am undergoing and, in case of necessity, hate your father, hate your mother, hate your sister, hate your brother, give them up, give up your property and your life and your race and your nation, or anything, why you cannot be my disciple. Don't let yourself be carried away by enthusiasm, because this is a lifetime business. It is going to cost all that you have, and you had better sit down and count the cost now."

I admire it, my beloved, because it is a statement of an honest man. He said, "If you are going to follow me, don't place any shackles on me by mentioning your father. If I call on you to do something hard for the Kingdom of Heaven, don't tell me what your mother wants you to do, because I am going to speak to you about the will of God. And when I let you know what the will of God is, all human considerations must be separated from it." You know I admire that. He desired no followers except those who would follow him for the sake of goodness and goodness alone, and for the reward of goodness that comes from God alone, and from no other human consideration. Oh, the sincerity of Jesus! Oh, that the world today were filled with such leaders who are willing to speak with absolute sincerity about the great spiritual realities of life.

Before I go on to the next point, let me pause to tell you that they nearly all left him. They nearly all left him. That is the way the multitude rewards sincerity. They nearly all left him. And after they left him, one day he turned around to a little handful that was left standing by him, Peter and James and John and the rest of the twelve, and he said, "Will you too leave me?"

Peter said, "Lord, where shall we go? Thou hast the words of eternal life." But even the man who made that deep confession on a certain day came to Jesus when men were saying evil things about him and when the multitudes were leaving him, even that man came to Jesus and said, "Lord, whatever other men may say about you, whatever other men may do to you, I will go with you until the end."

And Jesus said to him, "Peter, I know you better than you know yourself. You, too, will leave me." He said, "You will leave me; you, too, will leave me." He said, "The time will come when every one of you will go off and leave me alone." And then he took second thought and said, "But I am not alone, for the Father is with me."

My beloved, that is why you are here this morning. And that is why, when the endless ages continue to roll on and on, after your body and my body are buried in the grave and our names have been forgotten, men will be gathered together in little temples like this to praise the name of Jesus because he was a man so absolutely sincere. He was willing to stand and say, "I am not alone, for the Father is with me." He was absolutely certain that if he permitted all of his followers to leave him, every single one of them to leave him, and if he stood alone with God, he was absolutely certain that they would come back. And when they were leaving him, he said, "And I, if I be lifted up, will draw the whole world unto me." Why was he so certain about that? He knew that way down in the hearts of the men who would leave him on account of his hard words that they knew there was a loving Father, the living God. He knew that their hearts would lead them sometime or other back to the feet of God. And he knew that when they came back, they would find him there. That is the reason why we are here. We worship Jesus because of his absolute sincerity. Because of his willingness to stand alone and be mutilated and crucified and die an ignominious death and be buried. For he knew that the same men who crucified him and buried him would one day fall down and say, "This is the son of the Living God. Blessed be his name."

But you know Jesus did not make this statement—but before I go on I want to say, you and I have come into an age of the church in which we don't remember that part of Jesus. We don't remember that about Jesus. The world has been afflicted for 500 years with a mass of fallacy. Men have been telling about the pre-existent and glorious son of God who came down in trailing clouds of glory from a superhuman heaven and was crucified on Calvary to carry out a preconceived plan of the Living God, who was not subject to temptation as we are, and who on Calvary's brow executed our salvation and went on back to glory. They have been telling us that sweet story, and we have been very glad over that story because it is true. But they have forgotten to tell you that it was this same Jesus who stood up in the front of men and said, "I don't want a single one to follow me, not a single one to follow me, unless you are willing to hate your wife and your children and your brothers and your sisters, and to hate your own life. And if you don't take up your cross after I tell you that, you can never be my disciple." We forget that is what he told them. We forget it in our earnest desire to be beneficiaries of the salvation provided by the sufferings of Jesus. We have been led to stop comprehending the real, human Jesus who stood on the face of history and called on men to die.

And so we have got to be a flabby church. Forty million people in the United States belong to the church of the Living God by name, but that is no indication whatsoever of the number of followers of Jesus Christ. It may be that this whole fabric built up around these beautiful cathedrals and buildings will have to be destroyed before Jesus can really find out how many followers he actually has. One of the greatest blessings that could happen in this land today would be for some persecution to arise against the church of God and burn down its buildings, persecute its members, in order that the world might see the handful of men and women who really love Jesus Christ and are willing to suffer for his name's sake. But the world today has a flabby church. We have got multitudes of people on the rolls of the church of Jesus Christ who don't even think enough about Jesus to put in a dollar a year for the expenses of carrying on his cause, and don't become his followers until they are dead. Then someone sends in a marvelous and glorious obituary telling how they have followed the Lord Jesus Christ consistently for twenty years. I am glad that the obituary doesn't have to be prepared and sent to heaven, because I think it would be burned in the ashcan outside the back gate of glory.

Then there is a multitude of other people who pay their dues and are loyal to every external function in the church of Jesus Christ, but who wish to have the Gospel of Jesus Christ sugar-coated and sweetened and fixed up so that it won't hurt their past life. It "won't make me feel sorry for what I have done all my life; won't disturb any corruption that I may engage in; won't hurt my feelings and won't hurt my wife's feelings and won't hurt my children's feelings, and my brother's feelings, and my sister's feelings." We love the Lord Jesus Christ all right enough, but we want our salvation nicely done. We want it done according to the polite etiquette of the world. We don't want any more weeping and mourning and wailing, and washing tears, and agonizing groans over our sins, but we want to go to heaven by mechanics.

That is the reason the great Roman Catholic Church is so successful among a multitude of people today. It prescribes for you the kind of things that you must do—from one kind to a dozen—to get into the Kingdom of Heaven. Now if you don't miss mass once a month. If you take possession of the mass. If you pay your church dues, be obedient to the priest, say the rosary so many times, and go through so many forms of penitence, then the fathers will guarantee you that you can go into the Kingdom of Heaven. I don't say all of their religion, because some of the deepest and purest and most exalted souls in the world have come out of the Catholic Church. But so many human beings who have no intention whatsoever of following Jesus deeply down in their lives believe they are on the way to heaven by the performance of one or two or three or four things that can be done with the hands or the eyes or the lips or the feet.

So today we are living in a corrupt age of the church. The church itself has lost a great deal of its influence in the world because it has become, in many cases, a body of "respectables"—a body in which people come to signify to the world that "I am a respectable person." When a man wants to tell you that he is a "respectable individual," he tells you, "Now I belong to this, and I belong to that, and I belong to the other, and I belong to thus and so," and that is proof positive that that individual is a "respectable person."

My friends, way back yonder an old member of the First Baptist Church would never have bought his respectability at the cost of his life. The world today has become a sheepfold with a multitude of people covering themselves over with the respectable clothing of Jesus Christ while they continue out in the world. There are adulterous and guilty members destroying the Kingdom of Christ while they worship him in name. That is true not only of this church, but also of multitudes of churches all over the land. It is a great indictment against the Church of Jesus Christ today. And the one great need in the Church today—as it was in the day when Jesus was alive—is to have men once more know that they are deceiving themselves if they think that by any means whatsoever the doors of the Kingdom of Heaven are open to any man who puts his father or his mother, his wife or his children, his brother or his sister, his race or his nation, or even his own life before the will of God, he cannot be a disciple of the Lord Jesus Christ. And I am sent here to preach that hard gospel; to undeceive men; to tell men the hard, cold, literal truth that except you hate your father and your mother and your brothers and your sisters and your wife and children and your own life for Jesus, you cannot be his disciple.

Now let me go on. Jesus undoubtedly did not say this in order to prove his sincerity, because he was not so very much concerned about whether men said he was sincere or whether they did not say he was sincere. He said these things, my beloved, with several purposes in his mind. In the first place, Jesus wanted to weed out all hypocritical and wishy-washy and shallow-minded followers. Jesus wanted to get rid—at the outset—of anybody who followed him for any other reason whatsoever than believing in the thing that he preached. And you and I ought to get that today. Jesus does not care anything about our little gifts and our little compliments that we pay him when we get down and call him a multitude of beautiful names in prayer. And the world has got so low today that men feel they can patronize the cause of Jesus Christ; that is, they think they can say, "I believe in the church. Here is ten dollars."

But Jesus says, "Keep your ten dollars. Keep it forever. Keep your compliments. I don't care for your ten dollars, don't care for your compliments, don't care for anything you have but your soul, and I want all of it." Oh, no. The church can afford to be poor; she can afford to be a few in numbers; she can afford to be despised and rejected; she can afford to be persecuted; she can afford to suffer martyrdom; she can afford to suffer her members to be cast into prison, mutilated, burned, and crucified. There is only one thing that the church of Jesus Christ cannot afford and live: It cannot afford to be without men and women of conviction who love Jesus with all their hearts and souls and minds, and are willing to give up everything for his name's sake. That is the only thing that the Christian church cannot afford to do without. The reason why you don't hear many preachers say this is it hurts their salary; it hurts the collection. That is the reason I came into the ministry when I was young and in my vitality, so that I could go out and shuck corn, and set type, and sweep the streets, and do anything for a living in order that I might tell men the truth. The church can do without large numbers. It can do without money. It can do without everything in God's earth that men consider valuable but one: an absolute devotion to the soul of Jesus Christ with all one's heart and mind. The church can do without wealth; it can do without learning. For 150 years it was moved by common, ordinary fishermen. Even in his lifetime, Paul said, writing to one of the churches: "You will observe, brethren, that not many wives, not many immediately after the flesh, are among your number."

The church of Jesus Christ was founded and set on foot and brought to a glorious power in the world by slaves, servants, dishwashers, rude street sweepers, and the outcasts of the world. She can afford once more to go back to that place if only those people love the Lord Jesus Christ with all their hearts and all their souls and all their minds, and God will use them for a power. That is the only thing the church can't do without.

You know, the other day I heard an old-fashioned preacher preach, and he stood up and took this text: "You must be born again." And he just raised Cain with all of his younger preachers who received people into the church by shaking their hands. He said the time ought to come back when men would have to come to the mourners' bench, get down and cry as they did in the olden days about their sins, and come into the church of Jesus Christ. I sympathized with his purpose. The only difference between us younger men and him is that we believe a man can make that decision while he is standing up. But there is no question about the truth of what he is talking about. The only thing that God can be satisfied with about his church is that people be born again and have the spirit of God in them—not the spirit of the world or the flesh, but the spirit of God in themselves. The spirit of God in themselves. That is the only thing the church can't do without.

You can do without me. You can do without Professor Rice. You can do without any of those who are in official position. You can do without any human being who ever lived. You can do without any human learning. You can do without everything so long as you have a handful of people who believe in Jesus Christ and are willing to suffer all things for his Name's sake. Let us get that clear, and let us get the object of that clear. Jesus does not want any of us to compliment him, or to pay dues to him, or to put our names on the church books, or even to attend his services if we have any intention other than to follow him with all our heart and soul and mind. Is that right? I think it is right. I think it is right. The church has never been under constraint to have the world in its membership, but continually our Lord and Savior Jesus Christ has said to the church: "Resist the world. Separate yourselves from the world. And if you find worldly minded men among you, separate them from among you in order that you may be pure-minded people working on for the Master."

So Jesus was actually trying to weed out people. He was telling the flabby and the weak and the inconstant—who really were not in earnest about this business—to leave him from the very beginning, because he knew they could not be depended on in a crisis, and it would be better for them to leave him now.

In the second place, Jesus was saying, my beloved, that you and I should not be deceived about the nature of the Christian life. He did not want you and me to be deceived about the nature of the Christian life. He did not want anybody to get the conception that the Christian life was easy. Now why not? When men get the conception that a thing is easy, they don't put their strength into it, do they? They don't keep on their guard. And Jesus is trying to let you know in the very beginning of the Christian life that it is likely to cost us everything that you hold most precious. It is likely to cost you a disagreement with your father.

You hear men say today that men must not disturb the peace. "Don't disturb the peace." Why, what did Jesus say? "I came not to bring peace but a sword." Didn't he say that? He said, "My peace I give unto you, but not as the world giveth give I unto you. I came not to bring peace but a sword." A man's enemies, especially those of his own household, don't say that. "I came," he said, "to put enmity between a man and his father. I came to put enmity between a man and his mother. I came to make a man's children separate from him and cease to honor him. I came to split brothers from one another and sisters from one another, and I came to separate men from their own bodies. I came on a business that is the supreme business of life, and men must give up everything for it."

Let's re-estimate this Jesus. Let's re-estimate him. Now, if you and I start out on the Christian warfare knowing that we can't attain the prize by easy-going ways, then if we don't get the prize, it is nobody's fault but ours, is it? A man will walk along in the Christian life, and he will take steps that his own father will say he ought not to take. It says plainly that your father is your enemy. He is your enemy. I come to you and stand with you in this city, and I say to you, "Father, you stand in that city, and I will stand here just with Jesus." It is so hard, friends. But if you and I started out with that understanding, we will buckle ourselves up, won't we? We will be on our guard, especially against our most intimate associations. Those are the bitter things of this world: The people whom we love are the people who are our enemies.

One of the most disastrous things that could happen to a man who loves Jesus Christ is to be connected with a worldly minded woman whom he loves. It is one of the most dangerous things in the world. And if he fails to let that woman know that she is his enemy, he fails to let Jesus Christ have possession of his life.

Just a few days ago, I heard of a young man who had a splendid church in a most strategic place in this country and who was drawing to him a multitude of young people. His wife was a pleasure-loving woman. She wanted to go to all the card parties and dances. When they mixed whiskey with the punch, why, she wanted to drink that too. She didn't want anybody to disapprove of her conduct, and she kept saying to him, "You have got me hedged around so I can't enjoy myself." And he folded his arms, looked at the ministry of Jesus Christ, looked at his wife, and left the ministry.

Now, Jesus says, however commendable that man's love for his wife may have been, he failed to perform his duty. He ought to have told that woman, "Before I saw you, I saw God. I took my commission from Him, and I am willing for you to go and do what you please. I can't force you to deny yourself the pleasures of this world. I love you and will live with you, but I will treat you as the enemy of my soul and the enemy of your soul. Though you and I should be separated as far as the East is from the West, I will stay in the ministry, and my crucified body in the ministry will finally bring you back to me some day, if in the Judgment."

Now, my beloved, that is what Jesus means. He means that. There are all kinds of philosophies in the world today. There is the philosophy that a man ought to sacrifice everything for his wife; a man ought to sacrifice everything for his children; a man surely ought not to offend his mother; of all things in the world, a man ought not do anything to hurt his race; and, by all means, a man ought not do anything to hurt his country. What are you going to do when Jesus comes to you and says, "If you don't hate your father, if you don't hate your mother, if you don't hate your wife, if you don't hate your children and don't hate your own life, you cannot be my disciple"? What are you going to do? What are you going to do? What are you going to do? It is hard.

So Jesus gives us these pictures: the pictures of a man who went to build a house and went and got his lumber and started to build, and got half way through before he found that he hadn't figured out the proper cost of it. He couldn't get any more money and had to quit the job. And people stood around on the outside saying, "Aha, that old fellow started up with a mansion, and there he has only a little old log cabin standing on that hill, and he has no house." And they laughed at him.

Jesus said, "I don't want my people to be laughed at that way. I don't want the world to say that 'he went into the church and started out with a spontaneous enthusiasm and was getting along splendidly, but—well, he just didn't count the cost.'"

Count it now, brother. Count the cost now, especially being members of this race to which you and I belong today. We have suffered so much persecution; been hungry so many times; lived in poor cabins so many days;

and been just as anxious as we can be to get hold of a house, a home, and some good clothes, and to be respectable. Now Jesus Christ may bring you to the place where you have to separate from the deepest earthly desires in order to find out what is the truth and what is the joy and what is the glory of life.

In the history of this country up until this hour, there has never been a race philosophy that went along with Christianity. Now mark me. Let us study that over just a minute. Wherever in history men have put love of their race on an equality with the love of Christ, the love of Christ has taken a second place. The reason the Jewish race today is not the world's leading exponent of the Christian religion is because Jesus demanded of them that a man hate his own race if he would follow God. And they were not willing to give up their age-long devotion to the future of their race according to their own ideas. God pressed down upon the Christian church with such a mighty power that she burst the bonds of the Jewish race and leaped out among slaves in the Roman Empire, because the Christian religion cannot be kept inside racial bounds.

We have tried in Europe and in this country to carry along the Christian religion with the doctrines of the supremacy of a race. We have found out that from the far-flung mission fields, the Chinese and the Japanese are speaking in our faces telling us, "We want your Jesus, but we don't want you to bring him. We can't stand for your doctrine of race superiority along with the universality of the spirit of Jesus." You and I ought to be warned by that. The philosophy that we must do anything whatsoever out of the interests of a race is absolutely inconsistent with the spirit of Jesus Christ. There must come a time when a man will be willing to be hated by the leaders of his own people—despised, rejected, and spit upon in order that he may speak to his people about the salvation of their souls and the redemption of the world—which is the Christ Jesus.

I tell you that today there is more religious affinity, more true brotherhood between Albert Sweitzer, a white man living in the bowels of Africa as a missionary today, and those Negroes. There is more brotherhood between him and a Negro in the United States who has got the spirit of Jesus Christ in him. There is more brotherhood, more enduring and everlasting brotherhood, between him and those Negroes than any other Negro in the Negro race, because it is an affinity of spirit. And the only way that we can carry the doctrine of race love along with the Christian religion is to subordinate the love of race to the love of Christ. If we mean to make the race obedient to Jesus Christ who is the son of the Living God, then we can do whatever we can for our race in that regard. But if at any time, business interests or the social interests or the political interests of this race of ours stand between a man and Jesus, Jesus makes it perfectly clear that we must choose him, or we cannot be his disciple. Let us undeceive ourselves entirely about that.

Finally, my brethren, Jesus says these hard things, and the only reason I feel that he can say them with such complacency is because he knows—not believes—he knows that the price he calls upon a man to pay is not too large a price for what he gets. He says in one place that after he had made this statement, one of his disciples said to him, "Lord, what about us?" He said, "Some of us have left our fathers and our mothers for your sake. Some of us have left our wives and children. Some of us have left our houses and lands." He said, "What about us?"

And Jesus straightened himself and said, "Verily I say unto you, there is none who has left father and mother and brother and sister and houses and lands for my sake but shall have a hundredfold more, both in this present world and in the world to come."

Now, my beloved, it appears to me clearly that the rewards of the Christian life, both in this world and in the world to come, are so great, so satisfactory, so deep, so enduring, that it is worthwhile for a man to hate his father. It is worthwhile for a man to hate his mother. It is worthwhile for a man to hate his wife and his children and his brothers and sisters and, above all, his own life. It is worthwhile because of what you get in return.

Oh, that tonight you might read the life of the Christian martyrs! If I could tell you about old Polycarp who was seventy-six years old when he was ordered by the Imperial soldiers to Rome and was brought up before the Imperial Court. They looked upon his age and the grandeur of his countenance and thought of the multitudes of his friends and acquaintances who lived close to him. And they said to him, "Polycarp, the offense that you have committed requires that you be burned at the stake." He said, "It is awful to burn an old man like you with gray hairs, with a wife and children, and with so many loved ones." They said, "Listen, Polycarp. All that you have to do is just walk right over there by the altar and raise your hand and say, 'I forsake the name of Jesus. I take Caesar to be my national hero and my god.' Then sprinkle a little incense on the altar, and we will let you go."

The old man raised up his old shoulders, with this white hair hanging down over his head, and said to the man standing by the funeral pyre, "Strike your match. Bring up the stakes. Put your fagots on. I have been with Jesus and won't now deny him at this old age. He has brought me sweet peace and deep joy and gladness that passeth human understanding. He has brought my gray hairs down in glory before my children, and I love him so that I would not deny him for all the Caesars in the world." And they put Polycarp on the fire, they lighted the match, and his old body crackled and crumbled and became charcoal in the flame. The testimony in the little book written in Greek says that while they were burning him, he smiled and fixed his eyes on Jesus and said, "Lord Jesus, receive my spirit."

And old Paul—after having been beaten with forty stripes by the Jews many times, after having been stoned by the members of his own race and cast out for dead, after having been on a ship and cast into the bowels of the deep, after having been beaten and mutilated and cursed by all manner of men everywhere, after sitting in the prison cell at Caesar's court with chains on his arms, and after looking for the day when his own head would be cut from his shoulders—said, "I have fought a good fight. I have kept the faith, and I am now ready to be offered up. Henceforth, there is laid up for me a crown of righteousness, and not for me only, but for all that have loved his appearing."

As I look across history and see the testimony of those who have suffered all things for Jesus, hear their sweet words and the songs that they have sung as they were dying in his name, I know that when Jesus says that a man must hate his father and his mother and his wife and his children and his brothers and his sisters and his own life, it must be worth it. I don't know how you feel about it. I have lived thirty-four years. For about half of that time I have been trying to walk in his footsteps, and I have come to believe today that when he says that to me, my answer is "Lord, if my father gets in my way, I will hate him. If my mother gets in my path, I will separate from her. If my wife and my children come between me and Jesus, then they must be my enemies. If my brothers and my sisters and the members of my own race don't care to be with me, I will stick to Jesus." And if I be persecuted and all manner of harm be done to me, I am going to stick to Jesus, because I realize that I am making an experiment that is worthwhile.

I call upon those of you today who have the gray hairs of battle on your head: Don't give up the fight. Don't be led away by any smooth philosophies of this world. I call upon you young men and women who are listening to the philosophies of this world—the cheap and easy methods by which men seek notoriety and popularity and wealth and all manner of things. I call upon you to come to this Jesus who stands in the midst of your pathway and says, "I offer you not peace but a sword. I offer you not social prominence but social degradation. I offer you not riches but poverty. I offer you not glory in this world but shame. But for all these things I will give you precious gifts that no one in the world can give you." And, young men and young women, if you hear the minister of the Gospel stand in his pulpit some evening reaching out his hand in tenderness and saying to you, "Come to Jesus," don't misunderstand him. Don't think that he is asking you to get up from your seat, come forward, and simply take hold of his hand. In that smile of his and his low voice, he is asking you, maybe, to leave your mother, separate from your father, break up your home, cast your children from you, and maybe to lose your life. That is what he is asking you for. I think that any other leader would not be fit to follow, and I am glad that Jesus offers us a hard life, and a sweet, deep, and glorious reward.

Blessed be the name of Jesus Christ.

6. Chosen for a Purpose

In this sermon, Mordecai Johnson addresss crucial issues in cosmology and teleology. He maintains that the entire universe, including the stars in their courses, reflects God's purpose in creation. The essence of this sermon is derived from the writings of St. Paul. In summary, Johnson interprets Paul as saying that every true disciple of Jesus Christ is chosen by God to help Him carry out a supreme purpose that He has conceived from the foundation of the world. Since this is so, we are not products of mere chance. Rather, every "true disciple" has been singled out, "chosen" by God, from the foundation of the world. From a study of Johnson's life, it is apparent that the sense of being chosen, or of having an ordained mission, molded his life.

CHOSEN FOR A PURPOSE[6]

TEXT: Ephesians 1:4—"He hath chosen us in him before the foundation of the world."

"He hath chosen us in him before the foundation of the world." The city of the Ephesians was a most prosperous and religious city, and the inhabitants of the city as well as those engaged in business enterprises were profoundly interested in the worship of the goddess Diana of the Ephesians.

When Paul first went into the city, he was assailed by the businessmen of the city because his preaching disturbed their profits. They had been busy a long time making idols and images of Diana of the Ephesians. Paul came

---

[6]August 31, 1924.

and preached an invisible God who could not be worshipped in images made by men's hands, whereupon the image makers found that they were losing business. They sought to stop his mouth and stop the progress of his preaching because it was economically unprofitable to them.

You may judge, therefore, that the church at Ephesus was founded under some difficulty and that the few people who came into that church would be conscious all the time that they were at enmity with many of their brothers. No doubt there were times when they had their moods of despair—times when the everyday affairs of Ephesus were so much with them that the reality of this invisible and unseen God was a little feeble. In those moods, they would say to themselves, "How hard it is to cling to this invisible and spiritual religion. It may be that what it calls on me to do is too much for my feeble strength."

Paul in writing this letter undoubtedly had these moods of despondency in mind. He sets out here to tell these people, "You have not merely chosen God to be your God. You have not merely to cling to the skirts of some invisible captain that you cannot see. But I want to tell you another truth that goes deeper than all you think along that line. I want to tell you that he chose you in Christ Jesus before the foundation of the world to carry out his great purposes in Ephesus."

This particular sentence gives Paul's comprehensive view of the meaning of the Christian religion from the Godward side, and the substance of it is this: Every true disciple of Jesus Christ is chosen of God to help Him carry out a supreme purpose that He conceived before the foundation of the world. Paul was trying to say to this handful of men, "Your business is not simply to cling onto the skirts of a grandmotherly, invisible parent but your business is to realize that, however few you are, you are chosen people and that you are here to carry out the purposes that God conceived before the foundation of the world. Lift up your hang-down hands, your palsied knees, and get busy."

I want to analyze this statement for a few minutes as it applies to you and me, for there are no doubt times in which we are all possessed of this mood. Sometimes I go down into the prayer meeting and some brother, after he sits there for a while, rises and says, "We all seem to be so cold. The Holy Spirit does not seem to be with us."

Then somebody else will rise and say "Sometimes I wonder whether I am a Christian or not. I do not seem to feel these things that other people say that they feel. I just wonder whether I am a Christian or not. It seems to me if people are Christians and God's spirit is in their hearts, they ought to know it and feel it all the time."

If you and I will just listen to what Paul has to say here, it will help us in these moods of ours when we feel we are absolutely unworthy to be the children of God and doubt sometimes whether the spirit of God has ever entered into us.

Mark you the first thing that lies in this statement: Our God is a God with a supreme purpose that He conceived before the foundation of the world. Long before the stars ever came into being, long before the sun and moon ever shed their light, long before the mountains and hills were ever made or the ocean placed within its bounds, our God had a purpose in His mind. When He stood in the invisible presence of His angels and spoke the word that brought this universe into existence, He knew and knew beforehand what He intended to bring out of it. So we are dealing with a God who is in earnest, with a big job on His hands, and He intends to get done and has intended to get done before the foundation of the world.

My brother, that is a great consolation to me to begin with. So many of us have an idea that God is a kind of patient, indulgent grandmother; He loves us so that He will just help us along when we are sick, just forgive us when we sin, just help us carry out our plans no matter what our plans are. He just loves us and is tender with us no matter what we do. He is always ready to say, "Bless your heart! Come to papa and sit on His knee."

But Paul says our God is a God who is supremely in earnest, who has a great, supreme, and extensive program that He had in His mind before the foundation of the world. If you and I think He is just a kind, indulgent grandmother, we have just begun to get acquainted with God.

You can see something of that purpose when you intelligently look at the stars. Has it ever occurred to you to think of them and of the majestic harmony that prevails in this universe? So many millions of miles away from here, there is a star that we call the sun, which sends out from it millions and millions of units of supreme power. And around that sun are eight great worlds: Neptune, Uranus, Jupiter, Mars, Mercury, Venus, Saturn, and Earth—all circling with their thousands of millions of circumferences, all circling around that mighty sun. Not a single one of them conflicting with another; every one attending to its own business; every one turning on its own axis properly, keeping up a continual and beautiful but unheard music as they all carry out the will of the Invisible God. Trillions of miles away from that star, there is another star in the firmament thousands of times larger than that sun. It also has its worlds circling around it in majestic grooves. The astronomers tell us that there are a thousand million stars like our sun standing up in the heavens, each one of which has the Earth, Mars, Neptune, and the rest circling around in its majestic place. Yet all this universe stands together in harmony, rolls swiftly on singing its song and doing that because it recognizes the power of an Invisible Purpose and the powerful hand that has set it going and keeps it alive, waiting for the fulfillment of the purpose of God.

If you take your eyes off the heavens, you can go down and look at a little salamander egg or a little fish egg down in the depths of the waters. Take it out and put it in a little jar and turn your microscope upon it. Watch it and watch how one little egg separates into two little eggs, how two separate into four, how four separate into eight, eight into sixteen, and, finally, as if some invisible hand had laid hold on it, half of them come together and look like a head and half of them straighten out and become a tail. In a little while that egg, which was almost invisible to the eye, becomes a live fish swimming in the waters of the deep. Every salamander egg—as soon as it comes from the body—seems to have an unconscious knowledge that it was meant to be a salamander and not a perch or salmon, and it goes through all the processes of development until it becomes a salamander. It seems as if some invisible purpose spoke down in the depths and told it, "You came into the world for a purpose, and I am going on and fulfill that purpose. I am going on and fulfill His will." One standing here below looking up at the sun, down at the salamander, or up at the birds sitting on the mountain can say, "This whole creation is part of a wonderful plan waiting finally for the son of God, the man with the crowning face of the Invisible God—a plan that there should one day stand on top of this universe beings who would sing His songs, who would converse with Him with understanding and knowledge.

So if we take this Bible for it, when God created the universe, He had in His mind that out of material things should rise vegetable things, that out of vegetable things should rise animal things, that out of animal things should rise human things, and that out of human things should rise divine spirits who will associate with the Living God, sing His praises, and do His will throughout eternity. The purpose toward which He has been working through all the ages has been to create spiritual beings who would think and live like Him, be righteous like Him, and be full of compassion and kindness like Him. That is what the Bible says and that is what Paul is saying to these people.

Do you think you will cling to the skirts of some inevitable and kindly grandmother? You are dealing with a God who thought this thing out before the beginning of the world, who knew that Ephesus would be singing the praises of some unknown god. He also knew that there would be a handful ready to do His will and hear His voice.

I want you to understand that you ought to rejoice because God has laid His hands on you for the carrying out of His supreme purpose.

That is the way about us here in Charleston. As I said before, if you canvassed the tadpoles, they would not vote to be frogs because they do not have a wide enough vision. No tadpole would vote to be a frog. You would get an almost unanimous vote for all tadpoles to remain tadpoles. But they do not remain tadpoles because the purpose of God, before the foundation of the world, was that out of tadpoles should come frogs, out of immaterial things should come human things, and out of human things should come angels to do the will of God.

The second thing that is involved in this text is that in the very creation of the universe, God limited His own omnipotence. It is in the very nature of God's supreme purpose that it cannot be fulfilled except by the free will of His own creatures. Although the supreme desire of the Living God is to have all human creatures do His will and carry out His purpose, and although the happiness of every single one of His creatures is bound up with the doing of His will and the carrying out of His purpose, He has so fixed it that He cannot force His own will on His own creatures but must await their cooperation.

I want you to think about that. We are dealing with a God who has a supreme purpose. The limitations that He has placed on His own purpose require that He shall have the cooperation of His human creatures to carry out that purpose. That is why the world is full of misery, why sin stands up on every hill. It is not because the human who does sin is not a child of God. He is a child of God.

If I might speak in purely human language, I might say that there are in the galleries of heaven a portrait of Him when He grows up in Jesus Christ. God not only has a picture of you now but also has a picture of you as you will look when Christ Jesus controls your spirit and makes you an angelic creature. But that spirit picture will never be realized unless God gets hold of your will and mine. The very nature of His purpose is that He will let you go on and on without interposing his jurisdiction because His purpose is such that He cannot carry it on without your cooperation.

There are passages in the Bible such as "I stand at the door and knock." Do you see the Supreme Creator standing and knocking at the door of the heart of some degraded woman tonight, who is living perhaps in the "red light" district, who has gone so far that she has forgotten the teachings of her mother and of those in school and Sunday School, and who is living there in the cast-off district of some city. He does not take her by the hand and snatch her out and say, "You must come out of this because I created you to be an angel." But the High God stands there at the door with scarred hands and says, "Daughter, if you would just hear my voice and open the door, I would come in and sup with you, and you would sup with me. He desires nothing so much as to see that young woman come out of that place and cast all her sins aside and look up into the face of Mary, the mother of Jesus Christ, and be pure and clean and have some man respect her and have her become a wife and mother, but he cannot force it. He stands at the door and knocks, wanting to get into the woman's soul."

That is the second thing in this text: We are dealing with an earnest God who has made big purposes even before the foundation of the world but He cannot carry them out without the voluntary cooperation of the creatures He has made.

I do not know how to bring that closer to you than in dealing with your own children. Did you ever look at your little child playing in the yard— when you have read good books and heard good sermons—did you ever look at your little boy and say, "Oh, if I could make you like Booker Washington," or look at your little girl and say, "Oh, if I could make you like Joan of Arc"? And in that very hour, the little rascal goes out and disobeys you and does what it should not do—goes out of the yard that you say it should not go out of and sometimes almost gets itself run over by an automobile. For a few times you might shake it and whip it, but you will find there is something inside of that little child that can say to you, "I won't. I won't. I won't."

There are some parents today in the city of Charleston who have almost killed their children with switches trying to get the little child who says, "I won't," to say, "I will." You are just trying to do what God Himself has limited Himself in. He has put something inside the bosom of a little child, something like what is in the breasts of many women and many men that makes then say, "I won't; I won't," to the Living God Himself.

Therefore, our God is a suffering God. Therefore, He is continually crucified. Therefore, the blood of his agony is running down into the Kingdom of Glory. He knows that the only way He can change that "I won't" into "I will" is to make one fall in love with the love of God and to make one of his own freewill follow God's plan.

The third thing is—and here we come to the main point—that very few people have been chosen by God to help Him carry out His purpose, which He had before the foundation of the world.

Now, my beloved, I want to call to your remembrance certain passages of scriptures that will indicate to you that this is God's habitual method of dealing with the world.

Sometimes you and I, as we look around, see how few people there are who belong to the church, see how few people in that church are really serious, and we begin to ask ourselves such questions as these: "Is the church really a church of God? If it was the church of God, would it not get all the people somehow or other in the church? If the church of God was really what it ought to be and as the Bible says it ought to be, would not we have all the five thousand colored people in Charleston in the church?" Paul's answer is that this was not God's method: He looks at the city of Charleston today and says, "There are five thousand colored people there. Some are incapacitated by birth not to hear my voice though I should send my only begotten Son into the streets and knock on their doors." He might plead with them from the beginning of morning until the end of evening and from now until doomsday, and they would not hear because they are not prepared. We find this statement in the Bible, and we find it so often on the lips of Jesus Christ. Frequently after he had delivered a sermon to the people and made it as clear as sparkling daylight, he would make this statement, "He that hath ears to hear let him hear." He would say, "I have been talking to a multitude of five thousand. I am not deceived that all of you will hear me. Some of your ears are not deaf, but they are so shallow that as soon as the word falls, it will pass away. Some will hear me and start out with great enthusiasm and then break down. But you are so filled up with the things of this world that you will desert me before a few days pass away. I know only a handful of you will hear me and then go and bring forth fruit."

Go back to the very beginning of the Old Testament. There were certainly more people than Abraham. There were his whole family, his father, and the whole generation of Hebrews, but God called only one man out of that whole community to carry out His purpose. And he did not call a young man. I do not know what kind of a community it was but he picked out an old man, a man who had spent almost all of his days. He guided him out to the stars and said, "Abraham, look up at the stars."

Abraham said, "Father, I see the stars."

God said, "Abraham, you are childless."

Abraham said, "Yes, sir."

Then God said to him, "I propose to make a mighty family. I will make you not only a blessing to your children but also a blessing to the whole world. Rise and set out for the land that I will show you." All of Abraham's kin people were left behind and only Abraham launched out to fulfill the purpose of the Living God.

There were twelve sons of Jacob. Some were strong and some had fine intelligence, but God chose but one to go down to Egypt and lay the foundation for the work of Egypt. He picked out Joseph and put him in Potiphar's house where he was put in prison. God almost took Joseph's life away from him in order that he might lay the foundation for His work, carrying out the purpose of the High God.

There may have been a multitude of able men among the Israelites when they were in Egypt. There must have been some who were decidedly eloquent. There must have been some who had laid by a considerable sum of money and could have done considerable for those people. But God chose only one man, and He waited until he was nearly seventy years of age and called him on the mountain of Sinai and showed him His face in the burning bush and told him that He had heard the cries of His people in Egypt and asked him to be His special agent and deliver them from the bondage of Pharaoh. Moses said, "I cannot speak. I am not a man of much talent. I killed a man in Egypt thirty years ago and they must be laying for me."

The Lord said, "I do not care about that; you are a special messenger of the High God and I put the deliverance of the people into your hands."

Later there were other men. There were about 300 of them around Ahab's table and prophesied about the God but when God got ready to tell them, he picked out one man—Elijah—and drew him off and said, "I have chosen you. My people do not know me. They do not know the purpose that I proposed before the foundation of the world. I want you to get hold of them and speak to them and turn them onto the narrow path."

Then we come to the great eighth century B.C. when the people of Israel were in their great prosperity, had their golden and silver vessels, had a multitude of priests and songsters. But He had just about half a dozen men whom He had as his mouthpieces to deliver His people. He went out into the outskirts of Jerusalem where there was a man tending sheep. He said, "Amos, I have a big job for you. I have a purpose that I commenced before the foundation of the world. I want you to go to Jerusalem and tell them that God cannot use the kind of people they are making there today."

Then He had Hosea, and then Micah and the others—those seven or eight great prophets who were God's chosen men to carry out His purpose before the foundation of the world. Is it not true?

There must have been a multitude of people in the world when Israel had such a wonderful experience. Has it ever occurred to you that the religious experience of the people of Israel was so much superior to the religious experience of all the other people in the world? Has it ever occurred to you that there are only three great religions that worship only one God: Judaism, Muhammadanism, and Christianity? There is but one of them that grows out of the Jewish family. God chose one people out of all the multitude of races and nations that He might purify them in the fires of suffering to do His holy will.

Listen to the prophets: "All of you people say, 'We are the children of Israel. We are the children of Isaac. Surely our God will deliver us.'"

The prophet told them, "God does not propose to carry on this great multitude to do His law and will. He is going to destroy the majority of you, but out of that remnant will be born the Messiah and finally the Kingdom of God will come unto its own through Israel." But a little handful was chosen out of the chosen people. All of this was because that is God's method all the way through—to choose a little handful of people to carry out His will. He filled them with his spirit in order that through those people His great purpose, which He purposed before the foundation of the world, should come to pass.

Now getting down to the present. Just as God in days that are past and gone chose His groups to carry out His wish, so He did in Christ. When Jesus came to the people in Galilee, he did not choose them all to be his disciples. He picked out twelve first, and then he picked out seventy. Although there was a great multitude following him around wherever he went, it finally narrowed down to twelve people. He took them up on the mountainside and said, "Ye are the light of the world. Ye are the salt of the earth. Ye have not chosen me, but I have chosen you. I have chosen you not to stand apart but that you should go forth into the world and bring forth fruit and that fruit shall remain and whatsoever ye shall ask of the Father in my name He may give to you."

The world looked at them. They were insignificant—just good, hard-handed fishermen. The Romans were greater than they or their teacher. The politicians were greater than they or their teacher. Yet those twelve men changed the fabric of the world, established the church, and it has stood for two thousand years and is the strongest institution of the human race.

Has it ever occurred to you that the first and most important institution in the Western world is the church? Have you ever thought about it? Out of the chosen few that Jesus Christ took in his hands on the hillsides of Galilee has risen the strongest, most able, and most wise institution in the world today. The Roman Catholic Church has lived longer than any kingdom that is now living. The Roman Catholic Church has spread its influence over all the vast acreage of this Western land. And there is today no political institution, no business institution, or no educational institution in the world that can say it has stood as long as this church, which God founded through His twelve chosen disciples of the Lord Jesus Christ. From out of that church have grown all the other organizations that today constitute the strongest consolidated international body in the world, through the preaching of our Lord Jesus Christ and his twelve disciples.

Here we are in Charleston in this little church today built by the hands of slaves. Outside is a great multitude of people who have nothing to do with God, who hear preaching as often as most of us do but feel that they must get busy today and get hold of money, who feel that the pleasures of this life are sweet and that they must get the fullness of them today. Only a handful of people are in the church of Christ and, out of that handful, most of them are carried away by this world. Have you ever thought about that?

God knew that in Charleston there would be only a handful of people who would really fall in love with Jesus Christ, who would take up his banner as a soldier goes to the front. Paul says, "He chose you before the foundation of the world."

God said, "In Charleston in 1924 will be so and so. Those I have chosen will carry my truth and justice down to the next generation." It is wonderful to think about it.

What has He chosen us to do? Just a word on it. You know that whenever God gets hold of a man or a woman, there is no question about what the man's or woman's thoughts will be. There is absolutely no question that when the spirit of God lays hold of a man or woman, moral and spiritual consideration takes the forefront in that person's life. He begins to see that the character of a human being is the most important thing in the world. He begins to see that how a human being acts, what he really desires, what he thinks, and what he proposes in his heart are more important than the things that are going on around him in the world.

Whenever a man or woman comes to the place where he is mightily gripped by the moral and spiritual things of this world, he may know not merely that he has faith in God, but that God has chosen him and has faith in him and is using him as an instrument for the carrying out of the purpose that He had before the foundation of the world.

We might go back and find what He wants us to do. We will find that He has chosen you in Charleston to do justice, love mercy, and walk with your God. He did not choose your job for you. It does not make much difference—in the long run with the High God and His great purpose, it does not make much difference—whether you are working under a car with your blue and greasy overalls on, or in a schoolroom with tender children in front of you. It makes no difference if you are a member of a labor union or a man working out in the solitary places with a hoe in your hand. The supreme thing before God is whether you are dealing justly with the human beings with whom you come in contact. It makes no difference what the transaction is, deal justly. No difference who the man is, deal justly. No matter what he says or does to you, deal justly. Recognize that man as a child of God, and treat him so that when you see him before God, you will not be ashamed of your transaction with him. Deal justly. Deal justly! Deal justly with the men for whom you are working. Deal justly with the man who is working for you. Deal justly in your household affairs. Be ever sensitive of justice in every walk of life.

A man will cry because he has lost a thousand dollars. A child goes into his room and weeps because we have dealt unjustly with him in the backyard. I know in the last analysis, it is more important to me to get that thing right between me and that little child than it is to recover a thousand dollars in gold lost in a business transaction.

So it is, "Love mercy." You hear men say, "I deal with those who deal with me. I am not obligated to you or to that man who is not present." But to love mercy, God means that you will go out of your way to become interested in those who have need of your service although they have no obligations that they can lay upon you whatsoever.

Wherever you see the children of God in this world, they are people who are concerned about the sufferings of those who have no claim upon them. You will see them up here during the week in the Kanawha County jail talking to some mother's son who has no claim upon them. You will see them down in this dark alley where a woman has been afflicted with loathsome diseases and neglected by husband and children. You will see the child of God—upon whom she has no claim—take off the sheets and wash them, wash her sores, and feed her something because that child has learned of Jesus Christ that God loves mercy more than anything else in this world.

He has chosen us to walk with god. What does that mean? It means that when you find one that God has chosen, then he is an instrument in the hands of God. All the wealth and learning that he has belongs to the Lord. He will follow the dictates of the Holy Spirit and his conscience in the use he shall make of his wealth, education, and position in the work of the Lord.

To give you an illustration, over in Cincinnati there is a businessman named Nash. He is in the clothing business, and just a few years ago he looked at the misfortunes of the men who were working for him and said, "No man who is truly a servant of God has a right to have a group of men working for him, making money for him, without them having any claim on his heart." He went home and studied it over and said, "I am going to work this business on a new plan. There are three groups, and they are all God's children. There are the people who buy the suits—they are God's children; there are you who make the suits—you are God's children; and there is myself who owns the factory. We have to cooperate. I want to fix it so that every suit that goes out of this factory will be a suit that anybody would be willing to wear."

So they began to put out the very best suits they could put out. Nash said, "This factory does not belong to me only. It belongs to you, and I am going to fix it so that when we have good business and the profits roll in I will divide them with you. I will raise the wages as fast as the money comes in. When the business gets slack, I am going to cut down wages and I want you to vote to cut them down."

So they started out, and for five years they had each year twice as much business as before. The money began to pile in so that he raised wages 200 percent but in spite of that, the money piled up so fast that he found he was going to become a millionaire. He said, "I have no business with a million dollars. I am going to fix it so that all of this may somehow go back to the people." He called his men around him and said, "Every man who owns two shares of this stock; I want him to buy two more, and I will give him one more. And the time will come when we all own this together, and the profits will belong to all of you, and the public will be glad to purchase from us because we are putting out suits with God's approval on them."

So today Nash has a factory established in which 50 percent of the stock is owned by the men and women who do the work, 20 percent is owned by Nash, and 30 percent is owned by people on the outside. In five years more, Nash hopes to fix it so that, by the mercy of God, Nash's factory will supply 4,000 independent men and women in the clothing business with plenty of work, plenty of good homes, and plenty of education. And they will make plenty of garments that everyone is satisfied to wear.

That is what I mean by walking humbly. It makes no difference how many men are working for you. It makes no difference how much you have invested. You are still just a humble servant to the Living God. Everything you do is subordinated to that supreme purpose that God had before the foundation of the world.

I could go on with this, but let me recapitulate.

First, this text means that we are dealing with a God with a supreme purpose that He conceived before the foundation of the world.

Second, we are dealing with a God who has so much respect for my personality and your personality that He cannot carry out His plans without your cooperation and my cooperation.

Third, He knows from His own experiences that the majority of people in no particular generation will ever hear His voice. But He must choose a handful out of every city, state, and country in the world who shall be the special messengers of this generation to carry out His work in the world. And you and I in this church who really do justice and are doing mercy and are walking humbly with our God are the chosen ones in this city and in this generation to carry out the will of God.

Just a few applications to everyday life and I will be through.

In the first place, this message ought to give us great consolation when we think about our weaknesses. There is no true man or woman who serves God who does not sometime get to the place where he wonders whether he is fit to be used by God at all.

Bernard Shaw says that "every fellow who writes his autobiography is a liar." I want you to get Shaw's words. "Every fellow who writes his autobiography is a liar." It is perfectly manifest why he lies, because he will conceal the greater portion of the truth about himself. He will set forth only those things that the community in which he lives thinks are excellent. If he would tell the whole truth about his life, he would not lie willingly. But if he told the actual truth before the public, it would not be believed. They would think he was trying to get off a great joke. Shaw said, "In spite of my literary reputation, there are crazy people in my family. My first cousin is crazy and I have that blood in me." He said, "There are a couple of thieves right close to me that stole a lot of money and were put in the penitentiary, and I belong to that family." He said that when he told that to the reporter, the reporter laughed until he thought he would die.

The reporter said, "Mr. Shaw, you are trying to get off a joke."

Shaw replied, "No, I am trying to tell the actual truth." He said that when he printed the book, the people said it was the first book where a man told the truth about himself.

Suppose you read the writings of the Apostle Paul. He says, "I am the least of the Apostles. I am unworthy to be an Apostle of the Lord Jesus

Christ. You look at me in my strength but you do not know my weaknesses. When I go home and sit down, there is a battle going on within me all the time. I intend to do right, but there are many times when I do wrong and I know it. But there is something else you do not know about. I have a special thorn in my flesh that keeps me worried and troubled. I have gone to God and said, 'If you will just remove this from me, I can serve you better.' But after I had gone to him seven times, He said, 'Paul, just leave it there. My grace is sufficient for you.'"

If we would all look into our lives, we would find there is a lot that we would like to cover and a lot that you would not want the people of Charleston to know about. You go to your room and say, "Truly God Almighty knows all of that. Truly He knows I am a sinner and sometimes a hypocrite."

But the answer comes back from the Heavenly Father, "Bless you. I know all about your weakness. I know all about your sins but I have chosen you to be my representative, and my grace is sufficient for you. I know you cannot be perfect, but you can bear the cross in Charleston. You can carry it as no other man can carry it."

It is good to realize that God does so, not because we are perfect vessels. He has chosen us because by long preparation there is deeper down in our hearts a supreme love for justice, mercy, and humility before God.

Do you not know that God would rather have ten thousand weak and struggling servants who deep down in their hearts loved righteousness and justice than to have a million persons who had no righteousness and were not humble before God?

Another thing—and it will help us in our moods—we cannot all work with a Holy Spirit every day. You cannot be up on the mountainside all the time. A few days ago, there came to our prayer meeting an aged man who said, "I hear you talking about the Holy Spirit. I do not feel that. I wonder sometimes whether I have any religion at all."

A soldier of the Army of the United States may put his name down at the draft board with high enthusiasm and get his examination. On the day when he receives his uniform and his first gun and his insignia upon his shoulders, he feels as though he could whip the world. When the band is playing "The Star Spangled Banner," he goes down the street, marching erectly and fearing nothing. But when he gets over in Flanders Field with its mud and rain, when he is down in the trench and the shells are coming from the Germans and killing men by his side, and when he has not had a meal for three days, he feels sick at the stomach and dizzy in his head. He feels there cannot be anything that he can do for the government, that there is nothing in this business of "going over the top." But the captain comes at four o'clock in the morning and passes the word to the lieutenant that at five o'clock, he is going over the top and to let every man take his pistol and go with him. It is not because you feel like going over, not because of the spirit of patriotism, but because away back behind the line, the general had a plan. He wants you to charge this position and repulse the enemy and, whether you feel like it or not, you must go.

The Lord says, "I did not choose you to be always filled up with the Holy Spirit but with my plans, which I made before the foundation of the world. Whether you like it or not, you must charge. If there is injustice, you must charge on it. If mercy is needed, you must give mercy. If humility is needed, you must furnish it." That is the reason the church is so flabby and weak. We go up against the devil's organization and we say, "We must be tactful. We must be peaceable. Our Lord loves peace." He put a sword in your hands and he wants justice. He wants mercy, he wants righteousness, and he wants humility. He wants you to charge whether you feel like it or not.

Finally, my beloved, that plan was for you to obey God whether you like it or not, and then "the peace that passeth all human understanding" will be in your hearts.

Years ago when I was a boy, we used to have a mourners' bench along there. When you came to Christ, you had to feel that "peace that passeth all understanding." We had there for six or seven weeks a lot of people waiting every evening, waiting for God to give them beforehand that which is the reward for having done something for Him.

Mark me now! Mark me now! When did the heavens open and the dove come down on Jesus Christ? After he was baptized, was it not? When did the angels come and minister to him in the wilderness? After he had fasted forty days and met the devil in every high place and put him down. The scriptures show that he was among the wild beasts before the angels came and ministered unto him. The "peace that passeth all understanding" comes into the heart of a human being when he has done the will of God. He gets a telegraph message saying, "Well done, my good and faithful servant. I saw what you did and it gives me joy that passeth all understanding."

This heart of mine and your hearts are a kind of central station between this world and Glory. You and I get a message of need from some poor soul, and we launch out and meet it. Then the operator in Glory calls up and says, "The Father saw what you did when you touched that hungry man's lips with bread. When you did, you touched Him. When you visited that man in prison, you visited Him. When you did that good deed, the angles in heaven broke loose with an anthem."

You praise God and do His will and get a response down in the depth of your heart to let you know what is going on. Let me end this sermon. Do not spend your life sitting off in your room, trying to invoke the heavenly spirit to bless you when you have not done anything. Jesus Christ says, "He who does the will of God will know me." Charge on injustice and unmercifulness. After the battle is over, then the General makes his speech and gives the heart its peace.

Sometimes I stand in the city of Charleston, and I see sin marching down the street in glorious attire. Young men and women are marching along as happy as can be, and I see the leading citizens drawing profits from them and sitting up in the church with their arms folded and wondering why God does not come. Yet I know that no matter how many march, there are some who have not joined the hellish band wagon. There are some who will not take the profits of the people in this way. There are the decent ones who are chosen, not who are chosen for this time only, but chosen for this time and the time to come. Whatever Charleston is going to be that is worth while, you are going to lay the foundation for it.

Sometimes I get discouraged over it. Every time I do, God sends me a good funeral. I love to preach a good funeral. I have one this afternoon of a young man who looked at the filthiness and corruption around the world and never touched it with his hands. He never took a grain of corrupt profits from any man's investment and never touched the sacred body of an inviolate virgin. He never joined with any man in the corruption of this world. When he was dying in the hospital the other day, he said he came away from Institute, West Virginia, and sat in the back of the church to hear the Gospel preached. What difference does it make if 999 men go to hell if one man lives like that?

As God lifted up the children of Israel through Moses and Abraham, John the Baptist, and Jesus Christ, so He will lift up the world through young men and women like that in spite of all the devil can do.

During the Bible School meetings, there was a little boy with greasy overalls who came out of the "red light" district. In the first place he did not think he was wanted here, so he did not come in. He dallied around out front. Finally the principal of the Bible School brought him in here and told him that he had been chosen to carry the Christian flag. The little fellow looked around and finally he took it. I met him out of the door there with the Christian flag on his shoulder. I came back the next morning and that same little boy was here, but he did not have on greasy overalls. He had on a new white shirt, clean shoes, and clean trousers. He had made up his mind that if the principal of this Daily Vacation Bible School was going to trust him with the flag of Jesus Christ, he had better have on clean clothing, a clean shirt, and clean britches.

If God has chosen you out of the citizens of Charleston to carry on His work, He wants you to have on clean clothing. He wants you to take out of your life every sin that is in there. He wants you to take the money that you have invested in unholy places and take it out of there. He wants you to get all corruption out of your life. Get up every morning and say, "Father, here I am. I have put off my filthy garments. I have as clean a shirt and trousers as a man can have. Give me the flag of Jesus Christ that I may carry it down the streets of Charleston."

APPENDIX

B *Selected Significant Addresses*

B. *Selected Significant Addresses*

1. *The Faith of the American Negro*[1]

Representing the Graduate School, Mordecai Johnson delivered this address at the Harvard University commencement in June 1922, when he completed his requirements for the degree of Master of Sacred Theology. Its forcefulness made Johnson, at age thirty-two, a national figure. In the post–World War I climate of the 1920s, race relations in America were at a low point. Blatant discrimination and lynchings belied the United States' motto from that war: "To Make the World Safe for Democracy." Here Johnson shows that the Negro's faith in the American dream was being shattered, and he challenged the forces of Christianity to establish the conditions for the fulfillment that dream.

THE FAITH OF THE AMERICAN NEGRO

Since their emancipation from slavery, the masses of American Negroes have lived by the strength of a simple, but deeply moving, faith. They have believed in the love and providence of a just and holy God, they have believed in the principles of democracy and in the righteous purpose of the federal government, and they have believed in the disposition of the American people—as a whole and in the long run—to be fair in all their dealings.

---

[1] Cambridge, Massachusetts, June 22, 1922.

In spite of disfranchisement and peonage, mob violence and public contempt, they have kept this faith and have allowed themselves to hope with the optimism of Booker T. Washington that in proportion as they grew in intelligence, wealth, and self-respect, they should win the confidence and esteem of their fellow white Americans, and should gradually acquire the responsibilities and privileges of full American citizenship.

In recent years, and especially since the Great War, this simple faith has suffered a widespread disintegration. When the United States government set forth its war aims; when it called upon Negro soldiers to stand by the colors and Negro civilians—men, women, and children—to devote their labor and earnings to the cause; and when the war shortage of labor permitted a quarter million Negroes to leave the former slave states for the better conditions of the North, the entire Negro people experienced a profound sense of spiritual release. For the first time since emancipation, they found themselves comparatively free to sell their labor on the open market for a living wage, found themselves launched on a great world enterprise with a chance to vote in a real and decisive way, and, best of all in the heat of the struggle, found themselves bound with other Americans in the spiritual fellowship of a common cause.

When they stood on the height of this exalted experience and looked down on their pre-war poverty, impotence, and spiritual isolation, they realized as never before the depth of the harm they had suffered. And there arose in them a mighty hope that in some way the war would work a change in their situation. For a time, indeed, it seemed that their hope would be realized. When the former slave states saw their labor leaving for the North, southerners began to reflect upon the treatment they had been accustomed to giving the Negro, and they decided that it was radically wrong. Newspapers and public orators everywhere expressed this change of sentiment, set forth the wrongs in detail, and urged immediate improvement. And immediate improvement came. Better educational facilities were provided here and there, words of appreciation for the worth and spirit of the Negro as a citizen began to be uttered, and public committees arose to inquire into his grievances and to lay out programs for setting these grievances right. The colored people in those states had never experienced such collective goodwill, and many of them were so grateful and happy that they actually prayed for the prolongation of the war.

At the close of the war, however, the Negro's hopes were suddenly dashed to the ground. Southern newspapers began at once to tell the Negro soldiers that the war was over and that the sooner they forget it, the better.

"Pull off your uniform," they said. "Find the place you had before the war, and stay in it."

"Act like a Negro should act," said one newspaper. "Work like a Negro should work. Talk like a Negro should talk. Study like a Negro should study. Dismiss all ideas of independency or of being lifted up to the plane of the white man. Understand the necessity of keeping a Negro's place."

In connection with such admonitions, there came the great collective attacks on Negro life and poverty in Washington, Chicago, Omaha, Elaine,* and Tulsa. There came also the increasing boldness of lynchers who advertised their purposes in advance and had their photographs taken around the burning bodies of their victims. There came vain appeals by the colored people to the President of the United States and to the houses of Congress. And finally there came the reorganization and rapid growth of the Ku Klux Klan.

The swift succession and frank brutality of all this was more than the Negro people could bear. Their simple faith and hope broke down. Multitudes took weapons in their hands and fought back violence with bloody resistance. "If we must die," they said, "it is well that we die fighting." And the Negro American world, looking on their deed with no light of hope to see by, said, "It is self-defense; it is the law of nature, of man, and of God; and it is well."

For those terrible days until this day, the Negro's faith in the righteous purpose of the federal government has sagged. Some have laid the blame on the parties in power. Some have laid it elsewhere. But all the colored people, in every section of the United States, believe that there is something wrong—and not accidentally wrong—at the very heart of the government.

Some of our young men are giving up the Christian religion, thinking that their fathers were fools to have believed it so long. One group among us repudiates entirely the simple faith of former days. It would put no trust in God, would put no trust in democracy, and would entertain no hope for betterment under the present form of government. It believes that the United States government is through and through controlled by selfish capitalists who have no fundamental goodwill for Negroes or for any sort of laborers whatever. In their publications and on the platform, the members of this group urge the colored man to seek his salvation by alliance with the revolutionary labor movement of America and the world.

---

*The small town of Elaine, Arkansas, is near the Tennessee border and is where a horrendous racial incident occurred in 1919.

Another and larger group among us believes in religion and believes in the principles of democracy, but not in the white man's religion and not in the white man's democracy. It believes that the creed of the former slave states is the tacit creed of the whole nation, and that the Negro may never expect to acquire economic, political, and spiritual liberty in America. This group has held congresses with representatives from the entire Negro world, to lay the foundations of a black empire, a black religion, and a black culture. It has organized the provisional Republic of Africa, has set going a multitude of economic enterprises, has instituted branches of its organization wherever Negroes are to be found, and has bound them together with a newspaper ably edited in two languages.

Whatever one may think of these radical movements and their destiny, one thing is certain: They are home-grown fruits, with roots deep sprung in a world of black Americans' suffering. Their power lies in the appeal that they make to the Negro to find a way out of his trouble by new and self-reliant paths. The larger masses of the colored people do not belong to these more radical movements. They retain their belief in the Christian God, they love their country, and they hope to work out their salvation within its bounds. But they are completely disillusioned. They see themselves surrounded on every hand by a sentiment of antagonism that does not intend to be fair. They see themselves partly reduced to peonage, shut out from labor unions, forced to an inferior status before the courts, made subjects of public contempt, lynched and mobbed with impunity, and deprived of the ballot— their only means of social defense. They see this antagonistic sentiment consolidated in the places of power in the former slave states and growing by leaps and bounds in the North and West. They know that it is gradually reducing them to an economic, political, and social caste. And they are now no longer able to believe with Dr. Booker T. Washington, or with any other man, that their own efforts after intelligence, wealth, and self-respect can in any wise avail to deliver them from these conditions unless they have the protection of a just and beneficent public policy in keeping with American ideals.

With one voice, therefore, from pulpit, from press, and from the humblest walks of life, they are sending up a cry of pain and petition such as is heard today among the citizens of no other civilized nation in the world. They are asking for the protection of life, for the security of property, for the liberation of their peons, for the freedom to sell their labor on the open market, for a human being's chance in the courts, for a better system of public education, and for the boon of the ballot. They ask, in short, for public equality under the protection of the federal government.

Their request is sustained by every sentiment of humanity and by every holy ideal for which this nation stands. The time has come when the elemental justice called for in this petition should be embodied in a public policy initiated by the federal government and continuously supervised by a commission of that government, representing the faith and will of the whole American people.

The Negro people of America have been with us here for 300 years. They have cut our forests, tilled our fields, built our railroads, fought our battles, and—in all of their trials until now—have manifested a simple faith, a grateful heart, a cheerful spirit, and an undivided loyalty to the nation that has been a thing of beauty to behold. Now they have come to the place where their faith can no longer feed on the bread of repression and violence. They ask for the bread of liberty, of public equality, and of public responsibility. It must not be denied them.

We are now sufficiently far removed from the Civil War and its animosities to see that such elemental justice may be given to the Negro with entire goodwill and helpfulness toward the former slave states. We have already had one long attempt to build a wealth and culture on the backs of slaves. We found that it was a costly experiment, paid for at last with the blood of our best sons. There are some among our citizens who would turn their backs on history and would repeat that experiment. To their terrible heresy, they would convert our entire great community. By every sacred bond of love for them, we must not yield, and we must no longer leave them alone with their experiment. The faith of our whole nation must be brought to their support until such time as it is clear to them that their former slaves can be made both fully free and yet their faithful friends.

Across the seas the darker peoples of the earth are rising from their long sleep and are searching this Western world for light. Our Christian missionaries are among them. They are asking these missionaries, "Can the Christian religion bind this multicolored world in bonds of brotherhood?" We of all nations are best prepared to answer that question and to be their moral inspiration and their friend. For we have the world's problem of race relationships here in crucible. By strength of our American faith, we have made some encouraging progress in its solution. If the fires of this faith are kept burning around that crucible, what comes out of it is able to place these United States in the spiritual leadership of all humanity. When the Negro cries with pain from his deep hurt and lays his petition for elemental justice before the nation, he is calling upon the American people to kindle anew—about the crucible of race relationships—the fires of American faith.

2. Inaugural Presidential Address at Howard University[2]

The inaugural address of a college or university president is important for many reasons. It shows how he or she views the educational enterprise in general and the enterprise of the institution in particular. In this address, very carefully crafted, Mordecai Johnson gives recognition to all of his publics and outlines what he perceives to be the distinct mission of each segment of the university. While looking forward to the continued and increased support of the federal government, Johnson places the primary focus of his address on the opportunity and responsibility of the university to prepare graduates who meet the needs of the people in the communities they will serve.

INAUGURAL PRESIDENTIAL ADDRESS OF MORDECAI WYATT JOHNSON AT HOWARD UNIVERSITY (JUNE 10, 1927)*

Mr. Chairman, members of the Board of Trustees, and fellow citizens:

I wish first of all to express my very great gratitude to the Secretary of the Interior, to the representative of the faculties of the university, and to the representatives of the sister institutions who have greeted me with welcome today. Howard University is one among many agencies working for the development of the Negro people and for that enlargement of the life of our country, which must inevitably follow every step of this development. I am proud to be a part of these agencies. I am deeply encouraged by the welcome that they are giving me. And I hope that during my administration Howard University may prove an increasingly worthy cooperator in our great common undertaking.

---

[2]Washington, D.C., June 10, 1927.

*Reprinted and adapted from Michael Winston, ed., *Education for Freedom: The Leadership of Mordecai Wyatt Johnson, Howard University, 1926–1960.* Howard University Archives, Moorland-Spingarn Research Center.

Sixty Years of Struggle and Achievement

Howard University was conceived in the prayer meeting of a Congregational Church after the Civil War and the emancipation of the slaves. It was founded by a man who had been a soldier in that war, who rejoiced in the emancipation of the slaves and the preservation of the Union, but who wisely saw that these achievements were only the first and second steps toward a happy adjustment of the black people to the other elements of the American population. He believed that the next and most important step should be a strenuous undertaking to educate both the slaves themselves and the disadvantaged white people who, under the slave regime, had never had an educational opportunity. So, with a broad heart unembittered by strife, he spent the remainder of his life establishing educational institutions for the slaves and their children and for those disadvantaged whites.

This institution was originally planned to train preachers for the freedmen, but the plan was soon expanded to include all the training given by a comprehensive university organization.

The beginnings of the university were very humble indeed. On May 1, 1867, the normal department was established in a little frame building with four students, one teacher, and no money. Sixty years have passed since that day. What struggles there were during those years, what heroic sacrifices were made by presidents and faculties, and what joys there came as from time to time new sources of support appeared. These things are all well known to those who know and love the university's history. Today we are able to see that original normal department expanded into nine schools and colleges, embracing religion, medicine, dentistry, pharmacy, law, liberal arts, applied science, education, and music. The four students have grown to 2,268 students from thirty-seven states and ten foreign countries. The teaching facility has grown to twenty-five buildings and grounds valued at $3 million. The "no money" has grown to an annual income averaging $500,000. And now the university has 7,016 graduates living in every state of the Union where the Negro lives and working in every rank of life. Today 242 graduates go out to join that number.

But growth at Howard University has not been extensive expansion only. There has been intensive development as well. Little by little the curriculum has been concentrated and graded upward in quality. When Howard first opened her doors, the curriculum was thinly stretched all the way from teaching an illiterate slave how to read a few verses in the Bible to the degrees of Doctor of Medicine and Bachelor of Divinity. As the years have passed, the preparatory department has been taken away and the high school division has been taken away, so that now no courses are given in the university under the freshman year and every course given is of collegiate and university caliber. The standards of all the schools have been raised continuously, so that today at least six of the schools are rated in Class A by standard rating agencies, the seventh gives Class A work of its kind, and the two not yet recognized have come to the place where they can feel courageous enough to apply for Class A standing within the coming year.

There has also been a decided increase in the number of Negro scholars gathered on the several faculties, it being the purpose of the original white founders of the university not merely to train Negro men and women for practical life, but to train educational leaders who participate with them on a basis of uncondescending equality in the whole enterprise of Negro education. Here during the years has gathered the largest body of intelligent and capable Negro scholars to be found connected with any enterprise of its kind in the civilized world. Not only have these scholars been able to teach their subjects, but also some of them have ventured into the field of creative scholarship and have made original contributions to the knowledge of the world. Negro scholars at Howard University have made original and creative contributions in the fields of botany, zoology, sociology, and history. Just recently, a Negro member of the faculty was invited to share with a number of other scholars in the field of the natural sciences, including several Nobel prize winners, in preparing a volume that they in common believe will be a notable contribution to the world's knowledge of living things.

A Romance and a Monument

Howard University is the first mature university organization to come to pass among Negroes in the modern civilized world. Its growth from the humblest beginnings is one of the great romances of American education. During all the early years, while the founder and his associates worked, pseudo-scientific men were busily engaged in giving various reasons that serious education of the kind here undertaken should never be attempted among Negroes. History has answered their arguments. Howard University, with its high-calibered fruitfulness, is a justifying monument to the faith of the founder and to all his hard-working fellow laborers. It is a monument also to the far-sighted wisdom of the federal government, which, ever since the emancipation of the slaves, has not ceased to manifest an interest in their educational growth. Howard University has been made possible in its present efficiency very largely because, for a period of nearly fifty years, it has had the discriminating, judicious, far-sighted helpfulness of a sympathetic and understanding government.

Howard University is also a monument to the capacity of the Negro himself. The coming of the Negroes from 250 years of slavery (in which by far most of them did not know even how to write their names) in a period of sixty years to constitute the majority of the members of the faculty of a full-fledged university and to have their names recorded as original and creative contributors to the knowledge of the world is certainly an indication that the human mind—whatever the color and under whatever serious embarrassments it may have worked—is essentially a dignified thing and that all Christianity and other great religions have dared to believe about it can possibly be true.

Preparing Slaves of the People

The development of Howard University has not been, however, an unnatural thing, growing out of a desire to provide a monument. It has been a natural response to the clamant needs of a growing people. The Negro race today has needs that cannot be satisfied except by men trained in the way that Howard University attempts to train them. There are some needs of the people that may be met by servants trained in a brief period of time. There are other needs of the people that cannot be met except by slaves who spend one-third of their lives getting ready their powers to place them at the disposal of the people.

When a humble woman in her crude cottage in Mississippi stands by the bedside of her child threatened with death, her heart reaches out with a great desire to conquer the disease about to take away her most precious possession. But the mind is not able to respond. It takes twenty-five years of training to be able to meet the needs of that simple woman's heart. Howard University exists in order that—when the simple and the poor cry out for fundamental things that their hearts must have if they are to reach the goal of a normal and happy life—those slaves shall be prepared with competent minds to see that the heart's desire of the people shall not fail. If it be the ambition of any institution to prepare servants for the American people, I say that Howard University seeks the preeminent greatness that comes to those who try to make ready themselves and their associates to be the slaves of the people.

Professional Schools that Serve Great Needs

Medicine

The professional schools in Howard University have arisen to meet definite needs of the Negro people. Take the matter of health. When the Negro started out from slavery, it was freely predicted that physically he would not be able to survive in the midst of civilized life. He has survived, and nobly, but his health standard is far below the general health of the American people. His death rate is higher and his losses from all causes are greater than among the other sections of the American population.

Some 3,000 medical men have gone out to serve the health needs of Negroes, and the progress that they have made in winning the confidence of their people, in establishing hospitals, and in joining the public health service has been remarkable indeed. But their numbers are very inadequate. There is only one Negro physician to every 3,300 Negroes in the United States, as compared with one white physician to every 450 members of the white race. As important as dentistry is today, there is only one Negro dentist to every 20,000 needy Negro mouths. There is a great need to increase the number of efficient medical men, not only in curative medicine, but also in preventive medicine and for those public scientific measures by which we hope, in the long run, to prevent the rapid growth of disease among the people. Howard University is dedicated to supplying that need. This year her School of Medicine has been filled, and she has had to turn away thirty-two qualified candidates for lack of space in her laboratories.

Law

In recent years, there has been a decided increase in the accumulation of Negro poetry and a vast growth in business. There has been manifested also an increasing desire on the part of enlightened communities to have Negroes themselves in the legislative halls—to represent the real interests of their people and to see to it that these real interests are taken account of in the legislative process. There is only one well-qualified School of Law at work in the Negro race today. It is at Howard University. That the Negro shall have lawyers who are competent and who live up to the highest standards of the legal profession is the intention and one of the justifiably great measures of Howard University.

Teaching

I turn now to the profession of teaching. Howard University has been able to come to the place where it stands today because of the rapid development in the field of fundamental education for Negroes. We have been able to do away with the high school department of Howard because there has been a widespread increase of primary and preparatory education for colored people. The time has come when the system of Negro education itself demands that there shall be a university organization specializing in the preparation of teachers. There is today in the United States a deeply recognized need for teachers of a certain caliber of mind and spirit, not only among the high schools, but also among the growing colleges themselves.

A few years ago, here at Howard University, a number of college presidents met, and when they were asked to state in brief the one outstanding need in their institutions, every one of them, without previous conference, put his finger on this point: The greatest need is teachers who know their subjects, who understand the Negro mind and the difficulties under which our colleges labor, and who are willing to work with us, not counting hours or measuring units, but giving us all they have because they love the people. Howard University cannot presume to say at this moment that it is prepared to take care of that teacher need of the growing Negro colleges, but it is justifiable to hope that in this place in the coming years, with the proper class of graduate studies, there may be prepared a type of teacher—for high schools and for the growing colleges—whose competence and whose spiritual qualifications cannot be excelled anywhere in the United States.

Religion

I come now to the ministry of religion. There are 47,000 Negro churches in the United States, and there are in the whole country today less than sixty college graduates getting ready to fill those pulpits. The Negro church from every point of view is the most powerful and the most constructive organization now at work in the Negro race. There is no organization and no combination of organizations that can, at this stage in the history of the Negro race, begin to compare with the fundamental importance of the Negro church. And yet we can see what is going to happen to that church if only sixty college men are preparing to enter the Negro pulpit. The simple, unsophisticated, mystical religion of the Negro cannot continue to endure

unless it is reinterpreted over and over to him by men who have a fundamental and far-reaching understanding of the significance of religion in its
relation to the complexities of modern civilized life.

Here at Howard University we have the groundwork laid for a great
nonsectarian school of religion. It ought to be made a graduate school of
religion—seeking the truth about the meaning of life without bias, endeavoring to deliver the people from superstition and from uncharitable sectarianism, binding them into an understandable cooperation, clarifying their
vision, and releasing their energies for constructive service to the common
good.

The Work of the Colleges

This year there were 1,701 students in the colleges of Howard University.
That seems to be a large number, and to our hard-working deans and
professors it sometimes appears to be too many. But there can be no danger
in the next fifty years that there will be too many Negroes applying for a
college education. In all the days since the Civil War, only 10,000 colored
people have graduated from a college of any kind. Today in the colleges of
our country, there are approximately 800,000 youths studying for degrees.
Only about 10,000 of these are Negroes. This means there are eighty times as
many white young men and women studying in the colleges today as
Negroes—a far too great disproportion that must be remedied as rapidly as it
is possible for us to do so. There may be a danger in numbers for Howard
University but only the danger that comes from being overtaxed because of
our limited plant, limited faculty, and limited income.

Training in Sympathetic Understanding

There can be no danger here of that thing now so greatly feared in many
American institutions: that too many of our students will waste their time in
a thin, incompetent, and too liberal education. There is no leisure class
among Negroes today—students who are eager to come to a university to
produce a cultured aristocracy. Practically every Negro who comes to a
college knows that he must earn his living by the sweat of his brow, and that
whatever culture he gets must be in addition to fundamental and specific
preparation to do one thing by which he may earn his living.

The great danger that confronts Howard University and all Negro institutions of learning is not that we shall have too much liberal education, but

that we shall have too little of it—that we shall turn out competent physicians, competent lawyers, and competent teachers in their several specialties, graduates who are at the same time competent, shallow-sympathized men, ignorant of the fundamental human relations, and not knowing how to take their part in the general development of a community. At Howard University, along with the training of the individual to render specific professional service, it is absolutely necessary that there shall go studies to fit a man sympathetically to understand the kind of country that he is living in, the progress that the country has made, the direction in which it is moving, the nature of the institutions with which he has to deal, and the relations and possibilities of his own people to his government and to the progress of his country. This is what is meant by a liberal education—not the preparation of a leisured aristocracy simply spending its time in the discussion of things of cultural interest to incompetent men, but the broadening of the sympathies and the deepening of the understanding that will make the experienced physician able to cooperate with the experienced minister, lawyer, and teacher for the public good. Together they will endeavor to develop a country that shall have a deep sense of community and of brotherly cooperation.

The Common Problems of Negroes

Such preparation is all the more necessary by reason of the stage of development that the Negro himself has reached. A few years ago, it was customary to assume that the Negro problem was a sectional problem and that the development of the Negro and the development of cooperative race relations were matters to be handed over almost entirely to the southern states. But there are now two million Negroes living outside the boundaries of the southern states. It does not appear that there ever again will be a time when the Negro race will have a geographical unity and can be spoken of as involved in a mere sectional interpretation of the meaning of life. Yet these Negroes, distributed all over the country, from California to Maine and from New York to Texas, are more and more realizing that wherever they go, they have certain common problems. They are struggling today as never before to arrive at some unified understanding regarding what shall be their self-expression, what shall be their relation to the other members of the American population, and how they can maintain their creative self-respect in the midst of the communities where they live. These people must find some intelligent interpreter that shall not be sectional, some center of interpretation that shall look at the Negro question in its national aspect and that is acquainted with the problem of the Negro wherever he goes.

Howard University is the one great institution located and prepared by its history and organization to be that nation's center in which the Negro shall come to full self-consciousness about where he is, where he hopes to go, what difficulties are in the way, and how he can get there with the goodwill of his fellow citizens. It is of the utmost importance to the Negro people that whatever studies may contribute to this end shall be developed here on the highest plane of efficiency and as rapidly as possible.

Negro Problem of National and World Significance

This development is a matter of concern not alone to the Negro people themselves, but also to the nation as a whole, for the Negro question is now a matter of national and of international significance. When Howard University was first established in Washington, this was a capital that had been recently subjected to attack, was just recovering from the awful struggles of a civil war, and was looked upon with patronizing goodwill by many of the strong nations of the earth. But Washington today is the central, throbbing heart of the most powerful and most hopeful republic that now exists on the face of the earth. The urgent question that now confronts the world regarding this republic is "What is going to be its relation to the weaker and disadvantaged peoples of the earth?" The great nations of Europe for a century have been subordinating the undeveloped countries and the disadvantaged peoples of the world to the economic and political interests of the European powers. The urgent question today is whether the United States is going to follow this European practice, or whether there is going to arise in this place a country so deeply convinced of the possibilities of humanity that it is willing to keep its self-control, while having no relations with even the weakest of peoples except such as it can justify in the light of its deepest conscience, and while committed to none but a purely open and aboveboard practice of brotherliness to all men and to all countries of the earth.

America's Great Experiment

It is not necessary for the world to wait to see what we are going to do in our foreign relations in order to find out what the trend is going to be, because the United States of America has a barometer within the nation. It has twelve million of the disadvantaged peoples of the world in its own bosom. What is done as regards the Negro in this country is a signal and unfailing indication of the temper of the American spirit and of the character and intent of the American mind, and it will resound in the halls of all the world. It is in the interest, therefore, of our nation that it shall be assured from within not only that it is capable of getting along with a high degree of justice and goodwill in relation to Mexico, for example, but also that right here is the experimental crucible where the great race problem of the world is crystallized. It shall prove that it has the power publicly to assimilate twelve million negroes, to give them every form of public justice, and to give it to them in ways persuasive of their own free consent and cooperation, thereby making them an intimate part of the national life.

No Panacea

Years ago, when we were led by our infantile imagination, we were accustomed to suppose that there was some one panacea by which we could achieve this result. We now know that there is no such single panacea. The Negro is now intermixed with all the complex activities of American life. Nothing but the application of intelligence, persistent intelligence in a multitude of complex directions, with one solid goodwill, can possibly accomplish—even in a great length of time—the thing that we all desire and that we must have if the destiny of our country is to be fulfilled. Our country, therefore, needs an institution where those studies will be undertaken in a large and comprehensive way, which will prepare not only the Negro but also the nation to understand how the Negro is situated, where we want him to go, what the difficulties are in the way, and how, in spite of all the difficulties, by intelligence and persistent application of goodwill, he can get there.

Special Fitness of Howard University

I call your attention to the special preparedness of Howard University to undertake those studies in sociology, economics, social philosophy, history, biology, and anthropology—studies that may give us the facts, inform the public mind, and set forth a light by which both the Negro and the nation may be advanced. Here we have a great university, situated in a southern city so far as practice is concerned. Atlanta, Georgia; Nashville, Tennessee; or Natchez, Mississippi, can make no claim to be more southern in spirit than Washington. And yet in the midst of this southern city, you have something that you have nowhere else in the South. You have the continuously throbbing will of the whole American people, expressed in the executive government and in the Supreme Court. You have a constant stream of noble characters who represent the best sentiment of the nation, interacting continually with the southern mind, tending to assimilate and to transform it to the measure of the national will.

Here we have a university with 2,268 students—nearly one-fourth of all the Negroes in the United States engaged in college and professional education—taught by a biracial faculty, the white members of which constitute some of the most eminent minds in the life of America and the Negro members of which constitute the largest and most competent body of trained Negro minds engaged in educational practice in the United States. Negro mind and white mind work together without condescension in a living example of what intelligent men can do with the race question when they have freedom to undertake it together. There is also a biracial Board of Trustees—white men among the most distinguished in America and Negro products of higher educational institutions— working together with mutual respect, great capacity for cooperation, and a will to make this a creative, intellectual, and spiritual center that shall have not only the patronage but also the confidence of the Negro people.

Here is an institution partly supported by the United States Congress so that every student who comes here can have daily and continuous evidence of the persistent goodwill of an enlightened government, and yet such a relationship to the government as precludes any form of political domination. It is an institution, therefore, in which the teaching can have no suspicion of political supervision by the government and which, therefore, can commend itself entirely to the free and spontaneous affection of the Negro people and to the continuous confidence of those men of goodwill of all races who want to see the Negro problem brought out well. In such an institution, so situated, so manned, so supported, and, moreover, so richly blessed in having the resources of the Library of Congress and the other vast educational facilities of the national capital at its disposal, it is inevitable that far-reaching studies in race relations will be undertaken and that those studies will be of benefit to Negroes in all parts of the country and to the nation as a whole.

Possible World Fruits of Negro Thought

I have high confidence that these studies will add to the sum total of our knowledge of human life. If the Negro studies the human will, human motive, human organization, and human philosophy of social life in order to discover how he may become free—with the consent of the other elements of the American population—he is sure to discover something about the human will, something about human motives and human organization that may be to the advantage of mankind.

The President of the United States has recently said that there is a residual unconquered territory in human nature that prevents us from carrying out in practice the ideals that we know to be the ones to follow. The Negro situation is acute largely because the American population has not yet found the power to carry out its own ideals. If thinkers here can discover ways and means of eliciting that power and of bringing it to bear in race relations, they will make a contribution to the sum total of knowledge and to the ongoing of the human race.

Cultivating Natural Gifts of the Negro

As much, however, as the Negro may be interested in the professions and in those studies pointing to the solution of his problem, he must not forget to cultivate those natural gifts that have come with him from the days of slavery. Though he does not have health as he should have it, he must continue to sing. Though the social problem may not be solved in this lifetime, he must develop his talent to tell a good story and act out a good part. Though he may not for years be fitted into the texture of American life, he must still keep alive that simple and beautiful faith whereby he has been able to get along and to bear the cross with a gentle and kindly heart. Howard University should be the place where the undeveloped heritage of art in the soul of the Negro may be cultivated, a place where his music, his histrionic talents, and his instinctive kindliness of disposition may be brought to its fullest self-consciousness and competency.

The Support of Howard University

The support of an institution of this kind should be the common concern of all the American people. I do not hope that Howard University will become rich; I hope that it will always be poor enough to be responsive to the criticism and the stimulus of the current public will. But I do hope that it may be relieved from want. Howard University with its great mission today is in want. Over the heads of the people who work here hangs an accumulated deficit of $87,000 brought about by an annual current deficit over a period of six years. There has been an increase of 100 percent in the student body since 1919–1920, yet the faculty has increased not more than 28 percent, and the increase in equipment and in income has lagged far behind the needs. I should like to see that deficit removed. I should like to see an adequate income for maintenance. Every one of these buildings is in a low state of repair because we have but a minimum of 2 percent for repairs and maintenance of buildings and grounds.

Above all, I want that Howard University shall have salaries to give teachers a living wage. The work that it must do cannot be done by men who must be worried every night as to whether they can pay their board bill the first of the month. The highest salary for a professor at Howard University is $2,650—a salary below those paid in the public high school system in the city of Washington. There are teachers here teaching for $1,000 and $1,400 per year. How the work that we want to do can be done with these small salaries I am not yet able to say. But the gravest danger is not to the teachers themselves; it is to the product of the institution. Poorly paid teachers, who must work in the night to supplement their salaries by preaching and selling—even coffins—as some of them have done and are doing, will find it impossible to turn out anything other than a mass product. A mass product in industry is a good thing, but a mass product in education is an abomination unto God and sure to be a disappointment to the public good.

What we want to produce at Howard University is a self-conscious, self-directing, independent, responsible human being who knows how to act, who knows where he is going, and who has the courage to do what he believes to be right. Such a product cannot be trained in a machine university where the professors are financially strained and are obliged to spend their spare time in earning a living rather than in reflecting upon their studies and in personal conference with individual students.

Whence will come this support? For nearly five years, the major portion of it has come from the fees of students and from the government of the United States. I hope that during the next ten-year period the government will not cease its support. Howard University cannot live without that support, and the product already established here is too precious to be allowed to go backward.

I hope also that an increased sum will come from student fees. Already we have increased them far beyond the limit of most of our students to endure. Eighty-five percent of the male students are able to pay those fees only by working while they study. I hope an increased amount will come from the Negro people themselves. The way in which they have responded to the government's challenge and to the challenge of the General Education Board is a thing that should be precious to the heart of every American. By far, more than two-thirds of all the money now paid in the School of Medicine Endowment Campaign has been paid by the Negro people themselves.

Let me pause to say, to delight the hearts of those who are here, that the Endowment Campaign is now within $15,000 of victory. The acquisition of $15,000 more by the first of July will bring us the first half-million-dollar endowment for the School of Medicine.

I hope that discriminating philanthropy will supplement the gifts of the government and of the Negro people themselves. I have seen encouraging signs that philanthropy intends to do this. Nowhere in America and nowhere else in the world can funds be spent with greater productiveness for the common good than they can now be spent at Howard University. We are so happy to be able to report that under the supervision of the Department of the Interior and by the determined will of the administration, Howard University has a financial system unequivocally honest and open to the inspection of any representative of any organization that desires to make that inspection on any day.

The Destiny of the Negro

I am through now. Sixty-five years ago, the Negro came from bondage. In so short a time, he has come to this place. What is his destiny? I do not know. I hope, and I do not conceal my hope, that his destiny will be entire public equality and entire goodwilled cooperative relations with every element of the American population, and that he will be especially understood by those men who have been his former masters and who have been accustomed to making him a slave. I hope that he will be delivered entirely from every form of public servitude and that he will be redelivered spontaneously, by his own consent, into a willing slavery to the common good. I hope that this will be a moral accomplishment, not by amalgamation or by an expedient of any kind, even though that expedient should be brought to pass tomorrow morning. Amalgamation would be a beggarly solution of a problem that is essentially moral and that should be settled in a way that will result in strengthening the moral will of both of the peoples engaged in the enterprise.

I want my country to conquer all of the inhibitions connected with blackness and all of the fears connected with blackness, but I want the original blackness there, and I want that blackness to be unashamed and unafraid. That day is far off yet, but the existence of this institution tells something about the intent of the American mind. When I see that in sixty years it has been possible for such an institution as this to come to pass, I am encouraged for my country and my hopes are stimulated by a great inspiration.

The Responsibility of Howard Graduates

Fellow students of the graduating classes, you are among those who are prepared to take part in a great enterprise. You are going out to work among a people greatly undermanned. You are going to find it hard, most of you, to earn your living. You are going to be tempted to desert the public good and to seek merely your own self-aggrandizement. But I call upon you to keep in remembrance your university. Keep especially in remembrance those noble white men who founded it here. Existing in the form of Anglo-Saxons, they thought it not a thing to be grasped after to be on equality with Anglo-Saxons and to enjoy the rights and privileges of Anglo-Saxons. They humbled themselves, took upon themselves the form of servants, and made themselves obedient to the needs of slaves. They lived with us, ate with us, and suffered ostracism and humiliation with us so that by their personal contact with us they might teach us the truth and the truth might set us free. They did these things because they loved a country that has never yet existed on land or sea, a country in which all men are free, all men are intelligent, and all men are self-directing contributors to the common good.

That country has not yet been attained. It is still the goal of the American people. You are to participate in the bringing of that country to pass. You have here enjoyed the fruits of the labors of the founders. You cannot be self-respecting men and women unless you also participate in the spirit of the founders. Their country must be your country. You must salute it from afar. Even while you fight with every ounce of energy for those public equalities by which you cannot live, you must also take upon yourself the cross—your proportionate share of the responsibility of bringing that country of intelligent goodwill to pass. You will have to keep in remembrance that many men of other races who seek to do you injury are men who have not had advantages that you have had. They do so because, in their blindness regarding the meaning of life and the purposes of government, they think that their welfare consists in the subordination of your own to theirs. But if they be blind in the mind, you cannot afford to strike a blind man. You must be patient to be just to them while they get wisdom and courage to be just to you. You must remember that your disposition may be the decisive factor in the changing of their minds.

Keep in mind your university, and in all of your labors cast no shame upon her. So live out in the real world that travelers from your city may come to this place because you have been trained here. Your institution is large, but still it is little known. She is like some humble mother who washes clothes in a country place while you go out to share the honor and the glory of the world. The world will never know much about your mother or respect her except what you make it do so by the character of the life that you live.

So live that when you are done, men will eagerly ask where you were born, who were your teachers, and where were you trained. And in your prayers, when you strip yourself of all dress parade of every kind, mention your university before the God and Father of us all and especially mention your servant who now stands before you, deans and members of the faculties, the Board of Trustees, and all those men of goodwill in whose hands our destiny lies.

And now may the beauty of the Lord our God be upon you. May He establish the work of your hands. Yea, the work of your hands may He establish it.

3. *Prophets of Unsegregated Institutions*[3]

Mordecai Johnson recognized the contributions made by white northern missionaries who established schools for the freedmen following the Civil War. In this address he sets forth the ways in which those men and women, often at great personal sacrifice, sought to bring light, learning, and self-esteem to those whose lives had been so brutally demeaned. Moreover, he predicted with remarkable foresight that because of the progress, however so slow, that had been in race relations, in due course the walls of segregation in education would soon fall.

Following is part of a news reporter's account of some reactions to this forecast:

> I looked around at southern white folks and southern colored folks. President F. D. Patterson, Tuskegee, was leaning forward on the edge of his seat; a white person whose name I did not get sat on the front seat, laughing approvingly. Dr. Charles S. Johnson,

---

[3]Nashville, Tennessee, November 1947.

who was being inducted as president of Fisk University, sat with his right hand to his jaw and his expressionless face; President E. C. Peters, white, Paine College, August, Ga., sat tense. Dr. Johnson just stood there and stared at them as if reading them, weighing them.

"Did I say that the walls were falling . . . ? I amend that! They have already fallen!"

There was a burst of applause. Other speakers on the platform seemed concerned, uneasy. Harvie Branscomb, white, chancellor, Vanderbilt University and native of Alabama, presided. He seemed restless. Later, when he summarized remarks of the speakers on the panel, he quoted every speaker except Dr. Johnson. W. C. Jackson, white, chancellor, The Woman's College of the University of N.C., who spoke mostly on the democracy of Thomas Jefferson, twisted and turned in his seat. His facial expression was one of astonishment and concern. [Douglass Hall, *Baltimore Afro-American Magazine*, November 27, 1947.]

Seven years later, the U.S. Supreme Court issued a landmark decision in the *Brown vs. Board of Education* case, outlawing such segregation.

PROPHETS OF UNSEGREGATED INSTITUTIONS*

It is always thrilling for me to come to Nashville, for this is where I came when I was thirteen years of age, to what was then Roger Williams University, so I could continue my education from the sixth grade. At that time there was no education in my city or county for Negroes beyond the sixth grade, and I know now that the sixth grade training that I received was terribly watered down.

I am especially glad always to come into the walls of Fisk University and her related institutions, because in the perspective of a long and busy life, I have come to see clearly that it was in these walls—and walls like them—that the Negro people have received and enjoyed the highest friendship that they have known.

---

*Delivered at Fisk University at the inauguration of Charles S. Johnson as president, November 27, 1947.

In the days immediately after the Civil War—when the personality of black people was at a great discount, when this southern area was greatly troubled and suffering by reason of its recent experiences, and when there were very few to be found who believed that the Negro people would ever be able to stand erect and grow into full self-respecting and highly esteemed citizenship—there came down from the North representatives of the best educational system that the nation had ever known. Those representatives, being white, could well have taken great pride in their education and could have lived distinguished careers without ever touching this humble people. But they thought it not a thing to be grasped after—to be white—but humbled themselves and came here and made themselves obedient to the needs of slaves and the children of slaves. They saw all the deficiencies and warpings and shortcomings that the people in this region saw in us, but they saw what the people of this region had not yet come to see: Underneath our rude personalities, bruised and aborted by the slave system, there was the unrevealed and essential dignity of human nature endowed by its Creator with unlimited possibilities.

Education and Esteem

At that time the chief concern of white men in the South was to stay away from Negroes, except in the contact that inevitably took place between the working man and his master. This distance between the Negro and the white, throughout this whole region, was held to be necessitous for the preservation of what was conceived to be the dignity of the white race. But these men and women from the North, being constrained by their great faith in the high possibility of human nature as such, felt that it was absolutely necessary for them to come close to us. Disregarding all majority and agreed upon inhibitions, they took up their residence with the children of slaves. They lived with us, ate with us, slept in the same dormitories with us, suffered ostracism and humiliation with us, and staked their lives upon the faith that by their contact with us they would teach us the truth and the truth would set us free. When our clothes were unpressed and disordered and when our habits were the habits of men who had been inwardly bruised by slavery, they addressed us in class thus, "Mr. Johnson, will you read?"

Now by the common consent of the whole southern community, we were not that "Mr." Moreover, 99 percent of the time, we had a low esteem of ourselves. They must have known that, too. And they must have known that the southern world expected that relationship with us to be dragged to the lowest common physical denominator. But they disappointed and surprised all such expectancy. By their reverent courtesy toward us, they established a spiritual distance that evoked out of the children of slaves the deepest aspiration. Their pupils came to desire nothing less than to be able, clean, and strong like those who stood before them.

When, after some twenty years of labor, they had carried one of us from the humblest grades on up through the high school and on up through the college, and they thought that, at last, they had made a man, they were fearful to trust their own judgment. They all but literally laid their bodies down as a bridge between here and the North by taking part of their meager salaries to send their product to Harvard and other institutions, saying, "I think this is a man that we have made; you tell us what you think."

And the word came back, "You are right, you have done it; your work is good. This truly is a man!"

Then they met us at the station on our return and said, "My son, come now. You are no longer a child; you have become a part of us; and, henceforth, you will be a member of the faculty. You will join us in the most precious fellowship that exists among human beings and that knows no race or class. Together we shall work to make others like yourself." And so they established and maintained on this spot, for the first time in the history of this region, communities of the spirit transcending race, which have been until this day the most inspiring challenge to the dignity of the American soul ever planted on the soil of these states.

We know that this is the highest friendship that we have known. After a generation of life, we believe that it is the highest friendship that human life can know. We see now that what we met here was not merely a few northern white men and women; we met that city that we call "Democracy." We know now where that city is—not in the Declaration of Independence nor in the Constitution, which are paper rescripts. It lives in the souls of these men and women whom we met in this place, and this is our country that will hold our allegiance until we die. We shall never be able to live in any other country. And we shall never betray it. It were better to be dead than to be found loving anything less.

The institutions founded by these men and women are going to suffer physically during the decade now before us. They are going to find it a desperate undertaking to maintain their very lives. But I will venture to predict—and this is the heart of what I am going to say—that at the very moment when they are struggling to maintain their physical existence and when many of them may pass away, they will enter the most victorious validation of their educational purpose that has ever taken place in the course of their history. While the influences that have streamed out from this institution will meet a crisis in this decade, they will also be met by profound constructive influences of a world nature. Those influences will breach in principle and in fact the segregated system of education.

I predict that within this decade that system will be abandoned in principle, that it will be breached in fact and irreparably, and that from this decade on it will be in inevitable retreat.

This fact will be looked upon as a defeat of the South until it is observed that the "walls" were hacked on from within and that the breaching took place in the middle of the wall where those who were hitting on it from the outside were met by those who were trying to get out from the inside, because they could no longer endure the restriction of spirit that was imposed on them. What may look astoundingly like the defeat of the South will be the first great emergence of the uncompromising and naked soul of the South's best men and women. Once having breached that wall, they will never again retreat. They will become the center of a growing morale, rising out of real harmony with the world view of democracy in the deepest sense. And we shall have a birth of moral and spiritual solidarity, as between a growing group of Negroes and white people in North and South, unparalleled since the Civil War, and never again to be effectively compromised.

The physical fact that will precipitate the decision in a significant way will take place at the point where those schools yet remain defeated—on the graduate and professional level. The peculiar thing about those schools is the type of victories that they have won. At first, you know, they called themselves universities, but they were really sixth grade primary schools. The biggest battle they won was that which enabled them to give up the primary schools. They could not give up the primary school for fifty years because the South, still being hesitant over the question as to whether the Negro should be given anything approximating full education at all, found it extremely difficult to pass beyond the sixth grade. My town in Tennessee, for example, during my boyhood had two public academies for whites, but nobody had a thought that a Negro would go beyond the sixth grade.

There was a southerner who spent his life bridging that gap—Dr. James H. Dillard of Virginia. It was largely because of the inspired work of this great southerner that the gap between the sixth grade and the high school was bridged and that these schools could at last lay aside their work in primary education.

It took them quite a few years to do away with their high school work and to devote their full time to college work. But, at length, the stream of graduates began to roll out. The South at last was so much impressed by them that it could no longer resist the conviction that higher education was necessitous. Southerners began to choose the graduates of those schools, which they once despised, to be the principals and presidents of state-supported colleges for Negroes founded by southerners.

Advanced Education

A few years ago I had the privilege in New Orleans, Louisiana, of seeing a Board of Trustees for a school of higher education—a board make up of northern whites (that is natural); northern Negroes (that isn't quite so natural); southern Negroes (that isn't natural; that's an achievement); and some southern whites (that is a spiritual victory of a supreme kind). To cap the climax, they had elected a Jew as chairman of the Board of Trustees. If I had been a visitor from some far off Atlantis and had wanted to go to one place where I would see the essential heart of America nakedly exposed in one room, I would just want to look at that Board of Trustees.

Now those institutions could not finish their work. They slowed down at the professional and graduate levels. This type of education was too expensive. They could produce only two medical schools and two dental schools and two schools of pharmacy. They tiptoed up to the master's degree in a dozen places, but retreated where they had wisdom and repented even where they did not retreat. They have never yet looked at the Doctor of Philosophy degree except with an affectionate wave of the hand.

Now up to this time, the South has been able to validate every concession that it has made to this system of schools while at the same time maintaining the complete integrity of its segregated system. Just in proportion as those schools have succeeded objectively in seeing their work established, they have had to see what they have considered the essential element in it compromised and disappearing.

But today a great new fact is taking place. There are 78,000 Negroes in college as a result of the joint influence of those schools and the affection and confidence that they have drawn around them from southern leadership. The full consequences of that 78,000 do not appear on the surface. They will not appear until about 1950.

Two or three years from now there will be 5,000 Negroes—with a college degree in their hands—knocking on the doors of our two centers of professional education for Negroes. And they will find that they cannot get in. There were 1,351 applicants for medicine at Howard University in 1947, and we could take only 70. The same thing happened at Meharry Medical College. So this devoted system of schools will appear to have failed its students at the highest point of their achievement. But they will not have failed.

The Next Ten Years in Education

There will go up from these Negro students and their parents a most deeply felt disappointment and chagrin. Because they cannot help it, they are going to knock at the door of every professional and graduate school maintained by state and public funds in the South. They are going to say, "Let us in there. We have got to come in there. We have a right to be in there, and we must come in." Now they are not going to be received cordially, and this will not be because the people in there hate them, but because they are still afraid.

But these students are not going to stop knocking on those doors. They are going to sue, and the number of suits already in court will be multiplied by 100. They will sue for the inherent right of a citizen to come in contact with those highest personalities sustained by tax money, who have the power to transform their unfinished lives into that full capacity to serve their people and their country as they desire. They will sue with strength of conviction bought by their suffering in the war, where they paid with their blood the full price of admission.

A strange thing is going to happen. It is beginning to happen already. A considerable amount of the expense of those suits is going to be paid for by southern white students inside those institutions. And those southern white students are going to follow their professors into the court where, with their searching eyes made alive by deep reflection upon the meaning of embattled democracy in this world, they are going to subject the testimony of their professors to a scrutiny of the soul that will be unbearable.

The Negro's new and systematic intelligence will lay before judges who hear those cases, facts that they have long suspected, but which they will now come to know. And those judges will not permit points of order to interrupt the witnesses, for they will want to hear the full testimony. And, hearing, they will come to know that the segregated system of higher education, theoretically supplied as usual, in reality has no approximation whatsoever of equality.

That testimony will prove that the segregated system deprives Negroes of precisely the most precious element of education and in a way demonstrated by fact. It will be impossible for any judge who looks into the faces of those Negroes and at those facts to think otherwise. So those judges are going to rule that equality of opportunity must come into existence.

Build the Future

A bluff is going to be made to produce evidence that there can be equality on a segregated basis, but this effort is not going to succeed because, for the first time in its history, the South is going to learn the true expense of segregation. It is going to try to erect segregated medical schools in quantity sufficient to give the Negro his due chance. But such closed and segregated institutions of medicine, engineering, and law will require a good deal of money. It is all but inconceivable that the South will provide that money.

To obviate the necessity of paying that money, the leaders of the South are going to appeal to the federal government to appropriate money and to sanction to a regional allocation of schools for Negroes, theoretically supported by a program to establish regional schools for whites. I predict that the federal government will not do it. I predict that it will not do it, because it cannot do it. It will have the eyes of the world upon it. It will be confronted with a challenging system of life that says, "Watch them. They are going to do it. And they are going to do it because, in spite of all their pretension, they have no real care for the dignity and the freedom of the man lowest down. And they will compromise the very soul of their institutions before they will yield, in principle and in fact, the conditions necessary for every human being, who is a citizen and risks his life for his country, to have unlimited access to the resources of education afforded by his blood and his taxes." They will not do it. And because they will not do it, they will make a decision that we will be able to use as a final exposure of their lack of belief in their own system. We shall be prophetically armed to destroy it, because we know now that we are set out to destroy not a system that believes itself to be right, but a false and pretentious thing that does not actually believe in its own soul.

The Senators and Representatives sitting in the Congress will see clearly, and for the first time, that higher education segregated by race, however justifiable it may be as a political expedient, compromises the very substance of democracy itself. And they will not support it. I repeat—they will not support it. I predict they will not do it, because they cannot do it. And I predict that the Walls of Jericho will fall. Did I say, ". . . will fall?" I amend that—they are falling!

The Church and Education

In the city of Washington, the Roman Catholic Church, after 300 years of reflection, has come to the conclusion that, in the presence of the threat of Communism, it cannot longer compromise the dignity of its Master. And it has secretly reached a conclusion that segregated worship and segregated education are a blasphemy against God. In their leading American university, they have abandoned it. Within the confines of the South, they have opened the door of one of their great national institutions for Negroes on every level of instruction. It is no accident—what you saw happen in Missouri. They have done it in Missouri within the confines of the South, and they have also said at last on the primary level in their parochial schools, "Suffer little children to come together to the Master, for of such is the Kingdom of Heaven."

When their white parishioners got up a petition of 500 names and threatened to sue in the courts of the state, for the first time in 300 years the Catholic Archbishop unsheathed the sword of ecclesiastical discipline and said in effect: "In the presence of the principle explicated by this act, the Roman Catholic Church will not yield to the criticism of the state. There is One above the state. His voice only, speaking through the Apostolic Father, will we heed. If you sue the church while she is in the act of performing that duty, which is made necessary by her faith in the dignity of every human life, by that very act you will excommunicate yourselves from the church."

So southern Protestantism is already outflanked. It is outflanked on the right by the Roman Catholic Church and on the left by Communism, both of which have crossed the race line to establish brotherhood. Communism is the brotherhood of those that labor in the flesh, and Catholicism—those who have seen the great City of the Brotherhood that transcends the flesh— the brotherhood of the spirit, which is destined to supersede the brotherhood of the flesh.

I predict that if southern Protestantism tries to hold its segregated position for the decade now before us, she will be outflanked so effectively that the moral initiative will be taken away from her for 100 years and that she will never be able to recover.

But southern Protestantism is not going to do that. The Baptists may do it because the local preacher is isolated. But the Methodists are not going to do it.

I predict that the Methodist Church will abandon segregation. Did I say, ". . . will"? They are abandoning it. In the city of Washington, they also have opened their national university to Negro students on the graduate level. They will open more and more until their noblest men and women stand stripped of every physical defense, confident in the power of the spirit that they will not be degraded by contact with the Negro, but that by such contact both they and he will be mutually elevated and made unusually constructive in the South and in the nation.

The walls are falling in other states. They have already begun to fall in West Virginia. They have begun to fall in Maryland. A few weeks ago, the president of the University of Maryland said to me, "Be on your guard; we may surprise you." He said to another person, "During the current year, we shall open every division of the Graduate School of the University of Maryland to Negroes."

Now why are these things taking place? Because in the face of the war situation, America knows that she must reaffirm a world view that meets the issue raised by Communism. We must answer the question of whether the man who is on top of America can be trusted, unequivocally, to come in contact with the man who is on the bottom and to love him with persistence and strength enough to lift him to security and brotherhood. America knows she has got this to do. She knows that there must be no pussyfooting, and that she has got to do it now or her candlestick is going to be taken away from her and her own God is going to transfer the moral center of gravity to this universe clear out of the Western Hemisphere. In the presence of that challenge, America will not listen to a political and racial expediency that maintains those segregated institutions with their fears. She will listen to the prophets of unsegregated education, because she knows that in this way and in this way alone she will be able to explicate in fact and in content what she really means to this world.

Then we shall see, as I have said, not a defeat for the South, but the first emergence of the untrammeled and hitherto suppressed and crippled soul of the South's noblest people. Then we will all be on our way—South and North, black and white—to the city that Thomas Jefferson saw when he wrote the Declaration of Independence and that we Negroes have seen and loved in the hearts and lives of those who have taught us here at Fisk University and her kindred institutions.

★　★　★

4. *Interracial Contacts*[4]

In most of his addresses, Mordecai Johnson calls attention to the problems of race relations. Throughout his career, those were the most pressing problems of African Americans. It was an absolute necessity to present the facts and to analyze them in detail so that viable solutions might be projected. Because the patterns of racial segregation prevented whites from knowing and understanding fully the issues black Americans faced, the objective, honest, and forthright analyses of these facts opened many eyes and pricked many consciences.

More than in any of his recorded speeches to a white audience, this address to a group of Episcopalian women sets forth with clarity the basic issues in black-white relations, particularly those arising from economic and political disparities.

INTERRACIAL CONTACTS*

I feel a decided thrill in being able to speak to you today, for I think it is the first time in my life I have ever been permitted to address an Episcopal audience. That is not strange considering my background because, as Dr. Booker T. Washington said, most of us colored people are Baptists and Methodists. All my early life I generally regarded the Episcopal Church as the white man's church par excellence and as not much concerned with Negroes. But I have learned to know better as I have grown older and have appreciated the work that your church has tried to do among my people.

I count it as one of the great signs of advance in the matter of race relations that the laity of the Episcopal Church is becoming deeply interested in race relations.

Your chairman has rather defined the limits of what I shall say to you today by suggesting that I confine myself to two major aspects of the question, namely, the urgency of the problem, and an analysis of the problem so as to set it before you clearly as possible—leaving the solutions, for the most part, to you in your discussions.

Although I have strong convictions on race relations, I am quite willing to confine myself to those two areas because they are part of any effective

---

[4]Denver, Colorado.

*Presented at the Triennial Meeting of the Woman's Auxiliary to the National Council of the Episcopal Church, Denver, Colorado.

attack. Effective attack depends upon a proper conception of what the problem consists of and a powerful realization of the urgency of the question.

I am not among those who find themselves uncomfortable in calling this a problem. It *is* a problem. By this, we mean a set of human circumstances difficult in their first aspect, the solution of which does not immediately appear. But it is a problem that—when faced in all its difficulties—we believe we can attack successfully if we use all our powers. In the approach to a problem, we must be prepared to be as pessimistic in the beginning as facts require. I have learned from my long experience in tackling mathematical problems that one great danger is in allowing your optimism as to a final success to affect your judgment of the immediate difficulties. We must learn to run our fingers realistically over the rough edges of the problem and to see what the challenge is.

Part of the difficulty with regard to the race problem between whites and Negroes has been too much optimism in the statement of the problem. We have made it too simple. A very common statement of the problem that you can meet in America any day is this: The white people in America have achieved a high state of civilization, probably the highest ever achieved in the history of the world. Into that state of civilization have come—by means not too pleasant to reflect upon—a strange, undeveloped, and possibly inferior people. The problem of their liberty, brought about by the Emancipation Proclamation, raises a question as to whether they really have the capacity to live an American life. It is an open question as to whether full privileges should be granted until they have demonstrated their ability to live here. Therefore, for the time being, we withhold certain privileges pending proof of their real capacity for civilized life.

This is a beautiful statement and very calming to disturbed nerves, upset by the explosive power of the Gospel. It has made many willing to go on with the status quo because they have felt that a demonstration, which would finally define their duty in these relationships, was in process. God knows I should be glad to delight in so simple a statement of the problem. Some things of truth in the statement would make it appear plausible. We must not deny ourselves the pride of having achieved in America a high state of civilization, although it may not be the very best. There is no doubt that Negroes as a whole have not yet attained the full level of civilization that the best and most favored groups of whites in the United States have attained. However, it is altogether too great a simplification of this awful problem to assume that the white people, having attained their high state of civilization, are waiting with certain privileges in their hands to pass them on to this benighted folk as soon as those folks have demonstrated their ability.

The true statement of the problem is this: Here are two groups of human beings who daily and constantly live in an abnormal and unhealthy relation to one another, an unhealthy relation that hurts them both every day, that warps and injures and bruises their life, and that somehow or other we must find a way to heal.

The key to the understanding of the race question in the United States is the word "segregation." By segregation is meant that—in the relationship between colored people and white people—there is something deeper, first of all, than the personal equation. The unhealthy relationship that obtains between colored people and white people is a relationship that extends to the organized public life. The Negro in the United States—and I am going to put my finger primarily on the South—is actually cut off from normal relationship to the body of public life.

If you conceive of the public life—economic, political, and social—as a great spiritual body with a heart and pulse and blood stream passing through the arteries and veins, giving life to every portion of the body, you can better understand the interracial question. You should remember that the Negro is a limb in that body abnormally cut off from that body, and the circulation of blood that passes to the other members does not pass to him except in attenuated form. While his own blood seeks to cleanse itself, it does not pass in full force through the veins of the body and back to the heart, but struggles vainly to reach the cleansing chamber of the public lungs. It bulges blue in the small area of its abnormally restricted limb and, therefore, threatens constantly to weaken and poison the life it would naturally bless.

This is an abnormal relationship for colored and for white people to stand in and a relationship that deeply hurts them both. It took me a long time to see it, for the first thirty years of my life were spent in irritation and a vastly rising bitterness. It was long before I could see that this situation works as much injury to white people as to colored people. This I hope to show you by a bare and inadequate analysis of the problem.

First of all, I will take the economic side—that is, the bread and butter side, the job and homes, the business and bank account of racial relations.

Race relations began in this country by the enslavement of the Negro, that is, by the use of the black man's body and hands as a means of procuring wealth and well-being for white people, which they did not share with the Negro in full. The enslavement of the Negro needs not be defined. The injury that slavery worked upon the human being is too well recognized for me to spend any time talking about it. But most of us, when writing our histories or reading our histories, never think of the injury to the white people. I will not talk of the injury of the slave owner, but do you know that slavery actually impoverished 4.5 million white people? Not only did the 390,000 white slave owners keep in slavery about 4.5 million Negroes, but also they so dominated the economic life and markets of the South for 250 years with the slave labor so that a great class of people, now called the "poor whites," could not find enough work to do. They could not gain adequate substance for themselves, and so they had to live on the poorest land, going up into the mountains and the waste places to make their sparse living, with few or no schools, with no participation in the political life within a state of life in many cases more degraded than the state of the slaves.

These 4.5 million poor whites never had anything approximating economic and political liberty—to say nothing of human kindness—until the emancipation of the Negro. This we must keep in mind if we want to understand the terribleness of slavery.

In modern times the slave has been emancipated. Now for the first time also those poor whites have the opportunity to sell their labor for a living wage. But the black man is still in a state of semieconomic slavery in the southern states. Hundreds and thousands of Negroes on the farms in the South are in a state of semislavery called "peonage." They are tenants on the farm, but the masters so arrange the pay that the tenant never gets out of debt. No matter how much he may earn, he generally owes a little more than that at the grocery and feed store at the end of the year. These Negroes in the South have never had their liberty, even since slavery. If they wish to move, they must do it by night and even then subject to arrest and imprisonment for jumping the life-contract.

In addition to the thousands who suffer in this way in states like Louisiana and Mississippi, there are other thousands who own their farms and carry their produce to market but, having no power over market conditions, must sell their goods on the spot at the first price offered. Shrewd men, made shrewd by awful transactions akin to the spirit of slavery, are too often there with a price far below the real value of the commodity, so that hundreds of poor Negro farmers go back to their homes, while nominally enjoying liberty, having sold their produce at a price depriving them of all profit from their labor.

When they come to the cities to work, the Negroes are not included in a normal way in the economic life. Ordinarily, it is assumed that they are to be employed in domestic or unskilled labor. No consistent watch is made for manifestations of superior intelligence and skill whereby one may advance into a position of leadership in trade or business. Thus it is the experience of the majority of Negroes who work in the southern cities, with certain exceptions in the trades of carpentry, etc., that they may work a lifetime and manifest all intelligence and skill without ever having a chance to advance.

This method is systematically followed in the southern states—and I know I am talking in the presence of people who can challenge the facts if not true—and without any disposition to take advantage of their not holding the platform. As a matter of policy, you will find colored people employed in dry goods stores and other businesses as porters, cuspidor cleaners, sweepers, and elevator men, but almost never as clerks, almost never reaching a position of responsibility in the establishment. This means that they are deprived of the ordinary stimulus that comes from knowing that the highest posts are obtainable and are, therefore, kept on the lower levels of economic performance.

Knowing this, the Negro everywhere has attempted to establish a separate economic life. You will find all over the United States an effort to duplicate the system of drug stores, dry goods stores, groceries, and manufacturing establishments that white people maintain.

Those in authority in the white race habitually tell themselves that the Negro can do this, but sober reflection makes it clear that such duplication is impossible. American businesses today have reached such a state of organization that it is impossible not only for the Negro, but also for the poor white man to stand alone economically. Even grocery and drug stores are organized into great chains, backed by enormous capital. The Atlantic and Pacific stores, or the Kruger stores, with their organization and huge accumulation of wealth to back them, could enter a territory and crush a chain of Negro stores in ninety days by underselling. And in sixty days they could recoup their losses by raising prices on corn meal, potatoes, molasses, and other common commodities.

It is perfectly clear, therefore, that if the Negro is to be economically free in the United States, he must find a place in the economic system as it obtains. He must be permitted to enter on the ground floor. He must be recognized and advanced as an individual on the basis of his merits. Otherwise, he will be finally crushed in the attempt to build up a separate system. Every intelligent businessman recognizes this—when he thinks.

In Negro farm life where the greatest opportunity appears to exist, we all know that the individual farm has but a few years yet to remain. As you pass over the great prairie regions of Colorado and Iowa and see the enormous production of corn, brought about by machinery and artificial fertilizer—all organized by the best industrial processes—you know it is only a matter of time before the farm business is going to organize on the same industrial basis as steal, railroads, banks, and groceries. If the Negro cannot find his way into that new farm organization on the basis of his qualifications as a human individual, he will be economically reduced to a servitude class in spite of any powers he may possess.

This is the economic situation, but it is not all. The poor economic opportunity that the Negro has in the South makes him a poor buyer of goods. Because he is a poor buyer, he reduces the amount of goods that would naturally be sold in any one of the southern states. There are nine million Negroes in the South who have never lived a normal life and who have never had a normal amount of corn, bread, meat, shoes, machines, paint, and pianos. Because they never have had that normal amount of goods, that normal amount of goods has never been sold or manufactured in the South. The money represented by those goods has never passed through the southern banks, and the factories and machines; stores that might have been in action have never come into existence. Therefore, hundreds of thousands of poor white men in the South are deprived of their normal existence because they have never been called upon to prepare those things for the consumption of their millions of Negro neighbors. So you still find much of the poor white population in little better condition than before slavery, while those leaders who would control the white people and profit by their prejudice throw them against the black men and teach them that their prosperity depends on keeping the black man down. In a time like this, you have the awful spectacle of poor whites putting themselves into uniform and traveling about, demanding that Negroes be fired and that white men be given their jobs.

This abnormal situation—this antagonism—is produced by the simple fact that these two groups have never in their lives had enough work to be able to look at one another normally. I do not believe that in his heart the "poor white" man normally hates the Negro. He has been taught to hate the Negro because his leaders have never so governed the economic life of the South as to give him a normal chance to live and think like a normal man.

This is the economic situation. It is bald and bare. I can modify it some with encouraging color, but not enough to take away the awful bones of the fact.

Now for the political situation. When we come to the political life of the South, the Negro is frankly excluded from participation. The organized life of Mississippi, Alabama, Louisiana, etc., is run as if the Negro did not exist. In spite of the Constitution of the United States, he is effectively disfranchised. He, therefore, pays taxes without representation and has no say as to what shall be done with the taxes. The white people who control the system live daily under the abnormal temptation of using a greater share of the public funds for their own welfare than they are entitled to. This is what they do in every state in the South.

In practically every southern state, the Negro in the field of housing is crowded off into the most undesirable sections of the cities and deprived of a proper share of the public utilities. In Augusta, Georgia, for instance, you will find a street where many substantial Negroes own their own good homes. But that street is filled with mud and slush continually because the white people have determined that they will use no portion of the taxes to pave those streets where the Negroes are established. The most decent Negroes in Augusta must pass up and down through that mud as they go and come. This is typical of southern communities. Here and there some improvement can be seen, but not enough improvement to modify the fundamental conditions that prevail all over the South.

But the most poignant situation is the use of public funds is the development of public schools. In every state of the South with the possible exception of West Virginia and with North Carolina coming up and Tennessee following swiftly, an abnormal proportion of the school fund goes into new and beautiful schools for white children with well-paid teachers, while Negroes are left as much as possible in inferior institutions with the lowest pay for their teachers and, until the past decade, with little or no high schools at all. No southern state will admit Negroes to a state university, and no southern state has yet established and maintained a university for Negroes, not even North Carolina.

It would be a mistake to assume that white people do not suffer from this. Any man suffers when, in a situation that demands a fair and equal division of the public funds in the interests of the all-around human development of the community, he finds himself in a position where he can use an abnormal proportion for himself. Human nature in the mass has never showed that it could stand up under any such temptation. Wherever that condition prevails, you will find the endeavor to keep the public order so organized that the condition will not change. So practically all over the South, you have the suppression of free political discussion, the confinement of political activity to one party, and, therefore, the impossibility of that difference of opinion that underlies all healthy political development.

You from Mississippi, try to remember a time within the past fifty years when a presidential candidate has come to tell you why you should vote for him. It has never been considered necessary. The political organization is such that you know and the candidate knows that you voted against him, or that you voted for him before you were born and that you have no power to change that vote. So he goes to the states where the statement of his opinions may have some influence over the outcome. If a candidate for the presidency in the next campaign visits Mississippi, he will do so out of extraordinary courtesy, or to see the country, because he knows that what he says will not affect the situation.

That is bad for the country, because in the South we are born to those great political principles of Jeffersonian democracy that, in my judgment, still have a great career in this country if they could ever get pure expression in the public life. There is not a young white man or woman over twenty-one today who is not in some sense violently deprived of liberty by being unable to discuss those principles freely and to try to make them more effective in the public life.

So the political tragedy is enacted. And the South, which is yet largely agrarian and, with its humanity eager for development, would ordinarily be vigorously progressive and aggressive in political life, is a conservative political unity. It is always ready to make an agreement with any conservative political unity, and is always ready to make an agreement with any conservative political body that will not shake the boat too much—a political tragedy of the first rank as a result of its abnormal political domination of the Negro.

But more serious than that, the disfranchisement of the Negro in the South is one expressly deliberate violation of the Constitution of the United States by ways and means that judges, Senators, members of the House of Representatives, both in the state and nation, recognize to be a lawless violation of the law by men charged with the dignified honor of keeping the law. So you find that the root of lawlessness in this country is not to be looked for in small criminal bands such as those who seek to make money for themselves by selling liquor, but that the most serious source of lawlessness is the deliberate violation of the law by a whole section of judges, lawyers, governors, and mayors charged by the people with the holy duty of keeping the law in the southern states— and by the complicity of all the nation in that lawlessness. How can we make our own friends—how can we make our children—believe that we are in earnest about law observance when, for sixty-five years in order to keep the Negro from participation in public life, we have openly violated the law and have bragged of the success with which it has been done?

I want to close by calling attention to the personal element in race relations. The truth is that today we actually have in the United States an untouchable class. In our Christian meetings we talk about untouchability in India, but in the Negro and white relations in this country we have untouchability here. All who live in the South know that it is a social crime to call a Negro "Mr." or a Negro woman "Mrs." So all daily contacts in the South between the races follow the general rule of the colored man saying, "Good morning, Mr. Johnson," and the white man saying, "Good morning, Sam," or of the Negro woman saying, "Good morning, Mrs. Jones," and the white woman saying, "Good morning, Sally." Sally may be a graduate of the University of Chicago and a woman of refined and delicate culture. Sam may be a distinguished physician, doing his work in competency and in complete integrity. We will call him "Doctor," but not "Mr." Our contacts are filled with discourtesy and bitterness.

Every Negro who walks the streets of every southern state is hourly in expectancy of being called by that opprobrious term, "nigger." Someone may say at any moment, "Move, nigger; don't you see a white man coming?" Negroes and white people may not sit together, may not ride together on trains, and in many towns may not go up in the same elevator. It is still possible to see signs in the South: "Niggers and dogs not allowed." "Niggers and freight take the back elevator."

Not a Negro in America would take his wife on a trip through the South and go to a hotel, even if she were with child for seven months, with the expectation of being treated with courtesy. He must walk along the roadside, looking for some sympathetic friend to have compassion and to give that woman a chance to rest her head and rest without insult.

In actual practice, we have an untouchable class in America, and the Negro has not found that Christian white people in general make an exception to this rule of practice.

Remember I am speaking to you, not to make you happy, but to stir your conscience into revolt over a situation deeply injurious to the Negro every day he lives, and deeply injurious to every sensitive-souled white person living in Mississippi, Georgia, Alabama, or anywhere in the South.

When I plead for you to give your earnest attention to this problem, I plead not only for the Negroes but also for the white people of the South who are daily troubled, injured, and shamed by their personal and public participation in the crime of untouchability.

5. The Social Responsibility of the Administrator (Statement of Commitment to Academic Freedom)[5]

One of the highest compliments paid to Mordecai Johnson as an administrator was that he faithfully accorded academic freedom to the faculty, staff, and students of Howard University. He prided himself for this stance. This address, presented at the Fifteenth Annual Spring Conference of the Division of Social Sciences of Howard University, represents a major statement on the subject and is based on his experience of fifteen years in meeting charges of Communist influences and in defending the right of free speech at the university during the McCarthy era.

THE SOCIAL RESPONSIBILITY OF THE ADMINISTRATOR*

Mr. Chairman, ladies, and gentlemen:

I feel a very great sense of loss at not having been here from the very beginning. I know that I would have enjoyed the sessions and that my mind would have been illuminated. I am sure that what I am going to say to you this morning would have been greatly improved by having heard what has gone before. Nevertheless, what I am going to say to you is a matter of thought, and it is very precious to me because it has grown out of my experience.

I have two ways of discussing this subject. I can take it up theoretically and deal with it systematically from that point of view, but I can take it up also from the point of view of my experience. I have chosen to do the latter, because I have had quite an experience.

You see standing before you here now a man who has been for twenty-seven years president of an unorthodox institution tolerated and supported by the government of the United States. During these twenty-seven years, I think I have faced practically every basic question that involves academic freedom, and I have taken a position upon it.

I have had fifteen years of experience with Communism in its relationship to governmental institutions. I have taken some positions and actions that throw light upon the question at issue now and that make it far simpler to me than if I approached it now for the first time.

---

[5]Washington, D.C., March 14, 1953.

*Address delivered at the Fifteenth Annual Spring Conference of the Division of Social Sciences at Howard University, held during March 11, 12, 13, and 14, 1953.

This is what I am going to say to you: I want to deal with my practical relations as an administrator with academic freedom in five stages as related to Communism. The first stage arrived before Communism became an issue. At that time, the chief threat to academic freedom was from within the university and only in a secondary sense was from our relation to the government.

In the second stage, there came to be a concern about the mere presence of Communist ideas in the university. At that time, men in government became concerned as to whether we were even reading Communist books and talking about Communism here, and whether on a program here we had allowed a man who was a Communist to offer a point of view. We had quite a time.

In the third stage came a period when the government was definitely concerned with the individual Communist and was determined to get rid of him in all governmental areas. At that time the Howard University faculty was considered a part of the Civil Service of the United States.

The fourth stage came when the government became aware of the heavy infiltration of Communists in labor unions. It pounded on the national leadership of the labor union, which at that time was operating broadly throughout government and which had a local union on the campus of Howard University.

The fifth stage came after the government had determined that Communism constituted a conspiracy, was getting its instructions from a foreign power, and intended to be disruptive of the internal social order.

In each of those five stages, I have had to face problems in my relationship to the government and in my relationship to the faculty. In these five areas, I think I have faced all the questions—fundamental questions—that we have to face in the matter of academic freedom.

We do not need, I think, to define academic freedom at Howard University. The very existence of this institution is a testimony to the determination of the founders of this university to exercise academic freedom in the most radical sense.

This institution was founded against the mores. Its very establishment on this hill in a segregated community for Negroes—with Negro and white children enrolled simultaneously, with a Negro and white faculty—and the fact that it has persisted here for eighty-seven years in a community dominated by the mentality of the slave system that still controls the morals and habits of the community—I say the very existence of such an institution is testimony to the determination of the founders that we were going to think freely here, that we were going to have a right to think contrary to the mores, and that we have a right to have our actions in our community organization formed against the mores. Academic freedom is in the deepest sense a part of this university and a part of our mentality.

The very fact that such an institution exists in this community, that the federal government not only tolerates it but also supports it, and that among its supporters are men who despise the very idea for which it stands is a tribute to the tolerance and remarkable mentality of the American people and of American democracy.

In perspective, when I think that there are about a hundred institutions like this all over the South, and that for the first fifty years of their existence they were despised by the leaders in the southern states—and when I think of the fact that the southern community, in the days when it was almost wholly dominated by the ideas of the slave system, tolerated these educational institutions, although they ostracized the faculty—I know that I have before me a remarkable testimony to the constructive effect that democracy has had over the minds of even its most recalcitrant members.

The First Stage

When I first came to Howard University, this institution was in turmoil. The faculty and the students were in rebellion against the administration. I patiently looked at the institution work for one full year before I made up my mind as to the real nature of the problem before me and what to do about it.

I did not do anything for one year but oil the machinery that was in existence and resist being taken over by one of the two blocs of power that existed in the institution. This was the most dangerous period in the life of Howard University. The most perilous thing that has ever happened in this institution, as touching academic freedom, existed at that time, namely, the formation of blocs of power in the faculty itself.

For twenty years these internal blocs of power nearly ruined Howard University. The reason I came here to accept the presidency was the feeling that arose out of a sense of strong duty that the time had come for somebody who knew how to suffer to come here and solve the problem growing out of the existence of these internal blocs of power.

When I got here, I found that nearly every problem in the institution fell on the president's desk. There seemed to be no place in the institution where there was another person who would take responsibility for action, and individual teachers were ducking their heads everywhere with a sense of insecurity and fear.

I made up my mind that great thinking could not take place in such an atmosphere and that great thinking of a free and constructive kind could not take place at all except in an institution where the power was decentralized and where the individual faculty member could be assured of his security on the basis of his ability and character alone, without having to pay obeisance to any bloc of power whatsoever—whether in the administration or in the faculty. And I set out first of all to establish that condition.

The first great undertaking that I went after here was to establish the security and complete freedom of the individual professor. It took me ten years to do it. I did not start out by attacking these organizations. I attacked them only when they got in the way.

I knew they were here and I knew they were bidding for my support. They nearly worked me to death, bidding for my support. "Don't you have anything to do with that fellow," one would say. "He belongs to such and such an organization. Better watch him. He will cut your neck off."

I made up my mind that I was not going to take a single derogatory step in regard to any member of that faculty on the basis of anything anybody said to me about him. So far as he and I were concerned, we were going to begin life *de novo*, and we were going to build on what we knew about each other in action.

So I began the work of establishing the security of the individual professor. I worked on it for ten years until I got to the place in this institution where not only the individual professor was secure, but also the individual janitor.

You are now sitting in a university where it is impossible to fire a professor or a janitor capriciously. You cannot do it. If you start to push him out and he says you are wrong—if he says, "The thing I am accused of is not so"—you have got to stop right there. You cannot push him out until a committee of professors or of janitors, as the case may be, hears him. They are going to hear him.

That is true today with regard to the individual professor at Howard University, but it took a long time to establish such security. I started out to make it clear to the entire university that the president himself was not going to form an administrative block of power around himself. As a first step I undertook to convince the deans and teachers that the individual teacher owed no special personal allegiance to the president by reason of his appointment. I said to the deans, "Now, when a new teacher is appointed, I do not want to tell him that he is appointed. I have a right to do that, but I want you to tell him. When he is appointed by the Board of Trustees, I will tell you, and you will tell him, so that when he comes to the institution, he shakes your hand first.

"Whenever I see him I will let him know, 'You do not owe me anything. The reasons you came to this institution are simply two. You are a man of outstanding human competence in your field, and all that we had heard about you indicated that you were a man of integrity and that you could get along cooperatively with other people. That is all we wanted to know about you. As long as you proceed in that way, you are perfectly safe. You do not have to pay obeisance to the president or to any organized bloc of power. The president has no such organization. If any such organization on these grounds suggests to you that you have got to belong to it in order to be secure, it is not so. You do not have to belong to any organized bloc of power whatsoever.'"

This has been so now for twenty years. My next step was to have it made plain—not only to teachers, but also to students—that the right of open criticism existed here and that this right included the open criticism of the president.

I had not been here long before the student paper attacked me in a manner that was very drastic. A professor came to me and said, "Mr. President, did you see the student paper this morning?"

I said, "Yes."

He said, "The attack which it makes upon you is unseemly and improper. Mr. President, do you not want us to supervise the student paper and see to it that attacks like this do not happen again?"

I said, "I want to ask you one question. Are the students using any obscene or profane language that would disgrace us?"

He said, "No."

I said, "Evidently, they feel that way about me or else they would not run the risk of printing such an attack across the whole front page of the paper. Now I have a choice, it seems to me, of letting the students speak freely when they feel aggrieved by me, or of having them conceal their aggrieved feelings from me while they go about whispering them to others with the result that in the end the whole university may come to feel and think in the same aggrieved way.

"No," I said, "Let them come on out with it. Let them keep on coming out with it. If there is anything significant in the grievance, I will change my way of doing. If there is nothing significant in the grievance, the attack will make no headway."

In the same spirit, I went among the faculties saying, "Now, gentlemen, if I come here with a proposal for this faculty, however serious—

I may have worked on it for a month—and if I make the proposal and somebody rises in this faculty and seconds the motion, and yet you do not agree with that proposal, it is your duty to get up on the floor and to say, 'Ladies and gentlemen, with all due respect to the president, I have listened to what he had to say, and I do not think what he proposed will be good for the university. I hope you do not approve of it. If you have any disposition to do so, I hope you will lay it on the table for at least a while so we can consider and discuss it carefully and, if necessary, modify it or finally turn it down.'"

I have said, "If you do not have the belief in your own thoughts and the devotion to the university that is required to do this, you have no business here. If I do not have the strength to welcome your doing that, I have no business here."

It is that kind of procedure whereby we have established an atmosphere in this institution that makes it possible for a man who has a great mind, and who wants to devote his time to thought, to do so freely and with security.

I have not left it at that. This security does not depend on the benevolence of the president. We have organized laws and procedures within the university, which the president himself cannot violate and according to which the president and the Board of Trustees must proceed if the security of a man is brought into question in any way whatsoever.

There came a time, moreover, when the faculty thought that these procedures themselves were not sufficient, but that, in addition thereto, they ought to have a labor union. I brought about that. I was disturbed about the thought of a labor union here when the idea first came to me, because having spent ten or fifteen years of my life breaking up two organizations that were destroying the liberty and independence of members of the faculty, I thought maybe a labor union might become another organization like that and the union would itself destroy the foundations of academic freedom.

But after reflection, I made up my mind that any decent labor union would not want any more for the faculty and employees than I would want or ought to want. The only difference would be that the faculty and employees would now ask for these things out of an intelligent experience of labor unionism. I thought that if the labor union was a decent labor union, with its assistance the university should be able to know more quickly and more clearly what it ought to do in these matters than it would if it were dealing with the faculty without a labor union.

So I started to negotiate with the first labor union before it got a majority. Unfortunately, this first labor union greatly disappointed me. The very first time the union members had a significant case, they sent for one of their leaders from New York. When we were all gathered in the room, six or seven of us, I proposed an item for the agenda. The New York chairman banged upon the table and said, "We will not have any such item as that on the agenda."

I said, "Why, my dear brother, you are proceeding here with something that frightens me. Here is a university that is willing to negotiate with you before you secure the allegiance of the majority of the teachers. It is willing to have the organization bring you, the New York representative, into the university to preside on the first specific case, and you begin by telling the president of that university that he cannot even propose an item on the agenda."

I turned to the teachers and said, "Gentlemen, you have got the wrong man in the chair. I appeal against the decision of the chair."

And God be thanked, the teachers turned him down. His own teachers turned him down. This presiding officer killed that labor union in that meeting, because the teachers of this institution did not want a labor union here to bully the administration. They wanted a labor union to represent their legitimate interests in a constructive way.

It took me fifteen years to find out that the first union was a Communist labor union. I did not know it then, but it was. That dear presiding brother was beginning by practicing the dictatorship of the proletariat. This was a disappointing experience to me, but that experience did not destroy the opportunity for labor unions to function at Howard University.

When, at a later time, a CIO union came here, the Trustees of the university, following my recommendation, voted unanimously to establish this CIO labor union for both the teachers and the non-teaching personnel. Now not only did we have at Howard University the determination to make the individual teacher free, plus the tenure regulations to make him free, but also we gave him a labor union to see to it that he was free.

Well, that was the first stage. In that stage I had my first experience with the effort of certain political leaders in the government ranks to control important processes within the institution.

I had not been here three months before I was called down to the office of a very eminent member of the government who suggested to me that it would be very good for me to make an appointment of a certain teacher on the faculty.

I looked up that teacher and found out that he had a record of inferior mentality and performance. I found that he had formerly worked here and had been discharged by my predecessor. Thereafter, he had been down in the city and had taken the examination for a certain position in high school and had flunked that examination. He was now trying to use his political power to get back on the faculty of our university.

Well, I did not know anything then about academic freedom, but I told the eminent member of the government that I could not appoint that gentleman. I could not make such an appointment and continue to have the respect of the faculty.

The eminent gentlemen seemed to take this decision as the conclusion of the matter, but two or three days afterwards an intermediary brought me word that he very much regretted that I could not appoint this teacher, and he hoped I would reconsider. The intermediary was a powerful politician who looked me straight in the eye. There I made the first politically dangerous decision in my administration.

I got up out of my chair and said to this man, "Do you see that chair? You are in a position to know that I not only did not do anything crooked to get in that chair, I did not do anything at all to get in that chair. Now, God helping me, I am not ever going to do anything crooked to stay in that chair. This man who seeks this appointment is a man of inferior mentality. How in the world can I train the children of the Negro people with a man of inferior mentality who is politically appointed?

"If I were to appoint this man, the Negro people ought to come in here and start kicking me out of that chair. And they should continue kicking me until they have cleared me out of the entire campus."

I said, "I do not believe that this distinguished member of the government sent me that message. But if he did, then you tell him this: I am very sorry I cannot make this appointment. I cannot make this one, and so help me God, as long as I stay here, I do not ever intend to make such an appointment. If he considers this state to be a sufficient reason to merit my discharge, he may as well discharge me now, because every time I am approached in this way, this is what I am going to say."

I have been here for twenty-seven years. In all those twenty-seven years, I have had perhaps ten thousand communications from the most eminent men in the Congress and in the executive branches of government recommending persons and procedures. I have dealt with all these communications respectfully and thoughtfully on the merits of the matter alone, as I would with similar recommendations from any other eminent and honorable man in public life, depending upon him to respect the integrity and objectivity of my conclusions. Now this is my testimony: In all those twenty-seven years, I have had fewer than five men in government every try to push me beyond what was becoming of a gentleman.

This is a testimony that bears witness to the existence of a great reservoir of integrity, fine feeling, and restraint among the members of the government of the United States.

What would have happened if I had not laid down my job there at the very beginning, I do not know. The educational administrator has a very great responsibility, and my experience leads me to believe that he cannot discharge it and preserve academic freedom, without being ready to lay his job down over and over again.

The Second Stage

Next came the second stage. You remember when Dr. Ralph Bunche was here some years ago, we had a great conference on political problems in the southern states, under the auspices of this very social science division. In those days, the Communist Party was on the open election ticket. Mr. James W. Ford was the then-outstanding leader of the Communist Party. So he and one or two other Communists came to that conference— two or three sessions of it. As we discussed various items on the agenda affecting the relationship of Negroes to the life of America, these Communists would get up and participate. Sometimes they would vigorously criticize the present state of affairs. They would vigorously criticize the attitude of the Democratic Party and of the Republican Party. Of course, they were answered, and the give and take made that conference one of the most lively conferences we have ever had.

Well, some members in Congress became greatly troubled. They thought that something was taking place here that ought not to take place, and they pressed Mr. Harold Ickes, the then-Secretary of the Interior, to see to it that such things did not take place here. Mr. Ickes first of all inquired of me, "Dr. Johnson, do you say those speeches are going to be published, and the entire proceedings of the conference?"

I said, "Yes."

He said, "Would you let me see a copy when the printing is finished?

I said, "Yes." Being an old college debater myself and greatly enamored of the vigorous give and take of debate, I had no fear at all that he would be troubled by what he read.

When the proceedings came off the press, I handed a copy to Mr. Ickes. But Mr. Ickes surprised me. He did not read the proceedings at all. He said,

"Dr. Johnson, take this back. I do not want to read it. I do not want to carry out even a symbolic suggestion that I have a right to examine and to pass upon the thoughts that go on in a conference such as that. This is your academic responsibility. It is your freedom, and it is your risk."

He said further, "Now, that is what you have got to deal with, and you may as well know it. You have here to deal with the whole question of academic freedom, but you have more than that to deal with. There is a developing hysteria in this country and that hysteria may reach the place where it will imperil your appropriation. You have before you not merely a question of right, but a question of tactics. How will you proceed to preserve academic freedom without subjecting yourself to the loss of your appropriation by an irresponsible hysteria that is developing in this country and moving into the sphere of government? This is your problem. I have confidence that you will handle it wisely."

That was my second great experience with a major officer of government. I not only went through with it all right but also was inspired by it, for here again I found an administrator with understanding and integrity.

Some weeks after this the students of the undergraduate college arranged to hold a great mock national election here, and they put up candidates for the Republican Party, candidates for the Democratic Party, candidates for the Socialist Party, and candidates for the Communist Party. What did they want to do that for—just before I went down to the Appropriations Committee? [Laughter]

When I got down to the Appropriations Committee, one important committee member said to me very quietly, "Dr. Johnson—I would like to have this off the record—Dr. Johnson, I understand that the students are having election out there."

I said, "Yes."

He said, "I understand they have got a Communist candidate."

I said, "Yes, a Socialist candidate, a Democratic candidate, a Republican candidate, and a Communist candidate."

He said, "Dr. Johnson, do you think that this is wise? Do you not think that this might be injurious to the minds of the students?"

I said, "No sir, I do not. I think it would be greatly injurious to the students if I tried to stop them from holding this election as they have planned it. You want me to go out there and say to those young fellows, 'You go on and conduct this election but with this understanding: You can discuss only the Republican platform.' Do you know what will happen? There will be the greatest bootlegging of Communist and Socialist literature on the campus that you ever saw."

I said, "It is the very nature of the human mind. If you tell young people that there are some thoughts that are so dangerous that if they even look at them those thoughts will alter the whole course of their lives, many of them will never be satisfied until they have sought out and read those very thoughts, so as to alter the entire course of one's life."

I said, "Now, I suggest that we let those students alone. They are American students. They see all these parties on the voters' ticket, and they are trying to appraise the platforms of these parties just as adult Americans are doing. Let us leave them alone and watch the result."

At the end of the election 40 percent of the students voted Republican, about 48 percent Democratic, about 1 percent Socialist, and less than half of 1 percent Communist.

"There you are," I said afterwards. "What are you afraid of? Let the students think for themselves."

Well, this worked out all right for the time being, but there was to be an aftermath. Within a few days afterwards, I invited the Appropriations Committee out here, right on this very platform. On this occasion, this room was full of students and teachers. I had invited one member of Congress who was not a member of the Appropriations Committee. By the way, he was a member of the minority to which I belong.

The chairman of the Appropriations Committee acceded to my wish. The distinguished gentleman was invited, and I placed him in a position of honor among the speakers. He was to speak last. The Appropriations Committee was greatly impressed by the sight of these students. Some men from the West, who had never before had anything to do with Negroes, were so deeply impressed that they silently wept. Each man successively was deeply moved except the last speaker. When he rose, he said, "Well, I do not know about all this. I understand that there are some Socialist and Communist ideas out there circulating around, and that they are discussing Socialist and Communist thoughts here. I am just going to tell you right now that I am going to withhold my support of the appropriation until we can find out whether such ideas are circulating out here and until we can stop it."

Well, there I was. I had lost the appropriation right here and I could not adjourn, so I rose to speak. It is fortunate that I had had a great related experience with life when I first went to the University of Chicago, and I told the members of the Appropriations Committee about it.

When I first decided to go the University of Chicago, people who loved me said, "Mordecai, why do you want to go to that institution? It is a hotbed of atheism and socialism." When they found that I did not share their fears and had finally decided to go, they said to me, "Well, if you do go up there, there are two courses of study you must never pursue. Just put them out of your mind. If you study that thing called evolution, it will ruin your religion. And if you study socialism, then you will just be ruined in every way."

So I went to the University of Chicago, having duly taken this advice. When the dean of the graduate school said to me, "Johnson, you can take three courses. What are they?"

I said, "Dean Small, I do not know what the third course is. I have not made up my mind yet. But the course in evolution and the course in socialism—I want them right away." [Laughter]

So I took those two forbidden courses, and I will never forget as long as I live the profound creative contribution that those courses gave to me. I did not become an indoctrinated member of the Socialist Party. I was not converted to the materialistic theory of history. I did not lose my belief in God, because in the light of evolution, I saw that the universe was a magnificent thing that had taken hundreds of millions of years to grow. It enlarged my conception of God. After that, I could not put Him in my vest pocket. And I said to the members of the Congress, "Gentlemen, this whole position that you have heard here is based upon a genuine fear, however ill-advised it may be, that the human mind is of such a nature that if you expose it to a dangerous idea, the idea will stick to it in just precisely its original form."

I said, "The human mind is not like that. It is often stimulated by opposing systems of thought to deepen its original convictions and to think its ways independently on the basis of those convictions. Now this institution is erected for a minority who are segregated, discriminated against, and disenfranchised. There is no hope for us whatsoever unless we think in ways that are different from the majority.

"If you deprive us of the power to think independently and to search in every area of life to find the inspiration for our thoughts, it would be better for you to take the appropriation away from us, because the very meaning of education would be destroyed."

Well, you would have thought I had lost the appropriation. The fact is that I lost only one man on that committee. The majority of the Appropriation Committee supported me substantially and positively, and the committee members never thereafter said a single word to me about the content of ideas in the thoughts of the students here.

The Third Stage

That was the second stage of my dealing with academic freedom, but it was the first stage in my dealing with Communism as it relates to government and academic freedom. The third stage of my discussion, but my second stage in dealing with Communism, was the time when the government first became concerned about the Communist individual. This was after the war was over and it began to appear that the Communists did not entirely agree to love us after we had jointly won the victory over Germany.

At that time, Howard University's faculty members were considered to be members of the Civil Service, and an investigation of the teachers and employees of Howard University, including the administration, took place as part of a widespread investigation of government personnel.

Mr. Paul McNutt was the then-administrator of the Federal Security Agency. When the first investigation document came to Mr. McNutt, bearing derogatory information about one of our teachers, he read it. Then he wrote me a letter in which he said (I paraphrase from memory), "Dear Dr. Johnson, I have here a document on Professor so and so, filled with derogatory information that seems to suggest that he is a member of the Communist Party. What is your recommendation?"

I wrote back and said (I paraphrase from memory), "Dear Mr. Administrator, I recognize the validity of your concern, but you have me at a great disadvantage. You are looking at the original documentation of the facts, and you are asking me to make a recommendation on the basis of your appraisal of this documentation. I cannot do this very well. If you wish my recommendation, it is necessary that I see the facts you are looking at. Will you please send me the facts?"

Mr. McNutt responded to me promptly. He sent me a folder bearing the original documentation of the facts. I looked at it carefully. I saw that the man in question was associated in one way or another with one or more so-called "front organizations," but there was no index anywhere at all that he ever had anything to do with the Communist Party. There was no suggestion that he had engaged in any kind of subversive act.

I wrote back and said, "Mr. Administrator, knowing the teachers who are here at Howard University as I do, knowing the minority problem that is always on their minds, and knowing as I do how few people there are in the majority who are at all concerned to help this minority solve its problem, it is just as natural as some of these teachers live that—when they see a group of white and colored people trying to do something constructive about that minority problem or when this group says, 'Give us a dollar' or 'You come over to our meeting and speak'—I say it is as natural as they live that one or more of such teachers will have an almost irresistible tendency to give that dollar or to go over there. If he does not go or if he does not give that dollar, he cannot go to sleep because of a feeling that he has not done his duty."

I said further, "A man can make a contribution to one or more of those organizations and can be present at a meeting of one or more of those organizations. But these facts alone would never convince the Board of Trustees of Howard University that he was either a member of the Communist Party or a subversive. This document shows no sign of such subversion. It shows no sign of membership in the Communist Party. I recommend that this man be completely exonerated."

Mr. McNutt re-examined the material, concurred in my recommendation, and exonerated that man. Twenty-five such cases he sent to me. Twenty-five recommendations of exoneration I sent to him. For twenty-three of those, he and his committee concurred in and acted upon promptly. Two of the documents were so bulky and the material so involved that the committee felt an obligation to bring the two men thus involved down before the committee for hearings. Committee members heard the two men at length and finally exonerated those two also.

Mr. McNutt's procedure was one of the most decent, most honorable, and most helpful procedures we have ever had. It so deeply impressed one of the two last men involved that when later he actually decided to become a Communist, what did he do? He sat down and wrote Dean Price a letter (I paraphrase from memory), "Dear Dean Price: I have decided to become a member of the Communist Party. I can see that I cannot do that and at the same time remain a helpful member of the faculty of Howard University. I am, therefore, herewith submitting my resignation."

I shall always honor Mr. McNutt for the complete integrity and the dispassionate character of the procedures that he followed in these investigations. I sat down and wrote him and his family a letter of remembrance this Christmas. You do not forget such men.

Shortly after that, the chairman of the Un-American Affairs Committee sent out here for a list of all the books that were prescribed for study by the social science departments, and all the collateral books recommended for reading by those departments.

He said, "Send me a complete list of all the books on the book list of the department of sociology, economics, etc." And he named them all. Those books would have run up into the thousands.

Well, now, I have always had this attitude toward the members of Congress that the least thing you can say about them is that they are very distinguished men. Most of them have come to where they are because they have the confidence of the people of at least one district and often of an entire state. If such a man wants to see this list of books, and if he is in a position to demand it, well, I thought I ought to either send him the books or have a talk with him. So I decided to have a talk with him.

I called up the executive secretary of the committee, and I found that he was from Georgia. Since the chairman was out of the city, I thought it would be good to talk with the executive secretary.

I said, "You have the right to ask for this list of books, and if you demand this list of books, I shall send it to you. However, if I were you, I would withdraw this request. It is unworthy of you, and it is hurtful to a cause that you greatly value."

I said, "Now, you are from Georgia. I am from Georgia and Tennessee. Here I am working with all my might with some of my colleagues in this institution to help get a federal appropriation for education, precisely to help build up the crippled and underdeveloped system of education in the southern states. The one great opposition that I have and you have is that people are afraid that if the federal government gives money to the educational system of their state, it will next try to control that system. And now what are you doing? You are taking the first step to control the actual books that a teacher chooses to put up for reading by his class. Do you not see that by doing this, you are defeating the very major purpose for which we are both working."

He said to me, "Dr. Johnson, I never thought about that, but I will speak to the chairman about it just as soon as he comes in."

The executive secretary did speak to the chairman as he had promised. I do not say that what I said to him solely determined the decision the chairman made. I am sure that other persons in the field of education may have spoken to the chairman also, but the chairman later called on me to return that request. He said he did not want that list of books.

Maybe you would not have imagined that such a thoughtful and considerate thing would be done by the Un-American Affairs Committee, but it was.

Shortly thereafter, I had another situation to deal with. Just about the time the Progressive Party was up for election, a very distinguished member of the staff of Howard University became a member of the executive committee of the Progressive Party. Well, my telephone rang. A very distinguished person was on the line and said to me, "Dr. Johnson, it seems to me to be a terrible thing that while the Democratic Party here in power is doing all it can to give Howard University money for medicine, money for buildings, and everything like that, that this man, who is one of your important men, should become a member of the executive committee of the Progressive Party. Doctor, I have been called up confidentially to ask you to see if you cannot get him off there."

Academic freedom was certainly involved here. I said to my telephone correspondent, "Now just how would you proceed in this matter? When I asked this man to become a member of the faculty of Howard University, he was a citizen of the United States. In the invitation to join this faculty, I never said anything to him about giving up his citizenship. He has just as much right to be a member of the Progressive Party as the Democratic or Republican Party. Just how would I go about to exercise any authority over him in this matter whatsoever?"

The person said, "Well, Dr. Johnson, never mind. Just put the phone down and forget about what I said."

This member of the faculty went on with his membership in the executive committee of the Progressive Party. Here is one of the basic items of academic freedom: A member of the university staff has a right to belong to any party he wants to, as long as that party is openly on the ticket. He has the right to exercise his devotion to that party openly as long as he does not do two things: (1) he must not take up the university's time or use the university's money to pay for doing it, and (2) he must not stop his classes and take charge of an effort to organize support for his party right there in the classroom.

As long as he exercises his political rights out there openly in relation to the party of his choice, the president of Howard University has nothing whatsoever to do with that and has no power whatsoever to tell him that he cannot do it.

Now, you know, I would even be willing to go this far—you will have to listen to me very carefully—if the Communist Party were purely an American party and we were not in war, I would say that this principle applied to the Communist Party, too. I say deliberately that this principle would apply to them, too, even if they had in their declared platform that there are certain conditions under which they seek to overthrow the government of the United States.

The notion is preposterous that we can preserve democracy by batting every man on the head who has the idea that there are certain circumstances under which the government ought to be overthrown. It is impossible to legislate out of existence one of the alternatives that confront every honorable man when he is trying to reform an injurious situation and cannot get it reformed by due process. It just naturally occurs to him that he has got to change that process some way or other, even if he has to overthrow it.

The British have got a whole lot better system on that point than we have. I was lying down in Hyde Park one day. I shall never forget that day in London. I was tired. It was a hot day. Two policemen behind me were fanning themselves under the trees.

All at once I looked up and saw a man coming toward me with a stepladder in one arm, with a red flag in his hand, and with about four or five fellows who accompanied him. He came right there in front of me, opened his stepladder there, walked up on the stepladder, planted the red flag, and started addressing me, and these two policemen. He said to us, "Comrades:" By that time five or six other people were there. He said, "Comrades: I am more deeply confirmed than ever today in my conviction that this despicable British Empire ought to be overthrown. I have come here to tell you that there must be no hesitancy about it, that the sooner we overthrow it, the better, and the thing that has convinced me finally is an experience I had today."

He said, "I was coming down the street there. As hot as it was, I pulled off my coat and unbuttoned my shirt and the perspiration was just pouring down my breast. I passed by Buckingham Palace, and what do you suppose I saw? I saw poor George Rex coming down the steps with a great big overcoat on, one of these great big heavy Russian fur hats on, and the perspiration was just pouring off of him. I looked at him and I said, 'Poor George! You are a man just as I am and just because you are human, you ought to be free not only to pull off that big overcoat and that confounded hot bearskin hat, but also to pull off your other coat and vest and unbutton your shirt.'"

"But, Comrades," he said, "Poor George Rex will never have a chance to do that until this empire is overthrown, and George the man is let out of his imperial cage." [Laughter]

He said, "Comrades: For George Rex's sake, we have got to overthrow this vicious thing."

Well, he walked on away. I got up and I turned around to the two policemen. They were just standing there fanning themselves.

I said to one of the policemen, "Did you hear that man say he was going to overthrow the British government?"

He said, "Oh, yes, but he's just talking."

I said, "But he said he wanted to overthrow the government. He said so. He did not say he wanted to change it by voting. He said he wanted to overthrow it."

"Yes," said the policeman, "but he was just talking."

I said, "You would not arrest a man for saying right in your face that he was going to overthrow the British government?"

"I have no instructions," said the policeman, "to arrest a man for talking."

"Well, I said, "just under what conditions would you arrest him?"

"Nothing short of violence on the spot," he answered. "He would have to start to overthrow it right here. I am instructed to arrest him when he starts the overthrowing. As long as he confines himself to thinking about overthrowing it and talking about overthrowing it, I can just stand here and fan."

Now I want to suggest to you today that a great deal of the hysteria in America could be done away with if men would simply understand that a healthy government, which is fundamentally meeting the needs of its people, can stand a whole lot of thinking about violence and a whole lot of talking about violence. To be active in a conspiracy to overthrow a powerful government by force is a long way from thinking violent thoughts.

Most of the people who have violent thoughts are done with them when they do the violent thinking. All but a very few are done with such thinking when they find that they are free to say what they think. You have only a very small minority ever left who try to turn those violent thoughts into action. Most healthy governments find it relatively easy to defer them. If the Communist Party were just the extreme left wing of American politics and there were no suspicion whatsoever that it was a representative of a foreign power in the midst of a cold war and a hot war, I would say we ought to have no fear whatsoever of anything that it thinks. It ought to be equally tolerated and allowed to speak on the streets, in the churches, and in Congress. The net effect it would have would be to galvanize a predominantly liberal wing of thought. It might even have the effect of driving democracy forward at a rate that it would not otherwise have.

But I am getting off the subject now. This second stage in my experience with Communism was the third stage in my dealing with academic freedom.

The Fourth Stage

The fourth stage was when the government found out that the Communists were trying to infiltrate the labor unions, and the Congress of Industrial Organization voted that the CIO–AUW, a local unit of which we had here, was Communist dominated in its national leadership.

Phil Murray did that, and I had to face a decision. That local organization had never done anything since it had been here to suggest in any way whatsoever that it was subversive in any form. Quite the contrary. It conducted itself in an entirely honorable manner, not only seeking to take no advantage of the administration in any way, but also actually astonishing me on two occasions by an unexpected sense of responsibility. One time was when a man appealed to the union against the decision of an officer of the business administration to demote him. After looking at the facts, the union advised the man to accept the demotion. They said, "Brother, you ought to be glad to get off with the privilege of accepting demotion." On another occasion, when an employee's conduct was in question, the union members studied the facts and they themselves advised the appellant to resign.

The members of the local union here were entirely honorable in their conduct, but I knew what I would have to face when I went downtown before the Appropriations Committee. They would say to me, "Now, Dr. Johnson, have you got a labor union out there at Howard University?"

I would say, "Yes, sir, we have."

"Well, which one is it?"

"It is the CIO Union No. 10," I would reply.

"What?"

"CIO Union No. 10."

"Well, Dr. Johnson, don't you know that Phil Murray and the CIO have said that this is a Communist-dominated union in its national leadership?"

"Yes, sir."

"Well, why don't you get rid of it?"

I might say, "Well, I do not think it is Communist dominated."

I knew exactly what would happen to me. They would say to me, "Dr. Johnson, you know we have great respect for you as an educator. You know that because we have given you one thing after another to show you our confidence. Now if you were talking about education here today, we might be disposed to take your word as final, but you are not an expert in labor matters, Dr. Johnson. Phil Murray of the CIO is an expert in labor affairs.

"Phil Murray may be wrong, but in running this government we have got to take the advice of those leaders of labor in this country who have won the confidence of the American people. We are afraid of the Communist organization. We see that Communists are infiltrating certain great organizations like the electrical workers, where they could get their hands on the very substance of our war power, and we do not intend to tolerate them, Doctor.

You go on out to Howard University, and do not come back for your appropriation until you are able to tell us that this union is gone."

That was just as inevitable as day follows night. It was a legitimate concern of the federal government. There cannot be any doubt about it, a legitimate concern because by that time responsible members of the government had come to conclude in America that the Communists were infiltrating the unions in order to be able to sabotage the war effort as the source of production.

That is the ground on which I made my first decision in regard to the matter. I came into the Board of Trustees' meeting and had the board unanimously vote to cancel the contract of that union, not because I saw a thing to validate the suspicion the CIO had, but because I knew that the government's representatives had now reached a point in their own determinations about the cold war and Communist purposes that it would be impossible to reason with them that you could have a local of a Communist-dominated national union here and at the same time have their confidence.

The government had a legitimate concern. I must say for the faculty members that although they had some hesitancy about the validity of the CIO decision because of their acquaintance with the union, they cooperated with me apparently 100 percent in breaking away entirely from this union.

Well, I think I have finished all but the last stage.

The Fifth Stage

There came a final stage in which the courts of the land by a series of decisions determined that the Communist Party was conspiring to overthrow the government of the United States, a conspiracy actuated by instructions from a foreign power. On that basis the Congress of the United States made one appropriation after another on which it put this limitation (I paraphrase from memory):

> No part of this appropriation shall be sent to support the salary of any person who belongs to any party or group or organization that is either seeking to overthrow or advocates the overthrow of the government of the United States by force.

I had to face the question of whether I was going to recommend receiving the appropriation under this condition. The question was whether this was a legitimate and proper concern of the federal government. However extreme the position may have appeared to some, the government was not making it in relation to Howard University in the first instance. The government was making it to be applicable to the internal services of its executive departments, and Howard University just happened to be one of them.

To me, this seemed to be a legitimate concern of the government. I had no fear of it whatsoever, because my experience in the first investigation showed me that there were only twenty-five people in this institution who had any kind of derogatory information recorded about them, although at that time we had nearly a thousand people employed here. Of those twenty-five who had any derogatory information recorded about them—even of the slightest kind—only two had information of sufficient seriousness to cause them to be called for hearings before the loyalty committee.

I felt that there was no need for very great concern. I did not, therefore, ask the trustees not to accept the appropriation. I accepted the appropriation on their behalf, routinely, on that condition. Therefore, I acquired the obligation as the administrator of this institution to discharge from this faculty, or at least withdraw from the government payroll, the names of any members of the faculty of such description who received any part of their salary from the federal government. That obligation seems to me to be equitable, and it is my duty as administrator to carry it out.

The current situation comes upon us. Here we have an entirely different situation in which a committee of Congress gives notice that it is going to investigate educational institutions and bring up before its sessions members of the faculties and to question them on their affiliations.

I am afraid of that procedure, too, but I have not become excited because I have had fifteen years' experience with the federal government in every area affecting academic freedom. I venture to suggest to you that there is not an institution in this country that has a purer and more wholesome relationship with the executive, judicial, and legislative sections of government than I have at Howard University.

I have resisted every approach of any member of the government that, at any time, appeared to be an encroachment of any kind on the academic freedom of the institution. Instead of losing my job and losing my application, I think I have the respect and the cooperation of all the agencies of government.

That is the reason I am not afraid. I am not nervous. I have been conducting Howard University for twenty-seven years. I know as well as I live that if there are any Communists on this faculty, their numbers are so small as to be all but negligible. There is no possible way for an investigation—

however it is conducted—to end up with any effective indictment of Howard University. I know that even though it be conducted in a spirit and by a method that I cannot approve, and that I think is both dangerous to education and dangerous to the government, so far as the institution is concerned, I still do not fear it. But still it is a matter of grave concern to me. We have got to keep calm in order to put our fingers on the spot where the concern is, so we shall know what to do.

You see, I have already decided five or six times in the course of action, not theory, that the government of the United States is within its own proper rights in being very greatly concerned about the existence of the Communist Party in this country. The Communist Party is not on the same basis as the Republican Party or the Democratic Party.

The Communist Party has been determined, by thoughtful inquiry in many different directions, to be a part of an international organization headed up in Moscow, to be a party that acts on instructions from Moscow, and to be a party that has as part of its purposes in this country the intent to infiltrate the basic industries and to get into a place where Communists can sabotage the war effort of the United States. They have already been shown to penetrate the inner branches of the government and to turn over to the "the enemy" secret information of the greatest value to the United States.

It is a legitimate concern of any government engaged in a cold war and a hot war to locate, detect, and check the subversive representatives of a foreign power. I cannot escape this conclusion to save my life. It is impossible to escape it.

But there are two issues here. One is the inquiry as to whether the Communist Party has infiltrated education to such an extent that legislation is required. The other is the inquiry as to whether Mr. John Jones, who is a professor on the faculty of a particular university, is himself a Communist. There are two different inquiries. They require two different methods.

The chief difficulty at the present time grows out of the fact that a committee of the Congress is undertaking to do both things at the same time, when it is not qualified to do the second thing at all. It ought never to have been allowed by the executive branch of the government to touch the second inquiry at all. If the committee is permitted to proceed in undertaking to do so, that inquiry may possibly destroy the most precious thing in the whole American higher education, namely academic freedom.

The determination as to whether an individual is a Communist is of two kinds. The first is as to whether he is already a subversive and disruptive influence engaged in espionage and traitorous activity. That determination is no function for a congressional committee. That is what the FBI was created for. We have at the head of the FBI one the ablest, most restrained, and decent men that we ever had in that position since the beginning of the history of the United States. He knows who the men are that are engaged in espionage and traitorous activity, where they are, and when they got to the place of action. He knows that the government owes Howard University nothing, that it owes Yale University nothing, and that it owes Harvard University nothing. It has a bounden duty when a man is caught in that act—it makes no difference what organization he belongs to—to seize him, imprison him, stop him, and punish him through the courts. There is no doubt whatsoever of the right of the federal government to do this, whatever may be the name of the individual concerned.

But if the individual is a member of the faculty of a particular college or university, and if he is not found in active subversion, then the question as to whether he is a Communist or not and whether he ought to be discharged from the faculty is, first of all, a matter of concern to the administration of the institution and the faculty of the institution. The institution's examination of that individual should proceed with such decent and circumspect help from the government as the government can provide, and without such a blustering, blundering indictment of the whole faculty and the whole cause of education as is now going on at the hands of this committee.

There again the files of the FBI are a pretty definite repository of information. If the president of an institution or faculty committee were deeply concerned about Mr. Blank and felt that he was acting very suspiciously, as if he were a subversive member of the Communist Party, those officials of the institution might well go to the government and say, "You have got a bureau here that knows all the Communists in the United States. We are very deeply concerned. We do not want to engage in any espionage in our own institution. Would you let us see what you have on this individual? It would rest our mind."

The government might do that. If the files exposed only some suggestive derogatory information that had no subversive bearing in a fundamental sense, that fact would be an immense relief. The institution would be rid of the case at once. The government would be satisfied.

If the information indicated the man was seriously involved, and if it looked as if he were getting deep into the movement and was dangerous, then you would find an administration and a faculty committee in this institution and in every decent institution in America that would find a way to separate that man from the institution without imperiling all the innocent, constructive, and wholesome members of the faculty who had no business to be interrogated at all.

A process of that kind would have to be very careful to avoid a state of mind that sometimes appears in this congressional committee and that is really dangerous to this country. It is a state of mind that often rises in times like this, namely, when the feeling of revulsion, which naturally arises against the traitor in fact, is translated into a feeling of revulsion against a man accused of being a traitor. That feeling rises in a way so strong that the disposition to run over him and treat him as if he were a proven traitor is almost irresistible.

The process is mentally murderous in character, and all the checks and balances of our judicial system are set up to prevent an innocent human being from being confronted with that situation. The entire structure of American justice proceeds on the assumption that it makes no difference what a man is accused of, even of murder; he is innocent until he is proven guilty.

To accuse a man of being a Communist—to brand him as being a Communist in these days when Communism is identified with subversion and with subservience to a foreign power, and at the same time not to give him every conceivable opportunity provided under the judicial system to defend himself and to prove his innocence, is to commit murder upon him. No committee of Congress has a right to do that under the American system. And if this administration permits that to be done again and again to innocent and honorable teachers, the American people will not endure it. There will come a time when they will make that plain.

I believe, therefore, that it is the bounden obligation of the American Association of University Professors, of the presidents and trustees of institutions of learning, to call upon the existing government to confine the committee to the task for which it was appointed, namely to find out what quantity of infiltration has taken place in American institutions and to question such individuals with due and proper precautions as may give them that information. This approach does not include the exposure of innocent men to the murderous insinuation that they are traitors without giving them the opportunity to defend themselves.

It is perfectly possible to get all the information that is needed to guide the legislative mind without taking any such action as that against an individual.

If the administration will not change that process and there comes a time when some member of the faculty of a particular college or university, whom his colleagues believe to be innocent, is hauled up before that committee and attacked, brutally run over, and deprived of the privilege to defend himself and to answer questions with circumspection, then it would be the duty of the administrator of that college or university and of the Board of Trustees to refuse to discharge that man. And if their refusal should cost them a government appropriation, which is the very life blood of their institution, they should still refuse.

It would be better that our American institutions lose the last dollar than that we should turn our faculties into a group of frightened sheep, afraid to think independently, and afraid to go out to dinner for fear they may accidentally sit down by somebody who is a member of the Communist Party.

We cannot run American universities that way. We cannot carry on the process of democracy that way. Democracy will die unless, in these citadels of thought, men are at liberty to examine every area of thought and every institution on its merits in relation to the objective criteria of the mind, both intellectual and ethical, and to teach the students to think independently and to think dangerously.

I have only one final word to say: We could easily be subject to the illusion that the small numbers of Communists in this country are due to the effectiveness of the investigative processes and the propaganda we are carrying on. Brethren, it is not so.

Do you remember a man named Caesar? He was a great investigator. He had on his hands a far more innocent group of people than the Communists. He had the Christians.

The FBI of the Roman Empire ferreted them out and locked them up. The Romans harassed the Christians so that they had to go underground. They fed the Christians to the lions. They hung the Christians on crosses in Caesar's garden and saturated them with tar and burned them. But in a few short years those Christians had multiplied by such great numbers that in the days of Charlemagne there came a council of the Roman Empire in which the emperor threw up his hands and said, "Brethren, it is too late now. They are too many for us. We have got to capitulate."

The Roman Empire, run by the Caesars, the efficient Caesars, whose roads were so good you could roll your bicycle over them even today, nearly two thousand years after they were built—those Caesars cracked in spite of all the effectiveness of their investigatory processes.

The smallness of the number of Communists in this country is due primarily to the fact that under the administration of an enlightened government, step after step has been taken to change constructively the basic conditions of hunger and distress on which Communism thrives as a philosophy.

Communism is not an armchair philosophy taught in the philosophy department of institutions of learning. It is a workingman's philosophy. It makes its greatest progress when one workingman walks up to an inequitable and unbearable human condition, points to it, and says, "These people have had this going on for years and years and years, and they don't intend to change it."

Why, in Rome, you have got the Roman Catholic Church in practical control of all the churches and all the educational institutions. The Pope knows every night at midnight practically every structural thought that is going to be presented by every institutional person from that time until the next night at midnight. They are in complete control of institutional thought and no subversion is possible theoretically. But there are two million Communists in Italy. After working on it for years, we have not been able substantially to diminish the number of Communists in Italy.

Why? Because they still have the great estates that destroyed Rome in former times. The land has never been widely distributed, and the peasant classes daily have to till land that they have no hope of buying. Because of this and other economic injustices, two million of the Italian people have made up their minds that, so help them God, they are going to bring about a change. Now when men are so aggrieved, it makes little difference what is the name of the organization through which they are to function. They give their allegiance to it in the hope of change. Italy can have all the FBI it pleases and survey all the universities. Unless it changes these basically hurtful economic conditions, Communism will some day take over Italy.

There is only one effective defense against revolutionary Communism in America and in the world. It is the responsible discharge of the obligation to change whatever basic condition hurts human life, and to change such hurtful conditions by due process so steadily that there is no need to overthrow the government and no need to suppress the free thought of man.

Let the universities remember that. Let the governments remember that, and let the governments discharge their responsibility in the sight of the people and before the sight of God. Then we shall need no prolongation of these dangerous excursions of investigation into the thought of the people in America or anywhere else in the world.

6. Platform for Freedom[6]

In this address, Mordecai Johnson outlines some essential strategies for African Americans to obtain basic human freedom. Maintaining that the question of the leadership of the world by the United States depends upon how she handles her racial policies, he holds that we must work for complete elimination of segregation in all aspects of American life and must fight for equal economic opportunities in the southern states. Not until these goals are accomplished can African Americans be truly free.

Johnson maintains that we must recognize that the South has had no experience with real democracy or genuine Christianity. African Americans must become politically active and must vote only for those candidates who can be trusted to work to end segregation. Moreover, we must understand that all the darker peoples of the world are our actual or potential allies. Unless the United States demonstrates some sympathy for their situation, those people will be forced to accept Communism.

PLATFORM FOR FREEDOM*

Mr. Grandmaster, Willard Allen, Governor McKeldin, Dr. Byrd, distinguished guests, ladies, and gentlemen:

I am very happy for the privilege of being here today under the auspices of this great society.

My father was a member of this society, and I can remember that when I was a boy there were two things he held dear and kept close to his heart: One was his church and the other was the Masons. He let me see all the books and apparatus connected with the church, but what he had to do with the Masons, he kept locked up in a drawer. I don't know why. But I do know that he held it to be a highly constructive society, and he felt that its principles were such that they deserved the all-but-religious devotion of his life.

---

[6]Baltimore, Maryland, January 10, 1954.

*Emancipation Day Address, sponsored by the Masonic Order of Maryland and delivered at the Bethel AME Church in Baltimore, Maryland, on January 10, 1954. It is reprinted and adapted with permission of the Afro-American Company of Baltimore City, Inc., t/a the Afro-American Newspapers.

Governor Anticipated

I had anticipated that His Excellency, Governor McKeldin, would be here today. He was with us a few Sundays ago, not as governor, but as a religious man. We enjoyed him greatly, and he had said that he would be here today.

But I did not anticipate what is really joyous to me: that we should have on this platform the representatives of the two great political parties of America and of this state. I rejoice that this so. I do not hesitate at all. I was going to talk to the colored people about our program for the future. I am going right on and say just what I had planned to say from the very beginning, because I have long ago made it a habit to have no thought and no program in relation to the colored people that I wouldn't be willing to lay on the table with anybody present.

Dark Period Passed

What I think is highly significant is the remarkable development the southern states have undergone. Only eighty-eight years after emancipation of the slaves, we have on this platform in a great southern city the representatives of both the great political parties of America. They are bidding for the allegiance of all the citizens and have frankly and seriously come out here today to be present with the colored minority. That very fact tells us we have passed through a great dark period in the South. We are through it and are in another period.

There was a time when this gathering could not have been done in the South, when men would have feared to do it. But there is no fear here today. There was a time when both political parties would have thought it useless to be present—even though they had been in existence here—because they would have assumed to begin with that the colored man would have voted for only one of them. But there is no party in America that can assume this today.

Incalculable Vote and Important Program

The most important political fact about the colored man today is that his vote is uncalculable. Nobody knows where he is going to cast it next time. Because the colored man has at last come to the place where he has a program of his own, a political program of his own that he proposes to work for. He will work with the political party only in the proportion to which it helps him with his program.

Increasingly, we have come to know what that program is. Our political power, which we must not underestimate the necessity of developing, depends in my judgment, on the strength, intellectual power, and cohesive power with which we hold to this nonpartisan program of ours, and about which we propose to become partisan, only in proportion as either one of the parties helps us carry it out.

It is most important to have this program, and it is extremely important that we try to get both parties to stand for this program. I believe that the time has come in the history of this nation when the discussions made by these two political parties regarding the colored man and his relationship to the majority in these southern states not only is going to determine the future of the colored man, but also is going to determine the future of the leadership of the world.

I believe that the decisions made by the Republican Party and the Democratic Party on the question of segregation in institutions of public life and on the question of fair employment for the colored man not only will determine the future of the colored man but also will determine whether or not this nation will succeed in leading this world—or whether her leadership in this world is going to be superseded.

Humble People Commanded by God

We are a very humble people. At best, we constitute a tenth of the population of this country. We have no power whatsoever to force a program of any kind. We have only the power to persuade. But the obligation to persuade is upon us today as if God Himself had made us an assignment. We ought to be as near as we can, as clear as we can, about what it is that we want.

Point Number One

Desegregation

In all humility and with a spirit unembittered, I want to tell you what I think we must work for. It isn't going to be in ten points either—just two.

We must—when I say must, I mean must—believe that we are commanded by the Eternal God to work for the complete elimination of segregation in every institution of the public life. We must leave no doubt that desegregation is what we want.

We want the complete elimination of segregation from education. We are suing to get that now, and it is our sweet, calm purpose to continue to sue either until we get it or until the courts of the land and both the Republican

Party and the Democratic Party openly adopt desegregation as the fundamental pattern of this nation.

We must fight against segregation in parks, public places, swimming pools, hotels, railroad trains, and all avenues of public employment. We must not only be permitted to enter there but also be permitted to enter and to stay there as individuals on the basis of our merit as men, regardless of our color.

New Attitude

Now, politically, that is as far as we can go with our battle against segregation, but our prayer goes further than that. We want the white people of the South, in their hearts, to take an entirely new attitude toward us as individual human beings. Up to this time, they have been willing to receive everything from us—our labor, our love, our suffering on the battlefield—and they have received these things with a loyalty that is as unsullied and beautiful as any majority ever had coming, enslaving a minority since the foundation of this world, as they have not failed to testify. This is true.

In return, they have given us segregation in the schools, segregation in the streets, segregation in the graveyard, and segregation in the churches. The Christian Church, which they operate, operates in a field of consent that takes segregation for granted. That is why we left their church.

This is the only thing that we must let the white people know: in every other thing, they segregated us, but in religion, we segregated ourselves. In addition to the segregation that they have given in all the areas of public life, they have uniformly met our persons and the persons of our wives and our children with personal condescension and contempt.

We can't legislate that. We cannot enforce anything, but in our prayers not only do we want them to get rid of external segregation, but also we want them to substitute their contempt with respect and love for the persons of our children and our wives and our homes. There is no need for them to tell us that we have that, because we don't. If we say that we want anything less from them, we are liars and the truth is not in us.

Further, we want to get rid of segregation in all institutions of public life, and we want to get rid of segregation in their hearts. We long for the day when the highest aristocrat of Maryland upon meeting the humblest colored charwoman, the mother of a child, may be driven by his heart to lift his hat.

We may not get that respect this year. We may not get it next year, but if it takes a thousand years, we shall never be satisfied until we get it.

Now, that was number one.

Point Number Two

Labor Opportunities

Point number two is akin and part of desegregation, but it is so important that I'll separate it. We want white people to give us the same opportunity to work in these southern states that they give to their own children.

There is no need to try to deceive us. Eighty years ago—and that is one thing we admire about them—they stick to the policies they have made. Eighty years ago the leaders of these states made up their minds that they were going to confine colored labor to two or three categories: agricultural labor, domestic and menial labor, and such managerial semiskilled labor as they found they couldn't do without. They were going to reserve all unskilled labor in these states, so far as possible, for us. That they have succeeded in doing for eighty years. You go into the national capital and you see it. You go into all the department stores and no colored clerks, no colored buyers, no colored administrative officers, no colored managers but plenty of janitors, plenty of delivery boys. You go into the banks, and there is not a single black face in a skilled position in a single bank in the capital of this nation, unless it is in a colored bank. The banking fraternity has successfully excluded colored persons from any form of apprenticeship in the learning of banking.

White South's Progress

Those southern leaders have effectively excluded us from all employment One of the things that causes me great enjoyment is development of the industrial enterprise in the southern states. I think there is nothing in this country more remarkable than the development of textiles and other forms of manufacturing in these states.

Sometimes we colored people would do well not only to think about our own progress since the Civil War, but also to stop and think about the remarkable progress that the southern white people themselves have made and the progress that they have made in the industrialization of the South and the transformation of the one group cotton system to diversified agriculture. It is one of the most remarkable developments in the history of the world.

But with all that development, they have successfully excluded the colored man from all scientific and technical employment in these manufacturing establishments. You see colored people sweeping the floors, delivering the goods, and stoking the engines, but no colored skilled operators, no scientific and technical intelligence, and no managerial intelligence.

Economic Segregation

This not an accident. It is a deliberate policy. Today not only are they doing that, but also they are building down here plants that used to exist in the North, on condition that those plants subscribe to that doctrine before they come.

This is one of the most tragic aspects of our life in America. We colored people must know that if the South continues to be loyal to that policy, it can weaken us on every other front and, by that front alone, break our backbone and bring us down to a caste based on color, from which we shall have no power to recover.

The most important single platform in America, so far as we are concerned, is to break down this policy and build the South to the place where it will employ the individual colored man in any capacity whatsoever on the basis of his ability as an individual human being.

Now we must stick to that program. If we don't stick to both sides of it, we aren't fit to be Americans. There is no decent white man in America who will respect us or should respect us if we want anything less than that in the South and all over the country.

If I had time, I would point out remarkable progress. I would say that the progress that we colored people have made in the past fifteen years has been more significant than all the progress that we have made in all the other seventy years since the emancipation of the slaves.

One of the most beautiful things about that progress is the way in which certain southerners have cooperated. Even while the progress has come, apparently, against the will of southern leadership, it has been received with a dignity and restraint and fine feeling that is beautiful to look upon.

But we have not turned the corner. Unless we can turn the corner on these two fundamental things now—first the elimination of segregation from every area of the public life and by all means, and second the elimination of this wretched policy of economic segregation—we colored people are not yet free.

Democracy and Christianity in the South

That is only the introduction of what I want to say. There is, as you may expect it to be (it is not abnormal), a fundamental fear in these southern states to deal with this thing. It is a good thing that we colored people should recognize the naturalness of that fear.

The South has never had any experience with democracy. It does not, therefore, have the confidence in dealing with these matters that would come out of a long experience of democracy. That fear would especially arise in such a state as South Carolina, presided over by Mr. James Byrnes. It would be especially strong in a state like Mississippi and Alabama. For 250 years— do you realize it—these states have not had any democracy? They don't know any more about democracy than what they have read.

There has never been a two-party system in those states. Not for 250 years have the white citizens of those states ever had a chance to cast a real vote between two parties. In every presidential election, every candidate for the presidency passes by those states. Not only does he not go down there and make any speeches, but also he does not even ride through there on the back end of a Pullman platform and wave his flag.

He knows there is no use to do that—those people down there either voted for him or against him before they were born, and there is no way for him to change it now. So those states don't know anything about democracy.

They also know very little about Christianity, because they haven't experimented with it. We have to distinguish between being a Christian and being religious. We don't have any experience much with that distinction, because Christianity is of a radical, universal ethic. It is founded upon the conviction of the sacred and inviolable worth of every human individual. Any group of people, people who have never experimented with that, wouldn't know anything about Christianity except what they read.

We know what it is, as Jesus Himself said, only when we do it. "He that willeth to do the will shall know," said Jesus, "whether I speak of myself or whether it is God that speaketh through me."

In general, what I have said about Mississippi and Alabama and Louisiana is characteristic of the former slave states as a whole. We are just now making a tentative effort to experiment with democracy.

YMCA Segregation

I have just been invited to sponsor a statewide campaign for the YMCA in Washington with Mr. Eisenhower and Mr. Spencer and others. I wrote a long letter and respectfully declined. And, in declining, I said this, "Out of the deepest conviction, I can no longer endorse any Christian institution that bases its life upon the assumption of a segregated social order. I am convinced that this Christianity is a liability to Protestantism, a liability to Christianity itself, and a curse to the Western world."

These hesitations are normal, and we don't discount the human being because he has them.

South Carolina's James Byrnes

Take Mr. Byrnes (Governor James Byrnes of South Carolina). I have known Mr. Byrnes for twenty-seven years. He has been against everything that I have held precious in my life. But you can't, by that means, hate Mr. Byrnes. He's a southern boy—and nearly every southern boy in the last generation was born on the bottom of life.

He has come up intellectually to the height where he is capable of being not only governor of the state of South Carolina, but also Secretary of State of the greatest nation on earth and a member of the Supreme Court of the United States.

You cannot withhold a certain profound admiration from any southern boy who rises that high in the world. And you cannot fail to be glad that he was able to win that victory. You wish that, along with that victory, he could have won a victory in his heart.

After rising to that height in the world, he is probably the greatest enemy that we have. I may add, with all reverence, that in my judgment he is one of the chief and most dangerous enemies to the world of democracy now in existence in the world. I'll tell you why in a minute. And I say that with love. I wouldn't harm a hair on his head. I have no thought, even in the middle of night when I am alone, about him that his wife or his children or he would ever fear, because I know that he is suffering from one of the greatest diseases that can come upon human life.

His own Heavenly Father has blinded Mr. Byrnes so that he cannot see. In the most critical period in the life of this nation—when it needs nothing in this world so much as vigorous courage on this whole question of race, he is trying to lead us down a road that, if we would follow him as a nation, would destroy our leadership. That road would take the leadership of this country clearly out of Western civilization.

Mandatory Changes

So I want you to see how natural it is that we should be oppressed, because the South has had no experience on the basis of which she could go confidently ahead. But as the South goes ahead in these two main directions that I have stated here today (and I believe, under God, she must go ahead), she can walk only by faith.

The time must come, when the South, in her political and economical leadership, must really go into the prayer room alone and raise the question with herself as to whether she really believes in one God and one human family. She must consider whether she is willing to reach a course of action in this world on the basis of a belief. She must understand that this is the only course of action God will permit to succeed.

Now I have probably already spoken too long, but I want to leave the framework of what I have said.

People of the World

There are 2.4 billion people in this world today. We are so close together that any one of us in this room could get up and in twenty-four hours we could be sitting down, shaking hands, and eating dinner with any other group of human beings in this world. We are so indisputably associated that we never will get any further apart. As a matter of fact, the jet planes have put us only twenty-four hours apart, and we will never be separated.

This is going to startle you colored people—us colored people. Two-thirds of all the human beings in this world are colored. They are either black or brown or yellow. Only one-third of the human beings in this world are white. Two-thirds are black and brown and yellow.

Beauty in India

A few months ago, I went over to India. There are 400 million people in India, and I was astonished. It looked to me, as I got off the plane in Calcutta, that this little group of colored people had overflowed and flooded the world—400 million. If any of you colored people in here—we colored people—look in a mirror and are not satisfied with the way we look, it isn't on account of this color. Some colored people are the most beautiful creatures God ever made on this earth.

Intermarriage

Somebody said to me, "Dr. Johnson, do you believe in intermarriage?" I said, "Oh, yes. I believe the human race is one race. I believe in it. But now, personally, if you're asking me what my program is, I want to say to you, that I didn't marry the little brown skin woman that I married because she is colored. I married her after meeting two or three million women in the world, and because I think she is the most beautiful, sweetest, and most gracious creature the Lord ever made. If she should ever throw me over, I know ten other colored women by name in the United States I'd like to speak to privately. And since I have been to India, I raise that up to 100.

Powerful Nations

I repeat, three-quarters of all human beings are black and brown and yellow. In this multicolored world, the United States is the most powerful nation that ever existed. And you and I are voting members of that nation and candidates to be on the roll of the Republican and Democratic Parties to determine their policies.

The second most powerful nation in that world is Soviet Russia. That is extraordinary, because fifty years ago, that nation was made up, mostly, of freed serfs who came out of serfdom practically the same time we came out of slavery. They had no learning, no money, no skills, and no capacity for organization. Yet inside of thirty years they had organized themselves, built up the second most powerful nation in the world in a military fashion, and launched a program of economical and spiritual force on a worldwide scale, which in less than thirty years has 808 million followers. An additional 800 million people have not yet made up their minds which of these sides they are going to be on.

White People Divided

All but about 10 percent of that second 800 million are colored. The white people are divided. Not all the white people are on our side. The Russian white people; the white people of Latvia, Estonia, Lithuania, Poland, Czechoslovakia, Bulgaria, Romania, and Albania; a considerable portion of the white people of France; and almost enough Italians to control the Italian government are on the other side. Also on the other side are 450 million colored people in China.

On our side are some white people of the United States and Canada. Also on our side are the people who are technically from South and Central America and who are so much mixed up with colored people that they don't have any segregation down there among not quite as many as 450 million colored people.

Colored People on Our Side

The colored people, who are on our side, are divided into two parts: They are the colored people who are free and are on our side because they want to be, and the colored people who are on our side because our allies have their feet on those people's necks and they cannot get out. Also there are 600 million to 800 million colored people who used to have their necks under the feet of our allies. They are now free and nobody knows but God whose side they are going to be on. I want to tell you where they are. If you take a map and stretch it up and then let your finger rest on Afghanistan, just to the south of the western part of Pakistan, through India up through east Pakistan and down through Africa, you will see where they are.

They have no military power adequate to defend themselves from Russia and China. They have an undefended border of 2,500 miles. They have all been under the heels of imperial Britain or France or Holland. They have suffered from the same kind of segregation, the same kind of discrimination in employment, and the same kind of political domination that we have suffered from in this country.

Colonialism

Now let me say this to us southerners, all of us. We must not believe that this system of segregation and discrimination we have here affecting the colored people is peculiar to ourselves and is purely domestic.

Segregation is the product of the colonial system. Colored people are here because the British and the Dutch and the Portuguese and the whites—the great colonial powers—brought us here, sold us, and made more money off our souls than they made off anything else in their trade.

When they quit enslaving us, they began to operate the whole of the continent of Africa on this basis. You don't have to take my word for it; look at Africa today. Look at South Africa, where the Boers, who are Protestant Christians, are operating their relationships against the millions of black Africans in exactly the same way that Maryland is operating her relationship to colored people in this state. The French in Tunisia are doing exactly the same thing. The Belgians in the Congo don't talk about it much, but they are doing the same thing. The folks in North Africa are doing the same thing.

All the 200 million colored people in Africa, except the people of Abyssinia and Liberia, are being politically dominated, economically and socially segregated, and exploited by the European colonial process. Those colonialists are the same as the people who sold us into slavery, and they are doing that now. Fifteen years ago the British had 400 million black and brown and yellow people under their control in India, dominating them politically and making no offer to set up a democracy. Britain exploited them economically to such an extent that today the British have left 300 million peasants in India who make only $48 a year, only $24 of which they have to use for their families after they have paid their taxes and their rents. Certainly those people, all of them, know what economic segregation is, what political domination is, and what difficulties they are having today because they have suffered it for over 200 years.

Democracy Must Win

Now what chance have we to get those colored peoples to come on our side? We've got to win! We've got to win those very people. If we lose India alone, we're losing 400 million at one shot. That will give the Communists the control over half of this human race. And on what condition do you think they'll come on our side? Tentatively, the Indians are on the British side. Very soon there will be but one power in this world that is capable of winning those people for the democratic side. That power is the one to which we belong, the United States of America.

Power in Africa

What will the United States of America undertake with her military power? And I may say this now that the British and the French and the Dutch are so powerless that not only can they not regain India and China by themselves, but also they cannot hold Africa by themselves. Their military is now so reduced that they have to give up the colonial system entirely unless the United States of America supports them with her military forces.

The great question in this world at this hour—the most important question in this world at this hour—is this: Is the United States of America going to use her military power to support the political domination, the economic and social segregation, and the humiliation of the people of Africa and to undertake to restore the colonial system in India and China? Nobody knows. We haven't answered that question, and the people over there—550 million of them—are scared to death about that question.

Fear of Communism

They don't want to be Communists. They are just as scared of Communism as we are. But they are not going to run from Communism into the control of a new nation that segregates and humiliates them and robs them of equal opportunity to earn a living. You will see, therefore, that when the Republican and Democratic Parties are raising the question as to whether they are going to be for or against the continued segregation of the colored man in Maryland, Georgia, and Alabama, and whether they are going to maintain this system of unfair employment practices, they are not merely answering that question in relation to the colored man. They are answering it in the sight of Eternal God, and they are answering it for Africa, India, and China. Now that's where we are. Don't take my word for it.

Political Activity

It is a terrible thing to be in politics today. The leaders of the Republican and Democratic Parties have got to decide whether they are going to stay in their corners, or whether they are going to override segregation and set the colored man free. Now I'm through. We colored people should be as politically active in the next five years as we can conceive it to be possible. We must ask every candidate for governor, every candidate for Senator, and every candidate for public office in the state or nation these specific questions. If the answer is "No," we must prayerfully and lovingly vote those candidates down. If the answer is "Yes," we must support them because in them and them alone is all salvation. We cannot leave them alone to decide the salvation of our country.

Praise for Truman

I want to give you some encouragement before I sit down. I want to show you who is on our side, and this is very significant. In the past government, the President of the United States was on our side. The greatest progress that the colored people have ever made since the Civil War was made under the leadership of President Harry Truman. He was the only President since the Civil War who has unequivocally and repeatedly declared himself to be in favor of absolute equality of opportunity in every respect for the colored man. And he risked his political life and lost it.

It looks as if the present President of the United States [Dwight D. Eisenhower] is on our side. He is at least tiptoeing a little bit and is a little tentative. It looks as if he might be on our side if he is pushed a little more.

Support from Churches

The biggest organization in the world outside of the Communist Party is the Roman Catholic Church. The Roman Catholic Church is against segregation and is on our side.

Now here is something remarkable. The Episcopal Church has lately come up on our side. I am not talking about the American Episcopal Church; I am talking about the Church of England. The Church of England is just like a coin on one side of which you see "In God We Trust" and on the other side, "Glory Be to the King." The Episcopal Church is the religious experience of the British Empire whose bishops are appointed by the king. Its rectors are supported by the state taxes.

For years the Church of England has been sprinkling holy water and blessings. It was so in favor of segregation in India that it segregated Mahatma Gandhi.

The entire Episcopal faculty of a southern theological seminary in the United States resigned because the Board of Trustees would not receive a colored man into that school. Now the faculty hadn't read anything new in the New Testament. It's the same New Testament that they had been looking at for 250 years.

I could give you a list of ten more things but I'm going to give you only one.

Support from Britain

The British are on our side. When you see the Roman Catholic Church, the Episcopal Church, and the British Commonwealth on anybody's side together, you will know that God is on the loose and something new is taking place in this world.

The greatest question in the world is this: Where in the United States of America is this new determination? You know who will decide that. It will be decided by the Democratic and Republican Parties in Maryland and in the South. If you say "No," it won't be done. It was the fear that they would say, "No," that made Thomas Jefferson, the greatest southern President whom we ever had, say, "When I look at slavery and remember that God is just, I tremble for my country."

South Can Lead United States

The Republican and Democratic Parties in the South have it in their power to cement the world leadership in this country. If they undertake to support the continued segregation of the colored people in the public life, and if this support is continued, depriving the colored man of equal opportunities in employment, then there will be nothing for the darker people of this world to hope for. They can't depend on us for leadership. They—and you—will have to look somewhere else. There is nowhere else for them to look but to the Communists and to Russia. My God, my fellow men, don't force them to make that choice.

7. Aid to the Underdeveloped Countries of the World[7]

This address was given before 650 dignitaries from the fourteen nations composing the North Atlantic Treaty Organization (NATO) at a meeting in London, England, to establish cooperative efforts among them. Mordecai Johnson was one of the 110 U.S. delegates and also one of the fifteen persons serving on the Board of Directors of the delegation. He was chosen by the delegation to represent the Free World Committee as one of the five speakers at the Second Plenary Session of the Congress.

The primary theme of this address is a plea to the NATO countries to recognize the appeal that the Soviet Union was making to the underdeveloped countries and to accept the "moral responsibility" to use their scientific and technical resources to provide aid to those nations so that the ideals of a democratic society might prevail over the totalitarian incursions.

CENTRALIZED INTERNATIONAL ECONOMIC AID AND THE UNDERDEVELOPED COUNTRIES OF THE WORLD

Your Lordship, Mr. President, distinguished members of the NATO Congress:

I am glad beyond measure to be here and to speak to you on behalf of the Fourth Committee, which has to do with the relationship between the NATO countries, the Atlantic community, and the underdeveloped countries.

---

[7]London, England, June 6, 1959.

I suppose one reason you have been so kindly constrained to invite me is I am one of those underdeveloped peoples, and you would like to hear about the world from the way it looks down under. I am indeed from among the underdeveloped peoples; I am the child of a slave. My father was a slave for twenty-five years before the emancipation. My mother was born in slavery. I have lived practically all my life on the territory of former slave states, so when you hear me talk, you are dealing with the real underdeveloped thing.

Yet I have early in my life come into contact with what I conceive to be the noblest and best element in the Western world, namely those Christian educational missionaries who founded the first colleges and universities for Negroes. I am today working in a university founded by them on the basis of principles that are precious to the Western world. When those men founded Howard University, they put it on the cornerstone of the inherent dignity and immeasurable possibilities of the human individual. They enrolled slaves and the children of slaves along with their own sons and daughters without hesitation and without fear, being confident that on the Howard campus they would be able to bring them all to maturity, to responsibility, and to democratic and Christian creativity. I am indebted to those men for the development of my powers, for teaching me how to live freely from the deepest inclinations of my being, and for giving me the power to give my life away freely for causes that I love. So you are listening not just to the child of the slave who can give you authentic words from down under, you can give heed at this moment to one who knows the deepest and purest traditions, who reveres the men who handed them to him, and who loves the community of peoples out of whom they have come.

Cold War in Second Phase

Now I am very tired. It has been a struggle for me to be able to stay here, but I have a message for you. I have had it in my heart for a long time. But when a man is tired, he may speak poorly; he finds that his words are merely inadequate to say well what he wants to say. Please keep in mind that I speak with the highest esteem for the members of the Atlantic community. Whatever I say is intended, as my father used to say when he preached, to stir up your pure minds so the cause that is precious to you may come to victory on the highest level.

As I have read all the papers that have come into my section, I have found that they are all certain that the second phase of the war between the Atlantic community and the Soviet Union has already begun, and that it is an economic phase. I have always looked upon the economic purposes, so in my humble judgment we are just now beginning to confront the central and most powerful purposes of the Soviet Union and her allies.

In my humble opinion there is no appraisal of what is going to come to us better than can be found in the twenty-fifth chapter of Matthew in which it says, "And at midnight there was a cry made, 'The bridegroom is at hand. Go ye out to meet him.'" I have a feeling that the bridegroom of our Western civilization is at hand, and that we are now at the parting of the ways. When we meet this economic offensive, we are going to meet the most powerful opposition of ideas, the most vigorously intelligent handling of the economic and spiritual factors of life in a revolutionary way, that any group of people in the world has faced. Either we are going to adjust ourselves to meet that onslaught of idea power and economic organizational power with a vigorous readjustment of our lives, or we are going down and possibly lose any power to control the trend of history for years to come. But if we do meet it boldly, realizing from the beginning that it will involve the use of all of our powers to the maximum extent, we may be able to pursue a course of action that not only will lead to victory but also will lift our democratic life to a higher level of functioning than we have ever known before. It will give us a radiant power over the lives and affections of men around this world, a power such as we have not had in 500 years.

Reappraisal Necessary

Now if this is going to happen to us, I think we need to do two things that are somewhat uncongenial to us. We have got to go back and make a reestimate of our enemy, and we have got to acquire some humility in the appraisal of ourselves. Up to this time we have been looking at the military side of our enemy, his totalitarian organization and his aggressive subversion, and we have been filled with disgust and fear. We have been facing him primarily with military organization and with a cohesive and powerful economic organization. We have paid rather little or no attention to the central focus of what he is about in this world.

Now we have got to look at that central focus. If we are wise, I think we will allow our emotions of revulsion to prevent us from appraising him on the level represented by his highest and most intelligent and pure-hearted devotee. It is a great mistake to appraise any movement like the movement represented by the Soviet Union and the Chinese people by continually listing their faults. God has never yet been able to choose a faultless movement for the projection of His powerful purposes. One pure-hearted man at the hand of a thousand men, 50 percent of whom are full of faults, is able by the inspiration of his purity of heart, his moral power, to keep them in cohesive union, to bring to their assistance forces that are primarily selfish in character, and to bring about a change in human affairs that could not be calculated beforehand.

We must try to take a look at the Soviet Union through the eyes of their purest, most devoted, and honorable men. When you do that, you will see that at the central part of the Communist movement there is a simple and great faith. It is a faith that, with the scientific and technical intelligence that we have at our disposal in the modern world, if we put it in the hands of the right men, the struggle for existence in this world could be overcome in a worldwide way. Poverty, squalor, ignorance, disease, and early death could be conquered and the foundation laid for a great society in which culture would be available to all human beings.

Astonishing Achievements

These men believe this philosophy with a passion that is not exceeded by any movement in the world except early Christianity. They are all responding to it every day and every hour with an enthusiasm that is nothing short of remarkable. On the grounds of Russia and on the Chinese soil, they are making achievements of one kind or another that have astonished us. They are preaching it now around the world with an evangelistic enthusiasm that is immense. This message that they have is very fittingly addressed to the underdeveloped peoples of the world, of whom there are 1.2 billion, all of whom have a scale of living that is under $100 per capita per year. All of them are living in a primarily agricultural civilization and a very poor type of agriculture at that. All of them are living in countries in which there is very little industry to supplement agriculture. All of them are impoverished in the field of scientific and technical intelligence. And to most of them, it makes no difference how much money you would give them; they would have no governmental personnel prepared to make a wise and well-coordinated use of scientific and technical plans and projections.

Offer of Technical Aid

The Soviet Union is saying to these people, "Here we come to you from among those who, like yourself, have suffered. We have come not to make you strong and powerful so that you could dominate, exploit, and humiliate your fellows. We have come to show you how to treble and quadruple your agricultural production, to supplement your agriculture with the industries that we will show you how to establish, to lend you scientific and technical personnel, to sit down and talk with you about plans for the further development of your country, and to lend you money at rates so low that you will see in an unequivocally clear manner that we are not trying to make a profit on you. We are prepared to devote ourselves to this task for months and years solely because we believe that there is in you the power to conquer the struggle for existence in your country, and we want to have the joy of seeing you do that."

If we do not see that in them, we shall have no power to deal with them, because it is there—it is there. In pursuit of that purpose, the Communists are prepared to enter a pure-hearted relationship with the people of Asia and Africa. Now, what do I mean by that? In spite of the fact that they do not have any metaphysics akin to our religion, they have something that is very important: They have radical, universal ethics in their relationship to the black and brown and yellow peoples of the world. They have said in their literature—do not misunderstand this—"We take our position quite contrary to the Second International. We are not out to organize the white working people of the world; we are out to organize the working people of the world. We say it to all of our workers everywhere, in Africa, in Asia, and in the homelands of the colonial powers, 'Make solidarity with workers. Pay no attention to their national origin. We want to unite the workers of the world for a great society in which the struggle for existence is conquered, and all are led to a new freedom on the basis of that conquest.'"

They stand on a territory that constitutes one-fourth of the landed areas of this world. They have one-third of the population of this world, and they have now established themselves in a place where they know that we no longer have the military power to dislodge them. Of these 1.2 billion people that are underdeveloped, 800 million are on the border of the Soviet Union and of China, so close that the Communists have to cross no water to reach them. The Communists can also touch their hands any time of day and can speak to them without a long-distance telephone.

Apprehensive Millions

But all of these 800 million people are black and brown and yellow Asiatics, who in times past have suffered at the hands of the peoples whom we represent and who have some fear of us. [The people of color] look with admiration at what the Soviet Union and the Chinese people have done by their faith, and [the people of color] are proud to believe that if they could have the right kind of relationship with any group of people in this world, they themselves could do the same.

We are up against an immense antagonist. How many of the people does he have to win? Why, if he won India alone, he would all but tip the scales of the majority population of the human race and, in a few months after that, might turn the tables on us and put us in the minority of the world. We are up against a great antagonist with a great passion, with an immense achievement as a result of that passion, and with a profound faith that he is getting ready to turn the corner that leads to our graveyard—no, that leads to the graveyard and to the grave we are digging for ourselves. He believes that.

Need for Self-Appraisal

Now let us take a look at ourselves. I said the next thing we have got to do is to acquire some humility in the appraisal of ourselves. We are going to enter this contest with a great handicap. We speak of ourselves in a highly complimentary fashion as the free peoples of the world. Indeed we are, and the one who is speaking knows how true that is, for in our domestic institutions we are the freest and most flexibly organized people in the world. We are most sensitive to the will of the people, and we have developed parliamentary institutions that are precious to the whole of the human race and that we rightly want to preserve.

But it takes a great man like Toynbee to tell us that in our relationship with the people of Asia and Africa that sensitivity is not so of us. For 500 years we have been aggressors against them. We have attacked and conquered nearly all of them. We have exploited their natural resources in a manner that they consider to have been unjust. And we have often segregated and humiliated them on the land of their fathers and in the presence of the graves of their mothers. They remember these things, and in this hour when they are called upon to choose between us and the Soviet Union, there is in their hearts a fear of us that they cannot easily eradicate.

Western Nations Divided

In addition, we are still wounded; we are divided in our minds today by moral habits that have descended from a colonial system we have not yet been able to overcome. We present an equivocal picture in what we are doing now. The underdeveloped peoples of the world have only to look at Africa to see how divided our minds are. On the one hand, we see the noble British one by one freeing their peoples from the colonial yoke, freeing them deliberately, supporting them in their freedom, and inviting them in their freedom to come back to their mother country, which is now for them no longer an empire but a commonwealth. On the other hand, every now and then we see the noble French rise with a passionate gesture and say to their peoples, "Are we holding you? Then be free." Then under their breath, they say in prayer, "But do come back. We want you to be with us." The other day we saw a declaration from the Belgians saying, "This pathway of freedom is what we intend to pursue. Our plans are in the making and will be ready."

But you look at Africa. It is magnificent to see that some 70 million of the peoples have been freed under these circumstances by members of this organization. But here are 110 million Africans who are neither free nor under mandate, are still dominated politically, and are still having their natural resources exploited—not for their own good but for the good of those who exploit. We see on the shores of Africa instances of the most deliberate and cruel segregation and discrimination of the inhabitants of the country on the land of their fathers and in the presence of the graves of their mothers. Nobody can look at Africa without knowing that we are divided in our minds and that we have not yet been able to summon either the political power or the moral power to overcome that division. Though the God of our fathers has vetoed the colonial system and closed the open gates of the world against it, we are still reluctant to turn it loose. We may yet shame ourselves by admitting one more venture to reopen those gates.

May I say to you again, we have as yet been able to put no great world-enriching concept in the place of the colonial system to which we have been devoted for some 500 years and which is now fallen. What greater idea do we have now of a world-encircling nature that we can offer these underdeveloped peoples of Asia and Africa, of which they can be members just as we, in which they can be respected just as we, and by which they can move freely out of their own spontaneous enthusiasm just as we? I suggest to you that we do not yet have one. There are no great words coming from us today regarding the city that hath foundations that were made for the whole human race of one blood. And because we do not have it, we are in some difficulty in approaching these Asiatics and Africans.

Wrong Motives

I have sat often in these meetings when we talk about what we want to do for them economically. I have sat for a whole hour and heard us talk tactics, heard us talk self-interest, heard us say that we must do these things in order to protect ourselves—without one word of pure-hearted love for these people, without one single intimation that we are moved by a sense of obligation to do these things for them because it is a great thing to be in a position to create freedom in this world.

When those early white men came to the place where I was to be educated, they came to ask nothing—nothing. They looked at me when my trousers were not pressed and when my face was not clean and said, "Mr. Johnson, will you read?" They knew I was not "mister," but they knew what I could be. They came there for only one purpose, for the joy that was set before them in making a man out of me and turning me loose in the world. I tell you that one of the great, great differences in our preparations is that we seem to have lost the power to speak to these Asiatics and Africans that way.

Our program of economic helpfulness is an adjunct and a servant of our military activities. We talk about it that way in our congresses and parliaments. We say to our people, "Why are we asking you for $3 billion? Why? Because we have got to have it to defend ourselves, to take care of our self-interest." If we ask for a little more money in addition to that, attached thereto, we say, "Of course, we cannot give all of our money for that purpose. We have got to have a benevolent margin that we give away simply because they need it." I will tell you that up until this date, the greater portion of all that we are now devoting to the people of Africa and Asia in the field of economic help, even as an adjunct and accessory to the military, is in the field of benevolence that is not beyond condescension. There is as yet no substantial sum of money and no substantial program developed for them purely out of the motive to make them free from the struggle of existence and to give them a chance to be men.

Present Aid Inadequate

Let me say again—I told you that you must watch me and bear with me—only those who love greatly can talk this way. I say to you that as I look at this great economic program, it seems to me to be on the periphery of our interest, almost an afterthought. It has never sat in the chair directly in front of us and grasped the central focus of our hearts. We have a great military program, which represents the greatest power of provision planning and coordination that we are capable of. In the Marshall Plan and other great projects, we have had great programs of development protective of and stimulative of each other, which is one cause for admiration of each other, which—in turn—is one cause for admiration among men. But our program of economic helpfulness is a puny vein and comes into our minds as an after-thought, never having received prolonged thought from us, prolonged affection, and robust attention. Moreover—I am trying to be hard and my purpose is, as my father used to say, to stir up your pure mind—that program depends today too largely upon little droplets of annual appropriations that expire on June 30, that permit no planning, and that give no index that we have any purpose to devote ourselves to this objective in an unequivocal manner beyond one year.

Lack of Centralization

Again, there exists no central organization that is of our making and that plans to use and to coordinate all the economic powers we have for this purpose and to see to it that they work. I tell you, ladies and gentlemen, we are going into the fight of a determinative lifetime, and we are not prepared. We are not morally prepared. We are not purely prepared in our hearts in their orientation toward the thing that we want to do for these people. We are not committing ourselves to any long-range purpose when we know that it may take years and years to develop the economies of these people. We have no great central organization for talking with them, for listening to their ideas or exchanging ideas with them, for approaching cooperation with them, and for applying a fit measure to them.

It is hard for me to say these things to those whom I love, but it is so. It points to a weakness so great that God Himself, who loves you, must weep when He looks at it for fear that, walking too boldly and in such a self-congratulatory manner into the battle of your lifetime, you may fail and ruin the thing that He has loved you for from the foundation of the world.

Recognized Equality

If the chairman will bear with me for a minute, I will say swiftly what I think we have got to do. The first thing we have got to do is not economic; it is religious. The first step that we must take is to put the colonial system behind us in our minds and to renew our allegiance to the Christian world view regarding human nature and the possibilities of human nature and the possi-bilities of a free human society in this world as based on these considerations. The British know what I mean; you great Frenchmen, who pioneered the Illumination, know what I mean; you great Germans, who have meditated upon socialism long before the idea was born among the Russians, you know what I mean. I mean the thing that Abraham Lincoln meant when he said, "Government of the people, for the people, and by the people, dedicated to the proposition that all men are created equal, all men." And he said, "I have never had a political idea in my life that was not based upon the great proposition. When I read that proposition I see not only the slaves set free but also the last tyranny lifted from the back of the last man."

The world is in front of our eyes. We are just a few hours away from the children of any people on earth. Our missionaries and our scientists tell us that every child in this world who is normal shares with us the essential dignity and higher possibilities of human life that are immeasurable. Now we look this world in the face. Either we are going to dedicate ourselves to serve that world—on the conviction that all men are created equal—or else we are going to turn our faces away and morally die and deserve to die because having seen the God that we have seen and turned our faces away, it is better that we had not been born.

The next thing we have got to do—and we shall need the help of God to do it and the help of each other—is to give our consent to the Eternal's veto on the colonial system and to turn all the strength of these Atlantic powers to the liquidation of the remaining remnants of the colonial system in Africa. We have got to listen to the cries of those 100 million black Africans who are crying out against political domination, economic exploitation, segregation, and humiliation as if we were listening to the words of our children. We have got to say to them as we have never said, "I tell you, my son, this is Britain that hears you. This is France that hears you. This is Belgium that hears you. This is Portugal that hears you. This is Germany that hears you. This is your Uncle Samuel that hears you. And I'm coming and I am going to do what you want to be done, so help me God, as if I were performing a great act of expiation before God and making a demonstration before the whole world of the purity of my purposes toward you." We have got that to do. If we think that it is at all possible for us to influence the people of Asia in the way that we need to influence them without doing this, we mistake human nature and the order of this universe.

Moral Responsibility Cited

Next, we must accept the moral responsibility toward the people of Asia that is indissolubly connected with the enormous scientific and technical knowledge, organizational resources, and constructive powers that we have. We have got to go to them with a pure heart and say, "We have come to you not to offer you aid for the sake of your military helpfulness, not to hand you economic assistance as people put a halter on a bag of oats before a mule's mouth in order that, while you are eating the oats, we may lead you along the pathway to take up a load that otherwise, of your own free will, you would not take. We have come to offer men this program purely so they may be free in the same sense that we are free, so they may conquer the struggle for existence in their territory in the way that we are conquering it, and so they may be members with us of the great society that we have in our hearts and that we intend shall cover this world."

Coordinated Effort Needed

We ought in the next place to take this whole business out of the range of benevolence. We ought to put it before us not as an accessory to our military program, but as the greatest of all programs in itself—listen to me—for which the military program, as big as it is, is only a fence-building and protecting operation. We ought to handle the program in the central focus of our being, to accept it as an obligation not to be done with our cigar money, nor with our chewing gum money, nor our cigarette money, but to done, if necessary, with our very blood, because we cannot live in our hearts and see them suffer impoverishment the way they suffer and hold what we have and eat the bread we have in peace. We must cease to think about little benevolent annual drops of money. We are not mere jugglers of money.

We are the great producers of scientific and technical intelligence in the world, of the most diversified scientific and technical intelligence. We know more about the multiplication of agricultural products than any group of human beings in the world. We know more about building up great dairy herds and pure milk supplies than any group of people in the world. We know more about lending money, borrowing money, and the effective use of money. We know more about trade, and all these things that have to do with the building up of a great economic order.

The thing that I am talking about calls upon us to use all of these things in a coordinated fashion to an end that we determine to do or die if we do not do it. If we will do that, we have got to have an organization to do it with. I do not know enough to tell you what organization to use. It has got to be akin to this great military organization that spoke to us this morning. It has got to be led by minds that understand economic procedures through and through. It has got to be as diversified as the populations of the earth to which we go. It has got to be a planning organization that can send a team of men into any country and help them in a few days to discover the natural resources there, the soil there, and the possibilities of development there. The team can come back with a program that they have talked over with the people, and the team must have men who, after they have got the program, know which scientists and technicians to choose, know what administrative organizers to choose, and can send them there and keep them there until the work is done.

Costly Program

I see we have used up nearly all my time, and I have got to quit reluctantly. This program is going to cost you something. It may cost us as much as one-tenth of all the productive power of the Western world. It may even come to the place where it costs us the necessity to recoil from our high standard of living substantially so the money thus sacrificed may be put into this program—pulling back our standard of living so we may lift up the standard of life all over this world, and we may deserve the gratitude of the men who are looking to us for leadership. I tell you that this is the program for which we were born in the world. It is as if God were standing before us today saying to you, "My sons, this is what I brought you into the world for. Don't be afraid. Go on and do it for me. Nothing that you suffer will be too great. I'll give you the power to bear it, and I will make your name loved and respected and honored all over this world."

If we do it, we will entirely transform the relations that have existed between us and the peoples of Africa and Asia for nearly 500 years. We will give them hope such as they have never had in all these years, and they will know that it came from us because we loved them. It will infuse our democratic institutions with a new and radiant life and will put them upon a higher level than they have ever been in all their lifetime. It will place us in a position where we can look at the Communists and say to them, "Khrushchev, you miscalculated. You thought that we were morally incapable of this and, therefore, you had to deceive us. Now, let us sit down and talk. What you say you want to do for this world—can't you see that I am doing it? Why can we not do it together? What you say you want to do for the world and you say you cannot do without totalitarian power—do you not see I am doing it with freedom and flexibility and am listening to the wish of the people? Turn away from your methods, my son. Come with your brethren in the Christian world who are your brothers indeed, and let us do these things together."

Closing

Now you will forgive me, will you not, for taking the chairman's time, but I had a message for you that was so big that a stone would have burst unless it got that message out of its system. Hear me now, for even in these times men like you ought to listen to a stone.

Index

National Baptist Convention, USA, Inc.,
107
National Council of Christians and Jews,
104
NATO. *See* North Atlantic Treaty
Organization
"The Need for a Program of International
Economic Aid," 103
"The Negro and Our National Destiny,"
112
The Negro Caravan, 55
Nelson, W. Stuart, 124
The New Negro, 55
New York Baptist Union for Ministerial
Education, 32
New York Post, on MWJ as orator, 1
Newton Theological Institution, 30–31
Nonviolence, philosophy of, 116
Norman, Ruth, 124
North Atlantic Treaty Organization, 1, 103,
135
Nutter, T. G., 39

Oberlin College, 9
Obion River Baptist Association, 5, 10
Office of War Information, 111
Omicron Kappa Epsilon, 99
Order of the Star of Honor, 102
Order of Varco Vinez de Balboa, 102
Ovington, Mary White, 29
Owens, Samuel A., 21

Paine College, 28
Palmers Chapel (*later* Mt. Zion Baptist
Church), 6
Panama, MWJ honored in, 102
Paris, Tennessee. *See also specific institutions
by name*
historical background, 2
MWJ honored in, 2, 132, 134
Paris Lumber Company, 5
Parks, Rosa, 120
Patterson, Fred D., 111, 113
Paul (the apostle), 50
Payens, Hugh de, 41
Pearce, Richard W., 67
Penn, J. Garland, 61
Peters, E. C., 113
Phelps, Clyde Guiliemus, 45
Phi Beta Kappa, 44, 99

Phillips, Daniel William, 10
Pi Sigma Alpha, 99
Plessy v. Ferguson, 13
Poetry
Harlem Renaissance and, 55
MWJ's love of, 101
Politics, African Americans in, 4, 120. *See
also specific persons by name*
Porter, Nora, 8–9
Pound, Roscoe, 72
Prejudice. *See* Racial discrimination
Prillerman, Byrd, 40
Primrose Club, P4, 14, 15, 124
Providence Journal, 18
Psi Chi, 99
Public Works Administration, 90
PWA. *See* Public Works Administration

Quakers, 108
Quinn Chapel AME Church, 14

Racial discrimination
in armed forces, 40, 111–12, 119–20
assimilation and, 17–18, 130–31
Howard University School of Law and,
72–74
MWJ's concerns about, 62–63, 104,
110–17, 119–20, 133–34
Supreme Court decisions on segregation,
13, 73–74, 120–21
track system and, 121
training of lawyers and, 70–71, 120
university admission policies and, 30–32,
93–94, 97
by Washington, DC, hotels, 84
World War I and, 40, 46, 54, 57
at YMCA conference, 36, 37
Rankin Chapel. *See* Andrew Rankin
Memorial Chapel
Ransom, Leon A., 73
Rauschenbusch, Walter, 32, 41, 43, 110
Reddick, King D., 21
Reed, Daniel A., 67
Religion. *See also* Churches; Social gospel
movement; *specific institutions by name*
evolutionary theory and, 26, 43, 49
MWJ on, 48–50, 62, 108, 110–11,
113–14
MWJ's spiritual awakening and, 29–31,
33

Templars religious order, 41
Rice, Lewis, 38–39
Richardson, Scovel, 73
Roaring Twenties, 55
Robinson, Jack R. ("Jackie"), 105, 116
Robinson, Spottswood, III, 73
Rochdale Cash Grocery Cooperative, 41–42
Rochester Theological Seminary
    Bachelor of Divinity degree policy, 34
    founding of, 32
    MWJ at, 31–36, 40–42, 110, 119
Rockefeller, John D., Sr., 13, 25, 66
Rockefeller Foundation, Howard University
    funding and, 67
Roger Williams University (*formerly*
    Nashville Normal and Theological
    Institute)
    historical background, 10
    MWJ at, 10–14, 19
Roosevelt, Eleanor, 101, 105, 111
Roosevelt, Theodore (Colonel), 59, 60
Rosenwald, Julius. *See also* Julius Rosenwald
    Fund
    Howard University funding and, 65,
        68–69, 74
    Howard University presidential election
        and, 58, 60
    MWJ introduced to, 47
    offer to underwrite MWJ as lecturer and
        writer, 47, 64
Russia, MWJ on, 79, 86–88, 111–112, 115.
    See also Communism

Saint Elmore (*later* Mt. Zion Baptist
    Church), 6
Sale, George, 17
Sampson, Benjamin F., 9, 107
Sarah Lawrence College, 131
Schools. *See* Educational opportunities for
    African Americans; *specific institutions
    by name*
Science, conflicts of with religion, 26, 43, 49
Scopes, John T., trial of, 49
Scott, Emmett J.
    conflict with MWJ, 84–86
    at Moorland's retirement from YMCA
        position, 51
    offers MWJ Howard University
        presidency, 57–58

Second Baptist Church, 33
Segregation. *See* Racial discrimination
Sermons by Mordecai Wyatt Johnson. *See*
    Johnson, Mordecai Wyatt; Appendix A
Sherburne, John H., 84–86, 89
Sherman, J. H., 59
Sherman, William Tecumseh, 13
Shiloh Baptist Church, 101
Sierra Leone, MWJ travels in, 103
Slavery. *See also* Emancipation
    MWJ on legacy of, 110, 114, 121,
        131–32
    W. Johnson and, 1, 4–5, 31, 44, 135
    West Virginia history and, 38
Slowe, Lucy D., 90
Small, Dean (University of Chicago), 26
Smith, Emory, 64, 66
Snowden, Frank M., 75
Social engineers, lawyers as, 72
Social gospel movement
    Eddy and, 56, 60
    Harvard Divinity School and, 43–44
    MWJ's application of, 41–42
    popularization of, 32
"The Social Responsibility of the
    Administrator," 97. *See also* Appendix B
Socialism, University of Chicago course in,
    26. *See also* Communism
South Africa, AME Church and, 58–59
Soviet bloc, MWJ on, 1, 105. *See also* Russia
Speeches by Mordecai Wyatt Johnson. *See*
    Johnson, Mordecai Wyatt; Appendix B
Spelman, Laura, 13. *See also* Laura Spelman
    Rockefeller Memorial Fund
Spelman Seminary (*later* Spelman College),
    13–14, 20, 27
Spingarn, Joel E., 35
Spingarn Medal, 68
St. Omer, Geoffrey de, 41
Stanton, G. Frederick, 124
Storer College, 110
Strauss, Nathan, 47
Supreme Court
    decisions on segregation, 13, 73–74,
        120–21
    Thomas appointment to, 74
    training of lawyers and, 70–71, 120

Tagore, Rabindrianath, 101
Tate, Merz, 75